UNDER FIRE

Die Scholle: Monatshefte für aufbauende Arbeit in Erziehung und Unterricht, Juli 1939.
Reproduced by permission of the Cotsen Children's Library, Princeton University Library.

UNDER FIRE

Childhood in the Shadow of War

Edited by
Elizabeth Goodenough
and Andrea Immel

WAYNE STATE UNIVERSITY PRESS
DETROIT

LANDSCAPES OF CHILDHOOD

General Editor
Elizabeth N. Goodenough, Residential College, University of Michigan

Editorial Board
Louise Chawla, University of Colorado
Robert Coles, Harvard University
Donald Haase, Wayne State University
Gareth Matthews, University of Massachusetts
Robin Moore, North Carolina State University
Michael Nettles, Educational Testing Service
Zibby Oneal, author of children's books
Valerie Polakow, Eastern Michigan University
Roger Hart, City University of New York
Pamela F. Reynolds, Johns Hopkins University
John Stilgoe, Harvard University
Marcelo Suarez-Orozco, Harvard University
Jack Zipes, University of Minnesota

*A complete listing of the books in this series
can be found online at wsupress.wayne.edu*

© 2008 by Wayne State University Press, Detroit, Michigan 48201. All rights reserved.
No part of this book may be reproduced without formal permission. Manufactured in the United States of America.
12 11 10 09 08   5 4 3 2 1

Library of Congress Cataloging-in-Publication Data
Under fire : childhood in the shadow of war / edited by Elizabeth Goodenough and Andrea Immel.
p. cm. — (Landscapes of childhood)
Includes bibliographical references and index.
ISBN-13: 978-0-8143-3404-1 (pbk. : alk. paper)
ISBN-10: 0-8143-3404-0 (pbk. : alk. paper)
1. War in literature. 2. Children's literature—History and criticism. I. Goodenough, Elizabeth. II. Immel, Andrea.
PN1009.5.W35U53 2008
809'.93358—dc22
2007036409

Grateful acknowledgment is made to the Cotsen Children's Library, Princeton University Library,
for generous support of the publication of this volume.

Designed and typeset by Maya Rhodes
Composed in Adobe Garamond Pro and Orator Std

Contents

Preface ix
Introduction 1
    Elizabeth Goodenough and Andrea Immel

I. Hearts and Minds

1. Storying War: An Overview 19
    Mitzi Myers

2. Massacre of the Innocents? Sacral Violence and the Paradox of the Children's Crusade 29
    Gary Dickson

3. "Surely there is no British boy or girl who has not heard of the battle of Waterloo!" War and Children's Literature in the Age of Napoleon 39
    M. O. Grenby

4. Under Ideological Fire: Illustrated Wartime Propaganda for Children 59
    Eric J. Johnson

5. Shifting Images: Germans in Postwar British Children's Fiction 77
    Emer O'Sullivan

II. Representing Trauma

6. Baby Terrors 93
    Lore Segal

7. "No safe place to run to": An Interview with Robert Cormier   97
    MITZI MYERS

8. Picturing Trauma in the Great War   115
    MARGARET R. HIGONNET

9. The Shadow of War: Tolkien, Trauma, Childhood, Fantasy   129
    MARK HEBERLE

III. The Holocaust in Hindsight

10. *A is for Auschwitz*: Psychoanalysis, Trauma Theory, and the "Children's Literature of Atrocity"   161
    KENNETH KIDD

11. The Hansel and Gretel Syndrome: Survivorship Fantasies and Parental Desertion   185
    U. C. KNOEPFLMACHER

12. Gila Almagor's *Aviyah*: Remembering the Holocaust in Children's Literature   197
    NAOMI SOKOLOFF

13. The Anxiety of Trauma in Children's War Fiction   207
    ADRIENNE KERTZER

IV. Storying Home

14. A Physician's Take on *Ferdinand*   223
    JOHN GALL

15. Breaking the Cycle   227
    MARK JONATHAN HARRIS

16. Please Don't Touch My Toys: Material Culture and the Academy   231
    MITZI MYERS

17. "Appointed Journeys": Growing Up with War Stories   237
    MARIA TATAR

CONTENTS

Afterword   251
    PAMELA REYNOLDS

"Things by Their Right Names"   255
    JOHN AIKIN AND ANNA LETITIA BARBAULD

Works Cited   259
Contributors   277
Index   281

Preface

> Remember me & my friends
> —Ela, original cast member of *Brundibar*

Under Fire was conceived as part of a much larger project, which had its genesis in long-distance discussions between the late Mitzi Myers and Elizabeth Goodenough about the relationship of the war games children play to the secret spaces they create. What evolved from those conversations was the blueprint for an ambitious collection that would focus on truth telling and trauma in stories, films, war games, and oral histories by, for, and about children. Crisscrossing child and adult readers, the volume would combine critical approaches, seek connections between the media and memory, and investigate how children have been represented globally as killers and consumers, soldiers and refugees, victims and survivors. This book would also look at contested definitions of masculinity, including the fear that feminism threatens the male identity of boys. Its purpose was to challenge the boundaries of children's literature, redefining literary and material culture so that child studies would be repositioned at the heart of cultural experience.

Myers and Goodenough took the first step toward the realization of this project when they coedited "Violence and Children's Literature," a special issue of *The Lion & the Unicorn*. The next step was to be the conference "Under Fire: Childhood in the Shadow of War," co-organized by Myers, Goodenough, and Andrea Immel. Ambitious as ever, Myers expressed the hope that the genesis of what she called "our new American history" in a changing global order would emerge from this program. The participants' essays, she imagined, would spark the process of rethinking the field in order to enlarge the domain of childhood studies and, furthermore, to encourage those who work with the young. Just as fresh collaboration distinguished women's studies when it was launched in the 1970s and Gilbert and Gubar stood side by side behind a single podium at the Modern Language Association, this conference had the potential to inspire the flowering of new child-centered connections in the academy.

Preface

Yet as we three exchanged ideas about the program over the summer of 2001, it was clear that Mitzi's health was failing. Shortly after completing the conference program and less than a month after September 11, 2001, she succumbed to injuries sustained during a devastating fire eighteen months before. Thus she did not live to join the specialists on children's literature (among them a Vietnam veteran and a Holocaust survivor), augmented by a medieval historian, an anthropologist, a retired pediatrician, a distinguished novelist and translator, and a three-time Oscar-winning filmmaker who all assembled at Princeton University in 2003. There the group considered how children under fire have been represented for children, while also viewing two shattering documentary films about children's wartime experiences—"Behind Closed Eyes" and "Into the Arms of Strangers: Stories of the Kindertransport"—and propaganda from the two world wars in the exhibition "Brave New World," which was drawn from the collection of the Cotsen Children's Library. Mitzi's presence was strongly missed at the conference whose thrust she did so much to define in its survey of fairy tale and picture book, mythohistory and medieval chronicle, memoir and historical fiction for young adults, and visual culture, from children's drawings to book illustration and documentary film. She would have been pleased, we think, to have seen the conference participants discovering not only shared perspectives but also useful practices as professional veneers and dispositions fell away. It was almost as if they could hear Roald Dahl's mantra, "Get down on your knees for a week to remember what it's like when the people with power literally loom over you" (Talbot 2005, 94). This volume is therefore dedicated to Mitzi's memory but, more importantly, to her prodigal, passionate, restless intellect. We hope this book is worthy of her.

Introduction

Elizabeth Goodenough and Andrea Immel

> I feel homesick everyday but I don't know the way home.
> —Nhom, a thirteen-year-old Cambodian who lost his leg at nine

War, as Jennifer Leaning reminds us, is a "core human activity" (2003, 13). And in those nations where poverty, AIDS, or natural disaster has orphaned a generation, children are more likely to become caught up in warfare, as either aggressors or victims. In 1998, it was estimated that more than three hundred thousand children under the age of eighteen were serving in wars in forty-one nations. The reason that 60 percent of non-state-armed forces find child soldiers useful is because "They think it's a game, so they're fearless" (Singer 2005, 80). Twenty-three percent of those children are fifteen or younger—sometimes no more than ten. Evidence suggests that between 80 and 90 percent of people who die or are injured in conflicts are civilians, mostly children and their mothers. UNICEF reported in 2001 that "in the past decade alone, because of war, two million children were killed, six million were seriously injured or permanently disabled, and twelve million children were left homeless" (Bellamy 2001, 1). In the dark zone, "where children hunt for food, dodging mortars and snipers' bullets," observes James O. Grant, a former executive director of UNICEF, "harming children has become a strategy of war" (*I Dream of Peace,* vii).

Statistics like these suggest that childhood itself is increasingly under fire as a worldwide demographic, cultural invention, and social institution. Grim as the figures are, they only hint at the reality of growing up in societies disrupted by a kind of warfare where the notions of separation between combatants and civilians, between front lines and peaceful zones of support, have been so subverted that international law regulates them with intermittent success. Children's degradation in such conflicts has, conversely, been driven home in the electronic media. The coverage of events such as the 2004 Beslan school occupation in Russia included such brutal images of the abused child hostages—blood-soaked, used as human shields, forced to drink urine, exploded into the air—that the archbishop of Canterbury was moved to define the fifty-two-hour siege as "the most evil kind of action we can imagine" in an interview with the BBC (BBC Radio 4 programme, 2). Less exploitative but more searing are documentaries about children and war such as Duco Tellegen's "Behind Closed Eyes" (2000). The film focuses on four young people: Spencer, recruited at nine through terror by a gang of Liberian teenage fighters; Eranda, an eight-year-old Bosnian girl whose family was evacuated from Kosovo to a Dutch refugee camp; thirteen-year-old Nhom, a Cambodian boy maimed in a land mine explosion at nine; and the Rwandan Jacqueline, outcast at eighteen for having borne the child of her Hutu rapist. Their stories, shaped by a sensitive filmmaker, help us to "understand the position of children in war and so begin to know how to limit and/or cancel their participation, as well as to understand the reasons why some join in the conflict," as anthropologist Pamela Reynolds, a leading authority on children involved in warfare, civil war, and revolution in modern Africa, has urged (Reynolds 2002, 16).

Tellegen's portraits of youngsters under fire demand that we not only confront the changes in warfare since World War II but also revisit the questions about the representation of war's horrors through children's literature. Boys and girls have always been stirred by the accounts of war in the Bible, Homer, Xenophon, Thucydides, Plutarch, Caesar, Vergil, Livy, Shakespeare, and Milton, to mention just a few authors that generations of young people have read in school or for pleasure. Child characters may even figure prominently in them. In the fourth chapter of *The Adventurous Simplicissimus,* H. J. C. von Grimmelhausen's picaresque novel about the Thirty Years' War, the protagonist (then a ten-year-old boy) describes how the marauding band of soldiers tortured the men and raped the women as they sacked his father's farm. But these canonical works typically neither make concessions to young readers nor unambiguously celebrate the martial, even as they chronicle the fates of nations, glorify carnage for a just cause, perpetuate the memory of heroic deeds and infamous atrocities, and, it should not be forgotten, revel in the brutal vagabond comedy of military life. We might consider the case of Rudyard Kipling, a jingoist imperialist who nevertheless produced a picture of army life before World War I in *Barrack-Room Ballads* (1892), which, George Orwell observed, can be as subversive as the antiwar books that came after it. The chorus in "Gentlemen-Rankers," one of the volume's best-known pieces, reveals through an apparent show of bravado how military service can affect men. The narrators' outburst may be rowdy boasting, but it is also strangely poignant because of their ironic identification with characters in Victorian nursery lore (gentlemen rankers were typically the black sheep of their families). Swagger tinged with desperation also betrays feelings of guilt for acts committed but never described, and they try to escape from those memories for a time, now that they can no longer take refuge in youthful idealism:

> We have done with Hope and Honour,
> We are lost to Love and Truth,
> We are dropping down the ladder rung by rung,
> And the measure of our torment is the measure of our youth.
> God help us, for we knew the worst too young!
>
> We're poor little lambs who've lost our way,
> Baa! Baa! Baa!
> We're little black sheep who've gone astray,
> Baa—aa—aa!
> Gentlemen-rankers out on a spree,
> Damned from here to Eternity,
> God ha' mercy on such as we,
> Baa! Yah! Bah! (Kipling 1892, 32–49)

So, can authors of war stories for young readers risk the dangers of representing the ambiguities of putting a life on the line for some other national cause? The genre is often characterized as the stuff of Victorian boys' serials, dime novels, and series fiction—formulaic adventure yarns set in combat zones, filled with stock types, laced with plenty of derring-do, and shot through with mindless national ideology. Authors of juvenile war stories are assumed to have been obliged, in the way those writing for adults are not, to soften the subject's harsh contours to protect the audience without extinguishing the dreams of glory through service to the nation. Mitzi Myers argues against this simplistic conception in her survey of the genre, "Storying War," this volume's opening essay. Such writings may be inherently didactic, but the genre typically questions the morality of war as often as it inculcates unswerving patriotism. The modern war story for children and young adults is, Myers notes, a comparatively recent phenomenon, whose proliferation has coincided with "accelerating late-twentieth-century violence and reflects preoccupations with human evil: all forms of moral, psychological, and material destruction; past and present genocides, from the Holocaust to more recent 'ethnic cleansings'; the ever-present possibility of nuclear disaster." The most compelling twentieth-century children's narratives about war in her view are not the classic stories about espionage or battlefield experience—historical novels such as Esther Forbes's *Johnny Tremaine* or Rosemary Sutcliff's *Lantern Bearers*—but rather tales of survivors, whose heroism is so often modeled on the castaway Robinson Crusoe. Ian Serraillier's *The Silver Sword* is a good example of the kind of novel Myers admires. When the three Balicki children are marooned in the middle of Warsaw, they take shelter in one room of a bombed-out building. As resourceful as Crusoe, they manage to furnish the space so that it re-creates some semblance of the home they have lost and allows them to extend a measure of civilization to their fellow homeless children. It is characters like the Balicki children—civilians determined to somehow outlast the hostilities—who dominate this volume's wide-ranging discussion of the modern juvenile war story. The essays collected here offer compelling reasons why the authors of so many fine modern war stories for children, whether realistic fiction, picture books, fairy tales, or heroic fantasy, chose not to shield readers from the heart of darkness. They believe that children, like adults, can be offered challenging texts showing the tragic interplay between private lives and impersonal forces that suggest just how complex negotiations between the demands of memory, imagination, and historical truth can be.

Part 1: Hearts and Minds

> Death is clean compared to war.
> —Eranda Barisha, 8, refugee from Kosovo

In part 1 of this volume, contributors problematize the ethics of mobilizing children for war efforts. To muster support by exploiting childish vulnerability using any available means—preaching, processions, narratives, images, or toys—may be seen as the flip side of adopting the child's innocent eye to expose the horrors of war. Instilling in children a high degree of unquestioning faith in the cause has always depended on cultivating what Mary Gordon has described as an "appetite for the absolute." She recalls believing as a child during World War II "that I was meant to pray for what was called the grace of a martyr's death." She confesses: "if the Russian Communists held a gun to my head and demanded that I deny Christ, I would gratefully have my brains splattered all over the streets of Long Island. The secular world provided fantasies of martyrdom as well. Mine were concerned with Hitler, dead before my birth. I used to fantasize about parachuting into the bunker, killing Hitler, gladly being shot by the Brown Shirts for the sake of having saved Anne Frank" (Gordon 2005, 91).

Gordon's expressions of childish loyalty sound remarkably similar to the ejaculations of the child crusaders of the twelfth century, an unanticipated mass response to papal appeals that quickly gained momentum before the church could contain it. Gary Dickson's consideration of this puzzling episode, which has appealed so powerfully to the popular imagination for eight hundred years, allows us to see surprising affinities between the modern child soldier who operates outside the laws of war, such as the twelve-year-old twin "holy warriors" who led a rebel crusade against Myanmar's military, and their medieval predecessors caught up in a campaign of sacral violence with no official sanction. Child war heroes can be profoundly troubling figures, because their emergence in war-torn societies seems to depend on a volatile fusion of ideology, mysticism, and charisma. In Western Europe, the teenaged combatant Joan of Arc has been held up alternately as a symbol of transgression, a chosen agent of radical change, or a model of selfless devotion to the state, as in Maurice Boutet de Monvel's celebrated picture book.

Introduction

The inculcation of fealty has been central to twentieth-century governmental campaigns garnering support for national military priorities among their young citizens. But secular quasi-religions, however, are usually substituted for established faiths: the real-life exploits of boy patriots Li Feng and Mal'chish-Kibal'chish, for example, have been retold many times in Soviet and modern Chinese children's books to inspire zeal for Communism. Eric Johnson shows how modern war propaganda for youngsters relies heavily on the highly sophisticated politicization of familiar children's genres and canonical stories. The examples Johnson analyzes include picture books that stirred up anti-Semitism to instigate the persecution of Jewish peers, elementary school texts that portrayed the dictator Mussolini as the child-loving warrior-father of the nation, alphabet books that romanticized American military technology, and the retellings of classic fairy tales that projected national yearnings as they demonized the enemy. Based on materials from the Cotsen Children's Library 2004 exhibition "Brave New World," Johnson's essay demonstrates how little has been off-limits to the modern propagandist wooing children, as did the 2005 exhibition "Wearable Propaganda," with its stunning array of Japanese fabrics promoting militarism that were made up into boys' and girls' kimonos. The essays by Johnson and Dickson provide a broader context for the essays that follow in part 2, in particular those by Margaret Higonnet and Mark Heberle, who examine the impact of trauma upon French children in the Great War and its most famous soldier-author, J. R. R. Tolkien, as well as Kenneth Kidd's survey of children's books about September 11, 2001.

It is easy to denounce the wrong side's efforts to woo young hearts and minds—but what of the rhetoric produced by our own, with whom we identify and hope will prevail? Matthew Grenby and Emer O'Sullivan examine British children's fiction about the Napoleonic era and World War II, two "just" wars waged against forces threatening European civilization. On the one hand, Grenby tries to account for the surprising absence of the juvenile war story during the early nineteenth century—the same period that is the setting for Thackeray's *Vanity Fair* and Patrick O'Brian's Aubrey-Maturin series. Children were certainly possessed by war fever, judging by anecdotes from autobiographies and memoirs by writers who were young during the Napoleonic era. In addition to the excitement of tracking the conflict's daily progress in the news, children read about the great victories British military commanders had won in their schoolbooks and in works of biography and history tailored for young readers. But expressing antiwar sentiment via children's fiction was controversial during the Napoleonic era, and Grenby suggests why most writers would have refrained from deflating romantic ideas about military service. Only a few leading authors were bold enough—most notably Charlotte Smith, John Aikin, and Anna Letitia Barbauld—to encourage children to think for themselves about the morality of nations waging war.

Emer O'Sullivan, on the other hand, combines rigorous quantitative analysis of a 250-volume corpus of children's fiction featuring German characters from 1870 to 1990, with close readings of selected novels about World War II published decades later. She shows how writers have used national stereotypes for more than projections of the other as enemy. British novelist Robert Westall, for example, undermines the negative stereotype by isolating the other from the feared group, so the adversary emerges as an individual once his enemies observe how much they have in common. Joan Lingard and Eve Bunting, conversely, caution against faith in stereotypes in their novels about girls gripped by the romantic intrigue they read about in espionage novels. Only as adults do they discover that they had wrongly persecuted Jewish refugees from Nazi Germany, confident in their ability to detect the enemy among them. When novels such as *The File on Fraulein Berg* or *Spying on Miss Müller* acknowledge that the shattering of cherished beliefs is an integral part of being traumatized, we can see how they complement nonfiction works such as Trevor Grundy's surprisingly moving *Memoir of a Fascist Childhood*. Although Grundy came to reject the movement that was his raison d'être until early manhood, his loss of faith in Oswald Mosley was no release from the straitjacket of fanaticism but tantamount to being on the barricades once again.

Part 2: Representing Trauma

> We were afraid as we built the barricade
> under fire.
> The tavern-keeper, the jeweler's mistress, the barber, all of us
> cowards.
>
> The servant girl fell to the ground
> as she lugged a paving stone, we were terribly afraid
> all of us cowards—
> the janitor, the market woman, the pensioner.
>
> The pharmacist fell to the ground
> as he dragged the door of a toilet,
> we were even more afraid, the smuggler-woman,
> the dress-maker, the streetcar driver,
> all of us cowards.
>
> A kid from reform school fell
> as he dragged a sandbag,
> you see, we were really afraid.
> Though no one forced us
> we did build the barricade
> under fire.
> —Anna Swirszczynska, "Building the Barricade" (1979)

Under fire young and old, "all of us cowards," shield ourselves side by side. Yet suffering and remembering longest, children lose most in war. "We look at the world once in childhood. The rest is memory," says Louise Gluck in "Nostos." Terrible fear barricades memory and silences who "we" become. Grown children, not yet adults, perpetuate war while children endure it. But "though no one forces us," who among "us cowards" tells of the fright and bewilderment of childhood in the shadow of war? Readers may demand, as François Mauriac tells us, what was demanded from the prophet Isaiah: "Tell us pleasant things. . . . Deceive us by agreeable falsehoods" (Mauriac 1969, 481). Luckily that demand, an imperative to forget rather than to understand terrible things, has been countered by child and childhood specialists who have tried to provide answers. Yet rarely do they admit to the difficulty in seeing beyond their own purposes and conceptions. In order to come to grips with the loneliness, abandonment, and betrayal integral to "this little world of the past," the focus of the volume's second part examines the relationship between wartime trauma, whether experienced on the battlefield by soldiers or behind the lines by children, and its representation in war stories for young readers.

But how far can writers for children go in showing young people's responses to wartime's unspeakable experiences? It is ironic that in the literature of violence the representation of traumatized children should resonate with such "special symbolic value" when the ethics of writing about the subject for young readers remains so murky (Higonnet and Rosen 1987, vi). In the current climate of information overload and image shock, will such works plunge young readers into despair, exploit a mindless taste for the shocking, or dull their sensitivities? Will reading the literature of violence prepare young people to think beyond the thrills to the underlying moral problems? Or should they be spared exposure to horrors in fiction that they may never encounter in real life? The contributors to the second part of the volume address problems like these in light of how children came to embody trauma in literature about war as it has evolved through a cross-fertilization of psychology with philosophy, politics, art history, and narrative study. The essays in this part argue against the nostalgic notion of children's books as a safe haven when they demonstrate how picture books and fiction since World War I have offered a dynamic space to process trauma and actualize resilience through portrayals of juvenile agency in the face of betrayal, grief, terror, and dehumanization.

Yet, to write these kinds of stories, authors have to overcome the natural reluctance to tell children that evil is real, instead of pretending it is a nightmare that can be dispelled by turning on the light. Translator and novelist Lore Segal eloquently addresses this issue in "Baby Terrors." At the outset she admits that pussyfooting around ur-terrors in front of children is perfectly understandable. But, she points out, it also denies the reality that children know to be afraid of monsters before they can recognize them as projections of human evil. A parent will reassure a frightened child that there is nothing dreadful lurking under the bed, knowing all the time that the paths of monsters and humans do indeed cross. Most adults hesitate to communicate this truth to children because it involves explaining that monsters are unlikely to take shapes the child imagines but may assume instead the familiar forms of friends and neighbors. And yet there is always the possibility that an adult may betray inadvertently their own fears about monsters to the child. Segal recalls such an incident when she was eleven that involved her British foster mother, whose duty it was to protect her from extermination. When little

INTRODUCTION

Lore was being fitted for a gas mask in anticipation of Hitler's declaration of war against England, Mrs. Hooper suddenly panicked. Yet Lore, whose family had been dispersed by the Anschluss, was obliged to reassure her that nothing that terrible was going to happen: the little Viennese girl suddenly found herself parenting an adult. The well-meaning attempt to defang monsters, Segal warns, always risks leaving the child deeply conflicted by what she has already learned but senses must be concealed. As Maurice Sendak has remarked, "It is a sad comedy: the children knowing and pretending they don't know to protect us from knowing they know" (1994, v).

Protecting children from the knowledge of trauma may also deny them opportunities for resistance and perhaps heroism. For better or worse, combat zones have traditionally been among the most arduous of testing grounds of character, partly because wartime's inevitable social disruptions destabilize the bonds of authority between adults and children. Yet the portrayal of these zones of violence, where young people are thrust outside the cocoon of childhood safety, are not unique to the juvenile war story: they can also be found in Robert Cormier's controversial young adult novels set in small-town Massachusetts. Mitzi Myers believed that representations of traumatized characters in the modern juvenile war story should be compared with Cormier's exploration of characters' decisions to act or to be acted upon in circumstances where peers and authority figures may be complicit with the villains. Reprinted here is her interview with Cormier, in which striking parallels emerge between the characters who function within different kinds of total institutions, whether the Catholic boys' school Trinity High, the setting of the *Chocolate War* novels, or the camps and internment centers represented in Holocaust fiction. Much like the characters in Jane Yolen's *The Devil's Arithmetic*, Cormier's boys have figured out whether they will play the games of man, the devil, and God when the odds are against winning or surviving with dignity. Similarly, the crises in Cormier's novels, where adults frequently traumatize children by abusing their authority, point to the war novel's exploration of trauma inflicted in domestic circumstances. A World War II novel such as Miriam Magorian's *Back Home*, for example, focuses on a mother and daughter's painful readjustment to peace, a bewilderingly difficult transition punctuated by petty cruelties and further complicated by both women's unwillingness to reassume the more subservient roles they unquestioningly assumed before the war.

Representations of the frequently painful interactions between child and adult in the juvenile war story can also expose violent ambivalences underlying cultural fantasies of childhood. In her essay about French visual culture during World War I, Margaret Higonnet analyzes the cultural work performed by the representation of traumatized children and soldiers. In World War I, new connections were being posited, however, between the mental conditions of the shell-shocked soldier and the traumatized child. Attitudes toward these sufferers—formerly regarded as shirkers or hysterics who were little better than traitors to national honor—began to soften. Scientific observation increasingly confirmed that the characteristic form of regression was a medical, not moral, condition—a response to exposure to extreme violence or the radical erosion of belief systems. Learning to tell stories was seen as a critical part of rehabilitation for both soldiers and children by allowing them a therapeutic space to work through their pain. Higonnet shows how the propagandist, physician, teacher, and the picture book artist all exploited the parallels revolving around the difficulty in constructing coherent narratives about horrifying personal experiences. Among Higonnet's sources are archives of drawings produced as school assignments by children under fire across France. Remarkable as documentation both of physical damage to the French landscape and of emotional response to the devastation, the children's drawings may be difficult to interpret, but they open a window into the minds of children under fire. Some children were deeply troubled by what they had seen, but others, like Yves Congar, took to the streets to defy the enemy. The diary Congar's grandmother had him keep during the occupation of the Sedan is a remarkable testimony to the resilience of children growing up in the shadow of war. Little Yves' patriotism, close family ties, and ability to make fun of the enemy sustained a spirit of resistance, justice, and hope, not only through boyhood but also during his career as a Catholic archbishop.

Not all veterans of World War I who wrote about their experiences turned out realistic novels or memoirs. Mark Heberle examines the case of J. R. R. Tolkien, traumatized veteran of the Battle of the Somme, philologist, and creator of one of twentieth-century literature's greatest imaginary worlds torn by wars. Orphaned early, Tolkien found in the literary manipulation of language "a symbolic authority and security that supplied the place of his missing parents." His consuming fascination with words, which prompted him to construct the stories to contain them, offered him a means for working through anguish and anxiety at different stages of his life between the two world wars. After Tolkien's ghastly experiences during World War I (by the spring of 1918 all members of his battalion still in France had been either killed or captured, including two of his closest friends), he began composing the fragmented and elliptical fantasies that were never finished, the so-called Lost Tales, the genesis of the mythology underlying the trilogy that was to come. Heberle reads the heroic fantasies as "displaced accounts of the horrors that Tolkien had barely survived," but also as "post-traumatic responses to a half-century of civilized butchery." Although Tolkien chose a different form of expression from his contemporary soldier-poets or later writers such as the Vietnam vets Tim O'Brien and David Rabe, he nevertheless shares certain preoccupations with them. The search for a safe space where a fit audience can be assembled to hear the story, as Heberle suggests in his analysis of "The Cottage of the Lost Play," is especially interesting in Tolkien's case. It was essential to him that children be not only members of the fictional audience but also the real-life audience for his own works in development.

At the same time, Tolkien anticipated the critics who now see his work "as commentary upon the situation of endless war," currently extending into the worldwide "war against terror." Would he, for example, have disapproved of the recent *Lord of the Rings* movies or deplored the simulated battlefields of interactive video games, rated for "Realistic Blood, Realistic Violence?" How would he have accessed efforts to demarcate children's books according to age-appropriate levels when the material available on the Web, film, and television seem increasingly to subvert those standards by teaching the young how to exercise power to hurt and maim, not to mention promoting socially acceptable forms of aggression such as salesmanship, sport, and sexual recreation? Would developments like these have caused him to qualify his later meditations on what to read children in times of crisis, where he recommended fantasies that cast the "shadow of death" before some happy end is wrested from the unbearable? Yet Tolkien's rich vein continues to be mined by writers like Diana Wynne Jones in novels such as *The Dark Lord of Derkholm,* which celebrates familiar fellowship and adolescent agency during a frequently comic resistance against a never-ending war waged on behalf of commerce.

Part 3: The Holocaust in Hindsight

> Dwell on the past and you'll lose an eye
> Forget the past and you'll lose both eyes.
> —Russian proverb

Nowhere is the demarcation between books for the child and the adult reader more easily shattered than in fiction about World War II, which is often haunted by the memories of national betrayals and the Holocaust that mock "the whole heritage of European culture" (Milosz 1983, 82). The subject imposes formidable ethical, therapeutic, and aesthetic obligations upon any author. Adrienne Kertzer reminds us that *trauma* derives from a Greek word referring to the act of wounding and that "to represent trauma as objective fact—something that happens as a consequence of war—is quite different from representing trauma as subjective experience." When writing about the Holocaust for youngsters, the author's burdens become even greater, especially if he agrees with critics such as Elizabeth Baer, who have argued for the revelation rather than concealment of genocide's most appalling aspects. The "split agenda" between truth telling and reassurance underlying the rationale for a children's literature of atrocity, Higonnet points out, recapitulates "the tension within modern trauma theory, between those who believe that true trauma (as in the Holocaust) is unrepresentable and those who believe that the memory of a traumatic experience can and should be relived and narrated in order to put it to rest" (2005, 151).

As the contributors to part 3 grapple with the implications of carrying out this split agenda in World War II fiction for children, they also demonstrate why constructions of childhood have become central to literary re-creation of trauma. The etymology of *infant,* which means "not speaking" or "without language," reflects the central paradox in writing about the collective traumas of World War II. Relying heavily on oblique and fragmentary utterances, authors must speak about things that defy coherent communication and require the reading of silence. Narratives about characters' traumatic wartime experiences are not invented per se but woven of strands from psychoanalytic theory, personal testimony, and archival evidence so that they can assist the critical cultural work of truth telling, remembrance, and healing. Such texts are sites for contested understandings of trauma and shifting representations of survivor suffering as observed through the reflexive relationship of child and adult. As in part 2, the subject of families under fire recurs, particularly those circumstances where a mother abandons a daughter, as in the Grimms' *Hansel and Gretel,* Gila Almagor's novel *Aviya* about Israeli Holocaust survivors, and Mirjam Pressler's tragic *Malka Mai.* Kidd, Knoepflmacher, Sokoloff, and Kertzer take divergent stances on such topics as the relationships between the kinds of truth embodied by historical fact, historical novels, and fairy tales; the uses of transference, retelling, and forgetting in therapy and literature; and the ethics of happy endings. The variety of critical approaches drawn upon in this section—psychoanalysis, gender studies, sociohistorical, cross-cultural, and psychohistorical analysis—attest to the complex ethical, narrative, and pedagogical issues raised by efforts to represent and manage the incommunicable in literature for young people.

In part 2 Lore Segal argues in "Baby Terrors" that ignorance is no protection against monsters. What sort of fiction, then, should be written to help children comprehend the kind of atrocities that an authoritarian government like the Third Reich sanctions to further political policies and imperial mandates? Does a novel such as Doris Orgel's *The Devil in Vienna* go far enough in its restrained but moving portrayal of two girls' friendship unraveling during the uneasy months culminating in the German occupation of Austria? Kenneth Kidd addresses in his essay the concept of sufficient confrontation with the Holocaust through a literature of atrocity for children championed by critics such as Elizabeth Baer. In a wide-ranging essay considering the trope of the wounded child in psychoanalysis, literary criticism, and trauma theory, from Freud to Jane Thrailkill to Shoshana Felman, Kidd suggests why trauma theory, with its focus on the private self rather than public person, has become critical in coming to terms with the Holocaust. Central to his argument is the evolution of a concept of transference as "an enabling anxiety of influence" between a traumatized individual (or a literary representation) and another agent. Because this process is supposed to spark ethical responses, it argues for the superior ethical and therapeutic value of the literature of atrocity, as opposed to fairy tales and fictions based on them, which can be regarded as exercises in imaginative denial. Nevertheless, Kidd is troubled by what he calls the "sentimental unconscious of trauma theory" underlying this concept of transference, because it seems to have facilitated the development of what Laurel Berlant terms infantile citizenship. Kidd sees this debased idea about activity in the public sphere reflected in the "empty rhetoric of sharing and caring" of books produced in the wake of September 11, as well as novels about atrocities that are half problem teen fiction, and half historical fiction. He sees a better alternative in novels like Lois Lowry's *Number the Stars* or *The Giver.* While Lowry deals more indirectly with the Holocaust than novels set in German or Polish concentration camps, she avoids privatizing the public sphere through the banalization of trauma and asserts the importance of collective memory and will.

INTRODUCTION

Is there, alternatively, a role for forgetfulness, even though it may constitute both a denial of and assent to atrocity? Are there situations where a victim might be justified in forgetting trauma in order to put the past behind him? U. C. Knoepflmacher poses this difficult question in his essay on the fairy tale "Hansel and Gretel," which has just such a happy ending, implying that forgetting is a kind of forgiveness. The children's willingness to repress the memories of parental desertion when the family is reunited might be read as a therapeutic model, a view Bruno Bettelheim found sympathetic. The tale's troubling ambiguities about child abandonment have also inspired several powerful retellings with explicit allusions to Holocaust trauma, including poems by Randall Jarrell and Anne Sexton, a novel by Louise Murphy, and *Brundibar*, a picture book version of the Theresienstadt child opera by Maurice Sendak and Tony Kushner. Knoepflmacher scrutinizes the way these authors confront the moral and aesthetic choices of reworking "Hansel and Gretel" within such a context. Only one of the texts he discusses is explicitly for children, and not surprisingly, he discovers that *Brundibar*'s apparently joyful celebration of juvenile resistance against the forces of darkness is nevertheless highly conflicted. Although Sendak has stated that *Brundibar* represents to him "closure from lifelong cultural and personal traumas inflicted by the Holocaust," the picture book's happy ending is as problematic as the ending of the Grimm tale standing behind it. Sendak has admitted it was impossible for him to forget how the real story ended, even as he and Kushner tried to hold out reassurance to *Brundibar*'s readers. Adults familiar with the circumstances surrounding the original opera's conception read the story knowing that defiance of tyranny through art at Theresienstadt was fruitless, because its creators and young performers all died at Auschwitz. Only children who are ignorant of the opera's history can read the ending as a victory for the plucky Anniku and Pepicek.

As Knoepflmacher's discussion of *Brundibar* makes clear, indirect portrayals of the Holocaust for multigenerational audiences can founder when historical facts are muted or ignored. A cross-written text such as Gila Almagor's *Summer of Aviya* suggests just how powerful a novel that is based on actual experiences of traumatized individuals can be. Naomi Sokoloff's analysis of *Aviya*'s various layers, rewritings, and reconceptions for different ages in various media suggests why Almagor's depictions of Holocaust survivors' readjustment to peacetime have been received so enthusiastically in Israel. Almagor, like Tolkien, found storytelling a means of working through personal trauma over the years. But she was also motivated to write to create greater understanding for the European Jews who immigrated after World War II to Israel, which did not welcome them with much sympathy, fearing that they would never become the new kind of citizen the state required. Almagor's *Aviya* turned out to be instrumental in changing the sabras' attitudes toward the dispossessed refugees in postwar World War II Israel. The novel is unusual, then, in its honest depiction of the traumatized mother Henya's attempts to pull herself together and adjust to living in a new place and the effect her erratic behavior has on the young daughter who desperately wants to love her. Because *Aviya* confronts the social and personal realities of dealing with trauma by acknowledging the reality of unrelieved grief, while also allowing space for anger and questions, Almagor avoids promoting anything resembling infantile citizenship.

In the final essay of part 3, Adrienne Kertzer argues that novels for young readers about Holocaust trauma such as *Aviya* remain the exception, not the rule, in spite of authors' increased willingness to take on a subject considered taboo for children until quite recently. Kertzer takes issue with Kidd's contention that recent works of historical fiction "demand pain from readers as proof of their engagement." In her survey of contemporary writing about the world wars, she sees many books in which the line between young and mature reader are as sharply drawn as ever. Pondering "the adult reluctance to look at images of traumatized children," whether on the news or in war fiction, Kertzer takes account of what is left out. Precise historical context, she argues, is almost never provided, whether in a picture book such as Rukhsana Khan's *The Roses in My Carpet* about an Afghanistani child living in a refugee camp, or the pioneering novel about a concentration camp survivor, *I Am David,* by Anne Holm. Such texts, whose endings typically hold out the prospect of hope, are generally defended on the grounds that their authors are trying to educate children about evil without causing them to despair about the future. Yet Kertzer insists that when authors set out to teach about trauma but avoid explaining the historical conditions that gave rise to atrocities, they introduce inaccuracies that will give readers confusing ideas about significant events in modern history, as well as misrepresent the suffering a trauma victim endures as something that ultimately subsides and can be "cured." Casting a wider net, Kertzer notes the systematic omission of vicious secrets when adult books about the Holocaust are rewritten by their authors for children. The characteristic pattern of muting (or what Lore Segal would call pussyfooting) that emerges "in the shift from what we perceive as individual trauma to cultural, historic, or collective trauma." In discussing conventions specific to war fiction, as well as the power of fantasy to convey complex representations of trauma, Kertzer sees Mirjam Pressler's novel *Malka Mai* as exemplary for having created "a space in which trauma is one of the truths of war, and neither parent nor child is safe."

Part 4: Storying Home

> He is sitting there still, under his favorite cork tree,
> smelling the flowers just quietly.
> —Munro Leaf, *The Story of Ferdinand*

Hitler burned it, Franco banned it, Stalin named a field artillery piece after it, but Gandhi called *The Story of Ferdinand* his favorite book. After the surrender of the German Army in 1945, Major Munro Leaf, serving at Occupation Headquarters, was approached by two women psychiatrists requesting that *The Story of Ferdinand* be given to the children of Berlin, who in addition to being traumatized by death and the destruction of their city, were burdened by responsibility for surrender and national defeat. Leaf commandeered the military's Stars and Stripes mobile printing press to enable every child to receive a personal copy for Christmas. Although more than seventy translations appeared before Leaf died, this German edition remained his favorite. Leaf's gift of books to children at risk—no matter that they were the children of an enemy nation—is testimonial to our culture's faith in bibliotherapy to touch battered heart and mind, reanimate hope, and kindle the desire to strike truce with the past so that something like a normal life can resume. In part 4 of this volume, four contributors explain their belief in sharing stories as a way through dark woods, even though they are well aware that storytelling alone cannot release the traveler from memories of suffering or reconcile him to either inhuman cruelty or monstrous miscarriages of injustice. Gall, Harris, and Myers attest to the healing powers of storytelling on the hospital ward, on a film set, and at the site of a suburban home burnt to the ground. Looking back to Tolkien, Maria Tatar offers a moving defense for the great-hearted adventures that can only be undertaken "once upon a time," as holding out greater potential for consolation than "treacly sentimentalism or stern political correctness."

Decades of experience as a pediatrician spark John Gall's meditation on Leaf's bull Ferdinand who refused to be a killer and to be killed. In retirement, Gall finally had the chance to begin watching years' worth of tapes recorded from a camera that had hung above the examining table. The tapes revealed a telling difference he had never noticed between the behavior of a normal baby, who "danced the dance of life," and the traumatized infant, who could not move with joy because of wounds from wartime experiences to body and mind, life and landscape, home and family. What had effectively been wrested from those children, Gall believes, is the choice Ferdinand was free to make: to take a stand against violence and to return to smelling the flowers—his variation on the dance of life. Yet Gall expresses cautious optimism about the prospects for damaged children when he recalls the case of a traumatized boy he treated for whom an integral part of the cure was telling the story of what happened to him over and over again.

In a similar spirit, Mark Harris reflects upon making the documentary "Into the Arms of Strangers: Stories of the Kindertransport" (2002), which brought him into contact with the apparently lucky Jewish children who escaped Hitler and the concentration camps sixty-five years after being carried to safety in England. Nothing prepared him for the surprising disclosures after the film's release. The elderly interviewees revealed to Harris that their lives had been spent in the shadow of their memories of loss and loneliness, especially those who were never reunited with their families after the war. As children they suffered almost as much as if they had been deserted by their parents, not sent away on the Kindertransport as a desperate gamble to save their lives. Even the most resilient were too deeply scarred to want to say much about this rupture, even to children and grandchildren who wanted to know about this episode in the family history. Apparently, the film has encouraged many other elderly survivors to break the silence they had maintained for decades to protect their families from the past, which actually facilitated the transference of those unspoken anxieties to their children.

Introduction

Opening a space for inquiry into such secret pain is how Mitzi Myers framed "Please Don't Touch My Toys: Material Culture and the Academy." Her valedictory essay begins with a celebration of the "wear and tear and the grimy defacements" in which the hidden history of childhood might be recovered (she herself delighted in the spontaneous exfoliations of fluorescent self-adhesive notes, annotated with her unmistakable scrawls, pasted all over the pages of any text she was reading or writing). But she also argues that such "marks of personality and usage" delve directly into the reasons why children under fire need stories. She sees her own tale of loss, when her home and library burned to the ground one night, as a fairy tale in reverse: unlike Ashbottom, she'd fallen from "riches to rags" to find herself "naked, bereft, selfless and terrified." Going straight to the orphan-heart of kids' books, as one who suddenly discovered what it really felt like to be "homeless, a war victim, a refugee, a displaced person," Myers makes an impassioned plea "for the primal importance of the book and the tale," not just to grow a mind or to make a self but to save a life.

Lessons of storytelling thus transcend the literary, as Maria Tatar contends. Of fairy tales, she points out, "The morals of these stories are communicated not through the words on the page, but in the conversations that take place about the stories." Just as fairy tales offer "portals" through which children can venture into the dark and forbidding realms of adult experience, folkloric codes provide spaces for adults to frame, interpret, and relieve anxieties related to shock, exile, and even Auschwitz. As in part 3, narratives such as Lois Lowry's *Number the Stars,* Sendak's *Dear Mili,* and Innocenti's *Rose Blanche,* which share a sheltering impulse and utopian function while they efface to varying degrees their historical grounding, are singled out for praise. The dialogue these works inspire suggest that matters of life and death have always inhabited the heart of enduring works for children, but perhaps it is adults' compromised understanding of tragedy that makes the use of fairy tales in the representation of the Holocaust provocative. "Fairy tales don't promote violence," Tatar contends. "In fact they enable children and adults to discuss life's dangers in the remote world of 'once upon a time.'"

Children will always be hostages to fortune, whether they number among the perpetrators, victims, or survivors. Their stories will always inspire powerful fictions. In the afterword, Pamela Reynolds meditates about the future of the war story in light of late twentieth-century conflicts in Africa, where the social dislocations have been the most extreme. "Children," she notes, "depend on an ethical attitude, which is the basis for sociality." She asks, "What happens when that ethos is eroded by conflict (as it always is)" when they become "the targets of and/or participants in war?" If, as Stanley Cavell argues, children are led to a moment in which they consent to adulthood, what is the nature of that choice when it occurs during wartime? Because war removes the possibility of choice for many youth, Reynolds insists that we consider the following: "What for the young (or any of us) are the limits of consenting to horror? Or adapting to it? Should we credit the revulsion of youth to horror as conceivably political responses, even as they participate?" How much inner turmoil can or should be reflected in children's stories about the horrific conflicts of our times, if indeed they are told? Memoirs and novels about African conflicts of the late twentieth century are slowly beginning to appear—works such as Ismael Beah's *A Long Way Gone: Memoirs of a Boy Soldier;* Jean Hatzfeld's *Machete Season,* a collection of interviews with Rwandan fighters; or *Sozaboy,* Ken Saro-Wiwa's novel about a young Biafran soldier. How much will authors writing for young readers know of those realities, and how much will they choose to reveal to their audience? What effect might telling stories about these wars have on young readers—or, for that matter, anyone wishing to understand how war devastates societies and individuals? Because every generation must renegotiate the answers to these questions, we conclude *Under Fire* with the first antiwar story for children in English, "Things by Their Right Names," by John Aikin and Anna Letitia Barbauld, accompanied by an image of a battlefield from the border of an eighteenth-century writing sheet filled in by a child. Published in 1792 at the beginning of the Napoleonic wars, Aikin and Barbauld's riddling dialogue is a powerful reminder that any honest writer for children who takes on the subject of war cannot avoid the issues that Reynolds—and all the contributors to this volume—have so eloquently raised.

I

HEARTS AND MINDS

1

Storying War

An Overview

MITZI MYERS

What counts as a representation of war? What kinds of war stories have found favor over time? What trends emerge, and what genres and themes appear worldwide? War stories encompass varied fictional genres and perspectives as well as quasi-fictional autobiographical accounts and settings include not just the actual war zone but also the home front (as in World War II's many hiding out stories); war's aftermath at home or conflicts of the future are related topics. Tales featuring armed conflict, usually from an antiwar perspective, as in "Things by Their Right Names" and "The Price of Victory" in Anna Letitia Barbauld and John Aikin's *Evenings at Home* (1792–96) have contributed to juvenile literature since its late eighteenth-century takeoff. The American Civil War starred in many children's magazines; adventures tales, usually nationalistic, were popular in the later nineteenth century, an approach that also resurfaces during the earlier years of twentieth-century wars. Although war stories are sometimes categorized as pure adventure or combat zone tales, they are inherently didactic: they inculcate patriotic moral values or, more often, question the morality of war. Most are variants on the oldest adult genre borrowed by children, the Robinson Crusoe survival story, often directly alluded to within texts, as in Uri Orlev's *The Island on Bird Street* (1981, trans. Hillel Halkin 1984). Although tales may be overtly aimed at boys or girls, war stories are read across genders, and war activities frequently allow fictional protagonists (like real-life girl readers) participation in heroic activities, from nursing under fire to escaping enemy pursuers.

W. E. Johns's Biggles books are set in both twentieth-century World Wars and are still avidly read. Johns remarks that his flying hero may seem to give young readers merely the excitement they want, but "I teach . . . under a camouflage." British girls' series stories, such as Elinor Brent-Dyer's *The Chalet School in Exile* (1940) and Dorlita Fairlie Bruce's *Dimsie Carries On* (1946), feature war too. Evacuation and spy catching were big war themes in British tales, as they were in national propaganda. World War I fiction still comes out, as in Michael Morpurgo, *War Horse* (1990), but World War II generates the most literature, although the United States has much Revolutionary War and Civil War fiction. Vietnam and later wars attract some writers, but earlier conflicts still generate fine work, as in Mollie Hunter's tale of Robert the Bruce, *The King's Swift Rider* (1998), or the very different recent spate of young adult books concerning the early twentieth-century Armenian massacre, the attempted extermination of a whole people that Hitler explicitly cited as precedent, useful evidence that genocide could be perpetrated successfully because so few protested or remembered.

The platitudes that war books fascinate young readers because they provide risk-free real events more exciting than any make-believe, yet appealingly predictable because the audience knows who "won"; that they evade serious moral issues or reduce these to good guys versus the bad, thus serving as conduits for national ideologies; or that they are usually escapist (combat books from "over there" for boys) or gendered (domestic contribution stories for girls on the home front) need scotching. Current proliferation in war writing for the young coincides with accelerating late twentieth-century violence and reflects adult preoccupations with human evil: all forms of moral, psychological, and material destruction; past and present genocides, from the Holocaust to more recent "ethnic cleansing"; the ever-present possibility of nuclear disaster. Adult social history, cultural studies, and postmodern/postcolonial literary theory—all much concerned with redefining what counts as "war" and with exploring how conflicts escalate and how war is represented in history, memory, and words—filter into the expanding and impressive volume of war stories for the young. Not always comfortable or reassuring, many recent publications contrast sharply with previous simpler works in war genres that were in essence familiar forms such as school tales or horse stories. (One of the earliest British World War II novels, for example, is Mary Treadgold's 1941 *We Couldn't Leave Dinah,* the invasion of the Channel Islands in the guise of a pony book peopled by youngsters who help out the Secret Service and even decrypt German military codes.)

Within the exciting and comfortably familiar conventions of quest narratives, war stories move from harrowing escape and survival to a redemptive reestablishment of home, family, and friendship, whether in frigid Siberia, as is Esther Hautzig, *The Endless Steppe: Growing Up in Siberia* (1968); Tamar Bergman, *Along the Tracks* (1988, trans. Michael Swirsky 1991); or in the refugee trilogies of Sonia Levitin and Judith Kerr, whose German-Jewish families came, respectively, to America and

England. Reissued as *Escape from Warsaw,* Ian Serraillier's pathbreaking fact-based tale of *The Silver Sword* (1956) features a strong heroine among the fleeing children and is early in viewing some Germans sympathetically. Clever children and cross-cultural friendships elude Nazi terror in Claire Huchet Bishop, *Twenty and Ten* (1952); Doris Orgel, *The Devil in Vienna* (1978); and Lois Lowry, *Number the Stars* (1989). The difficulties of growing up German are explored by Barbara Gehrts, *Don't Say a Word* (1975, trans. Elizabeth B. Crawford 1986); Ilse Koehn, *Mischling, Second Degree: My Childhood in Nazi Germany* (1977), the German term alluding to the technically Jewish heroine's camouflage within the Hitler Youth movement; Laura E. Williams, *Behind the Bedroom Wall* (1996); and Jürgen Herbst, *Requiem for a German Past: A Boyhood among the Nazis* (1999). Through brilliant time-slip narratives of switched identities, Jane Yolen's *The Devil's Arithmetic* (1988) and Han Nolan's *If I Should Die before I Wake* (1994) transport inside the concentration camps, respectively, a modern Jewish girl bored with old woes, "tired of remembering," and a postmodern neo-Nazi skinhead.

Confusions of national identity and religious affiliation, especially when Jewish youngsters grow up abroad or hide out as Christians, are often notable in refugee tales, as in Johanna Reiss, *The Upstairs Room* (1972), and its sequel on war's aftermath, *The Journey Back* (1976); Elisabeth Mace, *Brother Enemy* (1979); Joan Lingard, *Tug of War* (1989) and *Between Two Worlds* (1991); Renée Roth-Hano, *Touchwood: A Girlhood in Occupied France* (1988); and Anita Lobel, *No Pretty Pictures: A Child of War* (1998). Returning to the devastated European homeland after the war, strong young people nevertheless locate alternative "relatives" to love in Tamar Degens, *Transport 7–41-R* (1974), and Peter Härtling, *Crutches* (1986, trans. Elizabeth D. Crawford 1988); or finally get "home," only to discover that their solitary heroism has matured them beyond the adults, as does the astonishingly resilient protagonist in Tatjana Wassilejewa, *Hostage to War: A True Story* (1999, trans. A. Trenter from the German trans. of the original Russian 1996). The lone child traversing combat zones has long been a motif of exciting stories that implicitly question war ideologies, from Meindert DeJong, *The House of Sixty Fathers* (1956), with Tien Pao and his pig wandering China during Japanese occupation (illus. Maurice Sendak) to Tomiko Higa, *The Girl with the White Flag* (1991, trans. Dorothy Britton), the child behind the famous army photographs of a youngster amidst battle on Okinawa.

Perhaps the first entry in the evacuated-British-child World War II genre is P. L. Travers, *I Go by Sea, I Go by Land* (1941). In a variety of psychologically sophisticated narratives, juvenile evacuees deal with loss and abuse and transgress class and gender norms, finding alternative homes and families in Canada in Kit Pearson's trilogy about working-class youngsters who must eventually leave the posh new world for home; discovering liberatory love and literacy after maternal maltreatment in Michelle Magorian, *Good Night, Mr. Tom* (1981), and renegotiating restrictive English gender and class codes after American freedoms in her *Going Back* (1984); or retrospectively engaging autobiographical guilts and attachments in Nina Bawden, *Carrie's War* (1973) and *Henry* (1988). Hardy juveniles rescue grownups from Dunkirk in Jill Patton Walsh, *The Dolphin Crossing* (1967), or furtively prowl blitzed London in search of love in her *Fireweed* (1969). Street children rebuild the secret garden amid the bombs and win over genteel adults in Rumer Godden, *An Episode of Sparrows* (1955), and wartime communal solidarity is symbolically enacted through the adventures of *Blitzcat* (1989), one among many revisitations by Robert Westall of his adventurous youth amid bombs in a port town.

Westall, the dean of British war novelists, features encounters with the "enemy" on the home front in his most familiar war story, *The Machine-Gunners* (1975), and its sequel, *Fathom Five* (1979), a spy story entangling the young hero in moral ambiguities. Westall's recurrent lone German and problematic father motifs also characterize perhaps the most often cited American World War II fiction, Bette Greene, *The Summer of My German Soldier* (1973), and its sequel, *Morning Is a Long Time Coming* (1978). Greene's Jewish heroine is persecuted by a punitive father and the Arkansas community as well; when she falls in love with a German POW and hides him after his escape, she is sentenced to a reformatory. Westall; Greene; Magorian; Mary Downing Han, *Stepping on the Cracks* (1991) and *Following My Own Footsteps* (1996); and most recently Carolyn Reeder, *Foster's War* (1998), link abusive parents and international abuses of power. The parallels between youthful war games at home and bloody combat abroad and the exploration of how war develops and of the human capacity to hate are worked through not only in much of Westall but also in John Malcolm Rae, *The Custard Boys* (1960); Susan Cooper, *Dawn of Fear* (1970); and Marion Dane Bauer, *Rain of Fire* (1983), among others. Boys in modern works typically learn that combat sickens; girls reveal formidable resilience and courage; both frequently show themselves as wiser than their elders, able to rekindle hope. Disenchanted soldiers star in Harry Mazer, *The Last Mission* (1979); Walter Dean Myers, *Fallen Angels* (1988); Cynthia Rylant, *I Had Seen Castles* (1993); and Robert Cormier, *Heroes* (1998), the latest in Cormier's trademark positioning of young people within larger cultural contexts dominated by institutionalized violence. Cormier explores the home-front fallout of World War II in *Tunes for Bears to Dance To* (1992).

New Zealand authors Eve Sutton and Joanna Orwin treat early Maori intertribal warfare. Mid-nineteenth-century New Zealand wars over land and sovereignty inspired Mona Tracy (pro-English), with Anne de Roo and Ron Bacon taking a Maori perspective on war's stupidities and children's plight. Maurice Gee, Jack Lasenby (most notably in *The Mangrove Summer,* 1988), and Winifred Owen deal with World War I and World War II. Distant combats from the Trojan War to the European Children's Crusade are featured and reinterpreted by Ken Catran and Michael Joseph. More recent conflict in Bosnia is complexly developed around a Maori protagonist in Kate de Gold, *Love, Charlie Mike* (1997). The distinguished Australian John Marsden, *Tomorrow, When the War Began* (1993), and the German Gudrun Pausewang, *The Fall-Out* (1987, trans. Patricia Crampton 1994), consider future wars.

Translated continental works have long set a high standard for stark realism, formal experiment, and moral engagement, from Rudolf Frank, *No Hero for the Kaiser* (1931, trans. Patricia Crampton 1986) to Max von der Grün, *Howl Like the Wolves: Growing Up in Nazi Germany* (trans. Jan van Heurck 1980), to the remarkable trilogy by Hans Peter Richter, whose three slim volumes vividly miniaturize Nazi triumph and ultimate demoralization, bearing witness against his country's and his own crimes in *Friedrich* (1961, trans. Edite Kroll 1972), the emblematic Jewish victim's story related by his "friend," the young German narrator; *I Was There* (1962; trans. Edite Kroll 1972), the older author's indictment of misled German youth, himself included; and *The Time of the Young Soldiers* (1967, trans. Anthea Bell 1976), in which early on the conscripted youngster watches his amputated arm casually tossed in the garbage. Frank described his first fiction as "an antiwar novel to warn young people"; Hitler imprisoned him in 1933, and his book was publicly burnt, vivid testimony to the public impact of war representation for young readers. Especially noteworthy contenders concerning war trauma include the two disturbed Davids of Anne Holm and Claude Gutman. Holm's fugitive in *I Am David* or *North to Freedom* in the United States (1963 as *David*, trans. L. W. Kingsland 1965; repr. 1993) painfully acquires an identity; Gutman's rebellious hero fills *The Empty House* (1989, trans. Anthea Bell 1991) by writing his own allusion-packed story. Gudrun Pausewang, *The Final Journey* (1992, trans. Patricia Crampton 1996), winner of the Marsh Award for best translated work of the year, sends her uncomprehending Alice to the gas chambers expecting a cleansing shower, a wake-up call to readers who know what she does not. Appropriately, the best and the most relevant war stories in an increasingly violent world share didacticism with earlier forebears, but they seek, as many authors and illustrators avow, to teach the skills of peace.

Revelatory and riveting, the diverse contemporary genres encompassed by war stories at the twentieth century's close are arguably the most relevant "didactic" forms for young readers who will shape the new millennium's global, multicultural society. Such works ask, like Primo Levi upon his arrival at Auschwitz, "warum," "why?" Surprisingly often they translate the notorious sign at the entrance to that camp, *Arbeit macht frei* ("work makes freedom"), in terms of the work of writing, bearing witness in the form of autobiographical or factually grounded fictions, actual journals, diaries, memoirs, letters, poems, and drawings. Anne Frank, *The Diary of a Young Girl* (1952; critical edition 1989; definitive edition with restored passages, trans. Susan Massotty 1995), is the most famous example. The author also produced an alternative imagined reality, with fables, dreams, a table personifying her diary as a girl named "Kitty" who is blessed with a "glorious future," and another creating a magical fairy who can dispense happiness for everyone (*Tales from the Secret Annex,* trans. Ralph Manheim and Michael Mok 1983). Anne's diary is itself atypical in the hidden child protagonist's relative insulation from brutal Nazi realities (the record ends before the capture and deaths of all but the father) and its normalizing, or what one critic calls "Americanization," a packaging of specific anti-Jewish horrors in the palatable universalizing form of identity crisis, sexual awakening, and family tensions. Even Anne's story, now the icon of World War II tales and a major source of young people's knowledge about that conflict, barely made it into print, despite its relatively upbeat tone and emphasis on hope for the future rather than guilt for the past. Because she has come to represent the liberal ideal of individuality, progress, and the right to happiness, Anne is also, paradoxically, widely taught as relevant to recent immigrant students in the United States. (She is the frankly acknowledged model for later young war writers, too, as in *Zlata's Diary: A Child's Life in Sarajevo,* trans. 1994.) In the award-winning *Behind the Secret Window: A Memoir of a Hidden Childhood during World War II* (1993), Nelly S. Toll, who survived hiding out, as Anne did not, vividly demonstrates the power of words and art to preserve and heal both the young writer and the young reader. Her little black journal of heartbreak is juxtaposed with exuberant paintings fantasizing school friends, happy families, and bright skies, ending with a Goddess of Freedom, produced just before the Red Army liberated her in 1944.

Current understanding of Anne Frank may, as some critics suggest, downplay mass destruction to celebrate resistance, rebirth, and renewal, as expressed through juvenile autonomy and freedom. Some Holocaust specialists (Lawrence L. Langer, among others) insist that World War II atrocity has no parallels and yields no lessons. Young authors and writers for the young feel otherwise. Most often, they foreground what Nina Bawden calls the more inherently interesting "outside child," the conscripted, the evacuee, the persecuted wanderer or hide-out, the spy seeker, the refugee, the exile, the immigrant, the orphan. War stories provide paradigmatic initiation or coming-of-age stories for both sexes and frequently sidestep gender and class codes normative in peacetime. Recent work often transcends patriotic nationalism, introducing multicultural themes and international issues. Shedding innocence and discarding naïve notions of what counts as heroism or legitimate authority, protagonists search for alternative values and communities, friends, and surrogate families who typically help them to survive and affirm, despite graphic horrors, that the humane and the spiritual matter and still exist. More than any other juvenile category, war stories foreground basic questions: What counts as "children's literature," and how does that literature differ from works for an adult audience; what constitutes permissible subject matter and how may horrors like Nazi crematoria and American atomic destruction be represented for young audiences so as to inspire and not paralyze moral action; and how can juvenile literature foster humane thinking and global peace when youngsters grow up saturated with media violence? More too, perhaps, than any other genres, war stories embody techniques of "cross-writing" that make permeable the boundaries between "fiction" and "history" and between audiences of children and adults. Specifically addressing a mixed readership, as does Janina Bauman, *Winter in the Morning: A Young Girl's Life in the Warsaw Ghetto and Beyond, 1939–1945* (1986), a quest for identity in Nazi Poland, war stories are often dual audience works, especially in the almost innumerable lost childhoods and teen survival and rescuer narratives, typified in Aranka Siegal's prizewinning two volumes on a Hungarian girl's survival and United States immigration, *Upon the Head of the Goat* (1981) and *Grace in the Wilderness* (1985). Documents from youngsters whose words alone outlived the Holocaust furnish both adult historians and teenagers drawn to horror stories. Moving accounts from the youngest survivors, such as Inge Auerbacher, *I Am a Star: Child of the Holocaust* (1966), and Milton J. Nieuwsma, ed., *Kinderlager: An Oral History of Young Holocaust Survivors* (1998), are accessible for quite young readers.

War works also transgress expected norms in appropriating picture books and cartoons for appalling contents and transferring moral authority and decision making from adults to younger protagonists, children wiser than their elders. The young heroine of Roberto Innocenti and Christophe Gallaz, *Rose Blanche* (1985), feeds concentration-camp inmates and gets shot herself at the very moment of German defeat, her improbable but inspiring domestic heroism in stark contrast to the hyperrealistic illustrations of city life under Nazi rule. When the narrative changes from first person to third, readers know that she is dead, but, the war over, the last illustration affirms the coming of spring and peace. Toshi Maruki explains why *Hiroshima No Pika* (*The Flash of Hiroshima,* 1980) impressionistically represents naked, burned, or vaporized bodies from the viewpoint of seven-year-old Mii: "It is very difficult to tell young people about something very bad that happened, in the hope that their knowing will help keep it from happening again." Less terrifying but equally educative, Eleanor Coerr commemorates the dead and disfigured of Hiroshima and Nagasaki in *Sadako and the Thousand Paper Cranes* (1977) and *Meiko and the Fifth Treasure* (1993); depositing the life-preserving cranes is now an annual child's celebration in Hiroshima Peace Park. For adolescents and their elders, Art Spiegelman, *Maus, A Survivor's Tale, I, My Father Bleeds History; II, And Here My Troubles Began* (1986, 1991), creates via the comic strip a multiaudience animal fable of Auschwitz and after, updating the ancient convention with Jewish mice, Nazi cats, and American dogfaces. Raymond Briggs, *When the Wind Blows* (1982), predicts nuclear holocaust via the destruction of Hilda and Jimmy Bloggs, a nice, elderly provincial British couple, in another highly sophisticated comic book replete with multilayered ironies. Directed at much younger readers, Dr. Seuss, *The Butter Battle Book* (1984), harks back to Swift's mortal combat in Lilliput, with the Yooks and Zooks escalating their weaponry over which side of bread the butter goes on. As the open ending makes clear when the child questions Grandpa whether he will drop the "Big-Boy Boomeroo," it is up to the future generation to decide: "We will see."

Outgrowing the generic staples of combat novel, spy story, or boyish adventures familiar from old favorites such as G. A. Henty and the Biggles books, recent war stories thus experiment with representational form as well as didactic content. They increasingly feature strong heroines, instead of soldiers, and often confront the moral dilemmas posed by more modern wars, with no simplistic accounts of good guys versus bad and no pat definitions of what constitutes heroism. Indeed, the convention of the patriotic youth off to help his country through battlefront combat abroad, returning home to applause, is becoming as suspect in juvenile fiction as it has been in adult fiction since Stephen Crane wrote *The Red Badge of Courage* (1895). Six million Jews died in the Holocaust, two of every three in Europe, a million and a half of them children; five million Gentiles also were systematically killed. Casualties in World War II were 44 percent civilian; the percentage of civilians and noncombatants in later wars has risen to more than 90 percent, a large proportion of whom are very young. For many writers, the most important lessons for humane living evolve through storying war and death. Whether picture books deliver their messages visually for older as well as younger readers, or pioneering realistic analysts of war, violence, moral responsibility, and heroism code their work in symbolic analogues, as does, most notably, Robert Cormier, today's best war storying vigorously negates Peter Pan's gush, "To die would be an awfully big adventure."

Further reading, including comprehensive bibliographies

Cadogan, Mary, and Patricia Craig. *Women and Children First: The Fiction of Two World Wars.* London: Gollancz, 1978.

Danks, Carol, and Leatrice B. Rabinsky, eds. *Teaching for a Tolerant World, Grades 9–12: Essays and Resources.* Urbana, IL: National Council of Teachers of English, 1999.

Holsinger, M. Paul. *The Ways of War: The Era of World War II in Children's and Young Adult Fiction.* Lanham, MD: Scarecrow, 1995.

Johannessen, Larry R. *Illumination Rounds: Teaching the Literature of the Vietnam War.* Urbana, IL: National Council of Teachers of English, 1992.

Kennemer, Phyllis K. *Using Literature to Teach Middle Grades about War.* Phoenix, AZ: ORYX, 1993.

Lenz, Millicent. *Nuclear Age Literature for Youth: The Quest for a Life-Affirming Ethic.* Chicago: American Library Association, 1990.

Marten, James, ed. *Lessons of War: The Civil War in Children's Magazines.* Wilmington, DE: Scholarly Resources, 1998.

Overstreet, Deborah Wilson. *Unencumbered by History: The Vietnam Experience in Young Adult Fiction.* Lanham, MD: Scarecrow, 1998.

Robertson, Judith P., ed. *Teaching for a Tolerant World, Grade K–6: Essays and Resources.* Urbana, IL: National Council of Teachers of English, 1999.

Stephens, Elaine C., and Jean E. Brown. *Learning about the Civil War: Literature and Other Resources for Young People.* North Haven, CT: Shoestring, 1998.

Stephens, Elaine C., Jean E. Brown, and Janet E. Rubin. *Learning about the Holocaust: Literature and Other Resources for Young People.* North Haven, CT: Shoestring, 1995.

Sullivan, Edward T. *The Holocaust in Literature for Youth: A Guide and Resource Book.* Lanham, MD: Scarecrow, 1999.

Taylor, Desmond. *The Juvenile Novels of World War II.* Westport, CT: Greenwood, 1994.

U.S. Holocaust Memorial Museum. *Teaching about the Holocaust: A Resource Book for Educators.* Washington, DC: Resource Center for Educators, U.S. Holocaust Memorial Museum, 1995.

Walter, Virginia A. *War and Peace Literature for Young Adults: A Resource Guide to Significant Issues.* Phoenix, AZ: ORYX, 1993.

Werner, Emmy E. *Reluctant Witnesses: Children's Voices from the Civil War.* Boulder, CO:

Westview, 1998.

———. *Through the Eyes of Innocents: Children Witness World War II.* Boulder, CO: Westview, 2000.

Whitehead, Winifred. *Old Lies Revisited: Young Readers and the Literature of War and Violence.* London: Pluto, 1991.

Note: The World Wide Web has numerous sites on wars, including those that focus on individual Japanese internment camps, featuring growing-up narratives and otherwise available documents on Vietnam and other wars and elaborate hypertext for many conflicts and individual battles, some of them created by youngsters themselves, class projects, and so on. Especially valuable are the National Council of Teacher's of English (NCTE) guides (Dans and Rabinsky and Robertson), both of which situate racism, violence, and war topics within a rich milieu of related current areas and are both strong on resources, including Web sites and teaching strategies.

2

Massacre of the Innocents?

Sacral Violence and the Paradox of the Children's Crusade

GARY DICKSON

The year 2012 will be the eight hundredth anniversary of the Children's Crusade, an episode of crusading history that is both known and unknown, famous and obscure.[1] How and why its memory remains alive in the popular imagination of Western Europe and North America is something of a mystery. There is no doubt that people have heard of it, but when and from what source is usually buried too deeply in memory's archaeology to unearth. Perhaps it is dimly recalled from illustrations in children's literature, from children's encyclopedias, or from popular histories such as H. G. Wells's unlikely bestseller *The Outline of History* (1920). Somewhat more recently, public consciousness of it was reawakened by Kurt Vonnegut's powerful novel *Slaughterhouse-Five or the Children's Crusade; a Duty-Dance with Death* (1969).

In fact, it was during the 1960s, a time of radical youth movements—antiwar and pro–civil rights—that a new surge of interest in it began, and George Zabriskie Gray's amateurish *The Children's Crusade* (1871) was reprinted unrevised in 1972. Dubious parallels were drawn by 1960s journalists between the so-called college kids who espoused radical causes and their putative medieval counterparts who set off, starry-eyed, on the Children's Crusade. The moral of this comparison, which was self-evident to sermonizing newspaper editors, was that idealistic movements of this sort invariably ended in tears, meaning that those naïve enough to be caught up in them are bound to suffer disillusionment or worse. Consequently, what was true for the child crusaders of the Middle Ages would also be true for the radical youth of today.

But the historical Children's Crusade is not that easy to pin down. The contemporary evidence we have for it is opinionated and patchy, consisting mostly of the terse reports of monastic chroniclers, many of whose fragmentary narratives are embellished with mythistorical motifs. These motifs increasingly gained the upper hand so that by around the middle of the thirteenth century the mythistory triumphed over the history. Let us, for the moment, close our eyes to its mythistory; its history is intriguing enough not to need the embellishments of fiction.

The Children's Crusade of 1212 was the first, though certainly not the last, medieval European youth movement.[2] Young people, both male and female, were the most conspicuous element in it. The acknowledged leaders of this crusade enthusiasm, the French shepherd boy Stephen of Cloyes and the German peasant lad Nicholas of Cologne, were described by the chroniclers as children or young people, in a word, *pueri*. Not all who joined it, however, were youths; for rather quickly the Children's Crusade became a mass movement. Elderly folk and entire families, including mothers with babes in arms, found themselves swept up in the collective excitement. All generations may have flocked to it, but the same could not be said of all social levels.

On the contrary, of the enthusiasts participating in the *peregrinatio* (pilgrimage-crusade) of the *pueri,* the vast majority belonged to the lower orders of medieval society. As a social group, the *pueri* comprised shepherds, landless peasants, artisans, and impoverished urban and rural laborers. Typical crusade armies, in contrast, often contained a popular element—including female camp followers—but were predominantly composed of a sprinkling of great lords, followed by lesser nobles, knights and their retainers, and then common soldiers, all accompanied by a scattering of clerics acting as chaplains, preachers, liturgical morale boosters, plus the odd high-ranking papal legate or two. This means that the Children's Crusade or *peregrinatio puerorum* can be termed a "popular crusade" in two senses. It was "popular," first, because those taking part in it were people of lowly social origins and, second, because it was unofficial. No one but the pope had the authority to summon a crusade, and Pope Innocent III (1198–1216) had not authorized the so-called crusade of the *pueri*.

So from its inception the paradoxical nature of the *peregrinatio puerorum* is clear. It arose as an unanticipated popular response to papal crusade appeals that were directly aimed at recruiting knights, the traditional arms bearers of Christendom. The Children's Crusade thus contradicts the notion that medieval peasant society was far removed from the world of major events and existed in a timeless world of its own. Not so. The response of the youthful peasant enthusiasts of 1212 demonstrates that at times of crusading crisis peasant society could be stirred; and this, indeed, was just such a time.

The crusading fervor that animated the Children's Crusade is directly traceable to the twin techniques utilized by the papacy for mobilizing mass support for the crusades, preaching, and processions. In this case, however, the consequences of collective arousal were wholly unexpected. Recruitment campaigns for the Albigensian crusade—the war against the heretics and their supporters in southern France—intensified during the winter of 1211–12. Preachers toured the same regions of France and Germany that in the coming months would produce juvenile crusaders. Then, hard on the heels of the Albigensian crusade, came the even more momentous Spanish crisis, triggered by the invasion of the formidable North African Almohades. Christendom's western frontier with Islam looked fragile. Emissaries were dispatched from Spain. A decisive battle, later to result in the great Christian victory of Las Navas de Tolosa (July 12, 1212), was imminent. Innocent III's anxieties about the endangered Spanish church were communicated to all of Christendom. Proclaiming an Iberian crusade, Innocent ordered supplicatory processions in Rome in which barefooted men and women—fasting, praying, weeping, and groaning—processed along a designated route (Dickson 2000a, 352–56; Maier 1999). Innocent next called upon prelates beyond Rome, including the archbishop of Sens, within whose province lay the diocese of Chartres, to organize similar processions. Such processions were probably held at Chartres around May 20, 1212.

Although we cannot be certain, it seems highly likely that from these liturgical processions, which became increasingly ardent and ecstatic, the Children's Crusade was born. As they marched in procession, the youthful enthusiasts fervently shouted out their supplications: "Lord God, exalt Christendom! Lord God, restore to us the True Cross!" (Dickson 1995, 47–49). These outcries articulated their beliefs. "Exalt Christendom!" points to a crusading crisis, while "restore to us the True Cross!" recalls the painful loss of the chief relic of crusader Jerusalem, the cross believed to be that upon which Christ died and which was seized by the Saracens at the Battle of Hattin in 1187. Everything indicates that the appeal of the Spanish crusade rapidly receded, its place taken by the imaginatively more compelling crusade to the Holy Land, which had been in abeyance since the crusaders captured Constantinople in 1204.

Apparently, at some point the processions at Chartres passed out of ecclesiastical control. Seemingly acting on their own without clerical supervision, the laity retained liturgical forms and props, while directing their footsteps where they chose. Once roused, popular enthusiasm proved difficult to contain. Prominent amongst these troops of marchers were wonder-working *pueri*.[3] If this is so, then the earliest phase of the Children's Crusade appears to have been leaderless and directionless, consisting of itinerant, processional bands of crusade enthusiasts.

The second stage of the movement (beginning in June 1212) witnessed the coming of charismatic direction. A leader emerged, who, although we cannot be certain, most likely participated in the processions at Chartres (Dickson 1992, 84ff). The anonymous chronicler of Laon tells us that Stephen of Cloyes, a young shepherd, was instructed by Christ in the guise of a poor pilgrim to deliver letters—contents never disclosed—to the king of France. Stephen then led a troop of *pueri* to King Philip Augustus at Saint-Denis and presumably handed over the letters entrusted to him. Mission accomplished. What followed, according to the Laon Anonymous, was that the king sought the advice of his university intellectuals, the Masters of Paris. Thereupon the king ordered the *pueri* to disperse and return home.

That is the last we hear of Stephen of Cloyes. But not of the Children's Crusade, which is next documented at Rocourt, near Saint-Quentin in northern France. Here a civic disturbance broke out between the canons of Saint-Quentin and the townsmen while the *pueri* were there (see Alphandéry and Dupront 1995, 345). Although the *pueri* are not accused of having taken part in the violence themselves, scholars have argued that it was their presence in the town that provoked a quarrel between the laity and the clergy over the question of donations. Should the *pueri* be treated as poor pilgrims and crusaders and given alms? If so, good Christians should be encouraged to give generously. But if not, Christians were not bound to donate. That the clergy might have been expected to decry the expedition of the *pueri* as illegitimate as well as harebrained makes this argument plausible. The canons might also have been expected to have argued that good Christians would be better advised to give their money to the church. In contradistinction to the canons, at least some of the townsmen would surely have been sympathetic to the youthful crusaders, inclined not only to contribute to but even, perhaps, to join their novel pilgrimage-crusade. However persuasive this hypothesis about the causes of the fracas at Rocourt may seem, like most interpretations of the Children's Crusade, it is impossible to verify.

After Saint-Quentin we lose track of the *pueri* until the Rhenish phase of the movement begins with Nicholas of Cologne. It is reasonable to believe that Nicholas's child crusaders came into contact with their French counterparts. Otherwise the origins of the German *peregrinatio puerorum* remain inexplicable. During the German phase of the movement the self-belief of the *pueri,* already apparent with Stephen's followers, strengthens, just as their crusader identity becomes more transparent. Under the leadership of Nicholas the bands of German *pueri* came to see themselves as neo-Israelites journeying to the Promised Land. Wearing pilgrimage and crusading insignia, including crosses and banners, Nicholas of Cologne's followers headed southward through the Rhineland to the Alpine passes leading toward the Mediterranean, convinced that they, too, would cross the sea to the Holy Land dry-shod, just as the Israelites had done.

Which brings us back to the paradoxical nature of the Children's Crusade. The crusades, from their inception at Clermont in 1095, were armed expeditions of knights intent upon the just reconquest of territories that were once Christian. Of course there was a pious and penitential aspect to the crusades. Indeed, they were described, somewhat euphemistically, as armed pilgrimages, and crusaders, before there was a specific word for them, were called "pilgrims." Yet the crusades were also a new kind of holy war. Central to them was sacral violence. Originally, their intended targets were the Muslims of the Levant. By the second crusade (1145) the Moors of Iberia plus the pagan Wends of Slavdom were added to the list. During the era of Innocent III—and the Children's Crusade—this list grew to include the Baltic pagans, heretical Cathars, schismatic Greeks, and Christian political enemies of the papacy. Although the papacy never meant the European Jews to be targeted by the crusaders, from the first crusade onward the Jews were often massacred just the same.[4]

Here we find the fundamental contradiction of the Children's Crusade. At no stage of their movement do the chroniclers mention or hint that the *pueri* bore arms. Now it would not have been unusual for peasants and artisans such as the *pueri* to have carried homemade arms—farm implements, cudgels, and the like—but there is not a word to indicate that the peasant crusaders of 1212 did so. Paradoxically, this was an unarmed response to a crusading crisis. Would it therefore signal a "crusade" with a pacifistic intent? Only one late and unreliably mythistorical source, the Austrian Rhymed Chronicle (c. 1270), suggests that this might be so by pretending to reproduce their very

> cries of *Pax! Iubilacio! Deo laus!* . . .
> Pagans and the perfidious will all be baptized.
> Everyone in Jerusalem will sing this song:
> "Peace is now, o worshipper of Christ; Christ will come
> And will glorify those redeemed by his blood.
> He will crown all of Nicholas's *pueri.*" (*Chronicon rhythmicum Austriacum*, 1880, 356)

Assuredly, this is not peace or peacemaking as we know it. The peace being heralded is eschatological: it is Christ's peace of the Last Days. Instead of this millennial vision of the Children's Crusade, perhaps a more plausible interpretation of what it represents is a reversion to the precrusade ideal of nonviolence, an ideal inherent in classical pilgrimage. Paradoxically, however, in this instance it is manifested in a context of crusading sacral violence.

In its final phase, the *peregrinatio puerorum* assumed a new guise. Trekking painfully southward, the *pueri* crossed the Alps into Lombardy. Some former child crusaders remained there, while others moved on to Genoa or Rome or Brindisi, perhaps also to Venice, Ancona, and Marseilles. It is during this period that the nature of the movement changed. As it approached the increasingly prosperous port cities of southern Europe, the mass migration of the *pueri* mutated into an influx of northern laborers. Unofficial, youthful crusaders had become cheap migrant workers in search of a livelihood. By mid to late September when the tattered remnant of these troops of would-be crusaders reached the shores of the Mediterranean, their extraordinary pilgrimage was over.[5] As it was and would be for countless immigrants, medieval and modern, they willingly exchanged rural deprivation for urban squalor.

On the road to their oneiric Holy Land, lives both young and old were lost or ruined. Nonetheless, granting the undoubted casualties of the journey, the heavy emphasis that the monastic chroniclers place on the miseries of the *pueri* still seems excessive. Again and again, they stress hunger and thirst, devirgination and exploitation, shipwreck and drowning, incarceration and enslavement, and, worst of all, the perpetual servitude of the *pueri* at the hands of Muslims in distant lands. As painted by the medieval chroniclers, this picture of the outcome of the Children's Crusade is an altogether dark one. Why was black the only color in their paint box?

The two reasons that spring to mind are clerical prejudice and lack of information. To the medieval chroniclers, the *pueri* were disobedient youngsters who, disregarding the warnings and commands of priests and parents, deserved their fate. For the most part, the chroniclers as monks were pledged to obedience and *stabilitas* (staying in one place) and so were bound to be hostile to anyone mocking these values. The *pueri,* moreover, were juniors who presumed to lead seniors. Plainly, this reversed the natural order of things. Crucially, in addition, their so-called crusade accomplished nothing, proving that God had not willed it. So its catastrophic conclusion was God's last judgment on it. Now, if such a venture was necessarily foredoomed, then an appropriate beginning was required in order to reinforce the godlessness of the enterprise and justify the disaster that befell the *pueri.*

The chroniclers answered the challenge with origin myths, demonstrating that the Children's Crusade was instigated as the result of a demonic conspiracy. According to the chroniclers who fearlessly named and blamed them, the perpetrators of the events of 1212 were the agents of Satan. Among them, naturally, were the Muslims and their allies, including the fearsome Old Man of the Mountain, leader of the Assassins. Also among them were various unidentified evil enchanters or magicians.[6]

In defense of the chroniclers, the idea of the catastrophic ending of the crusade of the *pueri* took root most strongly in the German lands, located far from the enthusiasm's Mediterranean terminus. So the chroniclers were poorly informed about what had happened to the Lost Boys. All they knew was that relatively few of them ever returned to their native lands. An explanation for their disappearance was called for, and providing an explanation in the absence of information is a well-known function of myth.

Contrary to the chroniclers' mythistorical constructions, a previously overlooked document suggests that, in reality, all was not doom and gloom for the crusade's participants. At least for some of the *pueri,* displacement and immigration might have brought fresh opportunities. A letter from the registry of Pope Honorius III, dated August 19, 1220, deals with the situation of a *pauper scolaris,* a poor student or scholar, named Otto. Otto was seeking and was granted dispensation from his crusading vow, which along "with a multitude of other *pueri,*" Otto had *imprudenter*—rashly—assumed. Otto most likely belonged to a band of German *pueri* who arrived in northeastern Italy sometime in mid-August, 1212. Pope Honorius, by absolving him from his vow to go on crusade, allowed Otto to continue his studies or pursue a clerical career without the threat of excommunication. Otto's children's crusade ended eight years after it had begun. Still, a clerical education opened a route to future prospects. Thus, for Otto, it cannot be called a tragic ending (Dickson 2002, 594–95).

Conversely, mythistory, not history, is what made the Children's Crusade memorable. And wonderful to relate, neither the mythistorical motif of its calamitous ending nor that of its diabolical beginnings exhausted the sheer inventiveness, the mythistoricizing creativity of the medieval chroniclers. Moreover, it should be pointed out that not all the medieval chroniclers were unsympathetic to the *pueri,* and where these more sympathetic mythistoricizing chroniclers excelled themselves was in smuggling the positive motifs of medieval childhood into their accounts. More particularly, it was the childhood of Christ that inspired them.

While it is true that not all of those participating in the crusade enthusiasm of 1212 were young people, the motifs of youthfulness and childhood surface repeatedly in the chroniclers.[7] The anonymous chronicler of Laon thus terms Stephen of Cloyes a *puer,* referring to his fellow shepherds as *coevis* or age-mates, without specifying what precisely their age was. Laon dubs them *innocentes,* however, and medieval ideas of sexual purity—*puer* was thought to derive from *purus,* pure—do suggest prepuberty.[8] Yet there are good reasons for caution in interpreting these writings.

The more mythistorically inclined the chroniclers were, the more they drew upon childhood motifs and heightened them. This is certainly true of the later chroniclers, but even the testimony of contemporary chroniclers such as Sicard, bishop of Cremona, should not necessarily be taken literally. Although he might have been in the region at the time, there is no proof that he actually witnessed the arrival of the *pueri* in Lombardy. In any event, when Sicard states that these German *pueri* were led by an "infant under ten years old," perhaps his terse remark was never intended to convey more than a sense of extraordinary youthfulness (*Sicardi Episcopi Cremonensis Cronica [to 1212]*, 1903, 180–81). The demands of numerical exactitude were not a preoccupation of the medieval chroniclers.

One year after the Children's Crusade in or near Paris, a recruitment sermon by an anonymous crusade preacher replicates the comment of the Laon Anonymous by describing the *pueri* as *innocentes parvuli,* child-innocents. Unlike the Anonymous, however, he also calls them *crucesignati,* crusaders; to him they were a positive example for encouraging knights and others to support the fifth crusade.[9] The midcentury French mythistorian Alberic of Trois-Fontaines adds a more specific gloss to the theme of childhood innocence by claiming that a church built in commemoration of the drowned *pueri* was dedicated to these New Innocents (*ecclesiam novorum Innocentum*).[10] Later in the century, another chronicler, Richer of Senones, compares the Little People of 1212 (*parva gens*) with the Great Innocents who were killed for Christ (*magnis innocentibus, qui pro Christo occisi sunt; Richeri Gesta Senoniensis Ecclesiae [to 1264]*, 1880, 301). Finally, the versifier of the Austrian Rhymed Chronicle confirms the same mythistorical linkage between the *pueri* and the Holy Innocents: "Nicholas with his Innocents (*cum innocentibus*) will enter Jerusalem" (*Chronicon rhythmicum Austriacum [to 1267]*, 1880). The medieval cult of the Holy Innocents, the child martyrs who were massacred in place of the Christ child, had a remarkable impact on popular veneration, art, and literature.[11] Because their cult also fell during the season of the Nativity (December 28), it had a strongly Christocentric, even Christomimetic dimension.

Devotion to Christ's nativity and infancy was an ever-strengthening aspect of thirteenth-century popular piety.[12] In this connection the role shepherds played in the art and theatre of the Nativity cannot be forgotten. Real shepherds could see themselves sculpted on church façades as well as represented in liturgical dramas. They were aware that God had chosen them to be the first to gaze upon the newborn Christ. According to the Anonymous of Laon, Stephen of Cloyes and his age-mates were shepherds, which would make the *peregrinatio puerorum* the first in a series of the medieval shepherds' crusades. Depicted as they were on the walls of the great cathedral at Chartres, Stephen and his fellow youthful shepherds would view themselves as enacting a privileged role in sacral history.

Last of all, what is perhaps the most intriguing Christomimetic childhood motif alluded to in any of the chroniclers' accounts of the Children's Crusade must not be overlooked, but it has rarely been discussed in the scholarly literature.[13] When the English "Barnwell" chronicler declares that none of the *pueri* was older than twelve years old,[14] and when the Franciscan Salimbene, decades later, begins his short mythologized narrative of the Children's Crusade, "In the same year, namely 1212, three boys of about twelve years of age . . . ,"[15] both chroniclers appear to be signaling the same episode in the Gospel. This is the sole incident that pertains to Christ's childhood, as distinct from his infancy. In it St. Luke recounts the pilgrimage of the twelve-year-old Jesus to Jerusalem, during which Jesus becomes separated from his parents, and only after three days is discovered putting questions to the teachers in the temple (Luke 2:41–52). Learned medieval treatises and commentaries were devoted to the subject of when Jesus was twelve years old.[16] Now could it be that when the Laon Anonymous relates the judgment delivered by the assembled Paris Masters on Stephen of Cloyes and his *pueri* that he is evoking the scene of the twelve-year-old, runaway *Christus puer* among the assembled doctors of the synagogue?

Crusading revivalism initially uprooted these young shepherds and peasants and directed their feet toward the Holy Land, indisputably demonstrating the power of the idea of the crusade to transform young shepherds and peasants into aspirant, if unlikely, Christian crusaders—unlikely because crusaders were supposed to be professional warriors, the *milites,* the knights of Christendom. Unlikely as well because, paradoxically, the unarmed *pueri* were responding to a crusading crisis in a manner reminiscent of the nonviolence associated with the classical idea of pilgrimage. And further paradoxes remain concerning this unauthorized, unanticipated crusade. Pope Innocent III, who never summoned the *peregrinatio puerorum,* but whose Spanish crusade processions probably triggered it, also learned from it.

Historians have attributed Innocent's new papal policy of socially and generationally inclusive recruitment to the fifth crusade, announced in 1213, to the influence of the *pueri*.[17]

But the history of these unlikely crusaders is not terminated in 1213. Their afterlife also belongs to their history, that is, the persistence of their mythistoricized memory. For the remarkable fact is that the *peregrinatio puerorum,* which its contemporary chroniclers consigned to oblivion—while, paradoxically, their vivid mythistorical accounts ensured that they would never be forgotten—survives in the collective memory of educated Europeans and Americans. To the disapproving, moralizing chroniclers, the *peregrinatio puerorum* became a sermon story or exemplum, a cautionary tale, just as it did centuries later in more sentimentalized Victorian children's literature. As such, it was perfectly designed for dissuading other would-be runaways. It was this semifictionalized or at the very least extravagantly embroidered account of the *pueri* that provided the medieval chroniclers with their morally satisfying unhappy ending and thereafter became the accepted conclusion of the Children's Crusade in the public consciousness of later generations. While the mythistorical tradition may view the *pueri* as the naïve or sublime victims of the machinations of satanic men, historical interpretation adopts a less lurid, but no less fascinating, perspective.

Notes

1. A full account of the *pueri* of 1212 and their afterlife can be found in Dickson (forthcoming). Material has also been drawn from Dickson (1992), reprinted in Dickson (2000a, cap. 5); Dickson (1995), reprinted as "The Genesis of the Children's Crusade (1212)" in Dickson (2000a, cap. 4); Dickson (1999–2000); Dickson (2002). For other views, see Zacour (1969) and Raedts (1977).
2. For later medieval youth movements (1333, 1393, 1441–42) as shrine-directed revivals, see Dickson (2000b, 487–90).
3. Shinners (1997, 395–400), offers a good selection of chroniclers of the Children's Crusade in translation. For the Laon Anonymous, see 395.
4. For good general histories of the crusades, see Mayer (1988) and Riley-Smith (1987).
5. A preliminary attempt to trace the route of the *pueri* appears in Dickson (1997, 121).
6. A brief overview is in Dickson (1995, 2–3).
7. But Raedts's notion that the *pueri* belonged to a marginalized social group of the same name, and so were not children, goes much too far: see Dickson (1992, 95–97).
8. For Isidore of Seville, prince of medieval etymologists, see Lindsay (1911, xi.ii.3–4 10; 11–12).
9. For a brief extract, see Bériou (1998, 60n188).
10. Further on Alberic describes the eighteen enslaved Christian *infantes* who were executed at Baghdad for failing to convert to Islam as *martirii.* Translation of Alberic (as Aubrey) in Shinners (1997, 396).
11. For example, see Dudley (1994).

12. For one aspect of the growing thirteenth-century cult of the Christ child, see Sinanoglou (1973).
13. For one exception, see Dickson (1999–2000, 98–99).
14. *Walteri de Coventria Memoriale* (1873, 205).
15. Salimbene de Adam (1966, 42): *Eodem anno, scilicet mccxii, trium puerorum quasi duodennium* . . .
16. Especially note Aelred de Rievaulx (1958).
17. See Powell (1986, 8–9) and Dickson (2002, 595).

3

"Surely there is no British boy or girl who has not heard of the battle of Waterloo!"

War and Children's Literature in the Age of Napoleon

M. O. Grenby

In 1824, Grace Kennedy began her best-selling children's book, *Anna Ross,* by claiming, "Surely there is no British boy or girl who has not heard of the battle of Waterloo!" (1824, 5). The French Revolutionary and Napoleonic wars (1793–1815) were such all-encompassing and nation-forming events—in many ways the sort of "total war" not seen again in Europe until the twentieth century—that it is difficult to believe that she can have been wrong. It is the task of this chapter to investigate first how British children living at the time of Trafalgar and Waterloo understood the wars, and second how they learned of them. This will lead into a consideration of how children's literature constructed the wars for its readers and whether the Napoleonic era witnessed the development of the war story genre, so central to children's literature in the nineteenth and twentieth centuries.

What is certain is that some children knew more than enough about the French Revolutionary and Napoleonic wars from their own personal involvement with them. With the army and navy so hugely enlarged during the wars, containing up to perhaps a tenth of the able-bodied male population, a very substantial number of children must have grown up without fathers or brothers present in their lives (Harvey 1981, 5). Further, with casualties of more than two hundred thousand during the wars, many children would undoubtedly have been orphaned (a partial explanation for the high incidence of orphan stories in the children's literature of the period). Moreover, in the eighteenth and early nineteenth centuries, children actually went to war themselves. On the high seas, each line of battleship in the Royal Navy generally carried upward of fifty boys aged between six and eighteen, some as "powder monkeys" or servants, others in training to be officers.[1] George III was told that "fourteen is as late as so hardy a profession can be embraced with the smallest chance of success," and Nelson and most of the other successful officers of the period were in command of many men by the age of twelve (Hill 1995, 150). On land, too, boys joined the militia and the army and might command their elders before they reached an advanced age.[2] A significant portion of the boys' literature of the mid-nineteenth century was founded on the reminiscences of these juvenile combatants.[3]

That many civilian children, and those whose families were not in the forces, were also drawn into the wars is demonstrated by many subsequently written memoirs, even if it is not unlikely that retrospective prominence might be given to such legendary events as Trafalgar and Waterloo. Napoleon's threatened invasion looms especially large in these accounts, clearly terrifying some children. It was, after all, a genuine danger in 1803 and 1804, especially for those, like Harriet Martineau, who lived in East Anglia. Although Martineau was only one or two years old at the height of the invasion scare, she claimed to have remembered her parents talking of the expected landing, and her father noticing her "standing staring, twitching my pinafore with terror." A few years later, after Wellington's Iberian campaigns had instilled more optimism, she remembered how she "used to fly into the kitchen, and tell my father's servants how sure 'Boney' was to be caught,—how impossible it was that he should escape,—how his army was being driven back through the Pyrenees,—or how he had driven back the allies here or there." She "liked the importance and sensation of carrying news," she remembered (Martineau 2000, 123 and 146–47). Equally perturbed by the prospect of invasion was the Taylor family, living at that time in Colchester. Almost every day, remembered Isaac Taylor, then fifteen years old, a rumor would be spread from the officers in the garrison that the arrival of the invasion force was imminent (Taylor 1841, 45). Children were evacuated. Three of the Taylor children—aged fifteen, nine, and five—were packed off to Lavenham, twenty miles inland, to be looked after by their older sister, Jane, then nineteen.[4]

Other memoirs record how the bogeyman Napoleon militarized more than frightened children. Charles Loftus, a schoolboy in 1808, wrote of the "patriotic enthusiasm which had been excited throughout Great Britain by the threatened invasion of the French," a pitch of excitement "kept alive by the accounts which were constantly reaching England of fresh triumphs for our arms both by sea and land" (see figure 3.1, p. 143). It meant that "every boy at school was ardently looking forward to the time when he should be old enough to join either the Army or the Navy" (Loftus 1998, 29). Similar martial sentiment is evident in many of the broadside ballads warning against the invasion in the collections of the British Library, including one purporting to have been written by a sixteen-year-old, "The Minor's Soliloquy," that sold for 3d. per dozen. "My Countrymen dear," it begins,

40

Brave BRITONS give ear:
A Tyrant severe
Now threatens to steer
Hither his career,
With monstrous idea,
Your Freedom to shear,
Your Country make drear
And, what is more queer,
Be sole Financier,
Of all the wealth here.

So it goes on, culminating in the author's boast that

Ev'n I, though just clear
Of my Sixteenth Year,
Would grasp the bright Spear
Without the least fear
Of the funeral Bier,
To prove I revere
My Liberty, Prince, and august Overseer!!! (Anonymous, n.d.)

Most boys, though, remembered the war as above all exciting and even fun. John Flint South (born 1797) recalled that, as boys, he and his friends "thought more about the warlike news than anything else . . . and were always looking for victories, illuminations and fireworks" (South 1884, 20). Thomas Carter (born 1792; his father enlisted as a soldier in 1794 and did return for four years) was also "much amused with the novel spectacles" he witnessed at the (temporary) declaration of peace in 1802: "The town was generally illuminated; the streets were filled with people; the church-bells were ringing; bonfires were blazing; and everybody seemed to be happy" ([T. Carter] 1845, 17 and 43). Thomas Cooper, the incipient Chartist, born in 1805, likewise remembered that during his childhood the town was "kept in perpetual ferment by the news of battles" and that the streets would be lined with people to see the postman "ride in with his hat covered with ribbons, and blowing his horn mightily, as he bore the news of some fresh victory." He and his friends incorporated such news into their play. They spent their time drawing soldiers and horses and Wellington and "Boney," or, on one occasion, dressing up as Wellington, Blucher, the Emperor of Russia, Bonaparte, and others and singing hymns outside the houses of local notables. They would give three cheers, he recalled, shout "Peace and Plenty! God save the King," then hold out their hats for coins (Cooper 1971, 17–18 and 23–24).

Perhaps the fullest account of children's response to the wars, and especially the invasion, is to be found in the memoirs of "Charlotte Elizabeth," Mrs. Tonna, born in 1790 and also living in East Anglia. She and her siblings felt the threat of Napoleon to be very real, "and many a time did we withdraw to the shelter of the old hay-stack, where we had hollowed out a little alcove, and hold converse, with breathless anxiety, on the probable future." Sometimes they sought out secure hiding places to flee to when the invasion came, but mostly they were determined "to stand by our mother to the last, and to try, if we could not, by some means, ourselves kill Bonaparte." Her brother went further still, she wrote.

> [He] assembled all the little boys of the neighbourhood, addressed them in a patriotic speech, and brought them to the unanimous resolution of arming in defence of their country. Those whose finances extended so far, bought real wooden guns and swords; others, impoverished by the allurements of an old dame who vended lollipops, were obliged to content themselves with such weapons as they could shape out of the hedge; a sixpenny drum, and a twopenny fife completed the military equipment, while on me devolved the distinguished honour of tacking sundry pieces of silk to an old broomstick and presenting these colours to the corps, with an oration breathing such loyalty and devotion to the good cause of liberty and Old England, as wrought to the highest pitch the enthusiasm of the regiment, whose colonel was ten years old, and very few of the officers or men much younger. ("Charlotte Elizabeth" 1841, 46–47)

Such playing at soldiers is very similarly described in a children's book called *The Little Deserter; or, Holiday Sports*, probably published a year or two after Waterloo (see figure 3.2, p. 43). There too the game seems to be simultaneously comic and deadly earnest.[5]

Although patchy then, the available evidence indicates that the war loomed large in children's minds. Their memoirs also reveal something of where children got their information from. Martineau overheard her parents speaking about the war; Charlotte Elizabeth learned much from the prayers said in church; Thomas Cooper learned of victories from the postman riding through the town but also gained much information from old soldiers, pensioned off and living in his neighborhood, whose tales he much preferred to "the fairy tales told by wandering peddlers and beggars" (Cooper 1971, 10). John Flint South recalled subscribing to a weekly newspaper with his schoolmates, then, when the Peninsular campaign got really exciting, a thrice-weekly paper (South 1884, 20). The most famous literary response to the wars, Samuel Taylor Coleridge's "Fears in Solitude," written during, and about, the invasion crisis of 1798, also suggests that it was from their reading that children came into contact with the war: "Boys and girls . . . all *read of war*," he claimed. It was something he deplored, grieving that

> The poor wretch, who has learnt his only prayers
> From curses, who knows scarcely words enough
> To ask a blessing from his Heavenly Father,
> Becomes a fluent phraseman, absolute

War and Children's Literature in the Age of Napoleon

Figure 3.2. *The Little Deserter; or Holiday Sports.* Edinburgh: Oliver & Boyd, 1825. Reproduced by permission of the Cotsen Children's Library, Princeton University Library.

And technical in victories and defeats,
And all our dainty terms for fratricide.[6]

If Coleridge is right about children reading of the war, the question is where? Ballads, newspapers, and other kinds of popular literature were evidently consumed by some children. But discussion of the war, or even any mention of it, was far scarcer in literature produced especially for children in the years leading up to Waterloo. Texts such as Kennedy's *Anna Ross* and Marryat's naval stories, which directly immersed their readers in the French Revolutionary and Napoleonic wars, began to appear only in the 1820s, after a decent interval had elapsed. Indeed, in Mitzi Myers's survey of the war story in chapter 1, just one pre-1900 text is identified, John Aikin and Anna Laetitia Barbauld's *Evenings at Home* (1792–96): one of whose four short war stories is reprinted at the end of this volume. Most other studies on the subject have also, somewhat surprisingly, been unable to discover the roots of the war story genre in the Romantic era or earlier.[7] It is in fact possible to identify several children's texts that do engage with the military concerns of the period, and what follows is in part an account of some of these. But what remains striking is how seldom either war in general, or the French wars currently under discussion in particular, formed a part of children's literature.

One kind of children's literature to which readers eager to hear of stirring martial exploits could confidently turn was history and geography schoolbooks. Some of these were blatantly militaristic. Thomas Mante's *Naval and Military History of the Wars of England,* published around 1803, is typical of these.[8] Written for "the Rising Generation," it offered what its subtitle called "An accurate and lively Description of the Sieges, Battles, Bombardments, Sea Engagements, Expeditions, and extensive Conquests of the British Arms, in all Quarters of the Globe." Its six lengthy, handsome octavo volumes covered the period from Julius Caesar to the Falklands War of 1770. Its most striking feature was its many copperplate engravings, which made no concession to the putative innocence of its intended readers, but tendered plenty of images of blood and gore, corpses and explosions.[9]

Less overtly militaristic schoolbooks often offered this kind of bellicose delight too. The most successful of all of them was probably William Guthrie's *Geographical, Historical, and Commercial Grammar,* first published in 1770. In the successive editions that appeared every few years until well into the nineteenth century, the accounts of British and French history were updated with news from the wars. Accounts of military engagements were highly dramatic, reading more like movie-makers' pitches for proposed war films than schoolbooks. In the twentieth edition printed in 1806, for instance, pupils would have found this: "In the course of the preparations made for the invasion of England a number of transports had been fitted out [by the French] at Flushing, and some other of the ports of Holland. . . . An expedition was therefore fitted out in May 1798, under the command of captain Home Popham, and major-general Coote, which landed a body of troops at Ostend, who blew up and entirely destroyed the sluice-gates and works of the canal at that place, and burnt several vessels that were intended for transports."[10] Throughout the war, then, children could be certain that such schoolbooks would provide them with tales of derring-do from the battlefield, the accounts often including transcripts of letters from the commanders, statistics about artillery and manpower, and comments on military strategy.

These schoolbooks are often unexpectedly blunt in telling young readers about the threat of invasion. The Reverend John Evans's *New Geographical Grammar,* designed for use in schools, informed his readers of "Vast preparations . . . made in all the different sea-ports of France," of "a great number of flat-bottomed boats and transports . . . fitted out," of "a formidable force . . . assembled near the sea coast to which they gave the appellation of the army of England," and of "rafts of an immense size, in which they were to float over to England, and to carry terror and dismay to her shores" (Evans 1811, 676). This account was published in 1811, after the invasion crisis had abated. But earlier accounts, printed before the victory at Trafalgar, all but ending fears of invasion, must have alarmed as much as it reassured its young readers. Here, for instance, is the 1806 edition of Guthrie's *Grammar*: "The people of Britain, roused by insult, and animated by conscious integrity and honour, have risen as one man, and with patriotic enthusiasm taken up arms in defence of their king, their constitution, and their liberties, convinced that the most wretched of slavery must be their lot, should the despot of France succeed in his ambitious and ferocious designs. But that he can succeed must be impossible, while the natives of this free and happy country retain one particle of their antient [*sic*] spirit" (Guthrie 1806, 291). There is a decided bravado here, masking a genuine anxiety about Napoleon's power. Within the year, the Battle of Trafalgar had made this unnecessary. Later editions of Guthrie's *Grammar* give a much more concise, confident, and blasé treatment of Napoleon's invasion plans.[11]

With Nelson victorious at the Nile (1798), Copenhagen (1801), and finally Trafalgar (1805), shrewd publishers and authors began to realize that there was a market for war stories, or at least they tried to develop one. Elizabeth Kilner's *A Visit to London* (1805) purports to show this demand with a description of a family's trip to Tabart's London children's bookshop. One of the protagonists, Edward, has "a very great desire to go to sea" and was enchanted when he read of the life of Nelson in a book called *The Juvenile Plutarch*. But, alas, says his sister Maria, who wishes to buy him a book, he now finds pleasure only in reading books that relate to the sea, and these, she says, are either scarce or too voluminous. Not so, says her fellow shopper, who has been scanning the shelves. "I have been fortunate enough to find two beautiful bound books, which I think will exactly suit him."[12] These are *The Naval Heroes of Great Britain; or, Accounts of the Lives and Actions of the Distinguished Admirals and Commanders who have Contributed to Confer on Great-Britain the Empire of the Ocean* (1806) and *The British Neptune* (1807), both by William Burney, master of the Naval Academy at Portsmouth, and published by Tabart's associate, Richard Phillips. In these Edward might have read to his heart's content of naval battles both historic and contemporary. Burney had brought his history up to date, his entry on Nelson, inevitably, being twice as long as any other in the book and culminating in a eulogy surely designed to fire the reader's martial ardor. "May future admirals emulate his valour," Burney writes, just as if he were recruiting for his Naval Academy from among his readers (Burney 1806, 435). *The British Neptune* was tamer, offering a straightforward history of the Royal Navy, but with compensations in the shape of luridly violent engravings, long lists of French and Spanish ships destroyed, and fully 120 pages dedicated to the wars with Revolutionary and Napoleonic France (Burney 1807).

In the fiction designed for children during the war years, however, representations of warfare were rarer and, when they did occur, much less bellicose. One exception, unapologetically pugnacious despite its lighthearted tone, was *The History and Adventures of Little Henry* (1810), produced by S. and J. Fuller at their "Temple of Fancy" and consisting of a verse text written to accompany a paper doll and its several paper costumes, all included in the price. Henry's final costume is that of a midshipman in the Royal Navy, a role in which "he performs prodigies of bravery to the admiration of the whole crew." He leads boats into battle, "And takes, in spite of all the thund'ring forts, / Ships with rich cargoes from the Gallic ports." What is striking is the strong endorsement of martial nationalism:

> Yet still [he] resolves with patriot ardour warm,
> To save his country from a tyrant's arm,
> He hopes in time to raise a nation's wonder,
> On Ocean's bosom 'midst the cannon's thunder;
> To Gallic territories to advance,
> Clip bold Napoleon's wings, and humble France. (*History and Adventures of Little Henry* 1810, 15 and 20)

Being a doll book, though, it seems unlikely that this could have been the sort of text of which Coleridge was complaining as encouraging militaristic inclinations. In any case, the military ardor on display here is unusual in the children's fiction produced during the war years.

Outright pacifism was also not common. Intriguingly, it would become more so after the end of the wars, paralleling the rise of the war stories of Marryat and others from the 1820s. Open pacifism was most often to be found in books produced by either Evangelicals or nonconformists. *The Good Child's Delight,* for instance, published around 1822, exhibits the shared ground between Evangelical Christianity and pacifism, linking the conflict with man's inherently corrupt nature. "Oh! what a dreadful thing is war!" reads the caption to an image of warships that, in other contexts, might have been designed to inspire patriotic pride. "JESUS says it comes of men's lusts," the text goes on, "meaning the lust of ambition, of power, and of oppression" (Anonymous ca. 1822, 32). Likewise, in Mary Elliott's *Plain Things for Little Folk,* published by the Quaker William Darton Jr. around 1823, the caption to another image of warships unequivocally advises the reader, "Go not on board this man of war / Its freight is only wounds and scars."[13] While the war was still being fought, most Quakers and Unitarians, as well as a significant number of other nonconformists and Evangelical Anglicans, had been opposed to it.[14] Perhaps it was at least partly because of publishers' unwillingness to seem unpatriotic that children's books seem not, as a rule, to have then included direct antiwar material.

However, the four antiwar stories (out of a total of ninety-seven) of Aikin and Barbauld's *Evenings at Home* were the exception (see Mahon 2000a, 2000b; and White 1999). What is striking is how well they mesh with the actual experiences of children. In Aikin's "The Price of a Victory," from the fourth volume of *Evenings at Home* (1794), a child, Oswald, bursts in on his father, gleefully telling him the news of a great military victory with thousands of the enemy killed and bonfires and illuminations planned for the evening. His father refuses to rejoice, pointing out the many that have died and been injured. His son asks if it is not right to celebrate a nation's victory, but his father thinks not, when so many must suffer on all sides, most of whom will not have gone to war willingly.[15] Aikin's story recalls the delight of John Flint South and Thomas Carter in victory celebrations, but it was apparently specifically designed to undercut their unthinking delight. Oswald's father's position, at least according to the Unitarian Harriet Martineau's memoirs, is typical of the dissenting response. The Martineaus did not celebrate the news of

Waterloo as a glorious victory. "It was the slaughter that was uppermost with us," she remembered, "though we never had a relative, nor, as far as I know, even an acquaintance, in either army or navy" (Martineau 2000, 147).

The antiwar stories of *Evenings at Home* may have been unusual, but they were not unique. Charlotte Smith produced what was probably an even more brutally pacifist discussion of the realities of war in her *Rural Walks: In Dialogues* (1795). However magnificent the sight of a fleet might be, Mrs. Woodfield tells her pupil, a view of warships should convey "only painful ideas." When she had seen the ships preparing for departure from the harbor, she recalled,

> I figured to myself how many of those brave thoughtless beings, who were now rending the air with shouts of triumph, proud of the splendor of that shew of which every one considered himself as a part, and elate with the grandeur of his country, whose strength lies in its navy, would, within a few days, perhaps, become mangled carcasses for the prey of the monsters of the deep, and dye, with their blood, the waves over which they were now so gaily bounding; inflicting, at the same time, equal evils on an equal or more considerable number of human beings, whom they never saw before, and with whom they have no manner of quarrel. (Smith 1795, 2:62–63)

Smith was no dissenter, but she had her own reasons for pacifism in 1795. Her son had been injured in battle with the French in 1793, resulting in the amputation of his lower leg.

Why were the sorts of bald militarism to be found in *The History and Adventures of Little Henry* and the open pacifism of Smith and Aikin and Barbauld so unusual? Sarah Trimmer's comments on the antiwar stories in Aikin and Barbauld's *Evenings at Home* in her children's literature review journal, *The Guardian of Education* (1802–6), suggest one possible explanation. The question of war, she wrote, "is of so intricate a nature, that *children* are not capable of comprehending a discussion of it" (Trimmer 1803, 345). She proceeded to mete out some very hostile treatment to *Evenings at Home* in a series of reviews. She accused its authors of being both seditious and blasphemous and of preying on the young and innocent. War was "both *lawful* and *necessary*," she declared, basing her argument (as she always did) on the scriptures, where war functioned as "one of the JUDGMENTS of the Almighty." It was very wrong, she said, "to inspire children with a *prejudice* which will . . . lead them . . . not only to be discontented with the government they live under . . . but to arraign even the Almighty himself." Indeed, she went on, war was often of great spiritual benefit to those injured and killed. A soldier's injuries, she wrote, could cure him of his former profligate behavior, and his death in battle might smooth his passage to heaven.[16] In addition to stating a political and scriptural position (with much modern resonance), these reviews were designed to intimidate other authors and publishers. The absence of much war literature in the first decade or two of the nineteenth century can be taken as an indication that she succeeded.

Conversely, Trimmer's central conviction—that children's innocence should be protected from any discussion of war because they cannot fully understand it—was essentially nonreligious and apolitical. When we ask why authors and publishers produced so few war stories in the 1790s and 1800s, the answer is probably less that they were intimated by Trimmer and more that they agreed with her. Maria Edgeworth and Richard Lovell Edgeworth, to take an example from toward the other end of the political spectrum, agreed that "the simple morality of childhood" could be shocked by books full of "assassinations, battles, revolutions" and so on (Edgeworth and Edgeworth 1798, 351–52). It was as a consequence, we might presume, that Maria Edgeworth's own children's stories did not touch on the subject. Yet the Edgeworths were not wholly opposed to the idea of war featuring in children's lives, offering in their manual, *Practical Education,* an endorsement of the sort of rational treatment of the subject provided in *Evenings at Home* or *Rural Walks.* They suggested that a teacher might present a pupil with a plain historical account of a battle. The child's surprise, and then grief, at learning of the "hundreds and thousands that were put to death by a conqueror, or that fell in one battle" would impart a valuable lesson—a useful channeling of trauma (Edgeworth and Edgeworth 1798, 351–52).

The lesson proposed by the Edgeworths and actually put into print by Aikin and Barbauld and Smith is fundamentally antiwar. But what the Edgeworths' commentary exposes is that more important to these stories than the serving of any pacifist agenda was the way in which they taught children to think. It is in this that the fundamental disagreement between Trimmer, on the one hand, and Aikin and Barbauld or the Edgeworths, on the other, lies. While Trimmer wanted to close down debate, the others were adamant that children should be encouraged to dispute and deliberate. The dialogue in Smith's *Rural Walks* between the wise Mrs. Woodfield and her intelligent and inquiring daughters and niece exhibits this perfectly. After hearing Mrs. Woodfield's opinions on the barbarity of naval warfare, the niece, Caroline, objects that "if every body reasoned in this manner, there would be no wars."

Mrs. Woodfield. And if there were not?

Caroline. Why then there would be no occasion for either armies or navies.

Mrs. Woodfield. And what would there be in that to lament?

Caroline. Dear aunt, I don't know. But other nations would fall upon us and destroy us, if we had neither.

Mrs. Woodfield. Not if all nations would be equally reasonable, and learn that there is nothing to be obtained by our cutting each other's throats.

Elizabeth. But, mamma, there have always been wars.

Mrs. Woodfield. And one blushes, as a human being and a Christian, to trace those wars to their sources.

Henrietta. But, mamma, is it not true that the English have always been glorious about fighting?

Mrs. Woodfield. Really, Henrietta, your ideas of glory are worthy of a little amazon. . . . I assure you, that the laurels of Britannia by no means compensate for her scars. (Smith 1795, 2:63–66)

Smith's dialogue closely resembles a longer debate between Commodore Freeport and his son Constantine to be found in a story called "War and Peace," translated from "La guerre et la paix" in Arnaud Berquin's *Ami des enfans* (1782–83; *The Children's Friend,* 1788, 3:64–73). Both offer rational debates about war, encouraging children to think freely about the place of warfare in history, even if the adults' views are finally allowed to prevail. There are some significant differences between Berquin and Smith. The commodore designs his lesson to teach his son to be a good soldier, for he is intended for a military career. Smith's decision to put Mrs. Woodfield in the place of Berquin's naval officer, and girls in the place of Constantine, is an intriguing feminization of the debate. Making Caroline so central is also important, as Smith has already established her as the recipient of a conventional and fashionable—which is to say faulty—education (Smith 1795, 1:2–9). She therefore stands for the prejudices of the public as a whole, and it becomes more obvious that society's received attitudes are being put on trial rather than merely those of Berquin's untutored child.

The antiwar sections of *Evenings at Home*—dialogues, like Berquin's and Smith's—were likewise designed to encourage discussion and to generate challenges to received opinions. Barbauld's "Things by their right names" and Aikin's "The Two Robbers" both try to teach children how little distinction exists between a battle and a common murder. While the antiwar tendency is manifest, readers have also been offered a riddle or an exercise in lateral thinking. As several critics have pointed out, these are stories about the vexed relationship between naming and knowing (see Mahon 2000b, 166; Summerfield 1984, 108). Aikin's "The Cost of a War" discusses the brutality of Louis XIV, leading to his conclusion that "Right and wrong are no consideration to a military man." Such an immoral axiom was designed to shock readers into disgust (Aikin and Barbauld 1792–96, 1:150–52, 2:148–52, 5:54–63).

All these dialogues invite children to try to distinguish convention from truth and appearance from reality. The ways in which children were challenged to think originally by Aikin and Barbauld's stories (although not only those about war) is generally significant in the history of children's books.[17] Within the context of this chapter what is most significant is how the stories tie in with what was probably the most recurrent motif of the children's literature about war during the French Revolutionary and Napoleonic eras, namely the frequent warnings to boys not to be seduced by the glamour of a military life and not to run off to join the armed services.

In fact, this motif features prominently in one of the *Evenings at Home* war stories. Aikin's "The Price of a Victory" can be divided into two parts. The more famous section is the first, already discussed, in which Oswald is made to question his initial unthinking celebration of a triumphal battle. In the second, longer section of the story, Oswald's father proceeds to recount the story of a boy named Walter, "a good and dutiful lad, and a clever workman," who ran off to join the army after he had been plied with "fine stories about a soldier's life." Crippled in battle, Walter limps back to his home village and soon dies, the rest of his family quickly following him to his grave (Aikin 1792–96, 55–56). While the first half of the story had proffered a theoretical lesson about the real meaning of war, the second half was a practical warning against allowing military zeal to dupe one into enlistment. It was advice much repeated and much amplified in other children's novels of the period. In *My Real Friend; or, incidents in life, founded on truth, for the amusement of children* (1812), Jem Wild joins the army because, like other "silly youths," he "had heard of honour, of fighting for one's country's cause, and of the gentility of such a life." Clearly they had not been so fortunate as to read the dialogues of *Evenings at Home*. "They had often heard of battles, and of fields being won," the reader is pointedly advised, "but the thoughts of bleeding in great misery and fatigue, or of the instant deprivation of life . . . did not form any part of their discussion," nor did the sinfulness of killing others. Worst of all, the grief they would cause "to a careful and affectionate mother and tender sisters . . . was, alas! unhappily overlooked." Indeed, the story ends not like "The Price of a Victory," but more pathetically, with the reproaches of the mothers and sisters left behind, "upbraiding in their heartfelt grief, those who were so estranged to the feelings of another's woe, as to allure them"—their sons and brothers—"into so fatal an adventure" (Anonymous 1812, 27–31).

My Real Friend, as the title hints and its publication by Darton confirms, was an utterly Quakerish production, just as *Evenings at Home*, published by Joseph Johnson, was thoroughly Unitarian. But it was neither the religious nor the political convictions of their authors and publishers that were generating such antienlistment texts. Much more conservative authors and publishers were producing very similar material, for instance, W. F. Sullivan, whose *Pleasant Stories; or, The Histories of Ben, the Sailor and Ned, the Soldier* appeared shortly after Waterloo. Sullivan was a convinced anti-Jacobin, the author of several satirical attacks on the French Revolutionaries and the successful poem *The Test of Union and Loyalty, on the Long-Threatened French Invasion,* written out of a "spirit of Loyalty and Patriotic Zeal . . . at a time the most critical and opportune, when our very existence as a nation is avowedly threatened by despotic presumption, personal enmity, and disappointed ambition." He had himself enlisted in the navy at the age of nineteen to fight in the American War of Independence (Sullivan 1803, vii–viii; and 1805). Nevertheless, *Pleasant Stories* was clearly designed to prevent boys from being seduced by the war. The uncle whose story opens the book could not have stated this position more emphatically (see figure 3.3, p. 144). He bitterly regrets that he ran off to sea when a child, for "all I have gained, after six-and-twenty years of hard service, is plenty of flogging, many hard knocks, and a broken constitution." He hopes that his misfortunes will be a lesson to his nephews, Ben and Ned: "I wish I was as young as they are, and had so good a birth," he says. "I'd see all the ships at Old Harry, before I would set my foot aboard one of them. . . . [I]f they know when they are well off, they'll stay where they are" (Sullivan ca. 1818, 12–14). The boys' tragedy is that, even with such an object lesson as the experiences of their ailing uncle, they are still not immune to the seductive power of his stories of "hair-breadth escapes" and daring victories that he also foolishly lets slip. They soon join up, Ben in the navy and Ned in the army, and, inevitably, both boys find their uncle's warnings to be accurate. Ben is maltreated by his shipmates, falsely accused of crimes, flogged through the fleet, cheated of his prize money, and heartily regrets his decision. Ned is tricked out of his bounty for volunteering, suffers from ludicrously severe military discipline, is half-starved, and is forced to march for miles carrying a heavy knapsack on his wounded back. Unlike the foolish uncle, Sullivan himself refuses to provide exciting accounts of any combat in the novel. When he does mention a particular military engagement, his description is clearly designed to depress the spirits of even the most militaristic boy. At the Battle of Corunna, for example, Ned reports that the army was "sadly misled by false friends," that they arrived at the battlefield "worn out and harassed," and that they were so doomed to defeat (Sullivan ca. 1818, 16–17 and 41).

Sullivan designed his ironically titled *Pleasant Stories,* with its bitter account of the boys' hardships and their painful regret about leaving home, to encourage boys to follow a more peaceable path through life. Many other children's novels followed exactly the same course. It is extraordinary that even at the height of the Napoleonic War, with Britain threatened by invasion and then economic if not military destruction, so much children's fiction was attempting to dampen martial ardor rather than enflaming it and to dissuade boys from enlisting rather than encouraging them. As the complicity of ex-soldiers like Sullivan suggests, no deep-seated pacifism lay behind this campaign. Rather, it was something more integral to Romantic-era children's literature: a fundamental disjunction between the overall purpose of the children's literature of the period and the glorification of war.

We get a strong sense of this from the Edgeworths' *Practical Education.* In their discussion of children's books they strongly inveighed against adventure stories. Such books, they said, preyed upon the natural impulses of a young boy, encouraging him to aspire to be "the soldier of fortune, the commercial adventurer, or the nabob" rather than to follow "the patient drudgery of trade, the laborious mental exertions requisite to prepare him for a profession" (Edgeworth and Edgeworth 1798, 337). In other words, tales of adventure and, by the same token, war stories, betrayed the whole purpose of the new children's literature of the later eighteenth century, which was to fit its young readers, particularly its male readers, for a secure, successful, and profitable adult life. This is, of course, a generalization, but it is surely not outrageous to suggest that by the 1780s and 1790s the central aim of most respectable British children's novels was to secure a future of stable and expanding affluence within a context of religion and morality. This was certainly the trajectory followed by the majority of the protagonists of the new generation of moral tales. Unlike the tales of the mid-eighteenth century, often designed to teach children how to work their way up from extreme indigence by learning to read and write, the lessons taught in the children's fiction produced in the decades just before and just after 1800 were more fitted to a middle-class readership. The virtues fostered were no longer patience and humility, gratitude and subservience, but much more commercial values and skills such as diligence and industry, trustworthiness and thrift, enterprise and ambition, prudent expenditure and judicious benevolence. It is easy to see why the Edgeworths and others would have objected to the war story as likely to undermine the entire raison d'être of this children's literature. Presenting a boy with tales of adventure and glory on the battlefield would be, it could easily be argued, very likely to inspire in him the desire to become a soldier or sailor. Even apart from the fact that these were arduous and hazardous professions and might be objected to by parents on those grounds alone, they were also in almost direct opposition to the sort of career that parents hoped the children's literature they were buying would encourage. A military career required daring not prudence, audacity not industry, and encouraged showiness rather than moderation. It was no wonder that those who were involved in producing this new children's literature shunned any text that they felt was likely to induce a martial zeal in its readers.

Concern about the effect of war stories on impressionable middle-class boys could produce several effects. First, there were some overtly pacifist texts such as the pertinent sections of *Evenings at Home.* Second, many books included depictions of wounded, impoverished veterans, and these in themselves, even if the war itself was not directly mentioned, taught a lesson about the dangers of combat and the ungratefulness of society.[18] Third, and probably the most prevalent response, was that exemplified by those texts that steadfastly did not refer to the wars at all. The disjunction between the purposes of children's literature and the representation of war was the cause, in other words, of the dearth of pre-Victorian war stories that is so conspicuous in histories of the genre. Fourth, some children's books did contain favorable accounts of the armed services, and even of children enlisting in them—but these texts showed only soldiers and sailors from social groups excluded from the main target audience of the new, respectable children's literature. For example, in one of Mary Pilkington's translated tales, a boy is recruited to the Royal Navy, proudly announces that "my ship has received immediate orders for sailing, and we'll try if we cannot give the French a drubbing," and then is prominent in a battle in which they take a "capital prize" of which his share is "near two hundred pounds." Such a glamorization of war was unusual but is allowed here, almost certainly, because the hero is no middle-class boy, one of the intended readers of such books, but rather Tippo, a black servant who has been turned out of his place by a cruel master.[19] Fifth, some texts were not antiwar but nevertheless warned against enlistment, Sullivan's *Pleasant Stories,* for example. It is to this kind of narrative, struggling to reconcile an anxiety about the damage war stories might do to the central aims of children's literature, the inevitability of boys' fascination with the military, and the needs of a nation locked into a protracted war with an indefatigable enemy, that best represents the relationship between war and British children's literature in the Napoleonic era.

One of the best examples of such a book is *Charles Lesson; or, The Soldier,* a novel by Harriet Ventum (1810). It is a much more balanced text than either *Evenings at Home* or *Pleasant Stories,* combining stern warnings against a military career and especially about the delusive glamour of the army, with a narrative in which the boy turned soldier is able, finally, to make a successful and happy career for himself in the army. The story proper begins when Charles, the son of a poor widow living in retirement in Westmorland, happens to witness the volunteers exercising in the local town. He is transfixed and reports, "If you please mother, I will be a soldier when I am big enough to enter: I should like it of all things." His mother's response accords exactly with those other texts that pointed out the difference between the appearance and the reality of war:

> It is the finery of the dress, Charles, that attracts you, . . . but, believe me, my dear, a showy outside frequently covers a sorrowful heart: there are few professions (I believe I may almost venture to say, not any) so laborious, fatiguing, or so hazardous, as that of a soldier; harassed about from town to town, and from one post to another; marching through all weathers, whether wet or dry, hot or cold; now drenched with rain, then covered with snow; at other times, parched with heat, and choaking [*sic*] with drought, either in pursuit or retreat; wearied and worn out by forced marches, harassed both in front and rear, exposed to the fire of their opposers, and frequently left more than half dead upon the field of battle; and then, Charles, some fiend, too frequently in the shape of a woman, for the sake of a little plunder the dead and dying bodies afford, will come, and, with cool, deliberate cruelty, finish what the bullet or sword of the enemy has begun: these, my dear boy, are but a few of the ills to which the life of a soldier is exposed.

If quite such a gruesome description of the horrors of the battlefield is unexpected, the account of the practical tribulations of the army is fairly familiar, echoing *Pleasant Stories* as well as the earlier, and apparently influential, Highlander's story in Thomas Day's *Sandford and Merton*.[20] Also familiar is the way in which Charles enters into vigorous debate with his mother. The army is surely a respectable profession, he argues, and soldiers must be "necessary to the good of the state." They are "the defenders of their country; and although they may be subject to fatigues and disasters of various kinds; yet if they surmount them, they return covered in glory." What is different here is that it is Charles's arguments that prevail. His sense of vocation is unshakeable. Pretending a pitchfork is a musket he teaches himself exercise drills, and he learns tactics from old history books (perhaps such as Guthrie's *Geographical, Historical, and Commercial Grammar*). Eventually Providence comes to his aid, in the form of a stranger who comes to his door who in return for hospitality pays for his commission as an officer in the army (Ventum 1810, 10–13).

Warnings about the dangers, hardships, and qualities necessary for success in the army now come thick and fast. Charles's benefactor, Lord D——, tells him that he "must be cool, firm, collected and intrepid in danger; regular, orderly, obedient to command; submissive to your superiors, and gentle and forbearing to your inferiors." His mother counsels him above all not to drink and not to gamble (Ventum 1810, 17–18, 29–33; see also 50–54). Given that Charles has already won his battle over his choice of career, this advice seems not so much designed to put off readers from enlisting as it is to perform two other functions. Lord D——'s advice is so practical that it seems actually intended to help a young recruit in achieving success in the military. Mrs. Leeson's cautions, though, are designed to bring this story of military adventure within the ambit of the conventional moral tale. Her warnings also build the foundation for the novel's plot. Charles is posted to the war in Spain. He is most in danger not from battle, in which he is successful, gaining several promotions, but from a fellow officer, Du Lasnes, who tempts him into hard drinking and then gaming. Their reason for doing this is to get Charles cut out of the will of the moralistic Lord D——, and a complicated storyline leads to Charles's imprisonment for debt, his righteous refusal to be suborned as a witness against his patron, and his eventual deliverance from the schemes of his enemies so that he can resume his successful career in the army. Despite this convoluted plot, the central theme of the book remains the tension between the morality of children's books and the values of the military. It is really the military life that tempts Charles into vice; Du Lasnes simply acts as its agent. When he taunts Charles for his respect for his mother's view, this disjunction between the two value sets becomes evident:

> Your mother again, Leeson! for pity's sake, do not shew your leading-strings, even if you chuse to wear them—Why man, you will be scoffed at and ridiculed by the whole army, if you are continually quoting the old-fashioned sayings of an old woman. We know very well, all mothers tell us not to do this bad thing, nor the other bad thing; but who minds what they say; they cannot see us; and it is very hard if we, who are exposed to a thousand dangers, and are fighting their battles, may not enjoy a drunken frolic now and then.

The dissolute army stands against the entire value system that children's books sought to foster: moral rectitude and parental monitoring—"mamma's schooling," as Mrs. Leeson calls it—as well as the tranquil, hardworking, prosperous life of a gentleman farmer, which Charles's brother Edward has chosen. This alterative career trajectory is periodically mentioned throughout the novel to make the contrast with Charles's folly absolutely clear (Ventum 1810, 65–66 and 92).

Ultimately, *Charles Leeson* is not wholly contemptuous of the military life. Its conclusion insists that Charles "was never, in his heart, either a gamester or a drunkard" and that "His real characteristics were afterward uniformly exhibited, in the brave and prudent commander, the zealous servant of his king and country, the affectionate son and brother, and the grateful acknowledger of past obligations." That "his promotion in the army far exceeded his expectations" is an indication that a synthesis has been arrived at: of the principles of the moral tale and the demands of the army (Ventum 1810, 164). It is the artificial synthesis of a contrived novel, but the point is that in this text at least, an effort had been made to reconcile the appeal of a military calling with the dominant values of children's literature. It would be stretching things to suggest that a text like *Charles Leeson* marks a turning point, when, under the shadow of Napoleon, a military career became a legitimate aspiration for middle-class children, and war became a fit subject for children's literature. But the novel does provide evidence that the exclusion of war from children's books, or its deprecation when it did feature in them, was becoming an increasingly difficult rule to abide by. Some boys did desire to go to war. Historical circumstance increasingly demanded that patriotism and militarism should be encouraged. Children's literature could resist, but the resistance was ultimately untenable.

One final example demonstrates this very succinctly. In an anonymous book called *Juvenile Stories and Dialogues,* published in 1801, the concluding story is called "Lord Nelson." In it, a father reads to his son Henry about Nelson's recent victory at the Battle of the Nile. Finding that the boy displays a strong wish to emulate the admiral and join the armed forces, his father and mother strongly counsel against such a move, rehearsing what we have seen to be the prevailing parental position in children's literature. You have been seduced by the glitter of dress, Henry's father tells him, and a steadier career would be greatly preferable. You will be wounded and left in pain on the battlefield, prophesies his mother. But, in yet another example of parent-child debate on this subject, Henry remains unmoved: "I could bear pain without complaint, surely in the service of my country," he argues. Again, the parental hopes that the new children's literature was designed to service come into conflict with both boyish enthusiasm and patriotism. In this case, it is patriotism that triumphs, the father suddenly giving way, overruling the "weaknesses" of the mother and giving his blessing to his son's career choice. He has been won over by the heroic and patriotic example of Nelson and the consideration that God has appointed some to be soldiers and sailors and some to live more peaceable lives. It is not even a father's place to gainsay this (Anonymous 1801, 152–53 and 163–67).

The existence of one or two isolated texts that sought to draw war into respectable children's literature should not, though, be allowed to disguise the main finding that surprisingly little war literature for children was published during the French Revolutionary and Napoleonic wars. An imaginative war literature for children developed only after Waterloo. This chapter has been largely engaged in listing to that silence and trying to explain it. Schoolbooks did offer militaristic thrills to young readers, but in fiction, Napoleon was conspicuously absent. Those children's fictions that did mention the war were surprisingly peaceable. Such stuff could hardly be accused of "swelling the war-whoop," as Coleridge had put it in "Fears in Solitude" (1988, l.89). A few texts were actively pacifist, but more were simply hostile to the idea the middle-class boys should sign up for active duty: they were antienlistment rather than antiwar.

The primary reason for this was that there was a fundamental incompatibility between militarism and what might be called the more "bourgeois" purposes of the new children's literature, particularly the books designed for boys. The desire of boys to go to war was a recurrent theme, but it was almost always represented as one in need of curbing. Books might include a very vigorous debate on whether a military career was acceptable for a boy, but only one or two were grudgingly willing to endorse such a course for middle-class children. Clearly, authors and publishers keenly felt themselves to be the surrogate guardians of their young readers' prosperous and uninjured futures. In an age when boys as young as five did enter the armed services, and with the long wars generating propaganda that glamorized military heroism, the danger of boys joining up was much more real than it would be after Waterloo. Thus children's fiction was enlisted to restrain boys' mobilization.

Perhaps what is most striking, though, is how out of touch children's literature was with children's lives. Their reminiscences tell us that children knew about the war. They were frightened by its menace, delighted to celebrate its victories, and quick to make up games about its heroes and villains. Many would have lost relatives or participated directly themselves. There would, in short, surely have been "no British boy or girl who has not heard of the battle of Waterloo." Yet in this matter, at least, their experiences were not being clearly represented in their literature.

Notes

1. See Rodger (1986, 68–69). On boys' duties aboard ship, see Lavery (1998, 266–67 and 292–93).
2. The hero of Charlotte Smith's novel *The Wanderings of Warwick* "had been a soldier from twelve years old" (1794, 10). Probably more typical was Philip Hamond, seventeen years old and still a schoolboy when he was gazetted in 1799 as a captain in the Norfolk militia. See Barney (2000, 29).
3. The most famous examples are the sea stories of Captain Marryat beginning with *The Naval Officer, or Scenes and Adventures in the Life of Frank Mildmay* (1829).
4. A letter from Mrs. Taylor explains that after the Colchester commander gave "the most solemn and decisive warning of our danger," all the principal families of the town hastily departed (Armitage 1939, 51–52). It was, in fact, in Lavenham that Jane Taylor spent her evenings "in composing her share of some little works which soon after appeared," as her brother recalled, referring to *Original Poems for Infant Minds* (1804–5) by Jane and her sister Ann. It would seem, then, that such classics as "My Mother" and "Twinkle, Twinkle Little Star" were written by an evacuee (Taylor 1841, 46).
5. Anonymous (n.d., but inscribed 1819). Full page images are available on the Hockliffe Project Web site at www.cts.dmu.ac.uk.
6. Coleridge (1988). Written in April 1798, "During the Alarm of an Invasion," lines 104–13 (emphasis added).
7. See, for example, Whitehead (1991), Fox, Leyson, and Koenders (2000), Eiss (1989), and Quayle (1973).
8. Mante (ca. 1803). Many of the engravings are dated, the earliest being 1794 and the latest 1803.
9. Similarly, action-packed images of warfare could be found in Trimmer (ca. 1800).

See, for instance, prints 28 and 46.
10. Guthrie (1806, 285). The episode was omitted from later editions, perhaps because the raid ended in British defeat.
11. For instance, Guthrie (1819, 239).
12. Kilner (1808, 153–54). Interestingly, this section was inserted only in the reprinted 1808 edition (it was first published in 1805). In the first edition, Henry had been judged too young to receive a book and had ended up with sheets of prints. The reasons for the attribution of this book to Elizabeth Kilner, Dorothy Kilner's niece, are given in Moon (1990, 74 and 69).
13. Elliott (ca .1823, opposite 14). There is in fact no evidence that Elliott was herself a Quaker. See Moon (1987, xiv).
14. See Cookson (1982), especially 4–8. Also useful is Macleod (1998).
15. Aikin (1792–96). All but thirteen of the stories in six volumes were written by Aikin, the others, including "Things by Their Right Names," by his sister.
16. Trimmer (1803, 345, 309, and 346). Her final argument here was exactly that which Coleridge railed against (1988, 11.117–23).
17. Such lessons in original thought go against what Andrew O'Malley has recently suggested to be the dominating theory and practice of later eighteenth-century pedagogy and children's literature, namely frequent repetition of the same lessons so that ideas could become physically fixed in the brain, a method based on David Hartley's theories of psychological materialism (O'Malley (2003, especially 66–67). These particles would subsequently vibrate in ways that they had become accustomed to. The important thing, therefore, was to accustom the brain to think by repetition.
18. See, for example, Anonymous (1816), about a disabled though jolly ex-sailor, or the more typical story of Ben Hallyard, an ex-seaman whose moving story of shipwreck, battle, capture by the French, and then poverty once back in Britain awakens the pity and benevolence of the well-to-do Danvers children in Ventum (1806, 5–25).
19. Pilkington (1799, 98). See also Anonymous (1808), in which a career in the army is depicted in glowing colors, as honorable and profitable, but only because the soldier was originally from the lower classes and has learned that he was wrong to have been "dissatisfied with the situation in which Providence had placed him" (26–27).
20. Day's Highlander was told before enlisting of "the dangers of the field, the pestilence of camps, the slow consuming fever of hospitals, the insolence of command, the irksomeness of obedience, and the uncertainty that the exertions of even a long life would ever lead to the least promotion," but feeling "an irresistible impulse . . . which urges me to the field," he ignored the warnings. As his father prophecies, he "purchased wisdom at the price of his blood," ending up a poor beggar after a catalogue of hardships and misfortunes (Day 1867, 416–18).

4

Under Ideological Fire

Illustrated Wartime Propaganda for Children

Eric J. Johnson

In 1922, Jean-Jacques Waltz and E. Tonnelat published a joint memoir of their service in France's Ministry of Propaganda during World War I. In it they describe the "first and fundamental rule of propaganda": "if you wish to reach the enemy's mind, write his language as well as he does." A further condition for propaganda's success, they explain, is variety.[1] Although they are specifically referring to their own experiences creating propaganda targeting German soldiers and civilians, their comments apply equally well to ideological works aimed at children, a fact that Waltz—better known to his young readers as Oncle Hansi, a famous author and illustrator of children's books—would have known well. The language of childhood is in many regards unique and specialized. Ideas that are crafted for adult audiences are not always equally attractive or understandable to children. Because of this simple truth, propagandists must insinuate their ideologically charged messages into forms that young audiences will instinctively recognize and accept.

Propagandists working throughout the first half of the twentieth century recognized this and were quick to exploit children and the language of childhood, conceptualizing the young as seeds that will grow to bear future ideological fruit and invoking childhood as a construct in need of political nurturing and military protection. In accordance with Tonnelat's and Waltz's emphasis on the importance of variety, they also recognized the utility of appropriating preexisting genres and forms of children's literature to package their ideologically charged messages in different ways. For instance, propagandists have used educational textbooks such as those teaching the alphabet and primers as ready-made instructional tools to inculcate basic political, military, and social ideologies in young minds. Readily recognizable formats such as picture books and genres such as fairy tales have also proven to be useful, offering ideologues the chance to disseminate their beliefs through familiar packaging, plot structures, and narrative techniques. As an established means of diversion, children's literature has also served as a vehicle for propaganda, presenting highly charged political and military philosophies in an entertaining format that encourages rereading. As both a literary and highly visual medium, illustrated children's literature has presented propagandists with a way to promote their messages in a mutually supportive way through the powerful combination of image and text.

The holdings of Princeton University's Cotsen Children's Library reflect the diverse ways that propagandists from around the world have targeted children and employed childhood motifs when fashioning their political and military messages for young audiences. What follows is a small sample of some of the many pieces of historical wartime propaganda in the Cotsen collection that draw upon conventions of children's literature to promote their own political and martial ideologies. I will focus on three methods propagandists used to disseminate their ideas: the use of politically charged texts modeled on traditional didactic works such as alphabet books and primers, the appropriation of picture books as a means of telling a particular ideological story, and the presentation of exemplary figures—both real and fictional—as models of proper thought, action, and behavior. In each section we will see that, throughout the first half of the twentieth century, propagandists did indeed master Tonnelat's and Waltz's "first and fundamental rule of propaganda." Regardless of what doctrine they spouted, they presented their beliefs in a language children could understand, using a variety of means to ensure that their messages would appeal to young readers. Whether fascist schoolbook, communist primer, or militaristic picture book, each of the works discussed in the following sections reveals that the pen can, indeed, be just as ferocious as the sword.

The ABCs of Ideology: Propaganda and Didacticism

An incredibly rich array of didactic propaganda materials targeting children were published around the world during the first half of the twentieth century, including ideological works produced in the form of alphabet books and elementary primers. From World War I– and World War II–era alphabet books touting the martial prowess of Britain's Royal Navy and the United States Army to radical primers full of ideological readings promoting the virtues of fascism or communism, such materials reveal how propagandists taught children different political, military, and social doctrines hand in hand with the basic elements of reading and writing. By conveying such messages in this didactic way, propagandists were able to force-feed their young audiences, nourishing their minds with politicized and militarized teachings that would help them grow into strong, loyal members of their respective states.

The Royal Navy: An ABC for Little Britons goes beyond offering children an introduction to the letters of the alphabet, indoctrinating its little readers into the military culture that dominated Great Britain during World War I (*Royal Navy,* ca. 1915). Presented in simple verse, the book's text describes predictable topics that relate to the Royal Navy: *A* stands for admiral and *B* for Britannia and her battleships, while *D* stands for destroyer and *T* for torpedo. Its rhymes are catchy, if at times awkward, and they lend themselves to easy recollection. But *The Royal Navy* alphabet does more than just identify naval officers and equipment. Its didactic message is also both overtly nationalistic and sentimental. For instance, the poem accompanying the letter *U* encourages patriotism:

> U stands for Union Jack, the best of flags on earth;
> O cherish it, my children, for 'tis yours by right of birth.
> Your fathers fought, your fathers died, to rear it to the sky;
> And we, like them, will never yield, but keep it flying high. (11)

A longer poem recounting the sinking of the German cruiser Blücher at the Battle of Dogger Bank in 1915 stresses the martial prowess of the Royal Navy, Britain's "bulwark and pride." But it goes beyond simple jingoism, showing the book's young audience that proper British sailors are not just brave in combat but also compassionate and chivalrous:

> We cheered; she sank, and then
> The sea was black around her
> With drowning sailor men.
> We put out boats to save them,
> For Britons, as you know,
> Show mercy to the vanquished,
> And spare the fallen foe. (7)

Other rhymes refer to further British victories, Admiral John Jellicoe, and the power of the Royal Navy to safeguard Britain's children from any and all harm. Such verses were undoubtedly intended to instill patriotism in children, pride in Britain's fleet, and a calm, confident assurance of their own safety in spite of the war going on in the ocean surrounding their island home. The book's final verse presents one last message encouraging all proper young Britons to think of themselves as sailors committed to the Royal Navy's fight:

> Now I am seven I mean to go
> On the Iron Duke with Jellicoe;
> I'll do my best to fire the guns,
> And sink the warships of the Huns.

> When I'm grown up, perhaps I shall
> Sail as a gold-laced admiral;
> I'll wear a sword and cocked hat fine,
> And never go to bed till nine. (See figure 4.1, p. 144)

This book's young readers may only recently have graduated from the nursery, but verses like this encouraged them to believe that like their elders they too were ready to defend Britain from her enemies.

Produced for an older audience than *The Royal Navy*, Edward Shenton's *An Alphabet of the Army* introduces military concepts to young readers in a much more sophisticated way, combining concise, detailed text with powerful illustrations that offered World War II–era American children an inside look at the U.S. Army (Shenton 1943). Written with the assistance of U.S. Army officers and the Army Bureau of Public Relations, the book's entries describe unique army units such as the Amphibian Engineer Corps, commandos, paratroops, the newly founded rangers and the Women's Auxiliary Corps (WAC); specialized military equipment ranging from bandoleers to walkie-talkies; weapons such as artillery, bazookas, flame throwers, and tanks; and more arcane topics such as *ack-ack* (colloquial soldiers' term for antiaircraft fire), *AMGOT* (Allied Military Government of Occupied Territory), *iron crab* (a mobile pillbox), and *zero hour* (the time of attack) (see figure 4.2, p. 145).

But this book provides more than descriptions of army units, weaponry, and equipment. It also offers readers a number of choice snippets of American World War II–era martial ideology. For instance, within the entry for "yesterday," a lengthy description of the history of the U.S. Army from the Revolutionary War through World War I, the text provides a lesson in duty and civics: "Our Armies have always been formed from citizen-soldiers. Today the men of the Armed Forces have been selected from all walks of life. Yet because this method truly represents our whole country, we can say that our Army is the Nation, and our Nation is an Army" (63). This lesson continues on the rear panel of the book's dust jacket, encouraging readers to fulfill their "duty of sharing in some degree in the great task" facing the nation by sacrificing some childish indulgence and buying war bonds instead. He concludes his sermon with an exhortation to all American children to overcome inertia, conquer selfishness, vanquish indifference, and "build [their] minds and bodies into strong carriers bearing [their] share of the struggle that will lead to final victory." Such ideological messages went hand in hand with the detailed technical literacy in military terminology and concepts the book provided. Together they would help young American readers identify with the soldiers fighting at the front lines while preparing them for their own future military service.

Alphabet books were not the only didactic medium propagandists used to disseminate their ideologies. Schoolbooks and primers also proved to be popular tools of political and military indoctrination, with the elementary textbooks published in fascist Italy providing some of the most fascinating examples of educational propaganda. The concept of youth lay at the very foundation of the fascist ideal, and Italy's children became special targets of the fascist government after it assumed power in 1923 and reorganized the Italian educational system under a centralized ministry that adapted national curriculum to conform to the Fascist Party's beliefs.[2] Two specific examples of instructional manuals published in the early 1930s celebrate the glories of Benito Mussolini and his regime within a didactic context, revealing the extent to which fascist curriculum mixed political, military, and elementary education.

Il capo-squadra Balilla is a veritable textbook of propagandistic discourse. This budding fascists' handbook presents a range of lessons intended to educate young squad leaders of the *Opera Balilla,* a paramilitary organization for Italian children established by Mussolini in 1926 to inculcate in Italy's youth the mission and message of fascism (*Il capo-squadra Balilla,* 1932). The book is filled with political and military instruction, including organizational charts detailing the hierarchy and structure of the *Balilla,* illustrations of the organization's different uniforms and insignia alongside descriptions of their significance, instructions on how to perform the fascist salute and how to execute commands, an account of Italy's role in World War I, a glorified biography of Mussolini, and a brief history of the rise of the Italian Fascist party and its successes during its first ten years in power. Illustrations of happy children exercising and executing close order drill appear throughout the book. On one page a trio of girls offers the fascist salute, directing the reader's attention to the description of the teaching the *Balilla* provides the future mothers of Italian fascism, including lessons in sewing, embroidery, hygiene, first aid, child rearing, home economics, and gymnastics (see figure 4.3, p. 000). Although not a traditional primer, *Il capo-squadra Balilla* presents modern readers with a comprehensive look at the basic tenets of fascist ideology that underlay didactic works for even the youngest of Italian children.

In contrast to *Il capo-squadra Balilla,* the primer *Sillabario e piccole letture* incorporates fascist propaganda in a more understated—but no less effective—way (Belardinelli 1931). Embedded within the book's more general educational message are overt lessons touting the virtues of *Il Duce* and the fascist state. Little children are shown making the fascist salute, and the book promotes an idealized, sympathetic relationship between Mussolini and Italy's children: "Benito Mussolini loves children very much. The children of Italy love *Il Duce* very much. Long live *Il Duce!*" (58; figure 4.4, p. 146). In addition to their blatant attempts to typify Mussolini as a friend and surrogate parent to Italy's children, such primers also promote a positive image of military life and activities. A reading in *Sillabario* titled "The Soldiers" tells the story of a band of children and their reaction to the sound of lively military music and the sight of a troop of soldiers marching down the street. The children rise up, each one clamoring that he wants to be a sailor, a member of the Alpine mountain troop, or a fighter pilot. The short tale concludes with an exhortation to its readers to meditate on the beautiful uniforms of these soldiers and to remember that eventually they should join their ranks: "Strong Alpine troops defending the doors of Italy; skillful artillerymen handling the guns; self-confident and fast cavalrymen; audacious infantrymen like Benito Mussolini.

Be valorous like the King. This is what you should strive to be!" (107). Materials such as *Il capo-squadra Balilla* and *Sillabario e piccole letture* went to great lengths to characterize Mussolini as a new Caesar, the founder of a resurgent Italian empire whose fascist creed had made possible this new resurrection of Italian political and military hegemony.[3] In doing so they thoroughly politicized and militarized Italian elementary education, shifting the focus from teaching children how to read and write to training them in the basic tenets of fascism: the state is supreme, individuals owe their primary allegiance to the state, and war is the natural state of existence (figure 4.5, p. 147).

At the other end of the political spectrum, Spain's communist Popular Front published *Cartilla escolar antifascista* in 1937, an elementary textbook whose traditional educational content is immersed in socialist rhetoric (*Cartilla escolar antifascista*, 1937). The primer combines what its editors describe as a "logical method" of grammatical instruction that incorporates basic lessons in the alphabet, syllable formation, and sentence reading with colorful photomontages and exercises that "in content and tone" reflect the Spanish communists' heroic fight against fascist traitors who attempt to control the population with the weapons of "ignorance and illiteracy" (3). All teachers and everyone who supports true Spanish culture, the primer's introduction explains, should work to destroy fascism with two of the most powerful weapons available: books and pens.

Unlike its fascist counterparts, the *Cartilla* conveys its ideological message through both positive declarations of communism's virtues as well as negative descriptions of its polar opposite: fascism. Whereas Italian textbooks such as *Il capo-squadra Balilla* and *Sillabario e piccole letture* solely concerned themselves with touting the virtues of fascism and the power of the fascist state, this Spanish text constructs its own left-wing propagandistic discourse in direct response to a competing, right-wing, antagonistic philosophy. The primer does teach its young readers the basic tenets of communism through various clichéd axioms such as "All people are comrades," "Proletariat of the world, unite!" and "The workers of the world are with us," but it also heightens its communist rhetoric by interspersing throughout its text fiery antifascist readings such as "Fascism is slavery and barbarism" and "After we conquer fascism we will have a prosperous and happy Spain." This twofold approach is effective because it reinforces the Popular Front's message by defining not just what communism *is* but also what it *is not*.

Perhaps the *Cartilla*'s most interesting aspect, however, is how it overtly politicizes and militarizes elementary education, likening the role of teachers to political officers, equating the classroom to the battlefield, and accentuating the importance of learning as a form of active fighting in support of communism and Spanish culture. One two-page selection, for instance, unites the concepts of fighting and studying, highlighting the symbiotic relationship between young students and combat soldiers by combining the readings "The rearguard must collaborate with the vanguard" and "We fight for our culture" with a photographic image of armed soldiers at the front line superimposed over a picture of children in a classroom (figure 4.6, p. 148). These pages clearly inform the primer's young readers of their responsibility to the Communist Party and the important part they will play in the continued existence of a nonfascist Spanish state and the future triumph of the Popular Front.[4]

Jingoistic works such as *The Royal Navy ABC, An Alphabet of the Army, Cartilla escolar antifascista, Il capo-squadra Balilla,* and *Sillabario e piccole letture* reveal that it is never too early to begin one's military or political education. They also show that the trappings of formal education can be used not just to teach children how to read and write but also to endow them with a deeper—and often problematic—ideological literacy, one that will help guarantee that the next war, whenever it might be, will have a full complement of soldiers and sailors ready to man its trenches and battleships.

Indoctrination through Illustration: Propaganda as Picture Book

Propaganda of all stripes lends itself well to the combination of illustration and text. Throughout the various conflicts of the twentieth century, but particularly during the first and second world wars, ideologues have put this maxim to the test in their efforts to manipulate their audience's emotions and engineer in them a willingness to support, kill, and die for their states. As I mentioned earlier, schoolbooks were ideal vehicles for the transfer of political and martial doctrines from propagandists' pens to children's impressionable minds. But the classroom was not the only place where young readers were exposed to jingoistic messages. Children's leisure reading—particularly their picture books—have also proved to be popular instruments of indoctrination, as the following examples of pro- and anti-German picture books published during World War I and World War II show.

One of a number of World War I–era picture books to use simple verses and large, colorful illustrations to proclaim Germanic military superiority, *Gloria, Viktoria: Ein Weltkriegs-Bilderbuch,* pits Franz, a German boy, and Michel, his Austrian comrade, against a hostile band of children representing the Entente Powers of Great Britain, France, Belgium, Russia, Italy, and Japan.[5] While Franz and Michel peacefully build a sandcastle at the beach, the six children representing the Allied powers look on enviously and quickly launch an attack against the Austro-German playmates. However, as the British, French, Belgian, Russian, and Italian children assault the fort, the Japanese child skulks among the dunes, biding his time for some unknown purpose. Franz and Michel repeatedly beat off all assaults, and in the end they defeat their attackers, round them up, and imprison them in their fortress. But during the chaotic battle, the Japanese child manages to sneak up to the sandcastle unnoticed by either Franz or Michel, snatch two pieces of fruit they had set aside for their lunch, and successfully flee back into the dunes (figure 4.7, p. 148).

Gloria Viktoria boldly proclaims the combined might of Germany and Austria to be invincible, even in the face of seemingly overwhelming odds. Franz and Michel struggle against six, the book proudly states, but they would gladly fight ten foes and still emerge victorious. The text also emphasizes Franz's and Michel's—

and by extension Austria's and Germany's—inherent moral and martial superiority, contrasting their industriousness, amiability, and strength with the envy, treachery, and belligerence their Allied foes exhibit.

On a more subtle level, however, *Gloria, Viktoria*'s illustrations convey a deeper, more sophisticated message than its text. Strangely, its verses make no explicit mention of the Japanese child who avoids participating in the free-for-all surrounding the sand fort. But while the text may not mention him, the book's illustrations emphasize his importance to its propagandistic message by placing him at or near the center of each picture. This concentration on the Japanese boy and his portrayal as a cunning and cowardly figure who waits for the battle to reach its height before swooping in and escaping with Franz's and Michel's fruit betrays a deeper preoccupation with the effects the Great War will have on European hegemony throughout the world. While the European children sit cowed and defeated behind the sand fort's walls, their supposed Japanese ally escapes, having avoided all risks yet still emerging with a succulent prize. As Europe fights amongst itself, the book implies, non-European nations will take advantage of the war to overthrow its colonial power and steal its wealth. Franz and Michel patrol their fort's parapet, not only guarding against any renewed hostilities from their European rivals but also protecting themselves and their vanquished foes from any threats the rest of the world might raise against them. The final message this masterful work of propaganda conveys to its young readers, then, is twofold: it confirms the unquestioned preeminence and assured victory of the Austro-German alliance, and it notes that in victory, Austria and Germany must also be the saviors, preservers, and protectors of worldwide European supremacy.

In direct contrast to *Gloria, Viktoria*'s strident pan-German ideology stands Jean-Jacques Waltz's equally harsh anti-German propaganda. Better known as Oncle Hansi, Waltz was born in Colmar, Alsace, shortly after its annexation by Germany at the close of the Franco-Prussian War in 1871.[6] Resolutely anti-German, he wrote and illustrated children's books pointing out what he described as the cruelties, excesses, and absurdities of German rule in Alsace. His books cover a broad range of topics, from crafty social satires attacking pan-Germanism and ridiculing Prussian educational methods (Waltz 1912, 1913), to pseudo-historical texts that cast the Germans as the enemies of civilization and highlight the age-old kinship between Alsace and France.[7] His works focused on traditional Alsatian values, customs, and traditions and became rallying points for the *revanchards,* Alsace's anti-German resistance movement. Waltz's works were read avidly throughout the war, and shortly after Germany's surrender in November 1918 he wrote what is arguably his most complex work of pro-French propaganda, *L'Alsace heureuse* (1919).

Written to celebrate the liberation of Alsace from nearly fifty years of what Waltz described in an earlier text as the oppression of German "criminals," "pillagers," and "assassins" (Waltz 1918, 9), *L'Alsace heureuse* offered young Alsatian readers a raw, heartfelt memoir of Waltz's own deep affection for his homeland and his hatred for all things German. He divides his autobiographical book into three parts describing his childhood, his military service during World War I, and his homecoming journey through Alsace at the close of hostilities. The flavor of the book's propaganda is unique in that Waltz wrote it from the perspective of one who has seen his beliefs emerge triumphant from a war of disparate ideologies. For Waltz, Germany's defeat reinforced his own beliefs, and what he offers his young readers in this book is a reaffirmation of German iniquity and a confirmation of French virtue.

Throughout the book, Waltz's words and illustrations combine to paint a vivid picture of the dark days of German rule. The text accompanying a drawing of the chief warden of Colmar Jail guarding an old door at the heart of the prison instructs readers to consider the image allegorically by imagining that behind the barred cell door lies a very sad little Alsatian girl lying in complete darkness. This image, he explains, epitomizes the oppression suffered by all Alsatians as a result of German rule. Other combinations of text and image lampoon German soldiers and government officials, while another depicts the fiery skyline of a burning French town.

But he balances such negative images with many upbeat illustrations of children in traditional Alsatian costume welcoming triumphant French troops; Germans leaving Alsace and crossing the border, presumably never to return; and pastoral scenes of an Alsace finally at peace. Perhaps the most dominant image in the book, a bold, colorful adaptation of the climactic scene from Charles Perrault's famous fairy tale, "Sleeping Beauty," communicates Waltz's nascent relief and joy now that pan-Germanism has been defeated (figure 4.8, p. 149).

In this powerful and many-layered illustration, Hansi politicizes Perrault's tale, depicting the awakening princess in Alsatian dress while portraying her prince as a smiling and attentive French soldier. Asleep under German rule for forty-seven years, France has succeeded in breaking the oppressive enchantment and rescuing Alsace. The princess's bed is decorated with one of France's national symbols, the rooster, while a pair of storks, Alsace's own avian emblem, sits above a window looking out on another of Alsace's most famous symbols, Strasbourg Cathedral. Directly above Beauty's bed, St. Odilia, the patron saint of Alsace famous for her ability to cure blindness, looks down on the princess as she opens her eyes to see the French soldier who has rescued her. But the specter of German oppression also remains, chiseled as spike-helmeted gargoyles in the decorated capitals surmounting the pillars flanking Beauty's bed. Beneath the illustration, Hansi uses Perrault's own words to amplify the scene as the princess asks her savior, "Is it you, my Prince? You were well worth the wait" (7).

Like Sleeping Beauty, Alsace has lain under a terrible enchantment. But the forty-seven years she endured under the German spell of oppression has been lifted, and she is now free to reunite herself with her savior, France. Waltz's complementary use of words and pictures and his skillful appropriation of this famous fairy tale scene encapsulate his own ideological beliefs, presenting them in a form that French and Alsatian children would have found easy to recognize and accept.

Nazi propagandists also found ways to employ the familiar medium of picture books in their pursuit of young hearts and minds. *Trau keinem Fuchs auf grüner Heid und keinem Jud bei seinem Eid!* (*Don't Trust a Fox in a Green Meadow or the Word of a Jew*) is a particularly vicious example (Bauer 1936). Written by Elwira Bauer, an eighteen-year-old art student, and published by Julius Streicher, a former elementary schoolteacher and producer of *Der Stürmer,* the Third Reich's most notorious anti-Semitic newspaper, the book became an important and effective weapon in the Nazi war against the Jews. Parents bought it for their children to read on their own and schools incorporated it into their curricula to teach young Germans the Nazi Party's political and racial stance on "the Jewish Question."[8] It proved to be so popular that it went through seven editions, with more than one hundred thousand copies in circulation at the height of its popularity.

Although it looks like a traditional picture book, *Trau keinem Fuchs* has no definite plot, instead presenting a loosely arranged series of two-page entries pairing inflammatory verse written in *Sütterlinschrift,* an old-fashioned Aryan form of writing popular in Nazi circles, and lurid illustrations to depict the perceived age-old antagonism between Aryans and Jews. The book establishes its severe anti-Semitic rhetoric immediately, using the first paired poem and illustration to identify the Jew as "the son of the Devil" while Germans are the "proud and beautiful" creation of God. The next eleven pairs characterize Jewish perfidy in a variety of ways. One page contrasts the strong, virile, hardworking figure of the "typical" blonde Aryan with the short, fat, lazy image of a balding, dark-complexioned Jew. Other illustrations depict Jews in any number of unflattering ways: a filthy vagabond, a sour-faced doctor, a cruel moneylender in the process of repossessing a German farmer's livestock, and a lecher who tempts a proper German maiden with a jeweled necklace while a Jewish boy leers knowingly at a bewildered Aryan girl. Such images efficiently summarize the Nazi attitude toward Jews, and the stereotypes they perpetuate provide a foundation of distrust and hatred upon which the book's young readers are supposed to build their own anti-Semitic beliefs.

But Bauer does not limit her rhetoric only to descriptions of Jewish deceit. Having firmly established the image of the Jew as a treacherous parasite, she uses the remainder of the book to promote a course of action that will rid Germany of its Jewish problem. She establishes this shift in tone with her depiction of an outraged German vowing to fight Jewish corruption and an illustration of a terrified old Jew sitting bolt upright in bed pointing at the approaching figure of death. Bauer even includes her publisher in the text, portraying a beneficent Streicher in Nazi uniform surrounded by a band of adoring German children. From this point on, the tables are turned as the Jews begin their inevitable fall. Bauer focuses on Germany's children for the remainder of her book. The final six illustrations portray little Aryans reading *Der Stürmer;* pointing at newly impoverished Jewish children who can no longer afford nice toys; taunting Jewish children as they are expelled from school; looking over their shoulders at a Jewish family brought up short on their way to a park by a sign reading, "Jews! You are not welcome here!"; and jeering at Jews as they are banished from town. One of the most powerful representations of this Aryan revival and the important part children will play in it shows a cheerful troop of Hitler Youth marching through the German countryside singing "Der Führer's Jugend" (figure 4.9, p. 150).

Bauer's picture book employs two distinct rhetorical strategies. The first casts Jews in a negative light, characterizing them as a parasitical infestation that must be purged if "real" Germans are to regain their God-given rights. The second firmly places Germany's children at the center of the Nazi vision of Aryan resurgence. With the Jewish threat identified, the future reclamation of everything Nazi ideology maintains the Jews have stolen—wealth, power, and liberty—depends on them. Germany's youth must prepare themselves for this approaching ideological and racial war, for as the book's final slogan maintains, "Without a solution to the Jewish question, there can be no freedom for mankind." Propagandists like Bauer who used virulent anti-Semitic writings and shockingly repugnant illustrations like those found in *Trau keinem Fuchs* proved to be devastatingly effective, a fact testified to by the Nazi party's official implementation of the "Final Solution" at the Wannsee Conference on January 20, 1942.

While Bauer's book proclaims German superiority, *Den onde Fyrste* (*The Wicked Prince*) transforms Hans Christian Andersen's famous 1840 short story about a tyrant who tries to conquer God but is instead struck down by a gnat into a dazzlingly illustrated picture book portraying the devastation that was the price of Nazi ideology and aggression (Andersen ca. 1945). Published shortly after the defeat of Germany and the close of World War II, the book is a celebration of sorts, but its tone is hardly euphoric. Unlike Waltz's jubilant portrayal of his liberated Alsace, *Den onde Fyrste* does not depict happy children, triumphant soldiers returning home, or peaceful scenes of pastoral tranquility. Rather, the book's illustrations emphasize terrifying and depressing scenes of Nazi power and oppression. Capitalizing on Andersen's description of the tyrant's soldiers as demons, the illustrator depicts German soldiers as devils rushing across a blasted, fiery landscape as if they had burst out of the very mouth of hell (figure 4.10, p. 150).

Flames lick at the sky while the grass Hitler's shock troops wear on their helmets for camouflage dances like flickering flames. This image of Nazi soldiers running amok across a war-ravaged Europe contrasts sharply with Elwira Bauer's happy band of Hitler Youth. While Bauer's illustration shows the troop of young Nazis proudly marching through a peaceful countryside, the illustration we see in *Den onde Fyrste* provides a chilling glimpse of what these proud German children will become once Hitler unleashes them on Europe. Other illustrations show Nazi troops preparing to ravage a young woman huddled amidst the wreckage of her house, a massive Nazi rally full of faceless figures saluting their leader, two German soldiers attempting to hang a portrait of the *Führer* above a church altar in spite of a priest's objections, and Hitler presiding over masses of troops whose ranks stretch to the horizon. The only two positive images in the book are of an immense, somber angel shooting down Hitler's bomber with a drop of celestial blood and the Nazi leader's ultimate defeat by one of God's smallest creatures, the gnat.

The book's editor, a minor Danish poet named Aage Hermann, adds his own words to Andersen's original text to help contextualize the fable for his young readers. In his brief foreword, Hermann praises Andersen's apparent prescience, noting that although the famous children's author wrote this story in 1840, his imagination still enabled "him to visualize the man and the weapons that, one hundred years later, would bring unspeakable misery upon the world." Hitler, Hermann explains, was motivated by an "insatiable lust for power," just like Andersen's evil prince. In his explanation of the fable's moral, he likens Hitler's hubris to the evil prince's challenge of God and warns his young audience that if they behave similarly, they too will meet a bloody end "in a ditch or in a bunker." He goes on, describing how proper leaders ought to act: "The wise statesman does not rely on power, but on authority. He does not compel respect with artillery, machine guns or bombs, but through those deeds that benefit the largest possible number of his fellow men." After this quick lesson in proper governance, Hermann reinforces this message, warning his young readers not to follow evil leaders, calling Hitler "the wicked prince of our time," and explaining that he did not commit his crimes alone but had help from many supporters (18).[9]

Although the war is over and Hitler is dead, *Den onde Fyrste* proclaims that it is too early to look past the devastation the Nazis have wrought in pursuit of their *Führer*'s dream. The message the book's text and illustrations combine to present is not one that looks forward to a happy, peaceful Europe. Instead, it exhorts its young readers to look back and meditate upon the negative examples of Hitler's motivations and the crimes he committed in his murderous quest for power. Only by doing so can Europe's postwar children ensure that a wicked prince will not take power again in the future.

Whether using simple verse, autobiographical text, or resurrected fairy tales and fables, the four picture books discussed earlier share one important quality: they all skillfully complement their texts with detailed, symbolic and visceral illustrations. The end result is a package that allowed propagandists to inculcate their ideological messages through a medium that children found both familiar and appealing.

The Cult of Heroes: Exemplary Figures in Children's Propaganda

For as long as propaganda has existed, those who have disseminated it have used heroic and charismatic exemplary figures—both real and fictitious—as models whose lives and accomplishments provide a paradigm of belief and behavior to be imitated. Propaganda targeting children is no different. Whether they highlight historical figures such as *Maréchal* Pétain or quasi-historical—or even outright fictitious—characters such as Ryuji, a Japanese boy who shows his father how to behave like a true Imperial Japanese soldier, ideological works such as those discussed in the following paragraphs taught their young readers that children can be as courageous, virtuous, and self-sacrificing as the adults who lead and fight for them.

Vichy France produced a wide range of propaganda aimed at children, including a seemingly inordinate number of works that focused on the exemplary figure of *Maréchal* Henri-Philippe Pétain, the heroic general whose defensive tactics were credited with defeating the Germans at Verdun in 1916 during World War I.[10] Such books stress Pétain's loyalty to France, his heroic military service, his unflagging wisdom and dedication to the preservation of French culture, and his apparent universal popularity among French children, all of whom, the various authors imply, ought to be devoted to the *Maréchal* and the ideals for which he stands.[11] One author even goes so far as to proclaim that the love the children of France should feel for Pétain can actually support the *Maréchal* and his tireless efforts to return France to her age-old glory: "Ah! If only the *Maréchal* knew that all the children of France already consider him their grandfather. What power, what energy he would he draw from them!" (Hérault ca. 1942, 32).

One book in particular, *Oui, monsieur le Maréchal!* offers a perfect example of how Vichy propagandists used the *Maréchal* as an exemplary inspirational figure (L'Oncle Sébastien ca. 1942). The book's pseudonymous author, Uncle Sébastien, places Pétain at the rhetorical center of his ideological message while following many of the fundamental tenets of effective propaganda. He begins by establishing a dark mood of desperation rooted in France's recent military defeat. He quickly extinguishes this hopelessness and misery, however, by introducing the proverbial hero with a plan, *Maréchal* Pétain himself, who presents himself as the savior of France: "I give to France the gift of myself to alleviate her misfortunes" (3; see also figure 4.11, p. 151). The author describes the immediate benefit of Pétain's sudden appearance: "And, solely on account of his presence, Uncle Sébastien and the children felt comforted because a thousand reasons for optimism arose before them" (3). He bolsters his readers' sense of patriotism with visions of idealized French greatness, including a parade of renowned French warriors and rulers such as Vercingetorix, Joan of Arc, and Louis IX and famous thinkers and cultural figures such as Pasteur, Colbert, Descartes, and others all touting the ancient glory and significance of France. He reinforces their national pride further by highlighting French culture and the six "traditional virtues of France": piety, loyalty, charity, politeness, industriousness, and courage. The economic riches of the provinces follow next, and the vision concludes with Pétain taking a seat at the foot of an oak tree while the ghost of St. Louis lingers over his shoulder to tell his enraptured audience how the good *Maréchal* will save France.

With his readers' hope restored and patriotism fortified, Uncle Sébastien shifts the emphasis of his ideological message away from proclaiming the strength of France to explaining what must be done if she is to recover her former glory. The first step, Pétain tells his listeners, will be to drive out all the "vermin" that have done so much to harm France, a classic propaganda technique that simplifies the political, social, and cultural issues that are really at stake by pinning responsibility for France's downfall on a mysterious, unwanted "other" that is the true reason for the nation's ruin. By this, of course, the author means the expulsion of Jews and other "undesirables" from French territory, a Nazi-inspired policy supported by a wide range of propaganda that was in full swing throughout Occupied France by 1942. Pétain describes this "vermin" as "spiders," "bedlice," and "termites," a trio of compelling metaphors for the undesirables the Vichy regime believed to be web-spinning and venomous conspirators; parasites who sucked the life's blood from their host, Mother France; and voracious destroyers who treacherously ate away at the foundation and supports of their own home, the French state. Immediately after a giant broom wielded by Pétain himself sweeps away these pests, the storm clouds disappear, the sun rises, and a fresh, clean air wafts its way across the countryside.

With the threat of the "other" eradicated, Pétain then explains the second step that needs to be taken to rebuild France, exhorting his listeners to purge themselves of their own defects. Such an action will require much suffering and self-sacrifice, the *Maréchal* states, but his audience willingly accepts his charge, reasoning that such suffering is only just and is "the correct punishment for our foibles and faults." Such a purging of "defects" follows a standard convention of propaganda, namely promulgating the understanding that each person should evaluate and remake him or herself not in terms of individual desires but in accordance with the ideological decrees and greater needs of the state itself. Inspired by the *Maréchal*'s words, Uncle Sébastien and the children form themselves into a work gang and pledge to do whatever they can to remake France in accordance with Pétain's vision. The author concludes his work with an exhortation aimed directly at French children everywhere: "My children, my dear little children, swear to do everything that brave children of France ought to do: render service, be polite, affectionate, gentle, courageous, loyal and disciplined. Long live France! Long live the *Maréchal*!" (L'Oncle Sébastian ca. 1942, 16; see also figure 4.12, p. 152).

Although *Oui, monsieur le Maréchal!* begins with a sad recollection of France's ignoble downfall with the signing of the Franco-German armistice on June 25, 1940, Uncle Sébastien quickly begins his task of rewriting history. In reality, he explains through the figure of Pétain, France has not been conquered. Rather, the armistice has given the French a chance to purge and reform themselves, to found a new society from the ground up based on the three core principles of the Vichy- and Pétain-supported *Révolution nationale: Travail, Famille,* and *Patrie*. In Vichy propaganda for children, *Pétain,* the hero of Verdun and the great leader whose vision was able to see ultimate cultural, social, and political victory for France in the face of military defeat, becomes the transcendent symbol of this new national revolution. The good *Maréchal* becomes the embodiment of and voice for the new France, the preeminent exemplary hero that all good French children should emulate and venerate.

Shina Jihen taishō kinengō (Sino-Japanese War), a book published in Tokyo in 1938 to celebrate Japan's military victories in China, offers a more nuanced example of how idealized heroic figures were used to inspire loyalty to the state and its ideals (Takagi 1938). During the 1930s, Japanese children's publications were forced to adhere to stringent censorship laws.[12] While many publications such as the well-known children's periodical *Kodomo no Kuni* modified their content to please the censors, other books were produced specifically to glorify Japanese military might, idealize the fighting spirit of the Imperial Army, and instill in Japan's youth a sense of martial pride and the obligation to serve their emperor faithfully. As General Sadao Araki, then minister of the Imperial Army, explains in his introduction to the book, the purpose of *Sino-Japanese War* was "to pour Imperial spirit into young children's minds . . . [for] the power of the Japanese future lies within the children who will be trained subconsciously" (Takagi 1938, 3).

The book attempts to condition its young readers by providing them with a variety of models of exemplary behavior, including portraits of famous military commanders such as Prince Kanin, the Japanese Army chief of staff, and Prince Fushimi, a fleet admiral in the Imperial Navy; jingoistic descriptions of the prowess of "heroic" Japanese soldiers and the corresponding inferiority of the "cowardly" Chinese; "true" military dispatches describing the bravery of front-line Japanese troops; and "emotional and admirable" stories celebrating the Bushido ("Way of the Warrior") spirit and self-sacrifice. The bulk of the book contains stunning and visceral double-page illustrations of Japanese combat troops in action. Serene and heroic Japanese soldiers capture a battle standard defended by terror-stricken Chinese troops; a small band of valiant Japanese commandos successfully defeats a Chinese force many times their own number; a brave and honorable tank crew rescues a European family from the depravities of Chinese troops; and stern-eyed Japanese cavalrymen overrun a Chinese entrenchment, sending their defeated enemy fleeing in panic. But the fighting prowess and spirit of Japanese troops are not the only virtues promoted through the book's images. Another illustration titled "Kind-hearted Japanese Soldiers" testifies to the inherent compassion of the ideal Japanese warrior, many of whom have taken it upon themselves, the illustration's accompanying text explains, to create and maintain graveyards for Chinese soldiers killed during the Battle of Shanghai. "Japanese soldiers are not only strong," the illustration's caption reads, "but also kind-hearted. That is what is so wonderful about Japanese troops" (35).

Perhaps most intriguing, though, are the book's exemplary stories of children doing their part to win the war on the home front. One such tale titled "Ryuji Cheers Up His Father" tells the story of a young boy who stoically accepts responsibility for his four younger siblings after his father is sent off to war in China and his mother dies following a long illness. Although consumed by grief, Ryuji calms his emotions, accepts his lot, and writes to his father, telling him that all is well and asking that he concern himself solely with winning a medal and bringing honor to the family. Tear-stricken and full of pride, Ryuji's father takes the letter to his commanding officer who proclaims that Ryuji's single-minded determination to act responsibly and free his father for the war effort reveals him to be an "admirable" and "excellent" example of a "true Japanese child" (Takagi 1938, 80; also see figure 4.13, p. 153).

The ideological messages that run throughout this book are at the core no different than propaganda for children from any other country. Courage, self-sacrifice, loyalty, and honor were all central tenets of Japan's national, military, and political faiths during the 1930s. But a hallmark of Japanese wartime propaganda, its "major goal," as Kushner explains, was its constant emphasis on "unifying the battlefront with the home front" (2006, 6). *Sino-Japanese War* embodies this strategy perfectly with its vivid, colorful, and exciting depictions of combat coupled with domestic scenes such as an illustration of a family—from young children to grandparents—tracing the progress of the war on a map and rejoicing at the news of further Japanese victories they have read in a letter from a family member fighting at the front (figure 4.14, p. 153). The home front and the front line, though geographically separate, are ideologically unified. While the book's illustrations of victorious soldiers provide vivid models of Japanese military might abroad, the story of little Ryuji provides the book's young readers with a model of how every good Japanese girl and boy ought to act and teaches them that events at home can have a major impact on conditions at the front.

Propaganda such as this helped create a vibrant and very personal relationship between Japan's civilian and military populations that helped reinforce notions of shared service and sacrifice. By the later stages of World War II the ideological connection between the front lines and the home front had become extremely real and tangible for Japanese children. Military training was compulsory in schools, with boys participating in live ammunition weapons drills and girls training to fight with halberds, bamboo spears, and hand grenades. After-school hours offered no respite, as both girls and boys were forced to work in factories helping to make clothes, weapons, ammunition, and other military equipment.[13] For the many young readers who might have been motivated by the inspirational story of little Ryuji, Japan's wars would quickly assume an even greater and more immediate importance in their lives as they were increasingly compelled to feed their country's martial ideology with their own bodies.

In the hands of skillful propagandists, *Maréchal* Pétain is not the venerable old hero of Verdun, and little Ryuji is not the fictitious creation of some unknown author. Rather, Pétain assumes the role of a kindly grandfather while Ryuji personifies the playmate every child longs for. Exemplary figures both, they become the literal embodiments of their states' ideologies, providing living and accessible models of behavior for all young children to emulate.

Conclusion

Effective propaganda offers easy answers in whatever forms it takes. And even if these answers are wrong, it is still useful and powerful in its ability to preempt questions, assuage doubt, and provide firm and fast guidelines concerning how one is supposed to feel, what one is supposed to believe, and the manner in which one should act. It is not concerned with discourse but rather with dictating manufactured, one-sided "truths." Its aim is not to inspire thought or consideration but to force its target to react emotionally and instinctively. As we have seen, children's propaganda adheres to all of these qualities. Each of the books discussed was designed to promote unwavering belief in a particular doctrine. Whether alphabet book or primer, picture book or biography, fable or fairy tale, the common element these works all share is their ability to speak to children in their own language. By dressing their various political and military creeds in the trappings of traditional children's literature, propagandists hoped to make young people understand that they had a direct stake in their community and an obligation to support whatever ideology it advocated. By reading—and rereading—such books, propagandists hoped, children would take one step closer to becoming active combatants willing to do whatever it might take to support their state and its social, political, and military aims.

Notes

1. Tonnelat and Waltz (1922, 10 and 18). Among the varieties of propaganda Waltz and Tonnelat used in their ideological war against Germany were false soldiers' letters sent home from the front, articles for fabricated German army newspapers intended to spread discord and lower troop morale, and posters and leaflets distributed behind enemy lines by agents, artillery shells, and aircraft.
2. For an interesting discussion of this curricular reorganization and a survey of some of the fascist textbooks used throughout Italian schools during Mussolini's reign, see Foss (1997). For an overview of the importance of the concept of "youth" (*giovenezza*) in fascist Italy, see Malvano (1997).
3. In his detailed examination of education during Italy's fascist years, Tracy H. Koon includes a passage from the "Balilla Creed," a bald statement of fascist faith, that reveals the importance of the idea of Rome's new empire and the extreme devotion young members of the *Opera Balilla* were required to show toward Mussolini and the state: "I believe in the genius of Mussolini, in our Holy Father Fascism, in the communion of its martyrs, in the conversion of Italians and in the resurrection of the Empire" (1985, 154).
4. In a concluding letter at the end of the *Cartilla*, Jesus Hernandez, the Popular Front's minister of Instruction for Public and Fine Arts, reemphasizes the role that children will play in the triumph of communism, exhorting the primer's young readers to commit to the fight against fascism in the same way they have committed to their own education: "With the same enthusiasm and sleepless hours that you have spent learning your first letters, you must ensure the defense of the democratic Republic and the independence of Spain, because in doing so you will forge the happy future of our land" (*Cartilla escolar antifascista*, 1937, 51).
5. *Gloria, Viktoria: Ein Weltkriegs-Bilderbuch* (ca. 1915) is an anonymous imitation and adaptation of Arpad Schmidhammer's better-known *Leib Vaterland magst ruhig sein! Ein Kriegsbilderbuch mit Knüttelversen* (ca. 1914). In this book a gang of boys in the attire of the Entente Powers assault a pair of German and Austrian boys in military uniform as they work peacefully in their garden. They defeat their attackers, imprison them in a cage, and return to their gardening. Schmidhammer (1851–1924) was a noted illustrator and regular contributor to *Jugend,* a popular German children's magazine published between 1896 and 1940.
6. For detailed discussions of Hansi's life and work, see Perreau (1962, 1994).

7. Waltz (1915, 1918, 1925). Hansi also contributed art to adult-oriented anti-German works such as Froelich (1913), a satirical exposition of the differences—ideological, political, and cultural—between Germans and Alsatians that ridiculed the perceived arrogance of pan-Germanism and Prussian hegemony.
8. For a detailed examination of Nazi and anti-Semitic children's literature produced in the Third Reich, see Kamenetsky (1984). For an analysis of the implementation of Nazi racist doctrine, or "racial science," in the German educational system during the Nazi period, see Michaud (1997, 257–80). For a fuller view of the Nazi ideological war against the Jews, see Herf (2006).
9. I am indebted to Professor Johan de Mylius of the Hans Christian Andersen Center at the University of Southern Denmark for kindly translating Aage Hermann's foreword and moral.
10. For a general discussion of propaganda in Vichy France, see Rossignol (1991).
11. Some of the more well-known examples of Pétain-focused children's literature include Hérault (ca. 1942), a patriotic coloring book titled *Présentez armes! Les voyages du Maréchal* (ca. 1942), Paluel-Marmont (ca. 1942, and 1942), and Roche (ca. 1942).
12. For an interesting and up-to-date overview of Japanese propaganda, see Kushner (2006). For a Japanese look at wartime Imperial propaganda, see Iritani (1991).
13. Iritani (1991, 179–81). For further information about the rise of militarism in Japanese school curricula during the Sino-Japanese War and World War II, see Ienaga (1978, 19–31 and 105–9).

5

Shifting Images

Germans in Postwar British Children's Fiction

Emer O'Sullivan

A sense of the shift in the portrayal of Germans in British children's fiction from the 1940s to the 1970s can be drawn from contrasting depictions in two children's novels published in 1941 and 1979, respectively, both of which are set during the Second World War. The following account of the enemy occurs in Captain Charles Gilson's *Through the German Hordes:*

> A man in his shirt-sleeves was cooking over the fire, and at a small table immediately opposite the door a fat man was seated who could not have been mistaken for anything else but a German officer, had he been found dressed up like a Chinese mandarin in a Red Indian's wigwam.
>
> He had a bald head with no back to it, though there was a roll of fat extended from his double chin to the nape of his neck. He had a waxed moustache, the hairs of which had been carefully brushed upward; and a pair of gold-rimmed pince-nez appeared to be somewhat precariously balanced on the bridge of a nose that was squat and discoloured. If one could judge by appearances, his complaint was probably a partiality to alcohol, since on the table before him was an empty glass and a bottle of wine. (Gilson 1941, 37–38)

This German is everything an Englishman, according to the projected norms and desired autostereotypes of that time, was not: fat, vain, unclean, and lacking in self-discipline. And no amount of dissimulation could disguise this fact. He is, unquestionably, the contemptible Other.

In Robert Westall's *Fathom Five,* a novel published almost forty years after Gibson's,[1] a young Briton looks on as German sailors captured during the Second World War come ashore, and his perception differs significantly: "The sailors seemed so ordinary. The fat one, who scratched his bum. The boy with terrible spots on his face that his fingers wouldn't leave alone. The dark flashy one with a thin moustache, who kept eyeing the legs of the girl reporter from the Newcastle Journal" (Westall 1982, 242). The German has metamorphosed from the "unmistakable Other" to someone who is strikingly familiar to the British observer's fellow countrymen. These passages illustrate the shift "from cultural certainties to . . . pluralism and ambiguities" (Agnew and Fox 2001, 1) behind the depiction of war in children's literature.

How are the Germans portrayed in British fiction for young readers? This question was the point of departure of a research project on children's books published since 1870, the year of the outbreak of the Franco-Prussian War and the eve of the foundation of the German Empire the following year, a significant date in the history of British-German relations, as Germany was for the first time jostling for a position on the world stage. In the research project, some 250 titles with a German connection were located and analyzed (cf. O'Sullivan 1990). In this chapter I address the relationship between the dual time axes of the period in which a narrative is set and its date of publication and reflect upon its influence on the image of the Germans in the texts. Asking how postwar British authors succeed in writing retrospectively about the world wars without employing a cast of familiarly evil German enemies, I identify two strategies authors employ to avoid negative stereotyping—revalorization of known images and negation of the stereotyped Germanness of individual characters—providing examples for each. Finally I address the correspondence between the location of the plot and the theme, which will be shown to prevail in spy stories set in Belfast.

Times of War as Most Prevalent Settings

A broad variety of genres and subgenres can be found in the corpus—historical novels, adventure novels, girls' stories, fantasy, school stories, detective novels, and so on. War stories are by far the most numerous, accounting for more than a third, and military and war themes occurred in two out of three texts. An examination of the dates of publication of all the texts in the corpus reveals that the periods of the two world wars, years of open hostility between the two nations, were ones of substantial production in Britain of fiction with a German connection. Thirty-five percent of all the books were published in the space of fourteen years, between 1914–19 and 1939–46,[2] just under 10 percent of the total amount of time covered by the corpus. In terms of the periods of time in which the stories and novels are set, the world wars clearly dominate, too, with over half of them set during these two periods.

The popularity of wartime settings in British children's books that feature Germans cannot be solely declared a consequence of the periods of hostility between the two countries. War settings have always proven popular in children's books, providing a context in which courage and cunning in the face of an enemy can be displayed, qualities emphasized by Maria Tatar in her contribution to this volume. However, the dominance of this theme and setting would seem to indicate a prevailing association of Germans with war in British children's fiction, which says as much about Britain's preoccupation with the world wars, and the importance of the perception of these periods for Britain's positive self-image, as it does about the image of Germany in Britain. The continuing pull that the period of the Second World War exerted in Britain in the mid-1980s has been interpreted as follows:

> Among the speculative reasons for this attraction are widespread disappointment with the post-war decades, the renewed experience of economic failure and social strife, this time accompanied by a staggeringly rapid fall from world power. And one may surmise that there exists a broadly based nostalgia, not so much perhaps for the days of the Empire themselves as for the days when people in Britain, though reeling under the realisation of just how much had been done amiss, though ferociously besieged and in deadly jeopardy, did pull together. . . . There are fairly good grounds to suspect a nostalgic feeling for the sense of national purpose and united effort that did seem to augur well for any future and at any rate, transformed weakness into temporary strength, made Dunkirk possible and enabled the country to withstand Hitler's Blitz. (Klein 1984, 45)

Attitudes toward the Germans

As the passages by Westall quoted earlier in the chapter indicated, not every portrayal of Germans in a book set during World War II is necessarily automatically and exclusively negative. There are novels and stories with this theme and setting that display a neutral or even a positive attitude toward Britain's adversary at the time. In order to try to ascertain the attitude toward Germans that prevailed in the texts of the corpus, and to quantify it in relation to the dates of publication and the periods in which the narratives were set, one of three evaluations—"positive," "negative," or "neutral"—was allocated to each of the 250 texts in the corpus. Such an allocation is ultimately subjective and, with only three points on the scale, undifferentiated. However, more discriminating ones—for instance, with a scale from -5 to +5—would only serve to mask the subjectivity of the undertaking.

The three evaluations were used as follows. Texts were deemed *positive* in which authors write about Germany or Germans in such a way that readers are likely to respond in an affirmative manner toward them. This does not mean that the author tries to *induce* such a response, although that is the case with many of the books in this category. An example is the girls' story *Sara Goes to Germany* (Allan 1976), a realistic novel in which a young English girl visits her married sister in a Germany of pleasant landscapes and people, and which, in effect, ignores the topic of the Second World War and how it affected the relations between the two countries.

Texts deemed *negative* present Germany and the Germans in an almost exclusively unfavorable light; they are often openly propagandistic. An example is the tale "The Perforated Helmet" by the blatantly chauvinistic Percy F. Westerman. On the battlefield in the First World War a public school boy comes face-to-face with his former German teacher, "the only member of staff towards whom the boys showed any real antipathy" (Westerman 1918, 71), a man described as a savage German without honor who rightfully, so the narrator intimates, gets his comeuppance.

In books evaluated as *neutral,* usually the most differentiated ones in terms of both story and discourse, the narrator neither comes down on the side of the Germans nor rails against them. They often present both malevolent and benign Germans. In *Tank Commander* (Welch 1972), a story set in the First World War, the fighting masses of the German Army feature, but no individual German is characterized, thus the anonymity of war is depicted, but attempts to elicit understanding or even sympathy for the antagonist or to incite hatred toward him are shunned.

Obviously not all texts allowed for as straightforward an assessment as the examples just given, but I suspect that the overall results would be reproduced by a number of independent evaluators of the same corpus.

Overall the most common evaluation of the 250 novels and tales, 40 percent, was "negative." Conversely, those that were not "negative" were in the majority at 60 percent (with roughly half of these "neutral" and half "positive"). Figure 5.1 shows a breakdown of the distribution of these attitudes according to the dates of publication.[3]

The lines on the graph represent the positive, neutral, and negative attitudes toward Germany in all the texts and show how the changes in attitudes correspond to historical events. The positive attitude clearly dominates in books published before the outbreak of the First World War, after which date it declines steeply. The types of books written before 1914 include fairy-tale type stories with German settings, historical novels—many with a religious theme published by the Religious Tract Societies, but also some chivalrous novels as well as historical tales of war. Characteristics attributed to the Germans in these books include piety, simplicity, honesty, love of nature, musicality, and homeliness; the emphasis is on gentle, traditionally feminine characteristics that can be subsumed under the headings of *Gemütlichkeit* and sentimentality. These are the Britons' German cousins (cf. Firchow 1986). The image is almost exclusively positive with scarcely an echo of the hysteria that manifested itself in the so-called invasion literature written for adults, the first of which, *The Battle of Dorking,* was published as early as 1871 (cf. Husemann 1986).

Germans in Postwar British Children's Fiction

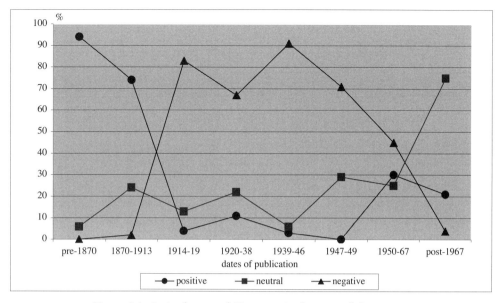

Figure 5.1. Attitude toward Germany in the texts of the corpus, according to periods of dates of publication (O'Sullivan 1990, 78).

Figure 5.1 reveals how this positive picture changes drastically with the outbreak of war in 1914. Four out of five books written during the First World War were evaluated as negative. They include several works for boys by authors such as Percy F. Westerman, Captain Charles Gilson, and Captain F. S. Brereton, "the best-known proponent of the invincible Empire" (Fox 2001, 5). Here the brutal, arrogant, military, heel-clicking Prussian German dominates, who terrorizes the lower ranks and grovels to his superiors. In his study of Anglo-German relations, Firchow writes that by 1915 "the German cousin was dead, never again to be resurrected except by cranks and Nazi-sympathizers at the fringes of British political life. From then onward, the German national character was to remain indelibly fixed in the British psyche. It was, in its main outlines and extreme form, efficient, disciplined, humorless; cold yet paradoxically sentimental; dull, vulgar, and barbaric, yet inordinately proud of its "Kultur"; viciously cruel on "principle"; unbearably arrogant when victorious, abjectly cringing in defeat. In short it was the "hun" (Firchow 1986, 178). The negative attitude prevails in the texts published during the interwar years, although the number of relevant titles issued then is not substantial and peaks at 91 percent during the period of the Second World War. Here Captain W. E. Johns, with his *Biggles* series, carries on in the Westerman tradition, and Elinor Brent-Dyer echoes the jingoistic sentiments for girls expressed earlier by Angela Brazil. Not until after 1967 do we find a pattern that resembles the one

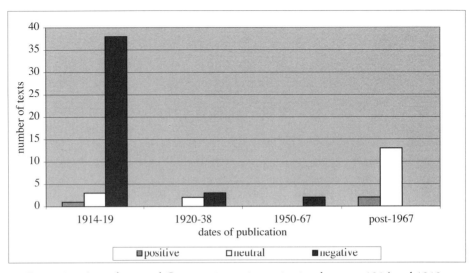

Figure 5.2. Attitude toward Germany in stories set in time between 1914 and 1918, according to the dates of publication (O'Sullivan 1990, 84).

observed before the First World War, the main difference being that the proportion of neutral and positive texts is inverted.

A hypothesis based on these figures might be that the war theme and setting disappeared after the late 1960s, with postwar Germany and Germans dominating in the neutral, modern texts. But this is not the case. From the late 1960s on, there was a sudden surge of interest in the topic of the world wars in children's literature, especially the Second World War. The twenty-five years that had passed is, according to Cadogan and Craig, the length of time a period takes "to progress from dullness or desolation to absorbing interest" (1978, 365). It is also the time it takes for a generation of writers to come of age whose formative childhood years had been spent during the war and who now wanted to write about it.[4] More than 60 percent of all books written after 1967 with a German theme deal with the world wars. These are the books in which a more positive, or at least a more neutral, picture of the Germans emerge. Figures 5.2 and 5.3 provide an illustration of the change in attitude in books with a world war setting according to their date of publication.

These two figures display striking parallels. Stories set in both periods written before 1968 reveal an almost exclusively negative attitude toward Germany. And, in the case of both time settings, the picture changes notably after that date.

This, naturally, does not mean that the First World War is seen in a neutral light and that the deeds of the Germans in the Second World War are praised in books written after 1967. According to the criteria for evaluating a book "neutral" or "positive" it indicates that, in the case of "neutral" books, the author neither sides with the Germans nor denigrates them and that the "positive" books with a

Germans in Postwar British Children's Fiction

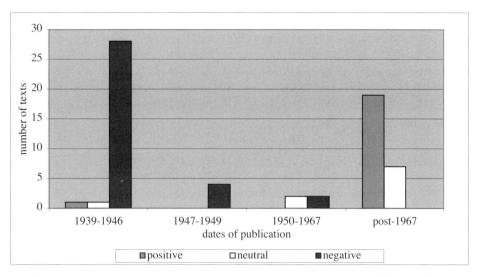

Figure 5.3. Attitude toward Germany in stories set in time between 1939 and 1945, according to the dates of publication (O'Sullivan 1990, 85).

Second World War setting are, for the most part, books in which one main German character, often a prisoner of war in England or a pilot shot down and now in hiding, is presented with almost exclusively agreeable characteristics and in such a way that readers are likely to respond in a positive way toward him. A batch of this type of book appeared in the 1970s, perhaps the most well-known of which is Robert Westall's Carnege-Prize-winning *The Machine-Gunners* (1975), in which a German pilot, shot out of the skies, drops into the lives of children. In their growing hostility toward the adult world, the children find a true friend in him, a father figure even. Other books of this type include *The Missing German* (Rees 1976), *Friend or Foe* (Morpurgo 1977), and *Willow's Luck* (Alington 1977).[5] The dark, negative side of Germany during this time also features in some of these favorably inclined books, but the overall positive power of the individual German character dominates and introduces with it an ethical dilemma for the children torn between national loyalty and personal feeling. Further sympathetic attitudes are shown in books such as *No Shelter* (Lutzeier 1984), which, inconceivable a couple of decades earlier, portray the war from the point of view of the suffering Germans.

Through the German Hordes (Gilson 1941) or *Biggles Defies the Swastika* (Johns 1941), published during the war years, wanted to keep their young readers' spirits up, wanted them to believe that the British cause was just, that the Germans were evil, and that Britain would conquer in the end. They were "an important distraction—or even a means of coming to terms with the war itself" (Fox 2001, 22). The writers of retrospective fiction about the Second World War, conversely, could describe the war from the tranquility of peacetime and could allow themselves to present a more complex and discriminating picture of events to readers who, more than twenty years after the event, were growing up secure in the knowledge that the war had been fought and won. These readers could be presented with a more equivocal approach, could be encouraged to question motives and accept the notion that good and evil could be found on both sides.

Given the tenacity of the images associated with the warring Germans, how could authors approach the topic of the world wars, whose history, lore, and literature had become part of the collective memory, complete with a cast of evil German enemies? How could they write in a different way about a national group fitted out with stock images traded endlessly in popular culture? Two strategies of dealing with these images could be observed in the corpus. One is to revalorize familiar images; the other is to negate the stereotyped Germanness of individual characters.

Revalorization of Familiar Images

The construction of national characters in literature often operates with binary opposites (active/passive, rational/irrational, positive/negative), a mechanism also central in the construction of gender, with male/female being the fundamental opposition. A characteristic can swiftly turn into its opposite or can be revalorized when there is a significant change in social, political, cultural, and especially economic relations between the group portraying and the group being portrayed. The German image in British children's literature since 1871 shows a clear development from "gentle," "family loving," "benign," "musical," "*gemütlich*"—traditionally more female—characteristics attributed during the late nineteenth century to the "brutal," "overpowering," "cruel," "loud," "unfeeling"—traditionally more male—characteristics of the threatening, Prussian German in literature written from the end of the nineteenth century until the 1960s. This development mirrors one of the structural factors involved in national characterizations, that of weak versus strong. As Leerssen (2000, 76–77) observed: "Images of powerful nations will foreground the ruthlessness and cruelty which are associated with effective power, whilst weak nations can count either on the sympathy felt for the underdog or else on that benevolent exoticism which can only flourish under the proviso of condescension." While in the early nineteenth-century representations, Germany had all the charms of a politically weak country, the same country of the Wilhelminian period had "all the repulsive hallmarks of efficiency, power and ruthlessness" (77). The shift in image is directly connected to the nation's rise in international stature. It also gave rise to the notion of "Two Germanies": that of the good German—poet, philosopher, and composer—on the one hand, that of the bad, militarist German, the threatening Hun with spiked or steel helmet on the other. This shift in German image from soft to hard, weak to strong, exotic to threatening can be observed by examining the valorization of the stereotype of "the musical German" in British children's books.[6]

The earliest mention of music in the corpus occurs in a story by Juliana Horatia Ewing, first published in 1862, of a young boy who grows up to be a great poet. In it the sensitivity of Germans to the arts in general is underlined with music especially being "innate in the German character" (Ewing 1912, 75); there are "a thousand airs floating in German brains" (56). We also find tales of poor musicians with magic violins (Goddard 1863) and of wandering minstrels who give up their traveling for the love of a woman (Roberts 1877). The musicality of the Germans is presented in these books—all written before and during the 1870s, before the Prussianization of Germany and England's reaction to it started to be reflected in literature—as exclusively positive.

The first discordant tones are to be heard in a story published in 1902, set during the Franco-Prussian War. The music here is loud and rowdy, produced by "rough drunken" German soldiers with their "shouts and songs and laughter" (Lucas 1902, 56). Music illustrates the uncouthness and arrogance of members of the German Army in books written and set during and just after the First World War. In *A Motor-Scout in Flanders* drunken Pomeranian soldiers sing "a very raucous and discordant interpretation of 'Deutschland über alles'" (Gilson 1915, 49), a song sung by soldiers, drunk or sober, in a number of books published during the 1910s and 1920s. This tradition is picked up again in the 1940s: British pilots who look down from their planes on a show parade in Germany in *Bombs on Berchtesgaden* see men in Nazi uniform goose stepping and "a typical German Band, blowing and swaggering" (Dupont n.d.).

What happens to this testosterone-charged musicality of the Germans after the war? As is well known, swaggering Nazis have become an important stock character in British comedy, escape stories, and the like. But parallel to the negative valorization of the musicality of Germans in the second decade of the twentieth century, we find a reinterpretation from the 1970s on. In many books the familiar stereotype of musicality is employed, but here its favorable properties are used as redeeming features of individual "positive" Germans in an apparent attempt to show young British readers that the Germans should not be exclusively associated with warmongering. The semantic core "music" remains the same, but the valorization has changed. The drunken, loud, nasty, raucous music of the bellicose Germans gives way, in books written after the late 1960s, to a recurrence of the gentle, sensitive musicality found in the earlier books, making the character endowed with the gift (usually a soldier or prisoner of war) almost exclusively positive. Rudi, in *The Machine-Gunners,* teaches his English child captors to sing the song *Ich hatt' einen Kameraden!* "The children took up the words of the sad old soldiers' song. They sang so sweetly that Rudi was close to tears. What was happening to him? He grew less like a soldier every day; more like a *lehrer* in some kindergarten" (Westall 1977, 132). In *Summer of the Zeppelin* by Elsie McCutcheon, Elvira is told that her father has been reported missing in action. Almost immediately afterward she hears music being played on the church organ. The rector tells her that the piece, *Jesu, Joy of Man's Desiring,* was composed "by a German musician called Bach. And you won't often hear it played as superbly as that" (McCutcheon 1983, 53). The organist is a German prisoner of war.

Negating Germanness

In these post-1967 British children's books set in periods during which Germany was Britain's prime enemy, we find English children who relate to a German soldier in their midst as they would to a father, a friend, or even a lover. The individual Germans in these books are marked sufficiently "German" to allow them to represent their nation, but at the same time their negative Germanness is disposed of. They are anything but Nazis. Robert Westall's Rudi, who literally falls from the skies into the lives of German-hating English children, is presented as an exclusively positive figure in contrast to "the Germans" as a collective: while they are faceless hordes, Rudi is an individual; while they are described as destroying everything around the children, he treats his young friends with the utmost consideration; while they are dedicated to fighting for their Fatherland and Hitler, he comes to reject both. When the children see him for the first time they think that he doesn't look anything at all like what a Nazi is supposed to look like: "And indeed the tattered wretch before them was not much like those black shiny-booted storm troopers who goose stepped nightly through their dreams. "He ain't got no swastikas!"—"He's not a blond beast!" . . . His hair was long, black and greasy, and going a bit grey at the sides, like Mr. McGill's. He really looked like somebody's dad; a bit fed-up and tired" (Westall 1977, 117). Rudi comes from Germany, but at the same time he is presented as a non-German, when, for the English characters in the book, "German" is taken to be synonymous with "evil" and "Nazi." To the same degree to which "the Germans" are dehumanized in English imaginations, the humane German is de-Germanized in Westall's narrative. The children's fear and hatred of the Germans in the novel and their desire to fight against them is presented as being valid during the time of the Second World War. So although they become very attached to an individual German, it doesn't ultimately affect the way they feel about "the Germans." The nice individual German in the story is a concession to the time in which the story was written, the late 1970s. Modern-day readers should be shown that there are "good Germans" too.

In contrast to the Nazis, the collective Germans whose maleness connotes aggression, Rudi and other individual Germans such as the kind pilots in *Friend or Foe* (Morpurgo 1977) and *Willow's Luck* (Alington 1977) don't pose a threat but have, symbolically speaking, been "emasculated"—often by means of a broken limb or other injury. And having being captured and held prisoner places even those not symbolically castrated firmly on the passive rather than the aggressive side. In order to transform their male Germans into positive figures during times of war, authors dispense with and indeed negate traditional elements of the social construction of masculinity in their characterization; they could be said to tinker with the gender of the male German.

Link between Location and Theme

So far we have looked at the correlation of world war settings with the date of publication and its influence on how the Germans are portrayed. If we look at the location of a narrative and its theme, an interesting correspondence can also be found. Examples of this are spy stories set in Belfast, the capital of Northern Ireland, during the Second World War. *The File on Fraulein Berg* (1980) by Joan Lingard and Eve Bunting's *Spying on Miss Müller* (1995) are both stories of schoolgirls who persecute their German teachers. The recent conflict in Northern Ireland colors these tales of how children can become caught up in the machinery of war in a manner that contrasts starkly with a nostalgic view of wartime childhood in England, such as found in Michael Foreman's *War Boy* (1989).

The File on Fraulein Berg tells the story of three friends: Kate, the first-person narrator and daughter of a financially struggling widow; boisterous Sally, one of five children of a butcher doing well on the black market; and posh Harriet. The socially unequal friends have three things in common: they are bored—things are too quiet in Belfast in 1944; they hate the Germans—as they are encouraged to do; and they devour contemporary spy stories. They also know that there is some "trafficking of German agents from Eire [The Republic of Ireland] into Northern Ireland" (Lingard 1993, 12). Into this explosive constellation, a new German teacher arrives, Fraulein Berg, smelling of Eau de Cologne: "Cologne. A city on the Rhine. No British woman would have worn perfume with a name like that, I felt sure" (25). The girls are convinced that Fraulein Berg is a Nazi spy and, with misplaced patriotism, stalk her. They are motivated by the notion of "doing their bit" mixed with romantic illusions from their favorite spy books and make Fraulein Berg's life miserable, even sending an anonymous note to a friend who accompanies her to a concert: "'Take care with whom you associate. Your country relies on you.' . . . signed . . . 'A well wisher'" (82). The novel skillfully contrasts the warm and lively friendship of the girls and their close family lives with the loneliness and isolation of the persecuted Fraulein Berg.

Religious conflict forms the backdrop to the novel. The girls, Protestants, are terrified when, on a trip to Dublin, they are spoken to by a Catholic priest. Sally insists that he was out to convert them, and Kate responds,

> "Don't be daft. How would he even know we were Protestants to start with?"
>
> "Oh, they know all right. They can tell. You can tell a Catholic, can't you?"
>
> That was true and I had to admit it. It's an odd thing that people who haven't been brought up in the North of Ireland might not understand. What it was exactly that enabled one to make the distinction I don't quite know. Perhaps it was simply that we had grown up looking for the differences. (Lingard 1993, 120–21)

Protestant and Catholic, British and German, enemy and ally; the girls' world falls into simple opposites. Everything seems clear when you know what differences to look for. When Fraulein Berg tells the class how happy she is that Paris has just been liberated, her spying pupils are confused: "Whose side is she on after all?"

(Lingard 1993, 150). Only decades later do they find out, and only at the end of the novel are the readers told, that she was a Jewish refugee whose family had been murdered in the concentration camps. That was a possibility they had failed to consider: "Fraulein Berg was Jewish! It was so obvious when one thought about it but it had not even crossed our minds that she might be. How extraordinary! We had been used to dividing up people into Protestants and Catholics in our minds but, somehow, Jews had never figured. . . . And of course we were young when we had pursued Fraulein Berg—when we had *persecuted* her—but even so . . . 'We didn't think,' I said aloud, and remembered my mother saying that not thinking could sometimes be a crime" (155). Her correction from "pursue" to "persecute" is apposite: "persecute" just as the Nazis persecuted the Jews. The novel is framed by a prologue and epilogue in which Kate, the adult narrator, feeling remorse and shame for their deeds, meets Sally in London thirty years after the events. Narrating the story and learning that Fraulein Berg has children and a new life of her own has a purging effect indicated by the final sentence: "At long last the file on Fraulein Berg could be closed" (159).

This is a differentiated and moving account of the effect of propaganda, hate, and betrayal on children during wartime, of how they can get caught up in the machinery of war and how the story they are left to tell is colored not by nostalgia but by shame. It is also a novel that is marked by its setting in Northern Ireland, with its binary thinking in religious opposites that cannot entertain a third possibility, and by the girls' misguided conviction that they could always tell whether someone was a German or not, a Catholic or not. But their judgment was flawed, and the flaw is specific to the location. This novel about the Second World War written in 1980 was inspired by the contemporary situation in Northern Ireland and is a plea, by an author generally committed to writing about political and social issues for children, for tolerance in the face of prejudice, an admonition to look at a person, regardless of the label one may think applies, to reflect whether it is justified to treat them according to that label—German, Jew, Catholic, or Protestant.

The confident propaganda of concomitant accounts of the world wars gives way to ambivalent feelings about the war itself reflected in the use, revalorization, or even negation of stereotypes in later texts. Authors of British fiction with a German theme have, since the late 1960s, gradually begun to functionalize dominant and prevalent national stereotypes in their narratives to serve different ends, one of them being to question how the war itself has been portrayed in the past, and to reject simplistic accounts in black and white. From a literary point of view, this development has generated texts that display interesting examples of a variety of aesthetic uses of national stereotypes; from an educational and political point of view, the development can be seen as promoting more peaceful interaction between two nations. What has not yet appeared on the literary scene are texts that blur the divisions inherent in national attributes in favor of a joint European image; today this notion sounds more like science fiction than a realistic reflection of political and social developments. But if it takes twenty-five years for a period or theme to progress to absorbing interest, then we might still have to wait a long time yet for a body of literature in that particular European vein to materialize.

Notes

1. The novel was first published in 1979.
2. For the periods of the dates of publication, the war years 1914–18 and 1939–45 were extended by a year to include books written in 1918 and 1945 but not issued until 1919 and 1946, respectively.
3. See O'Sullivan 1990, 59–64, for a discussion of the periodization, which follows along the lines of conventional divisions to be found in historiography, mixed with a bit of pragmatism in view of the texts of the corpus.
4. See Lathey (1999) on autobiographical children's literature set in the Second World War.
5. An American novel that uses the same device of the single German soldier is the classic *Summer of My German Soldier* (Greene 1973).
6. The following account of the metamorphosis of the musical German appears in a similar form in O'Sullivan (2002).

II
REPRESENTING TRAUMA

6

Baby Terrors

Lore Segal

Wordsworth said that we come trailing clouds of glory. And we also come primed with ready-made terrors—terrors for which the experience we cannot have had cannot be the source.

Why does the infant cry when its mother—its designated grown-up—disappears from view? How does the baby know enough to be afraid? Did it get in-utero reports about abandonment and deprivation? Why are little children frightened by strangers? Do they intuit kidnappings and abuse? I have an agreement with my three-year-old grandson Isaiah: I will let him know before I start grinding the coffee beans so he can escape into the next room. I will call him when the noise is over. Why does noise frighten him? He knows nothing about the racket of exploding bombs and antiaircraft guns. He has not experienced, near the end of World War II, the nightly, unmanned doodlebugs flying over our heads. They throbbed with a binary on/off, on/off drone. When the drone stopped we knew to count to fifteen before it exploded on us or somewhere else. What does noise signify to Isaiah?

My five-year-old grandson Benjamin passed through a phase in which he could not be persuaded to go into a corner to retrieve a toy. What lives in corners? Are babies born with intimations of the uncanny? I remember how the massive Viennese furniture in our pre-Hitler apartment creaked only when I was alone.

What acquaintance has the baby had time and occasion to make with the monster that lurks in every nursery?

What can we grown-ups—we ex-babies—do about the children's terrors except to comfort them with love and lies? We lie when we tell the child to check under the bed—when we tell them there's nothing to be afraid of. Anxiety attacks are the truth tellers. We have experienced the horrors of September 11, 2001. If there's no war here at this moment, there's one somewhere else. And there will be deaths.

My daughter—Benjamin's mother—was eight, her brother—Isaiah's father—was six when their father died. I looked for help for them from children's literature. Several books dealt with the subject, but it was always a bird that had died, at worst an ancient grandmother whose time had run its course.

Grown-ups pussyfoot around the ur-terrors, understandably, out of anxiety and out of tenderness for the little ones. Notice that the monsters in today's children's books tend to be good guys at heart. Sendak's "Wild Things" may have claws and yellow eyes, but they wear striped T-shirts. To expose the truth to the child—to expose the child to the raw truth—feels like an obscenity. I will confess to having started my own book about a father's death and stopped when I found myself pussyfooting. I was trying to be harmless, guaranteeing that I was also going to be useless.

Maurice Sendak and I did a book together. It was called *The Juniper Tree and Other Tales from Grimm.* Folk literature is braver than we are. It dares to tell the truth in the guise of a lie. Notice that the idea of a fairy tale is synonymous with dream/wish fulfillment and nightmare terrors. The fairy tale scares us to death before it tells us we will live happily ever after. In the Grimm stories it is a mother who dies or is already dead—a reversible, a negotiable death. There are mothers who come back to life after the witch is dead and the curse is broken; Cinderella's mother reaches out of the grave to supply her marriageable girl with a gown to catch the prince. These stories do what most of us do most of our waking lives. We know we will die, but we don't oblige ourselves to believe it. We believe we have a golden age to come, if not here then in the hereafter. We refuse to believe what we know, and that may be the best we can do for the children.

And what do we grown-ups do when war turns childhood's fears into facts?

I want to look at two brief episodes from *Other Peoples Houses,* my own autobiographical novel. Here is the child I used to be at dinner with the family, the year before the coming to Vienna of what Lucy Davidowitz called the "War against the Jews."

"Did you read this, Igo?" my Uncle Paul asked at dinner in the autumn of 1937. "Another speech and Hitler can put Austria in his pocket. I know the university; it's ninety per cent Nazi."

"You're talking about a handful of lunatics," said my father.

"We Jews are a remarkable people," Paul said. "Our neighbor tells us he's getting out his gun and we watch him polish and load it and train it at our heads and we say, 'He doesn't mean us.'"

"So what should we do?" said my father. "Go and hide in the cellar every time some raving lunatic in Germany makes a speech?"

"We should pack our rucksacks and get out of this country," Paul said.

"And go to the jungle, I suppose, and live off coconuts. According to your brother, Franzi," my father said to my mother, "every time a raving lunatic in Germany makes a speech, we should go and live off coconuts in the jungle."

"Is it going to be war?" I asked my mother, aside. I had a sick feeling in my stomach. I knew about the first World War. I had a recurring nightmare about my mother and me sitting in a cellar with tennis rackets, repelling the bullets that flew in through a horizontal slit of window.

"No, no, no, no. Nothing like that," my mother said.

I tried to imagine some calamity but did not know how. My mother was ringing the bell for Poldi, the maid, to bring the coffee. I decided there must not, that there could not be anything so terrible that we would have to pack and leave everything. I stopped listening to the grown ups.

On the eighth day of the following March I had my tenth birthday party. On the twelfth, Hitler took Austria.

By May, Poldi had had to leave our Jewish employ. I had to change schools and enroll in an all Jewish school, my father lost his job at the bank, and an SS sergeant commandeered our flat and everything in it, including my mothers Bluthner piano.

A year later I was living in England, having arrived on the *Kinder Transport* that brought some ten thousand children from Hitler-dominated Europe to England. I was residing with the Hoopers, the second of my four English foster families, when Word War II was about to start.

> Toward the end of the summer, Mrs. Hooper took Gwenda and me downtown to the Air Raid Precaution Head Quarters to be fitted for gas masks. We put on the black masks with their flat snouts; we looked hideous, strange, monstrous to each other. For the little children there were Mickey Mouse masks with blue snouts and pink, floppy ears, which didn't fool them. They howled in terror at the close, evil-smelling rubber over their faces.
>
> The experience jarred Mrs. Hooper and on the way home she kept asking me if there was really going to be a war. I said no, there was not. Hitler would never go to war once he realized the Allies meant business. Mrs. Hooper was relieved. I must know, she said, after all I came from over there.
>
> War was declared on September 3rd and Mrs. Hooper had hysterics.

A few years ago I was sitting in the dentist's chair. The dentist's face hung above mine like the face of the lord over primal waters. God, parents, doctors—they are going to take care of us, aren't they? They will put right what goes wrong. Won't they? I watched my dentist's sweat start on his forehead. His mouth took on a kind of rictus. This doctor—I could tell—did not know what to do about—what? What do you do when the doctor looks frightened? "Is it going to be all right?" I managed to ask around the fingers in my mouth. "I hope so," he said.

Grown-ups, it turned out, didn't know what was going to happen, couldn't stop whatever was going to be. Not only did they not make things all right for the children, but also they couldn't save themselves. Ninety percent of the parents of the *Kinder Transport* children were never seen again. They had been taken away by the vicious stranger. They were murdered by the next-door neighbor turned monster.

And what is the fate of the war-traumatized child? I don't know that you can tell us from other children grown into grown-ups, grown old. Some of us succumbed to a life of depression. Some have limped along for better and for worse. Some have lived vigorous, useful, creative lives. All of us, surely, were surprised, once in a while, by joy.

If some have responded with justified vitriol, others pity the world and yearn to do it good.

Our response to September 11 is, perhaps, interesting. The children of war never had the "innocence"—a misnomer, surely—that America felt itself to have lost. We were more likely to think, "So, here it comes again!" with a feeling not unlike relief. We say, "So this is the shape, sound, time, and place where this or something else was always going to happen." We relax. We wait for the other shoe to explode.

7

"No safe place to run to"

An Interview with Robert Cormier

Mitzi Myers

Robert Cormier is so well-known as the founding father of young adult (YA) dark realism, as the author of almost a score of award-winning and controversial novels, and as the lightening rod for recurrent censorship campaigns that it seems presumptuous to introduce him. With their stark and uncompromising challenges to conventional happy endings and their innovative intellectual and stylistic complexity, *The Chocolate War* (1974), *I Am the Cheese* (1977), and *After the First Death* (1979) made the 1970s landmark years and broke new ground for a whole genre. Never one to rest on his laurels, Cormier continues to shock and to provoke thought in more recent work, especially in *Beyond the Chocolate War* (1985), *We All Fall Down* (1991), *Tunes for Bears to Dance To* (1992), *In the Middle of the Night* (1995), *Tenderness* (1997), and *Heroes* (1998). Teen and world violence pervade these often brutal, always mesmerizing novels, which treat variously of youthful trashers, Holocaust survivors, maimed World War II veterans, and serial murderers and the girls drawn to them. Whether he's inside the mind of a young Protestant girl puzzling over the mysteries of Catholicism, alcoholic parents, and global warfare; a boy who kills to experience tender love; or a teenage runaway who doesn't know what she's getting into when she indulges her fixation, Cormier has an uncanny ability to write across decades, genders, and moral universes. He often works with alternating points of view, juxtaposing male and female voices convincingly. Most recently, in a lecture (*Probing the Dark Cellars*) at the University of California, Los Angeles, and in his poignant *Frenchtown Summer* (1999), a lyrical revisitation of youthful memories and fears, Cormier has explored the roots of his remarkable art, further developing the autobiographical elements in what might be called his postmodern, metafictional, or magic realist *Fade* (1988), wherein young Paul's environment bears much resemblance to French Hill, the close-knit community of French Canadian immigrants where Cormier grew up.

He lives only a few miles from where he spent his formative years and where he usually sets his work. That physical proximity emblematizes the adult's psychic kinship with the youngster inside who inspires him and the juvenile readers (and adult teachers and critics) in the larger world whom he inspires and empowers in turn. He manages to rivet both teen audiences and tough adult critics, who have both lauded and chastised his relentless and unflinching portrayals of adolescents who must somehow achieve selfhood in an intimidating and manipulative universe. If some critics and many censors have seemed as unyielding as the juvenile detention center inmates who read about their fellow detainee, Eric Poole, the antihero of *Tenderness,* in English class, Cormier most typically wins the minds and hearts of readers through his emphatic powers. The young prisoners thawed too when the author paid them a personal visit, though even some of them would have opted for the Disney or TV ending Cormier will never sell us. Cormier's chocolates always come bittersweet.

A working journalist for thirty years until he opted for full-time authorship, Cormier has always lived in Leominster, a small town in north-central Massachusetts, the fictional space of "Monument" in most of his tales. He still resides in the house on Main Street where he and his wife, Connie, brought up three daughters and the son whose disquietude about selling chocolates at his private school launched his father's career as the chronicler of adolescence's dark underside. Cormier had already published several adult novels, but his empathy with youthful consciences soon won him a national and now international reputation.

Because his body of work is at once outstanding and crucially relevant to the moral dilemmas and somber themes that this volume opens out for discussion, Cormier is an obvious interview choice. With characteristic generosity and grace, he answered formidable and perhaps impertinent inquiries. Cormier's readers always come away from his works asking serious moral questions of themselves; here he gives, with his usual ethical concern, considered answers to daunting questions about art and life. Escalating violence; intermittent wars worldwide; and "local," recurrent "police" action in racism, terrorism, or ethnic "cleansing"; and the attempted genocides of whole populations can induce what some investigators call *compassion fatigue.*[1] The question of how the unspeakable and the unrepresentable can be portrayed in an ethically responsible way is not just a theoretical problem for academics or a quandary for grown-up philosophers and journalists, however. It urgently concerns young people and their storytellers, parents, and teachers. As one

An Interview with Robert Cormier

who is a storyteller, a parent, and a teacher, Robert Cormier helps us think through ways in which history might not repeat itself so that we may be enlightened instead of "blinded by the knowledge that there was no safe place to run to."[2]

Q: In prefacing this interview by juxtaposing the child and adult photographs and reproducing the 1938 letter home from summer camp that you so kindly provided, we wanted to represent visually the roots of your moral concerns and the relationships between child and adult readers, and especially writers, links that seem especially foregrounded in your recent poetic reminiscence, *Frenchtown Summer* (1999). At the heart of your work, it seems to me, is an abiding concern with what makes a moral (or immoral) action, what kinds of heroism (however limited) are available to most of us. These are matters of permanent concern, of course, but they are especially pertinent now, as we face a generation of young people who have grown up, are growing up, with unprecedented exposure to violence. Theirs is a completely different experience, in many ways, from that of their older siblings, and certainly from people who grew up in small towns years ago as you and I both did.

I might say that I first came to the study of children's and young adults' literature from a historical perspective; I was (and still am) working in late eighteenth-century literature for younger readers, when realistic fictions were called "moral tales," so I've always been especially concerned with what kind of moral possibilities stories present. Moral then didn't mean piously moralistic but was concerned with social manners and the possibilities of juvenile agency: how shall I live my life, what's important, what values do I embrace? The central injunction of these Enlightenment writers is that you must "think for yourself," that there are no easy answers, and that you can't rely on pat rules. It has always seemed to me that you are probably the most centrally concerned with morality—in a philosophical sense—of all those writers who have defined what's popularly called the "new realism" in current young adult literature, by which is usually meant the introduction of darker themes and difficult answers, from sexuality and related gender issues to oppressive individuals and institutional structures to violence and war. And you do insist above all that readers think for themselves.

I suppose you get censored so often (and most recently very close to home) because many people don't trust younger readers enough to feel that they *can* think through the ironies and ambiguities in your fiction. Censorship is an issue on which you have written and spoken often, wisely, and well, but I don't want to get into whether the young *should* be exposed to war, death, violence, human injustice, and so on, because they are being so exposed in forms we cannot control and in ways that frequently deaden response. So I return to the notion of what books can offer to cope with the omnipresent visual desensitization to moral issues.

The arguments (and persuasive images) in your essay "A Book Is Not a House" could hardly be bettered, but do you want to comment again, however briefly, on these book censorship controversies before we move on to more substantive matters?[3]

R. C.: It's true that I am weary of censorship battles and, if it only concerned me, then I would remain silent and let the book, whether *The Chocolate War,* or any other, speak for itself. Not only weary, I guess, but angry. Why should I defend the book? The book is what it is.

Yet it would be unjust not to come to the defense of teachers or librarians who are under attack because of what I've written.

Why I've become increasingly weary is that the would-be censors (who never call themselves censors and I'm getting pretty tired of that too) are incapable of or reluctant to acknowledge any virtue at all—even a glimpse—in the books they challenge. If *The Chocolate War* has been taught in schools for a quarter of a century despite all the challenges, surely there must be virtues present. Why do they think teachers take the risk of presenting it to students if it weren't teachable? The responses to the challenges are also tiresome because most challengers have not bothered to read the book, take words and phrases out of context, and fail to see the whole. But these are tired old responses of mind, of course.

In a recent case where a fifteen-year-old boy said he couldn't finish *The Chocolate War* because the book offended him, I defended his stance. But the more I think about it, the more I believe that there were probably other reasons. I can't imagine a fifteen-year-old kid, in this age of MTV, video games, R- and X-rated movies that invade the home on cable, being upset by a book. I have a feeling that he just didn't feel like reading the book as a classroom assignment and used the protest as a cop-out.

Q: After all, the Internet can't be effectively policed, but you can do with printed matter what you cannot do with other media. In an omnibus review of recent books about adolescence that I did, I was struck by the disparity between families, how involved with their children a few were but how utterly detached or disconnected many were, completely "clueless." I know you have mentioned in past interviews that you felt such detachment was a factor in censorship, parents not really knowing what their children know, perhaps also parents thinking that they can control print if nothing else. Paradoxically, it may be getting worse, although one would think the post-Internet world would make the virtue vigilantes turn their energies elsewhere. I know this is an old topic for you, but you do seem to keep coming out with new books (*Tenderness*) that occasion concerned letters to young-adult publications that review you favorably, and your classic *The Chocolate War* seems to be one that even your neighbors can't let alone. Some people would feel that the subjects of this special issue, period, should be off-limits to young readers because it is beyond the grasp of meaning making for them.

R. C.: Nothing in my novels is gratuitous or titillating for the sake of titillating. Even in *Tenderness,* when I was dealing with a sexually precocious girl and a serial killer with a predisposition for necrophilia, I wrote it in minor key, using suggestion for the most part and being careful to avoid exploitation. But here I am in a defensive posture again, so let's move on.

The would-be censors, like the poor, we will always be with us, and my best response is to keep writing.

Q: We're especially interested in the relation between childhood experience and the emergence of a moral grown-up and how writing can foster that—also, to put that in aesthetic terms, how these matters constitute what might be called a poetics of memory. One of the big themes in this issue and in all the discourse on war, violence, genocide—the Holocaust in particular—is how do we find moral "lessons" in something so awful, how do we make it knowable to young people now, how do we translate the past into fiction that will make the future generation into thinking—and reading—people instead of passive responders, watching TV and netsurfing. Many of the essays in our journal issue and elsewhere foreground narrative, storying, as a foundational way of knowing, not just for youngsters but for all of us. It has always seemed to me that you are the preeminent novelist who simultaneously appeals to kids who just want a thrilling book and to thinking readers of any age.

R. C.: I regard myself principally as a storyteller. Someone once told me that "you are much more than that." A statement like that doesn't give storytelling the dignity it deserves. It's through sheer storytelling, holding the attention of the reader—young or old—that the great themes can be addressed. "Once upon a time" are still the most provocative words in literature—we want to be told stories, we want to hear the gossip of history, and I think that's how the big themes are translated into human terms, how we can take something like the Holocaust while seeming to reduce it to a story or even an anecdote, make it real and vital, whether it's aimed at a young person (particularly a young person, I guess, who has only a vague idea of the impact of the Holocaust) but older people too. Just as a grain of sand contains the entire beach, I think small incidents like the events of *Tunes for Bears to Dance To* can hold larger truths. The storytelling form of the novel makes it accessible and, I think, emotionally effective. But it's important to know that as I sat down at my typewriter, I was very much intent on telling a story, of what happened to Henry and old Mr. Levine, and Hairston the grocer. I had to begin with them, or the exploration of the theme would never have happened.

I'm not a "thematic" writer, and I am uncomfortable thinking in the abstract. That's why I'm a novelist and not an essayist. I don't like to analyze my work, and when I do so it's only in answer to interviewers. As a journalist during so much of my life, I feel that I must respond to inquiries. (And yes, I'm aware that a certain amount of promotion and exposure is necessary—my publishers do a lot to push my books, and I feel that I owe them that much at least.) I also feel that I owe a debt to teachers and professors (especially you, Mitzi, who have done so much to explore and interpret my work for so many, many students). So I find myself uncomfortably expounding and explaining and often feel I'm out of my depth. In fact, I feel like that comic character (Donald Duck?) who finds himself flying, suddenly realizes what he's doing, becomes self-conscious, and plunges to earth. So I might plunge—forgive me if I do.

Q: As you know, I have taught a number of your works over the years and for the last few years several of them together. For this interview, of course, I've reread everything, but I had never read your first novel before, although I knew you started out as an "adult" writer for the first few books and got great reviews. I am sorry that the title got changed to Now and at the Hour (1960)—I read the original title in *Eight Plus One: Stories* (1980)—and thought the verses from Auden's farewell for Freud perfect (and perhaps also important thematically in your body of work):

> Of whom shall we speak? For every day they die
> Among us, those who were doing some good,
> And knew it was never enough but
> Hoped to improve a little by living.[4]

I am amused now by the way that early novel and all your material that's in print get marketed as "young adult," but it's the cross-generational connections and what literary people call interreferentiality or intertextuality—cross-referencing between an author's texts and between those texts and an author's life—that I am especially interested in, among other things. A few years back, Uli Knoepflmacher and

I coedited a volume of *Children's Literature* that originated the term cross-writing for dual audience works, authors who speak to multiple audiences of different ages who might get very different things from a work, crossover writing of different sorts. I remember, having come up with the word, that I had to defend it to an editor, and now we see it everywhere in discussions of literature for younger readers. Among the many other pioneering things you've accomplished are all these kinds of crossing over (including gender perspectives) so that your adult work throws light on your books for youth (and also on your themes as a writer).

Eight Plus One, your short story collection, is a very interesting work from a cross-writing perspective, because you shift between; it also has a lot of moral relevance to other work. Did you envision a mixed audience, or what? It seems so from your introductory note.

I enjoyed the way that you prefaced each story with remarks on writing and was curious about the motivation for that. The comments provide invaluable commentary on your writing processes, but they could have arisen from impatience with the interview or from a need to speak to these questions on memory's translation into fiction, or from a wish to encourage young writers who'd written to you.

R. C.: When my editor at Random House/Pantheon suggested a collection of my short stories, I wasn't interested. I preferred to push ahead with my novels. When he persisted, I thought of writing introductions which would also answer some of the questions I'd been receiving from students in their letters. That's when I became interested in the project even though the stories were written at an earlier time with no thought of ever having them collected in a book.

Q: Although some authors devoured by the young are outgrown and wouldn't be interesting to adults except teachers, I've always found it sad that many YA authors—you are not alone here—would be devoured by grownups too, but because of market niches you won't get that readership. Does it ever bother you being called a YA author and thus losing some readers who would relish your work if it were marketed differently?

R. C.: Especially in earlier years and occasionally now, I feel regret and a bit of irritation about losing potential adult readers because of the YA label and finding my books in the back of the bookstore with the children's books. Yet I have come to appreciate and cherish the YA label because of the wonderful audience of young readers who are so responsive and loyal and the teachers and librarians who have spread the word of my writing all over the world. My books have been translated into more than a dozen languages—from Japanese to Swedish. Would that have happened without the YA label? Yet I do sometimes find myself wistful about the readers I have not had through the years who dismiss me as "a writer of kids' books." (I've heard them describe me that way.)

Q: You've remarked that "I have almost total recall of my emotions at almost any given moment of the past" and that you wrote the short stories when your kids were teenagers, which you have repeatedly called "lacerating" experientially. I liked the way you described "translating" your emotions of growing up and combining those with what was then going on into stories dealing with family relationships. You mention that the youngsters in the stories grow up and that the parents do too, and I admired the way some stories were from the young person's point of view and some from the parent's. I agree about the parents' growing up in these stories; would you apply that same comment to the adults in the *novels*? You know but too well that one of the criticisms leveled against your work is that it doesn't provide models of "good" adults.

R. C.: No models of "good" adults in my novels? Listen, I don't even worry about providing good models of young adults, either. I'm not in the business of providing good role models or models of any kind, old or young. If I neglect adults or parents, it's because I want the focus to be on my protagonists or connecting characters. For instance, in *The Chocolate War,* I wanted the boys to be judged by their actions and their own decisions, not by whether they came, say, from broken homes or overly affluent homes, or whether they were spoiled as children, et cetera.

Q: Yes, I love the way you won't let Archie or any other character off on the victimization or case-history-victim-of-circumstance dodge that permeates so much talk about young adult literature. That's a great touch that you show Eric manipulating the adults with just that gimmick. I am impressed by the way you foreground moral responsibility and get readers to recognize the consequences and implications of their actions, for bad or for good. Kate, in *After the First Death,* may not exit the bus a triumphant heroine who's saved the children, but she has tried and she has realized a potential within herself that she didn't know she had when she experiences her epiphany: "the possibility that hope comes out of hopelessness and that the opposite of things carry the seeds of birth—love out of hate, good out of evil. Didn't flowers grow out of dirt?" (Cormier 1979, 118). That really reverberates in your consciousness ever after.

R. C.: The writer owes the reader a climax or an epiphany or that internal click that provides satisfaction. But I think you can go beyond that, and that is exactly what I try to do. It's important to end the story as soon after the resolution as possible, but it's also possible to add something beyond the climax, something unresolved perhaps or a provocative afterthought—thus the book never really ends in the reader's mind and lingers after the last page has been turned.

Q: I remember a haunting passage in the short story "Mine on Thursdays" when the father (who is going to fail his daughter) recalls his father's saying that the important thing in life is being a man (or a woman like Kate, as the case may be): "to look at all the wreckage of your life and to confront it all without pity for yourself. Without alibis. And to go on. To endure." Even your first published book about the dying father is pervaded by the ordinary bravery of someone who is not a traditional hero but is a survivor, sometimes dealing with past failures, but who has learned from them. I think of Jerry's defeating or deflating Emile Janza by taking the blows in *Beyond the Chocolate War* or Henry's destructive act and his then saying no and praying for the villain in *Tunes for Bears to Dance To*.

   From your first novel on, something is implied about a kind of morality that's in all your books because we are all mostly cowards and complicitous in everyday or worse evils and certainly not the cowboy heroes of your childhood that you have often amusingly recalled. You seem very early to have seized on the issues of moral living and moral choice and what heroism is possible for us—these are behind all your books and, I think, are very relevant for everyone now, child and adult. I wonder if you'd comment on the general issues of moral living and heroism in your books especially, but also in general. It is not for nothing that you ironically title your recent war book *Heroes*.

R. C.: Here again I avoid talking in themes or about moral living, preferring to explore such questions—and even that not explicitly—in my work. But I do believe, sincerely, that we are all made up of the good and the bad, that we have as much capacity for evil as for good but a certain moral fiber steers us away from the evil. Some people are untested simply because they have lacked the opportunity not to be good. My generation, for instance. We were good kids growing up because our opportunities to go wrong were so limited—we lacked access to the many things that lead kids astray today—drugs, guns, even cars to transport us. And so I believe we have those capacities, but deep down in my bones I believe that the capacity for goodness outweighs the capacity for evil. (Religion also plays a part, but that's too big a topic to go into here.) And that's why there are so many good people, good kids out there—we mostly hear about the bad ones. But remember even those that aren't good are human. The monsters around us have that spark of humanity that somehow exists even as they deny it. But we simply never see their dark nights of the soul.

Q: I'm glad you stressed here the goodness or innocence also present in the "monster"—what people don't always notice in the presentation of Miro, Kate's killer. That Brother Leon gets to deliver a terrifying truth about the classroom's guilty "good" boys early in *The Chocolate War* or that Archie forces Obie to face up to complicity in the ruin of his high school years toward the end of the sequel always disquiets some readers. Possibly Eric in *Tenderness* appalls some censors because they don't want to grant a "monster" any tenderness. It's easier to think of black versus white until we remember the good Nazi John Rabe who saved so many Chinese lives amid the mass rapes and murders of the Nanjing Massacre during the Japanese invasion. I recall, too, Primo Levi's remarkable piece, "The Gray Zone," in *The Drowned and the Saved*: that he indicated the totalitarian system devised by the Nazis in the death camps but shunned judging those who might have been corrupted by the system.[5]

However, many critics have felt that you seem to specialize in what happens when the threat of tyranny confronts us, as in Stanley Milgram's notorious experiments a few years after World War II—when he paid volunteers (some university students, some townspeople) to give supposedly electric shocks to people apparently hooked to a machine. The volunteers were told by an authority figure that it was in the name of a scientific experiment. Contrary to predictions, most people went along and continued to administer increasingly powerful "shocks" as long as the figure in the white coat took the flak, even when the presumed victim screamed to be free or fell silent and seemed to have suffered illness, perhaps a heart attack. Very few walked out. Much has been written about the ethics or lack thereof of the experiments, but what's to the point is how willing most people were to conform, even when they were severely uncomfortable. Those experiments have often come up when my classes discuss your work.

Everyone likes to think he or she would have stood up to the Nazis or whatever other tyrannical force, but most of us, like your people on the bus confronted with the rowdy teens in an anecdote I think you have used, would look the other way or get off a stop earlier—nobody wants trouble. Many of us remember also the famous New York case some years back in which a woman was beaten to death and her screams heard by many, many on a hot night and no one helped—and there have been several other recent examples.

R. C.: The Genovese case in New York illustrated the themes in some of my novels—it's a simple truth that is a cliché simply because it is the truth—bad things happen when good people do nothing. Not only people but the individual. It can start with one person.

Q: I think you put that so memorably in an earlier interview, that effective action had to be collective but that it also had to start with an individual. People who want to interpret your work as unequivocally grim stories of doomed young people forget the narrative moments, the "what if" places, in your favorite phrase, when it might have turned out otherwise, as when the chocolate sale falters and some students begin to think. Someone said charitably of the New York case that maybe they all thought someone else called 911; but that doesn't help, because if I hear and don't call, it's my responsibility.

What seems really important is that you don't show easy victories or even victories. Sometimes you show failures and then go on to show some reparation, however small, and it's those aspects I'd like to discuss more specifically in relation to *Tunes for Bears to Dance To.*

You have mentioned in other notes from *Eight Plus One* that you are always looking for a "second level" of meaning in your stories and you are interested in "explor[ing] prejudice and the possibility of love—or compassion—overcoming it," two remarks that seem especially pertinent in asking you to address some key issues in relation to *Tunes*. I really think it a small gem of a book that encapsulates central moral issues in your body of work and is crucially relevant to the themes that are this special issue's focus. It is so elegantly done and feels, to use a pretentious word I don't like, almost archetypal in embodying not only Holocaust issues and their fallout but also the banality of evil and the many forces and constraints, institutionalized or informal, that adolescents grapple with in achieving intellectual and moral identities.

R. C.: The banality of evil. One thing I admit—I do try to show in most of my books that very banality, that evil doesn't creep out of a cage at midnight dragging a chain but is the clerk at McDonald's, the teacher in the classroom, the man next door who belongs to the Rotary Club and plays golf every Saturday afternoon. Brint in *I Am the Cheese,* I am sure, has a two-car garage, indulges his wife, and belongs to the Elks. Horror isn't a thunderstorm at two o'clock in the morning but the grocery clerk who delivers your order just before noontime. All of this is trite, of course, and obvious, but so obviously worth probing. The poet said, "I myself am heaven and hell." We contain all of that, and that is why we must love each other.

Q: Probably a four-car garage these days! I have to ask a question that I swore I wouldn't. You know what's coming, but what is the specific genesis of this story, and did it go through any metamorphoses along the way to get distilled down (as you've mentioned happened with *Fade* and other works). Not only Henry, the boy facing the choice, but also the banally evil employer, the racist grocer Mr. Hairston, with his threats, temptations, and attempt at a Faustian pact, and the survivor through art, Mr. Levine, wonderfully re-creating in loving detail his childhood village, making live again everything that the Nazis destroyed so that he can live himself: it's almost a parable. No one who has read Hannah Arendt and others on the banality of evil, the ordinary Germans, the bureaucrats who went along with mass destruction, can help being struck with how much philosophical weight you get into this story. Could you especially comment on these genesis, character, and connection aspects of *Tunes?*

R. C.: I didn't set out to write a "Holocaust novel" with *Tunes for Bears to Dance To,* but the Holocaust was very much on my mind. I'd been reading about it, and of all the horrors that I ran across, what struck me the most were the little horrors, the small things that haunt at midnight. The compulsive reactions, like the old man tipping his hat. That haunted me. What set me to reading about the Holocaust and stories about the death camps in the first place was my anger at reports that some people were saying the Holocaust never happened! I'm afraid of big lies (just as I'm afraid of anything big) because they're so big that they tend to be believed after a while. About the same time, a woodcarver friend of mine displayed his latest creation at a local arts and crafts show. His centerpiece was the re-creation of his hometown village in Canada, the house he was born in, the church, the town hall, et cetera. It was a masterpiece, so detailed and lovingly made. People brushed casually by the table on which it was displayed and where it remained on display for three days and nights. It seemed to be very vulnerable and almost welcoming an accident that would damage or destroy it.

From that point, I made the writer's leap through my Holocaust reading to that small hat-tipping compulsion of the camp's victim. Then came the final touch that sent me to the typewriter, and here's where Graham Greene's words echo [quoting]: I remember a grocer I ran errands for when I was nine or ten years old. He seemed to be a nice guy, but he was a practical joker. And his jokes, which he played on me and another boy, sometimes crossed the line between fun and cruelty. To go into detail would take up too much space, but let me say that one particular "joke" left me utterly humiliated, and it has remained with me through the years. Somehow, it came back to me as I was pondering what to do about the woodcarver's village and the hat compulsion.

Q: Some therapists have recently written about using this story with highly disturbed young people to help them work out their identity issues, including the notions that no one would believe their stories or that they could not question the controlling adult. The students in group therapy, by the way, all of whom were seventh and eighth graders severely "at risk," completely identified with the boy's plight and learned resistance from it. These were extremely aggressive and violent young people, and I found that especially worth remarking on because Henry is basically such an innocent, which is, of course, why Mr. Hairston targets him. I am a bit troubled, though, by the blatantly bibliotherapeutic use of the fiction and by the reading of therapists as its being about the ways that adults fail children (there is, of course, the daughter's abuse).

It certainly is a story of moral growth, but its implications, especially the end, go far beyond its reduction to a help for troubled teens. The events and last few chapters of the book poignantly evoke *Kristallnacht* in 1938 when the Nazis chose to shatter the fabric of Jewish life in a strikingly public way. When Mr. Hairston tries to seduce Henry into obliterating the village before the town award ceremony, it seems to miniaturize and to make legible for younger readers the horrors of that night. It's been rightly said, I think, that there is a political, in the most generous sense of that term, dimension to all that you write.

Your work began to open up a whole new terrain in writing about and in creating YA fiction because, aside from being strikingly vigorous stylistically and conceptually original, it made it possible to see what had formerly been considered a narrow, narcissistic genre as capacious enough to handle an intellectual novel of ideas. So there's been much interpretation of your work as a response to institutionalized tyranny—I suppose that got in high gear with *I Am the Cheese,* but it lends itself to other works equally well. The sociologist Erving Goffman has written brilliantly in *Asylums* about what he calls "the total institution," meaning a world unto itself where the individual is pitted against and overwhelmed by what I guess Marxist theorists like Althusser would call the "state apparatus."[6] Specifically, Goffman analyzes insane institutions, hospitals, and schools, and I think also the general media culture that environs everyone would count too. One fears the Internet is for many young (and older) users a "total institution." You must still get the occasional reader or parent who somehow thinks you're anti-Catholic schools, when that is not remotely the point of *The Chocolate War* or its sequel, which I and many classes, by the way, have virtually uniformly found a satisfying finale, instead of the letdown that many sequels turn out to be. No student has ever had anything positive to say about the movie's conflation, however. As the showing concludes, the classroom always erupts with outrage.

I wonder, though, if what was initially a liberating critical strategy isn't also in danger of reducing a multilayered and evolving body of work to a single trademark theme. What's fascinating is that you don't just repeat yourself—one of the things that amazes me is that, after all, I am an adult and a teacher with many years of analytical reading behind me, and you *still* "do a number," to borrow a phrase from one of your books, on me every single time. I confess I'm still a little bit stunned by your response to what research you'd done for the serial killer novel, because I was teaching several sociological studies at the time, and you were so dead right (sorry, I couldn't resist), and you smiled and said, "none."

So I want to turn from the "political" to the "personal" element that is always present in your writing.

It seems to me that in many ways your most recent work, *Frenchtown Summer,* like the column collection *I Have Words to Spend* and the wonderful address you gave at UCLA, *Probing the Dark Cellars of a Young Adult Writer's Heart,* not only are the kinds of cross-writing that speak to adults as well as to youth, but they also seems to re-create almost consciously the germinating context of personal childhood traumas, the fears and tests that ground your distinctive "public" and "political" themes.[7] It's as if you were pausing at a mature moment in your career to go back and say, this is where I came from, this is the matrix that makes sense of my work, this is where I get my ideas, this is what kind of person I am, this is the experience that I translate into morally responsible fictions.

I think at a certain point in life such reflection happens; I don't know how conscious it is. I was especially taken with the notion in rereading *Fade,* with its detailed background so much like yours, in conjunction with your most recent exploration of your early dreads and traumas, like your terror that your mother might be dead when she was napping or the pursuing bully you've wished dead who falls off a hill or returning from summer camp to find the cousin dying in horror of being buried alive, the "little" events that made you understand the world was fraught with threats.

Could you comment on those autobiographical or contextual issues? Because most readers will not have read the UCLA talk, to connect childhood trauma and adult themes would be most appropriate as exemplifying two kinds of cross-writing at once—youth and maturity, fiction and remembrance. You've mentioned that one woman who'd read some of your work had almost not attended a seminar because she feared meeting a "monster" and told you she was glad she came because she had met "another Robert Cormier." How do the two connect?

R. C.: I think my later (autographical) writings come from the critics who have questioned me about my work or from the talks I've made in recent years. Answering questions and writing talks like the one at UCLA caused me to look back and try to find links. At the same time, I've been aware of my age and the passing of years and even the passing of friends. In a way my writing has always been autobiographical. Graham Greene wrote: "The creative writer perceives his world once and for all in childhood and adolescence and his whole career is an effort to illustrate his private world in terms of the great public world we all share." He also quotes another writer (whose name I can't pin down at the moment): "In the lost childhood of Judas, Christ was betrayed." He also said words to the effect that "the writer must have a sliver of ice in his heart."[8]

These remarks echo in my life and in my writing. When I say that all my writing is autobiographical, I mean that I am in all my characters. I am Archie and Lori in *Tenderness,* and all the others *as I am writing.* I italicize these words because a distinction has to be made between writing and real life. I worry when I get into the skin of Eric Poole and have waking nightmares about identifying with some of my characters but also outside of my writing as well. I have never talked about this at length and resist even thinking much about it. What I mean is: I don't have to make a great leap about how a boy of fourteen feels at a given moment, I simply know. And so I know exactly how Eric Poole feels as he goes about his compulsions although I haven't done what Eric Poole has done.

Yet I *do* know, excruciatingly, and sometimes this knowledge is a terrible burden to bear.

Q: Finally, I can't help asking about the "didacticism" or teaching and learning function of your work, about you as a teacher. (I don't see didacticism as a "dirty" word signifying inartistic or moralistic, having originated as it did in the eighteenth century.) I've always found it especially wonderful when my students discover with shock that in the excruciating scene humiliating Gregory Bailey before the class, the "bad" headmaster, Brother Leon, is in fact delivering a key message about collective passivity and/or responsibility. You remark that action against evil starts with an individual. I think for readers *you* are that individual, the "good" teacher. Maria Edgeworth in 1798 wrote that the function of good teachers is to make themselves unnecessary (which she remarked in later editions many readers thought a typo but it wasn't). I know that teaching people is very far from your first motive in writing, that you write from emotions and fall in love with your characters, nevertheless . . . I don't think that some people are prepared to find such complexities, ironies, and ambiguities in young adult books; as with children's books, some people (including some students) want a rose-colored view. (I don't think such people remember very clearly the powerlessness and pain that is so much a part of being young.) You expect readers to *think*, to extrapolate beyond the end and connect what they have read with what they will do with their lives in the world, so that's why I think of you above all as a wise teacher (as opposed to some YA novelists who obviously write to teach and so don't). I hope "teacher" doesn't seem reductive to you but wish you would comment on that.

Also, ultimately, and I won't rehearse all the awards and so on, how would you like best to be remembered? Maybe as a magician rather than a teacher like Ray Bannister! I always think of you too in connection with Archie, the master manipulator, whom I love a bit, and I think you do too. (My students always misread that comment until I explain.) One of the horrors of the filmed version of *The Chocolate War* was that Archie would *never* get humiliated as he did there. Like Archie the artist, Cormier the magician always tricks the reader into shocked realization at his or her own complicity! None of your books end at the end. In your first published novel about the dying father, there's the line, "When a man dies, he leaves a legacy." What would you like your legacy as a writer to be?

R. C.: I don't, of course, regard myself as a teacher, although I suppose readers draw lessons from what they read. But, as I've said many times, I regard myself simply as a storyteller. I'm reminded, though, of fables which illustrate certain truths, and I suppose that if I try to write the truth, which I certainly try to do, then lessons are possible. I know from the letters I receive from young readers that they derive more than just the experience of a story from my books. A boy from Nottingham, England, recently wrote that I changed his life. More than one adult has told me that my books helped them through his or her adolescence. These are sweet to me. And so this answer about teaching life lessons is probably linked to the one about how I wish to be remembered and it may be this:

That I not only entertained but illuminated, that I somehow changed the way young people think and had a positive effect on their lives. As I write this, I am almost overwhelmed because I've frankly never thought about my writing in these terms before. I mean I am touched when I receive a letter with those sentiments, to listen to somebody saying them to me, but have never dwelt on them. Or put them into any perspective. Until this moment.

Q: I don't think you can separate the entertainment and the illumination. In setting up this interview, I mentioned briefly the exchange student I had at UCLA last spring in the adolescent literature class. Because foreign universities often do not teach such materials, almost everything we read was new and fascinating to her, but her response to *The Chocolate War* was at a whole different level. She and her sister British exchange student (actually one was of Greek and the other of Italian ancestry), both juniors (junior year abroad), always sat in the front row of a huge class because they can't ask questions or participate much at home, and I try to encourage student response. She seized me and said with this kind of dazed expression, "Dr. Myers, Dr. Myers, I could NOT put this book down once I started it. He is just an amazing man. I want to meet this man. I *need* to talk to him." Her intensity and urgency cracked me up, but I think they typify your effect on young readers. Thank you so much for giving us the time to talk to you.

Notes

1. See Moeller, *Compassion Fatigue: How the Media Sell Disease, Famine, War, and Death* (1999), especially chap. 5, "Covering War: Getting Graphic about Genocide." Important recent work covering American packaging and media management of the Holocaust in particular includes Cole, *Selling the Holocaust from Auschwitz to Schindler: How History is Bought, Packaged, and Sold* (1999; published in Great Britain under a different title); and Novick (1999). Contemporary Holocaust memorial discourse is especially concerned with the relation between representation and bearing witness past and present. See, for example, the anthologies edited by Leak and Paizis (2000), Rosenfield (1999), and Sicher (1998).
2. The title of this interview comes from Cormier, *Frenchtown Summer* (1999), chaps. 23, 82.
3. Cormier, "A Book Is Not a House: The Human Side of Censorship" (1992).
4. "In Memory of Sigmund Freud (d. Sept. 1939)," in Auden (1945, 164).
5. Levi ends his essay "The Gray Zone" provocatively by noting the difficulties of resistance, much along the lines of Cormier's thinking in this and other interviews: "Willingly or not we come to terms with power, forgetting that we are all in the ghetto, that the ghetto is walled in, that outside the ghetto reside the lords of death, and that close by the train is waiting" (1998, 69). A key "gray" and highly controversial case he discusses in detail is Chaim Rumkowski, dictator of the Lodz ghetto, whose quasi-collaboration with the Nazis in order to save Jews is also noted in Adrienne Kertzer's essay in the volume.
6. See Goffman, "On the Characteristics of Total Institutions" (1961, 1–124).
7. Cormier (1991, 1999b).
8. The Greene quote is from "The Young Dickens" (1951, 54); the other author on Judas is cited as AE (George William Russell) in Cormier (1999b).

8

Picturing Trauma in the Great War

Margaret R. Higonnet

As a number of French historians such as Stéphane Audoin-Rouzeau have noted, the war culture of 1914 to 1918 embraced children through toys, magazines, school lessons, and propaganda posters, relying especially energetically on visual culture.[1] Children were mobilized to become soldiers on the home front, while at the same time, as icons of innocence, they became ideal citizens. Thus the French minister for public education announced in September 1915, "In all France, the school will be the moral center of the nation" (Dancel 2003, 72). As the German invasion and French national mobilization engulfed children in harsh new necessities, they were asked to participate in the national sacrifice. The costs of war were felt on the home front as well as in the trenches, and school assignments often focused on that analogy. Drawing assignments explicitly juxtaposed scenes of sacrifice and deprivation in a trench with scenes at home.

    As children were being impelled into the adult culture of war, they also participated in their own specific war culture, as Audoin-Rouzeau has shown, through schoolbooks, leisure reading, and the production of their own visual record. Much of that material was devoted to violence. Only in part, however, did this visual and verbal culture acknowledge the place of trauma in children's experience of war. Often it was represented in indirect and symbolic ways. Almost a century later, scholars such as Olivier Faron have begun to study the impact of personal loss in an environment of violence on the children of war. Following the lead of Audoin-Rouzeau, scholars such as Didier Guyvarc'h, Frédérick Hadley, Brigitte Dancel, and Manon Pignot have also begun to explore imagery for and by children, whose representations record the sufferings of war, and in doing so frame them for further interpretation.

Violence is strangely unstable as a force in children's books. The bulk of war literature for children from this period indoctrinates them in politically acceptable history and builds adventure stories around child heroism, combined with the glamour of new technologies—from chivalric combat in airplanes to inexorable lumbering advances by tank. The vast majority of this literature is unrealistic and highly gendered. Poor children and those in the war zones had little access to these books, and they probably imagined this war through tales about earlier wars. Some war books, especially picture books for younger children, treat violence comically. Thus, during World War I, the French rapscallions called the "Pieds Nickelés" marched off to tweak the moustache of the kaiser, and the Breton housemaid Bécassine, through her inimitably triumphant incompetence, joined the domestic war effort and thwarted enemy spies. Her ability to screw things up became a form of patriotic heroism. When mischief is translated into patriotic mayhem, such books turn violence into slapstick and naturalize war as an expression of individual human energies rather than as socially implemented destruction.[2]

Often the humor rests on an analogy between child and soldier. The comic artist Poulbot, an icon of Montmartre, imitated a naïve children's style to depict in posters and newspaper illustrations the war games at home that echoed the war at the front, and in the process he blurred the line between the two. Children themselves relished comic elements in the new war economy. Thus Olivier Pérès, eleven in 1914, drew a picture divided into sections showing the dismayed reactions when adulterated bread became the norm in Paris and imposed "equality" between soldiers and their families: one little girl refuses to eat it and throws her slice on the floor. On the entry of the United States into the war in 1917, Pérès drew himself waking up tousled to find a beautiful Easter egg on his night table; in a second panel on the right a recognizable Woodrow Wilson sends a different kind of egg—a declaration of war—to the kaiser. These couplings of the child's world and the adult world reframe the war in a way that empowers the child.

Balancing exuberant comic modes, in which child heroes and tricksters exhibit their courage and cunning, are more serious representations of war and of the injuries it inflicts. The mobilization of millions of soldiers affected every family in France, creating an audience among children who needed to find imaginative means to express loss and the darker side of war. Thus in Marc Corelli's illustrated chapter book *Mémoires du Général Joffre en Plomb* (1917), a child's beloved but broken toy soldier (Général Joffre on horseback) becomes a silent model for the older brother, Christian, who has returned handicapped from the front, having lost one arm and a hand. Christian's struggle against depression and despair gives surprisingly detailed shape to the difficulties many families faced. "Joffre" exhorts him: "You are handicapped, yes, useless, no!" (48). Such representations for children of trauma reflect not only the growing recognition of the post-traumatic disorders that became hallmark diseases of World War I but also the desire to enable children to work through their exposure to that experience.

Nonetheless, some writers may strive to protect children by building a censoring screen around traumatic images, reinforcing the erasure that is one of the key traits of trauma itself (Kertzer 2004, 251; Bosmajian 2002, xiv). Especially in small children's picture books, strategies of indirection and substitution arise. In pictures drawn by children who have themselves been under stress, selective symbolic details without narrative integration become keys to our understanding. The many difficulties of representing violence, as well as the difficulties in reading violence, pose serious challenges to students of this war culture.

Children's trauma is more difficult to analyze than adult trauma because children are even less able than are adults to articulate their traumas verbally. As Jane Eyre explains, "Children can feel, but they cannot analyze their feelings; and if the analysis is partially effected in thought, they know not how to express the result of the process in words" (Brontë 1996, 31). In a 1918 article on children's experience of the war, René Dumesnil and Thomas Simon noted that many children simply listed telling details in their accounts of their war experiences, but the observed details of their drawings conveyed more than their words. "Certainly these children saw better than they knew how to say" (57). Likewise Victor Perrot, president of the Montmartre historical society, commented on the children's drawings collected in the schools of Montmartre: "The child has a marvelous sense of the actual. He listens attentively but sees precisely. If in his writings, he often simply reflects what he hears said around him, his drawings by contrast reveal an observation that is more direct, more spontaneous, more real" (1915, 4). Whether or not we agree that children's drawings are "real," alternative physical and visual means of communication such as children's drawings and picture books take on special importance in response to the hypothesis that one of the main features of trauma is the difficulty of verbal communication.

Given the difficulty of expressing trauma at all, one of the first steps to take in opening this topic is to consider our understanding of trauma as experienced by children as compared to the trauma of adults. Military doctors observed paralyzing "shell shock" among soldiers who suffered from protracted violence under exhausting conditions, or from the sight of intolerable mutilation that exceeded their grasp. Historians such as Jay Winter and George Mosse also speak of social trauma resulting from the loss of beliefs, the breakup of systems of power, economic chaos, and the decimation of an entire generation. When we speak of children, we may have in mind those who have directly witnessed terrifying events, or we may mean the cumulative impact of corrosive losses: of a home, of a parent or siblings, or even of the child's own limbs. Not until recently has children's experience of war been considered as forming part of collective trauma.[3]

Propaganda of the period, however, instead of distinguishing the soldier's shell shock from the trauma of the child, drew a parallel. Although Jacqueline Rose argues provocatively in *The Case of Peter Pan* that children's fiction hangs on "the impossible relation between adult and child" (1984, 1), it is surprising to discover just how tightly propaganda and fiction intertwined the shell shock of the adult and the trauma of the child. That juxtaposition of the child and the soldier is one of the prime tropes of the period (figure 8.1, p. 154). Civilian authors of the middle classes in particular tended to perceive soldiers as children and children as fellow combatants in a world struggle: the two groups shared a limited vocabulary, naïve simplicity in their observations, and victimization by the war. Thus Dumesnil and Simon saw in children's testimony a simplicity "a little like that of all soldiers, little actors in an immense drama" (1918, 77). In a strange reversal, trench propaganda targets soldiers as subalterns, simplifying and infantilizing them, while home front propaganda calls upon children to become adults and agents (see Isnenghi 1977). Conversely, propaganda interpellates the child, calling upon him to assume responsibility for the absent adults, sacrificed for the nation. In the years after the war was over, on monuments erected throughout France, the dead soldier became one of the lost "children" of his town.

Traumatic shock expresses itself as an inability to know or understand what has happened, and it may even impose muteness, like that of an infant (Latin *infans* means without speech). War reduces adults to the level of vulnerability of a child. The child, especially the injured or traumatized child, takes on symbolic resonance in a nation at war. The child is no longer a simple mascot. As in the famous British poster, his wound asks, "Daddy, what did you do in the war?"

Scientific study of trauma links the soldier to the child as well. Some psychiatrists have drawn a link between the expression of trauma by adults such as shell-shocked soldiers, and the expressive models of a child. Judith Herman, for example, links the two in her well-known book *Trauma and Recovery* (1997) and connects the functioning of traumatic memory to its value as testimony. "In their predominance of imagery and bodily sensation and in their absence of verbal narrative, traumatic memories resemble the memories of young children" (38). Herman comments on the performative and iconic nature of traumatic expression: children are "able to reenact these [traumatic] events in their play with extraordinary accuracy" (38). Likewise Dumesnil and Simon stress the "objectivité" of children's accounts of war (1918, 75, 77). Under traumatic stress, Herman argues, the inscription of memory may be particularly visual and "enactive," that is, recapitulated through performance. She draws upon Harvard psychiatrist Bessel van der Kolk to hypothesize that, under the impact of trauma, "the central nervous system reverts to the sensory and iconic forms of memory that predominate in early life" (Herman 1997, 39). Traumatic forms of memory then would correspond to the fragmentation of narrative and the dissolution of visual context.

Precisely such traits in the expression of trauma drew the attention of surrealists such as André Breton, who took down the ravings of soldiers when he was on duty as an orderly at the Val de Grace, and drew on them for his first surrealist experiments.[4] The drawings of children also served as models for the material, symbolic expression of emotion and dream. Is there, in fact, a parallelism between the iconic, truncated traits attributed to artistic productions by shell-shocked soldiers and to art by children? At least one observer of French children who had witnessed combat, Mme. Marie Hollebecque, specifically noted their difficulties in articulating historical events. A pedagogue, she interviewed children in hospitals—child soldiers who had run away to war, then been sent back wounded to Paris hospitals. Considering the cases of these roughly one hundred children who took off for the front in order to volunteer as soldiers or nurses, she comments that many, motivated by the unhealed wounds of the Franco-Prussian War, felt intensely the tragedy of war but were unable to articulate a unified story. "All felt stirred by this war tragedy, yet no one knew the events very well or was able to compose an account, however fragmentary" (1916, 73n).

One implication underlying Herman's thesis and Mme. Hollebecque's observations is that one might consider trauma itself, or its avatar "hysteria," not just in the usual way as a feminized set of symptoms but also as a mode of expression that signifies a general loss of power, like the helplessness of a child, as well as a loss of conventional powers of articulation or unifying control. These psychological observations in turn may be applied to the images that children used to express their experiences. Do formal features such as the lack of perspective in children's drawings, especially wartime drawings, correspond to the traumatic breakdown of unifying control? Perhaps an aesthetic approach to the way pictorial narrative disintegrates and decontextualizes images, together with a diagnostic approach, offers an alternative tack to interpreting these materials. Visual traits such as floating images may correspond to a child's difficulty in understanding the causes of the war and the damage it wrought. In turn, the therapeutic question arises whether a visual narrative of trauma may offer some form of healing agency or power to the child.

How was the range of traumas that struck them lived by children? One response of adults was undoubtedly to censor the griefs of children, whether because they were not thought capable of deep melancholy or because their sorrows were taken to be unpatriotic. The famous actor Jean-Louis Barrault, for example, recounts the death of his father three weeks before the armistice. His father, Jules, was a litter-carrier who at forty-two was caring for soldiers ill with typhus or the Spanish flu. Sent home, he was dead inside two days. When jubilation broke out on November 11 at school, the teacher, himself a soldier who had been invalided out, was horrified to find a child weeping in a corner. Without a moment's hesitation, the teacher beat the little Barrault boy until he broke his cane (cited by Faron 2001, 39). In a country mobilized for war, the grief that war causes may not readily find its place. Studies of war trauma by historians such as Annette Becker (on the occupied zone of France) and Paul Lerner (on German treatment of shell shock) concur in finding that soldiers' post-traumatic symptoms were regularly dismissed as effeminate shirking or suppressed as a part of the war that could not be integrated into a national narrative. To acknowledge trauma was especially problematic in the case of children, whom the nation—and indeed the war itself—was charged with protecting.

Yet French children's confrontation with trauma was not overlooked during the interminable years of war and occupation, from 1914 to 1918. Alfred Binet's

Société libre pour l'Etude psychologique de l'Enfant sought to gather information about the repercussions of the war on class size, absenteeism, discipline, games, academic progress, and so forth. It collected children's letters from the most severely affected regions but found them "difficult to analyse" (Société libre pour l'Etude psychologique de l'Enfant 1917, 6, 44). It also requested that teachers send drawings for which the war was "the occasion or the pretext" (8); the drawings that arrived, however, were not "spontaneous" as expected, but rather "school assignments, executed on request" (15). The historian Stéphane Audoin-Rouzeau has traced in scrupulous detail the mobilization of children by government propaganda, schools, the church, and their families. School assignments presented the justifications for the war, the barbarism of the enemy, the main battles, and the heroic acts of the war. These often focused on child victims as well as child heroes. Pictures here were indeed worth a thousand words to mobilize both children and adults, by showing scenes such as a dead boy lying next to a popgun and a toy horse.

This mobilization of children is manifest in the drawings by children collected and published not only during the war itself but also in recent years. Children's school drawings were part of the war effort. Mme. Hollebecque reviewed in 1915 a collection of 1,485 drawings by children aged seven to fifteen, a third of them girls, collected by the Larousse publishing house.[5] In May 1917, 147 children's drawings were assembled for an exhibit at Nantes, with reports by the directors of the schools (Guyvarc'h 1993).[6] The Montmartre archive in Paris has preserved more than one thousand drawings, of which Manon Pignot has reproduced 121.[7] Likewise at Breslau there was an exhibit of children's drawings that was published by researcher C. Kik in 1915.[8] In all these collections we can observe the impact of a war culture that sought to organize children psychologically and politically. At the same time, teachers, journalists, and psychologists expected that the very activity of drawing might offer children emotional release.

In fact, some of these drawings may depict scenes children had seen or heard about at home, according to reports from teachers. The director of a school at Nantes comments that the images "often are furnished by the children who recite on arriving in the morning what each letter delivered at home has told their mother, grand-parents, and the children—brothers, sisters" (Guyvarc'h 1993, 46). Word of mouth was especially significant as a source in occupied zones. In the rear, many strove to copy or trace images from news media, posters, and other sources, whether current propaganda or past history. Typically boys enjoyed depicting heroic individual duels or chivalric aerial combat, while girls were more likely to draw hospitals, as Mme. Hollebecque explains (1916, 86–87). Most often they follow assignments by their teachers. For example, they were encouraged to depict the refugees who flooded into their schools in 1914, seeking emergency housing in the classrooms. Drawings of "actualités" or current events from schools in Nantes show a mother comforting her child, mothers and children with bundles, and families trying to sleep on the floor of a classroom (figure 8.2, p. 154).

Many images respond to reports of specific incidents that were read in class by the professor (such as the bravery of a sergeant who picked up the wounded and brought them back to the trenches) and thus recur in drawings by different hands. Some are troubling, ambiguous depictions of violence in Paris: the collection at Montmartre includes drawings of a famous aviator named Navarre who on April 19, 1917, deliberately ran down several policemen, as well as drawings of deserters, one of whom killed four men. As the spring of 1917 saw mutinies in the army and strikes in Paris, the fourteen-year-old named Honoré who drew images of three of these may have found an indirect vehicle to condemn the demoralizing effects of the unceasing war effort. But the shocked bystanders in the image do not tell us how the child interpreted those homicides.

A particularly impressive assignment concerned the story of Théophile Jagout, a twelve-year-old scout who refused to tell German soldiers about an ambush a few yards further in the forest. When the Germans retreated, they turned against the boy and executed him. Since the story was not only published (Le Cordier 1918) but given as a class assignment, we know that this story resonated as a twentieth-century version of the French Revolutionary child hero Barra, who according to legend was shot by royalists.[9] It therefore captured the imaginations of students who were familiar already with heroic models of national childhood (Guyvarc'h 1993, 44–45). Although successive drawings of such stories tend to make the child ever younger, as Stéphane Audoin-Rouzeau has pointed out (1993, 141), the child victim Théophile Jagout symbolically becomes a soldier himself, assimilated by a scout's uniform to the uniforms of adults. Because the child is a volunteer, never a conscript, he incarnates the common will to defend an innocent nation.

Similar in its pathos to the execution of the young Théophile is the colorful if brief account in a children's journal of the execution of a fourteen-year-old Belgian farm girl said to have been falsely accused of passing information to French officers. She was shot "impitoyablement" (pitilessly) before her parents' eyes, as the farm buildings were set on fire, according to an illustrated cover story of December 12, 1914, printed in the children's magazine *Trois couleurs,* the first such magazine to be specifically devoted to the war. In a blue dress, the girl raises her arm almost in a salute as she falls back under the assassination squad's fire. We should note that the masthead of this magazine promises a mix of "episodes, stories, and novels" about the Great War (Audoin-Rouzeau 1993, 96–97), a blend that warns its readers to take its history with a grain of salt.

Internalized by schoolchildren, published images of child martyrs recur in children's drawings such as one made in 1915–16 at Nantes by an eleven-year-old child named Choffget, who illustrates a story about the execution of civilians, with a stoic mother and her son in a burning village (Guyvarc'h 1993, 46; figure 8.3, p. 155). Students also illustrated texts given them in dictation exercises or copied images from illustrated papers. The cultural work done by such images of child martyrs was clearly to consolidate the image of France herself as an innocent victim.

The narrative of France as a victim was even more important for those Frenchmen separated from France by the German occupation of the North and East. During the summer vacation of 1914, "Tere," mother of the future cardinal Yves Congar, asked each of her children to record their daily impressions. A remarkable child whose wartime sufferings influenced his religious vocation and later ecumenism as a Dominican, Yves, then ten, embellished his unusually vivid diary about the "Franco-Boche" war with drawings inset into an entry or at the bottom of a page.

On the day the Germans entered Sedan, August 25, 1914, he drew a broad line across the page of his journal and wrote below, "Here begins a tragic history, it is a sad and somber history written by a child who always has in his heart love and respect for his country and a just and enormous hatred for a cruel and unjust people" (Congar 1997, 30, 250). Thus he visually demarcated the political rupture between past and present in his notebook. Unlike most schoolchildren in the unoccupied parts of France, Congar lived in the "forbidden zone" of Sedan through repeated bombardments and the deportation of his father January 6, 1918—perhaps the hardest moment of the war for the family. His openly angry diary has exceptional value as the verbal and visual testimony of a child about his war experience. This ten-year-old's use of his drawings can be reflective, even analytic: on several pages, he drew the city of Sedan "before" and "after." One diptych from October 1914 shows a church in a landscape on the left, three ruins with no trees on the right (57). Another from November starkly contrasts a large three-story home next to a bench, with a horse-drawn wagon laden with goods and a woman carrying pails in front of the building on the left, with a roofless ruin on the right framed by unrecognizable wreckage, its surface cross-hatched and scored red to suggest the violence and fire that have assaulted the building. In this visual syntax, line and color inscribe the German invasion.

Enraged by the destruction of Sedan and his church of Fond de Givonne, Congar almost went to prison for using the term *Boche* and deeply mourned his father's exile as a hostage. Not only did he witness destruction, but he was also caught up directly in resistance to the occupiers. Defiant, he spat on a soldier and was called in to the police station. Yet Congar appears to have warded off trauma by his intensely patriotic and affective family ties, as well as by his lively sense of satire. His diary is full of caricatures of Kaiser Wilhelm, the Kronprinz, and of German soldiers of all ranks, one modeled on Pinocchio, others perhaps echoing caricatures in the comic strip adventures of the Pieds-Nickelés. When Germans march across the page, their square moustaches, goose step, and elaborately pointed helmets help identify them (figure 8.4, p. 123).

Clearly the diary offered a lifeline to the young Congar. When he witnessed an attack on September 17, 1915, by mounted Uhlans running down civilians in the town square, he hurried to record the event pell-mell on the page and to capture the chaos. This entry continues a series of earlier entries about harvesting potatoes (called "canadas" in the Ardennes) to be hidden from the Germans, but the pace has accelerated and the narrative overflows. "I return to the potatoes with the wheelbarrows I was already at the arch when I see a gathering, I wondered what it was and I see 300 women men children taken with their wheelbarrows or sacks, I hide mine behind the communal wash-basin [*lavoir*], I join the gathering and I watch people going by, we were about a hundred there wh'en the Uhlan arrives gives kicks

Picturing Trauma in the Great War

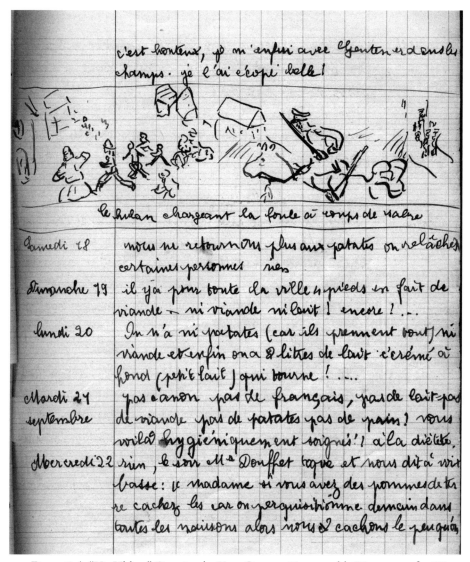

Figure 8.4. "Un Uhlan." Drawing by Yves Congar, 11 years old. Diary entry for 17 Septembre 1915. *Journal de la Guerre, 1914–1918.* By permission of Dominique Congar.

tells us to fucc ourselves, draws his sabber, and thrusts his horse at a gallop into the crowd 2 are hurt" (Congar 1997, 124–25).[10] Far from running away he joins the crowd. The child's outpouring of an almost unpunctuated present-tense stream of details about the German violence and his satiric verve, so visible in this entry, may have helped protect him from surrendering to the sense of helplessness that often accompanies trauma. In retrospect, he stressed in 1924 the steady hope that sprang from patriotism, religious faith, family solidarity, and communal exchanges; these sustained the brothers' "little acts of resistance" amid their "suffering and sacrifice" (253, 251). "We did what our brothers the *poilus* did: hold out" (250).

For other children we know little of the long-term impact of their sufferings under attack, even though we do have drawings that record such events. Thus it was "from memory" ("d'après les souvenirs") that the Belgian Célina Terrÿn depicted an aerial combat in August 1914 over Dixmude, with a French 75 mm shell aimed at a German plane by artillery hidden among trees on a slope. For such refugees, the plane was a "synonym of death."[11] This child was herself a refugee from Staden-Dixmude (at the line where the flooded Yser slowed the German advance), as her instructor carefully noted on the drawing of "trois aéros boche-belge-français (*sic*)" in August 1914. Above the crossed flags on the tower of the single building that signal the allies' joint resistance, the aerial combat and antiaircraft fire create a crossfire that would inadvertently threaten civilians. Such contradictions tacitly imply the terror of living through a military advance (figure 8.5, p. 155).

One of the most poignant drawings of airplanes in the collection at Nantes springs from the memories of the refugee named Marcelle Goupilleau. Her school principal reported that the only child who failed to receive her "Certificat d'Etudes Primaires" had returned after two years in Paris, where she had been under bombardment by German airplanes called Gothas and the long-range cannon known as "Big Bertha," which could reach Paris from German lines. She had caught typhoid, and more interestingly, she had become a stammerer (*bègue*). Her picture of Paris under bombardment (1918) shows a line of five planes all carrying the curious label "Paris" on their tails. As seven or more bombs fall, buildings disintegrate, people scatter in the street, and a woman lies bleeding on the sidewalk in front of the hospital. The multiple burning bombs (where the cause and effect are fused) and the hurried dispersal in different directions of horrified adults and a running child speak to a terror that destroys community literally and emotionally. Echoing the disintegration of this world is the way Marcelle's colors underscore and shadow the points of impact in her image. The smudged red hatching suggests the figures' haste and leaking blood. It may also indicate the artist's impulse to wipe away what she has drawn (figure 8.6, p. 156).[12]

Given the importance of visual communication for young children, the picture book, with its emphasis on imagery alongside verbal narrative, even though it depicts imaginative scenarios, opens up a strangely efficacious field for the exploration of traumatic memory for children. If we turn to such picture books, we can see that the propagandistic repertoire of motifs is rather similar to the repertoire of themes that were assigned to children by the schools. War is depicted episodically, generally one theme per page or opening, with separate scenes of fathers departing to join the troops, letters home, soldier pen pals, and some hardships, represented in part by other children who are refugees. The obligatory scenes include loss and fear.

Modern graphics as in Schaller's *En guerre!* dramatically invoke the threat of the German boot, and the invasion force at Liège (figure 8.7, p. 156). The gigantic, shiny black boots of the aggressor are cropped by the edges of the book, suggesting their nightmarish power to stamp on the miniscule figures who represent the defenders of the Belgian city of Liège. Thus even simplified formal effects are suggestive of the apprehensions with which children were burdened.

In Lucie Paul-Margueritte's *Toinette et la guerre*, illustrator Henriette Damart invoked trauma through nightmare and hallucination—visual figures or tropes close to the "intrusive" flashbacks and nightmares symptomatic of trauma among soldiers. Thus she framed the motif of little Nanon who has been driven into exile from Belgium, leaving behind her ducks and home, in a double-page opening that shows not only her flight on a wagon piled high with household goods but also the enormous forces that threaten from behind, depicted as a gigantic soldier on the horizon, like the boot in Schaller's book (figure 8.8, p. 157). The breadth of the Italian folio reinforces the sense of distance that must be traveled in order to escape. At night Toinette wakes up from a dream that a huge slug has invaded the French "hexagon," in a schematic echo of a two-pronged invasion represented on military maps, but she is consoled when her dog Jim jumps on her bed and licks her face.

One of the most interesting features of wartime picture books as well as wartime drawings is that they seek analogies between the sufferings borne by soldiers and the difficulties and sorrows borne by children. Artists such as Damart use their visual medium to focus on experiences familiar to children. Their purpose is double. These scenes at once give realistic form to troubling new conditions of daily life on the home front in wartime at the same time that they subliminally narrate the conditions of life at the battlefront that are experienced by their brothers or fathers. The result is a narrative that functions both directly and by displacement. For example, in *Toinette et la guerre* the bombardment of Paris forces Toinette and her brother Riri to take refuge in the cellar—cold, dank, under threat from spiders, amid bottles. Tame as it is, Damart's stylized illustration of the arched ceiling of the cellar silently invokes the harsh experience of the children's father under bombardment in a trench, besieged by rats, amid the refuse and cadavers buried in the half-frozen mud. Such scenes shape a solidarity between the home front and the battlefront, the children and their father (figure 8.9, p. 157).

Again, when their father is wounded and their mother leaves to care for him, the children are sent to their grandmother's home in the countryside, where they soon become embroiled in a snowball fight. The narrator's voice floats above the page, above the melee, above the "disobedient" children who have slyly slipped outdoors. When both are wounded, their figures are literally split apart into two separate vignettes on the page. They must learn to play peacefully, in visual symmetry, just as the dog and cat eat side by side—a message for adults as well, undoubtedly.

Far more serious are the losses incurred in one of the most powerful children's books of the period, *Jean sans pain* (1921), by Paul Vaillant-Couturier, illustrated in a striking modern style by Picart Le Doux, whose flat planes are outlined in black. The impoverished orphan Jean has lost his father, dead at Verdun, and within the first pages also loses his mother, her health damaged by factory work. The first image of the child shows him floating in blank space, alone. Through his double loss, Vaillant-Couturier inscribes a critique both of militarism and of capitalism. Transported magically by animal helpers, a hare and partridges, "breadless" Jean travels to the battlefront, where he initially is horrified by the sight of death, as he faces a "grimacing" dead soldier with a ball through his temple sprawled in front of barbed wire, who does not respond to his call. Picart Le Doux's illustration shows a dead soldier with a blackened mouth, in front of broken barbed wire and the boots of another cadaver. The next illustration distances us from the shadow of death, showing the shells that light the night sky, as if they were fireworks. Jean then smiles, for the first time in his life, when he climbs up into No Man's Land, his partridges flying like an aureole of stars above his head: for silence has announced the legendary Christmas truce, and the soldiers celebrate the child they believe Jean to be. His message to the soldiers (who perceive him as a modern, secular Messiah) is one of brotherhood (figure 8.10, p. 158).

Although the tale closes with Jean's departure to an unnamable other world (like the "little Prince" of Saint-Exupéry), the soldiers, we are told, will all go "East, where men learn to be free and good" (Vaillant-Couturier 1921, 52). Despite its fairy-tale structure, this story drives home a darkly Marxist vision of the war, and the boldly delineated watercolor images point to the poverty and pain of an unjust world. The angles of vision from above and below stress the child's perspective, both physically helpless and morally superior. Individual suffering is programmatically linked to social suffering. Such a book could be published only after the war, in 1921.

What conclusions can be drawn from these examples? First, drawings by schoolchildren do record their daily life in wartime. For Victor Perrot, the historian who published drawings collected at Montmartre schools, those drawings by children provided exceptional testimony about conditions in Paris: "Since iconographic documents about Paris especially during the years 1914–1915, are exceedingly rare, to paint Paris in its successive and diverse manifestations, oddly enough we must consult the drawings by young students from the Montmartre school of rue Sainte-Isaure" (1915, 4–5). Certainly the details of everyday life captured in children's drawings such as the lines of women queuing for food or a legless soldier selling vegetables do testify to the visible costs of war. Even today, we make use of these drawings to document children's experience of war.

At the same time, we need to approach children's drawings with some awareness of their political functions, as the great majority of those that have survived were produced on assignment. The themes and contemporary events correspond in most instances to an official school program of instruction that aimed to convey factual knowledge, patriotic attitudes, and moral uplift.

Yet even assigned work can be appropriated for private purposes, as Yves Congar's journal so clearly demonstrates. The mother who set the Congar children to this task never censored, never corrected them. The personal drawings of Yves Congar and Olivier Pérès remind us that not all witnesses to traumatic events are individually traumatized; nonetheless these boys use drawing as an outlet for their pain and their outrage. Although much more clearly subject to direction and control, some of the school drawings, such as those by Célina Terrÿn and Marcelle Goupilleau, appear to work through a memory of suffering. The traces may be very spare. As René Dumesnil and Thomas Simon comment, the child "does not tell us, or rarely tells us, his private reception of this upheaval deep within . . . a little like the bird that continues to sing between the firing lines. He tries to go on with life" (1918, 77).

Second, just as schools mobilized children through their assignments, so too picture books such as Charlotte Schaller-Mouillot's *En guerre* strove to mobilize the child through vivid phantasms of the enemy threat and cheerful depictions of patriotic tasks such as the collection of funds to support the war effort. Even so, the visual depiction of a child's fears, nightmares, and losses in a book such as *Toinette et la guerre* can be subtle and effective. Moreover, the symbolically transposed representation of wounds and bombardment can give imaginative shape to the soldier's war experience within terms that a small child can grasp.

My last suggestion concerns the way that picture books may use children's sufferings and war trauma to perform almost antithetical cultural work—to mobilize the child, on the one hand, for military patriotism or, on the other, for pacifist universalism. In a sense, *Toinette* does both: the children rehearse war games, yet their grandmother makes them learn to play "pacific games." In Vaillant-Couturier's text, the focus on a socialist critique of capitalism and militarism likewise aims to mobilize the child for political ends: a social struggle for economic justice is to replace the military struggle. The oppressive steel frame of the factory will be replaced by harmonious symmetry under an archlike echo of the rainbow that symbolizes peace. In their strikingly different modes, then, each of these politically charged narratives makes the child into an actor and shapes a narrative structure of hope. It is that ambiguity, subtly traced in the dialogue between text and image, I would argue, that made these books such effective agents in wartime culture.

I would like to thank Stéphane Audoin-Rouzeau, Dominique Congar, Françoise Lévecque of the Bibliothèque de l'Heure Joyeuse, Andrea Immel of the Cotsen Library, and the University of Connecticut Interlibrary Loan librarians for their prompt and generous help at every stage of this project.

Notes

1. Cf. Audoin-Rouzeau (1993, 1996), Historial (2003), Pignot (2004), Guyvarc'h (1993), Faron (2001).
2. See Higonnet (1998).
3. The Brauners, who worked with children in refugee camps during the Spanish Civil War, were among the first to study this group of casualties and to do so by collecting their drawings. Olivier Faron's book on French orphans is devoted to issues of mourning and recovery from traumatic loss.
4. See Becker (2000).
5. Hollebecque (1916, 86–87). The girls rarely represented military action; only two

dealt with German atrocities, in spite of massive propaganda, and most children stuck to individualist scenes of aerial combat rather than trench warfare.

6. Many of the drawings preserved in Nantes archives are reproduced by Guyvarc'h(1993). Others were exhibited and published during the war. See "La vie à Montmartre pendant la guerre racontée par les écoliers montmartrois de la rue Sainte-Isaure" (1915). For another recent catalogue see *Des écoliers dans la Grande Guerre, enfance et adolescence à Sainte-Croix-du-Verdon* (1997).
7. Selections from the collection preserved in Montmartre also appear in the Historial catalogue, *Les enfants dans la Grande Guerre* (2003).
8. C. Kik, *Kriegszeichnungen der Knaben und Mädchen* Leipzig 1915. Two images are reprinted by Alfred Brauner and Françoise Brauner (1991). Kik is cited by the Brauners on pp. 17–18.
9. Stéphane Audoin-Rouzeau suggests that the "Bara" of 1914–18 was Émile Després, who became legendary as a martyr, first after he offered water to a condemned French soldier then turned the German officer's gun on him, killing him, before finally suffering his inevitable fate. Thus the child martyr becomes a soldier and actor in the Great War mythology (1993, 146–49).
10. Congar's French includes misspellings that I imitate in the translation: "je retourne au pommes de terre avec la brouettes j'étais déjà à l'arche, lorsque je vois un attroupement, je me demandais ce que c'était et je vois 300 femmes hommes enfants pris avec des brouettes ou des sacs, je met la mienne derrière le lavoir, je me mèle à l'attrouppement et je regarde passer les personnes, nous étions là une centaine l'orsque le hulan arrive donne des coups de pieds nous dit de ourt, tire son sabbre, et élance son cheval au galop dans la foule 2 personnes sont touchés" (1997, 124–25).
11. The instructor at the Nantes school on the Boulevard de la Colinière has captioned the drawing: "Vue par une jeune Belge de Staden Dixmude, . . . d'après les souvenirs d'une réfugiée de Staden Dixmude" (Guyvarc'h 1993,42).
12. I have made this argument in an essay in *PMLA* (October 2006).

9

The Shadow of War

Tolkien, Trauma, Childhood, Fantasy

MARK HEBERLE

The subtitle of this volume includes a phrase used by J. R. R. Tolkien in his foreword to the second edition of *The Lord of the Rings* (1973). After vigorously denying that his masterpiece is an allegorical representation of World War II and its nuclear age/Cold War aftermath (the period when it was written), Tolkien continues with a striking concession: "One has indeed personally to come under *the shadow of war* [my emphasis] to feel fully its oppression; but as the years go by it seems now often forgotten that to be caught in youth by 1914 was no less hideous an experience than to be involved in 1939 and the following years. By 1918 all but one of my close friends were dead" (1994a, xv). Rather than address issues of literary interpretation, Tolkien refers to the experience of war. Rather than simply deny the significance of the Second World War, Tolkien subordinates it to the First World War. Rather than refer directly to his own experiences on the Western Front in 1916, he uses indefinite pronouns and passive constructions to generalize rather than particularize what happened to him. Rather than directly describe those effects, Tolkien recalls the deaths of others in the startling final sentence.

Tolkien's comment exhibits several characteristics of post-traumatic writing, a subject I have treated extensively in a study of another combat veteran writer (Heberle 2001). While others may have forgotten what World War I was like, Tolkien has not nor ever will, as reflected by this passage, written more than half a century after he participated in the disastrous Somme offensive. His "close friends" include those who died (Rob Gilson and C. S. Smith) as well as the one survivor still alive in 1973 (Christopher Wiseman), but they go unnamed, and the reflection is marked by an emotional constriction that serves to both distance and contain, if not to cover up, whatever personal trauma he may have experienced. Several phrases in the passage significantly register the war's personal effects, however. To be "caught in youth by 1914" is to see the war as purposefully predatory and punitive and the writer and his young comrades as its victims and prisoners, but also as its subjects. The signifier "1914" would seem to be a synecdoche for the entire Great War but also suggests that "youth" came to an end in 1914 and a new life or at least a new phase of life began then. The "shadow of war" suggests the pervasiveness as well as the darkness of that experience, a ghostly presence that may be associated with the dead friends but also quite literally with the land of Shadow—Mordor—and its all-seeing Dark Lord of the Rings, who covers his strategic operations beneath the dense clouds of Mount Doom.

Recent books by John Garth on Tolkien's World War I experiences (2003) and by Janet Croft on representations of both world wars in Tolkien (2004) illustrate the growing consensus among recent critics that Tolkien is a post–Great War writer whose works are suffused with reflections and traces—"shadows," we might call them—of twentieth-century war. Both Garth and Croft also reflect Tom Shippey's claim, in *J. R. R. Tolkien: Author of the Century* (2000), that Tolkien is among those post–World War II writers whose writing either represents or is significantly affected by combat traumatization, an insight that was first seriously broached in 1989 by Hugh Brogan in commenting on the earliest form of *The Silmarillion,* Tolkien's mythology of what he came to call the First Age of Elves and Men: "It was therapy for a mind wounded in war, and before that by deep sorrow in childhood and early manhood" (358).

Drawing upon Brogan's double reference to war and childhood, I would claim that Tolkien's career as a imaginative writer, and its culmination in *The Lord of the Rings,* is profoundly influenced by both sources of trauma, that his greatest and most influential work successfully incorporates but does not fully resolve these earlier anxieties through the creation of a heroic fantasy and that the persistence of at least the conditions for trauma—both within *The Lord of the Rings* and within the world inhabited by his readers—helps account for the extraordinary vitality and continuing significance of Tolkien's trilogy. While the Second World War may or may not have been its figurative subject, the war was on Tolkien's mind throughout its composition, reawakening, yet also helping to revise, the trauma of the Great War imaginatively and, in turn, his earlier mythology.

As Brogan has also noted, the crucial text in Tolkien's evolution from personal mythology to "author of the century" is a children's story, *The Hobbit.* In creating this remarkable and unexpected masterpiece, Tolkien found not only a variety of audiences eager to read more of his writing but also "his own literary voice" (Brogan 1989, 358). Writing *The Hobbit* also enabled him to revisit and create anew the art of fantasy that had captivated him as a child. Any full account of Tolkien as a post-traumatic writer must begin, however, by considering the mythological stories that he began to devise in the wake of his own breakdown in the Great War. The following brief account of Tolkien's movement into and beyond trauma will therefore focus primarily on *The Lost Tales,* written between 1916 and 1920, and their later metamorphosis into *The Silmarillion,* with a glance at *The Hobbit* and *The Lord of the Rings,* which anticipates that larger project.

Tolkien's childhood was marked by crises of dislocation and the loss of both parents, which are reflected in his later work. As a child, Tolkien's character and imagination were directed from the beginning by language itself, which may have provided a symbolic authority and security that supplied the place of missing parents and the lack of a home to call his own. His evolution from orphan to Germanic philologist and Oxford don to world-famous author has been traced in Humphrey Carpenter's authorized biography and selection of letters, to which I am indebted for much of the factual information that follows. Born in Bloemfontein, Orange Free State, he was taken back to England by his mother, Mabel, at the age of three to recuperate temporarily from the African heat. At the age of four, he wrote his father a letter dated February 14, 1896, looking forward to an imminent return. The very next day Arthur Tolkien died five thousand miles away after a bout with rheumatic fever. The remainder of his family never returned to Africa.

After her husband's death, his mother moved the family to the midland hamlet of Sarehole outside Birmingham, where Tolkien reveled in countryside excursions with his younger brother Hilary that included climbing and talking to trees. Mabel Tolkien enthusiastically encouraged and directed her son's linguistic precocity, teaching him Latin and French and doing everything possible to have him enroll at King Edward's, the oldest and finest public school in Birmingham. When he was ten, the Tolkiens moved back into Birmingham so that Mabel would be closer to the Catholic Church she had just joined and her son could walk to King Edward's. For Tolkien, the childhood spent in the countryside would remain a lost Eden that could only be revisited imaginatively: "Four years," he wrote later in old age, "but the longest-seeming and most formative part of my life" (Carpenter 1987, 32). The loss of places that were once "home" for the child would later be reflected in both the *Silmarillion* (where the world created by Tolkien's creator god Iluvatar is ultimately lost for men and elves) and *The Lord of the Rings,* where the Shire represents the earlier preindustrial world of England that Tolkien had faintly but crucially encountered in childhood. Ultimately, Tolkien would create places where his imagination could be satisfied forever, the world of Middle Earth and the Three Ages, with their associated languages, histories, and distinctive peoples.

Tolkien wrote his first story at the age of seven, a dragon tale based on Andrew Lang's version of the slaying of Fafnir by Sigurd. Forty years later, he noted how his response to Lang's fairy story exemplifies the power of literary "sub-creation" to imaginatively override and improve upon the world we inhabit physically: "Fantasy, the making or glimpsing of Other-worlds, was the heart of the desire of Faërie. I desired dragons with a profound desire. Of course, I in my timid body did not wish to have them in the neighbourhood, intruding into my relatively safe world, in which it was, for instance, possible to read stories in peace of mind, free from fear. But the world that contained even the imagination of Fáfnir was richer and more beautiful, at whatever cost of peril" (Tolkien 1984b, 135). Tolkien later noted that he did not write a story again for many years after his dragon tale (Carpenter 1987, 30–31) because he had become absorbed with the sounds and forms of words, an obsession that began with the Welsh words on coal trucks that he would see in the railyards of Birmingham, where the family had moved from the midland countryside when the boy was eight years old. In some sense, perhaps, words came to be loved in the absence of trees and meadows.

Creation of his own languages seems to have begun in earnest about the time of his mother's death in 1904, when Tolkien was only twelve. Tolkien's subsequent life as a scholar and writer can be seen as the carrying out of a childhood addiction to words, given additional impetus by orphanhood and dislocation. Mabel Tolkien had been his most important tutor, his dearest friend, and his most encouraging admirer, and the goddesslike figures of Arwen, Galadriel, and Goldberry in *The Lord of the Rings* may owe something to her inspirational power, influence, and love. Her place was inadequately filled by Father Edward Morgan, her confessor and executor and another early mentor, but more fully by Tolkien's wife, Edith, another orphan, whom he fell in love with at the age of seventeen against Father Morgan's wishes.

An at least equally important intimacy began the year after his mother's death, when Tolkien began a close friendship with Christopher Wiseman, a schoolmate at King Edward's, and the two classmates became the nucleus of a small circle of friends who called themselves the Tea Club and Barrovian Society (TCBS). Tolkien's most important associates besides Wiseman were Rob Gilson (the son of King Edward's headmaster) and Geoffrey Bache Smith, three years younger than Tolkien. The four of them became the "best friends" that he recalled sixty-eight years later in the foreword to *The Lord of the Rings,* and they continued to encourage each other's work in literature, art, drawing, and music after they had gone off to Oxford (Smith, Tolkien) and Cambridge (Gilson, Wiseman) and, eventually, to the Great War. If loss of parents and loss of homes were traumatic childhood sources for Tolkien's later stories, his youth and young manhood were shattered by the experiences of the TCBS in the Great War. The importance of their association for all four of the young friends, from grammar school to university to the Western Front, has been demonstrated by John Garth's meticulous biographical and historical account, *Tolkien and the Great War,* which he dedicated to the TCBS. On "the threshold of middle-earth" (Garth's subtitle), Tolkien found an intimate, encouraging audience for his early writing and began to compose and publish poetry, much of which was to incorporate scenes and situations that derived from the fairy world he was beginning to imagine as the backdrop to the languages that he was inventing. Until *The Hobbit* appeared in 1937, in fact, all of Tolkien's *published* imaginative work was poetry.

All four young men left university for the Great War in their early twenties. Wiseman enlisted in the Royal Navy, but the three who went to France fought in the horrific battles of the Somme River offensive in the summer of 1916. Gilson was killed on the first day of the British operation, Smith was dead five months later, and Tolkien was disabled by trench fever later that year and was sent back to England to recover. By the spring of 1918, in fact, all the members of Tolkien's original battalion still serving in France had either been killed or captured. The fate of the four friends as well as the human catastrophe that Tolkien went through in 1916 began to haunt him while he was still under fire in France and, of course, far outlasted the war. Tolkien's youngest son, Christopher, born in 1924, would be named after Wiseman, who also survived the war. Reflecting on Rob Gilson's death in a letter to Geoffrey Smith on August 12, 1916, to be passed on to Wiseman, Tolkien confessed,

> So far my chief impression is that something has gone crack. I feel just the same to both of you—nearer if anything and very much in need of you—I am hungry and lonely of course—but I don't feel a member of a complete body now. I honestly feel that the TCBS has ended—but I am not at all sure that it is not an [*sic*] reliable feeling that will vanish—like magic perhaps when we come together again. Still I feel a mere individual at present—with intense feelings more than ideas but very powerless. (Carpenter 1981, 10)

The collective dismemberment that Tolkien expresses here could only have been intensified by his incapacitation and return to England in November and Smith's death in France of combat-related gangrene in December.

Tolkien had been evacuated so that he could be treated and then resume his role as a second lieutenant in the Lancashire Fusiliers. During the next two years, however, every time that he was returned to duty, the illness reappeared and required hospitalization and rest. As if he were engaging in post-traumatic recovery during these years with Edith, Tolkien began to write his way out of the war, employing, revising, and extending his previously invented elvish languages and some earlier poems into a personal mythology. This work was to be revised and rewritten during the rest of his life but was never given closure. Instead, it was to both fertilize and be transformed by *The Hobbit* and *The Lord of the Rings*, the completed masterpieces through which Tolkien's traumatic experiences were ultimately given literary resolution.

Just before the outbreak of the war, Tolkien had become fascinated by an obscure Anglo-Saxon word, *Earendel,* and explored its apparent etymological roots and affiliations. His work took creative form in a forty-eight-line quasi-mythological poem that illustrates Tolkien's 1955 self-characterization of his procedure as an imaginative writer: "I am a philologist, and all my work is philological. . . . The invention of languages is the foundation. The 'stories' were made rather to provide a world for the languages than the reverse. To me a name comes first and the story follows" (Shippey 2000, xiii). John Garth has suggested that even "The Voyage of Éarendel the Evening Star," whose obscure passage across and beneath the world is dissolved by the rising sun, is a war-haunted poem. Written just after war had begun, during a period when Tolkien had delayed his enlistment in order to complete his last year at Oxford, the poem presents a hero who embodies "the idea of escape from oppression that Tolkien later celebrated in [his essay] 'On Fairy Stories'" just at a time when "his creator was defying universal blandishments to join Lord Kitchener's volunteer army in September 1914" (Garth 2006, 236). Although its inspiration may have been philological, the poem seems to anticipate the horror to come when Tolkien was shipped east to France in 1916.

After his return from the war and during Tolkien's convalescence in England, the medically disabled veteran began to incorporate Éarendel's voyage into a much larger mythological framework that grew out of his creation of two languages, Qenya (later Quenya) and Goldogrin (later Sindarin),[1] based on Finnish and Welsh, respectively. Just as the word *Earendel* had become the inspiration for the poem, the languages led Tolkien to invent a fantasy world generated by a creator god (Quenya Iluvatar) and populated by quasi-godlike Valar, immortal elves (the "first-born" of Iluvatar), and mortal men (the "second-born"). Edith transcribed this "Book of Lost Tales" over the next several years. The first story to be composed, "The Fall of Gondolin," an elvish city assaulted by the armies of the Satanic valar Melko/Morgoth, can be seen as a displaced account of the horrors of war that Tolkien had barely survived. Another, the story of Beren and Luthien, was likely prompted by a period in Tolkien's recovery when he and Edith used to walk through the woods near Roos, Yorkshire, just after their first son, John, had been born in November 1917, and she would dance and sing for him. Indeed, following her death in 1971, Tolkien had the name "Luthien" inscribed on Edith's gravestone and wrote a letter to his son Christopher the following July, about a year before his own death (details in Carpenter 1987, 104–5).

Thus, whatever else they were intended to be, *The Book of Lost Tales* and its eventual successor, *The Silmarillion,* began as works of post-traumatic recovery prompted by the Great War. To paraphrase Tolkien, the trauma of World War I was the foundation. The "stories" were made to provide a world within which he could recover from that experience. Their account of a world both destroyed and partially saved is a mythological reflection of the experience that Tolkien had undergone in France. Among other things, the Beren-Luthien story is at some level an acknowledgment of Edith's role in helping her husband to become whole again, and the nightmarish Fall of Gondolin figuratively relives the endless combat and flight of refugees Tolkien had experienced on the Western Front. As both Garth (2003, 220–21) and Croft (2004, 18) point out in particular, Melko's besieging bronze dragons clearly recall battle tanks, which the English Army used for the first time during the Somme offensive.

According to Christopher Tolkien's edition of his father's proto-mythology, the first two of the "Lost Tales" to be written date from as early as winter 1916, when Tolkien began his convalescence in England, and included Gondolin (1984a, 148) and "The Cottage of Lost Play" (1983, 1), which creates a narrative framework for the whole series of stories. Many of the other tales were written and/or transcribed or retyped during Tolkien's two years of service and/or convalescence in England, and more tales were added when he was working on the Oxford English Dictionary between November 1918 and spring 1920. The whole series was left uncompleted when Tolkien assumed his chair at the University of Leeds in that year, but he continued to reshape the material between 1926 and 1930 into what became *The Silmarillion* and subsequently revised and expanded that work over the next half-century before his death in 1973. Tolkien's early and later mythologies exemplify many typical characteristics of post-traumatic literature as well as the rhetorical conditions that generate such writing as they are identified in Kalí Tal's seminal article "Speaking the Language of Pain" (1994): the urgent need to tell one's story, the impossibility or difficulty of telling it, and the crucial need to find an audience willing to accept or acknowledge it. These conditions also mirror the elements of trauma therapy defined by Judith Herman and other clinicians, in which being able to first recover and then tell one's story of self-shattering encounter with death to others is essential to resuming a normal life. Tal's task in her later book *Worlds of Hurt* (1996) is to encourage and formulate critical methods for reading the literature of trauma, but her emphasis on direct representations by combat soldiers of their experiences is not very helpful in the case of Tolkien. Even though traumatic experiences typically both enforce and yet repress the desire for their representation, trauma can inspire or make necessary a wide variety of post-traumatic literary tropes, including, for example, Tim O'Brien's refabrication of his own experiences through protagonists who illustrate post-traumatic stress disorder (PTSD) symptoms; surrealism, absurdity, and parody in the Vietnam plays of David Rabe; and obscure and private symbolism in the poetry of Bruce Weigl. Tolkien's generation of World War I soldier writers characteristically employ invective, disenchantment, and irony (e.g., "Red lips are not so red, / As the stained stones kissed by the English dead" in Wilfred Owen's "Greater Love") as well as a minutely circumstantial realism.

Tolkien, by contrast, transmuted his experiences into myths and heroic fantasy narratives that show little direct impact of the war. Moreover, his later revision and expansion of the *Lost Tales* into *The Silmarillion* removed traces of his wartime experiences (including much of the horrific action of "The Fall of Gondolin" and the mythological tanks) and replaced the elaborate narrative framework of "The Cottage of Lost Play" with a single omniscient narrative point of view, as in Genesis, which authoritatively and impersonally traces the creation, destruction, and eventual rescue of a diminished earlier world. Insofar as writing the *Lost Tales* was necessary for personal recovery and their content was meant to reprise, however indirectly, the violence of the Great War, perhaps neither purpose seemed as necessary in 1926, when Tolkien began to compose *The Silmarillion,* or in the forty years thereafter during which he continued to revise it. Moreover, the final *Silmarillion* story represents a post-1918 viewpoint that reflects both the horrifying violence of the Great War and its victorious closure: the 1914 poem is transformed into a concluding quest narrative ("Of the Voyage of Éarendil and the War of Wrath") by the hero to find the quasi-angelic Valar and have them save elves and men from Melko. Éarendil's action not only brings the First Age of elves and men to a positive conclusion but also gains him immortality.

Nonetheless, traumatic signifiers remain noteworthy in both earlier and later versions of the mythology, including Éarendil's voyage westward. Here, as in *The Lord of the Rings,* the West represents an unfallen realm of beauty and original splendor, Valinor, the realm of the godlike figures who have created and sustained the fallen world of elves and men and a place associated with the best that may be desired or imagined, just as the Shire was later located in the extreme west of Tolkien's Middle Earth as a more homely ideal. Tolkien's imaginative moral geography may have been initially prompted or reinforced by his own escape from the war, a life-saving evacuation from France to England in 1916 that brought him to recuperate with his wife in Great Haywood, Lancashire, where much of the early mythology was created. It may also embody a return to the midland countryside southwest of Birmingham where Tolkien's imagination had been so stimulated as a child. Of course, following the path of the setting sun also suggests a desire for final rest and ultimate release that can be associated with Thanatos, and the departure of the elves (and eventually Frodo at the end of *The Lord of the Rings*) back to the West is always marked with solemn melancholy in Tolkien. More generally, his narrative of the First Age began in 1917–18 as a dark myth of creation and fall that involved nearly continuous violence and conflict after the separation from the other Valar of Melko, the powerful but evil figure who wages furious warfare against the elves and the small minority of men whom he is unable to win to his side. This endless, multiple violence is more formally articulated in *The Silmarillion,* with its Five Great Battles, than in the original postwar mythology and suggests that the Great War—and doubtless its successor—had darkened Tolkien's view of human history and projected it into his mythology, an endless cycle of organized violence that does not seem to have evolved significantly beyond the world represented in *Beowulf.*

The Lost Tales initially began with another voyage westward that Tolkien eliminated when he removed the storytelling framework of the post-traumatic mythology. In the "Cottage of Lost Play" episode (written as early as winter 1916, and thus perhaps just after "The Battle of Gondolin") the wanderer Eriol comes to the Lonely Isle, Tol Eressëa, a refuge for elves who are now exiled from their original unspoiled realm of Eldamar, much farther to the west in Valinor. The creation, darkening, and eventual cataclysmic wars that have changed the world are presented to him by various elvish storytellers as previous narratives marked by nostalgia for what has been lost. Indeed, they may be seen as a collective post-traumatic narrative. Eriol has voyaged west seeking to satisfy his desires, like Éarendil, who searches for his father (Tuor) and mother (Edril), but will never find them because they sailed "into the sunset and the West" and were "sundered from the fate of Men" (Tolkien 1999, 294), an indirect reflection of Tolkien's situation as a child and young man. Eriol's mother and father, however, have been slain in defending their castle when "war fell suddenly on that town amid its slumbrous peace, nor were its crumbled walls able to withstand the onslaught of the wild men from the Mountains of the East"

(Tolkien 1984a, 4). Both figures thus reflect the trauma of losing one's parents, but Eriol's story curiously combines his orphanhood with the hell of war, as if Tolkien were reflecting all his losses in a single figure. Eriol's name is glossed as "One who dreams alone" in "The Cottage of Lost Play," which is where he hears the mythic fantasies Tolkien was "dreaming" and writing down as he recovered from the war in late 1916.

As Christopher Tolkien has noted, "The Cottage of Lost Play" first appeared in a sixty-five-line poem written in April 1915 *before* Tolkien entered the army (Tolkien, 1983, 19). John Garth interprets "You and Me and the Cottage of Lost Play" as a love lyric written to Edith (2003, 72). Like the first full version of the story of Beren and Luthien ("The Tale of Tinúiviel," Beren's own name for Luthien), a later narrative of the same title was written during Tolkien's recovery from trench fever in England and was transcribed by Edith Tolkien for her husband (Tolkien 1983, 1; 1984a, 148–49). As one of the first "Lost Tales" written by Tolkien just after his evacuation from the Western Front, however, "The Cottage of Lost Play" becomes a fairy story narrated to Eriol by the elf queen Vairë that explains the origin of the very room within which Eriol listens to it. Both the explanation and Eriol's circumstances constitute a myth of inspiration that brings together children and adult audiences and storytellers. Eriol is told that the cottage is a replacement for an original house of storytelling that now rests empty to the west in Tolkien's Eden-like Valinor, a place where men and elves can no longer travel after the terrible wars waged in the Great Lands (Tolkien's original term for Middle-Earth) to the east. Vairë explains that the now abandoned cottage "was the Cottage of the Children, or of the Play of Sleep, and not of Lost Play, as has wrongly been said in song among Men—for no play was lost then, and here alas only and now is the Cottage of Lost Play" (1983, 8). But both cottages are identified as places where human children travel through dreams to experience fantasies: "and so here we builded of good magic this Cottage of Lost Play," Vairë continues, "and here old tales, old songs, and elfin music are treasured and rehearsed" (9). The myth suggests that such stories are secondary substitutes for original experiences (a Hall of Play Regained is also associated with the second cottage), but because the children who once traveled to Valinor either could not bear to leave it or remained forever unsatisfied with longing once they had, secondary fantasies are perhaps the only way in which men and women (in contrast to the immortal elves) can realize their deepest desires. Besides mirroring Tolkien's actual creation of the "Lost Tales" in 1916–20, this explanation may reflect how language and literature provided compensation for Tolkien's loss of his parents and the Edenic landscape of Sarehole as well as for the loss of innocence and whatever it was that the TCSB might have accomplished if they had not been variously consumed by the Great War.

Tolkien's metafantasy is most remarkable in effacing the distinction between adult and child audiences and narrators. When Eriol wonders how the cottage can fit so many children, the doorkeeper responds, "Small is the dwelling, but smaller still are they that dwell here—for all who enter must be very small indeed, or of their own good wish become as very little folk even as they stand upon the threshold" (1983, 3). The explanation recalls some of Jesus's Gospel characterizations of the kingdom of heaven (Matthew 18:1–5, 19:13–15; Mark 10:13–16; Luke 18:15–17). When Eriol enters the cottage he finds a mixed audience: "the hall and all its benches and chairs were filled with children of every aspect, kind, and size, while sprinkled among them were all folk of all manners and ages. In one thing only were all alike, that a look of great happiness lit with a merry expectation of further mirth and joy lay on every face" (1983, 4). Indeed, children, adults, humans, and elves (associated in all of Tolkien's writings with what has become purely imaginary) are gathered together to share stories throughout the *Lost Tales*. For example, the twice-revised link that introduces Tolkien's earliest narrative of the Beren-Luthien story (1984a, 2–6) involves an exchange between Eriol and Vëanne, one of a number of children who are eager to hear his story. He obliges with the account of his parents' tragic death, his involvement in subsequent wars, and his eventual voyage to the west that has brought him to Tol Erëssea. In turn, he is eager to have the children tell him a tale, and Vëanne, assisted by her brother Ausir and another unnamed boy, obliges with "The Tale of Tinúviel," Tolkien's most direct tribute to Edith's role in his postwar recovery.

Not only the "Cottage of Lost Play" but the entire metanarrative framework of the *Lost Tales* was eliminated from Tolkien's later versions of them in *The Silmarillion*. Eriol, the orphaned, postwar figure who most clearly represents the traumatized author, is absent as well. The omniscient, impersonal, third-person viewpoint of the later mythology provides a more seamless narrative coherence, but it also effaces the traces of personal trauma and recovery that its creation incorporated. Indeed, the fictional narrators and audiences of the original stories reflect the rhetorical conditions of post-traumatic therapy, as Eriol tells the elves about warfare and the death of his parents while they recount the creation and fall of their earlier world into civil war among gods, elves, and men. One of the effects of that fall is the "loss" of "tales" that human children could once experience directly and must now recover through secondhand storytelling of the sort that the *Lost Tales* dramatizes. Despite their often violent and dark content, the stories are shared equally with eagerness and joy by immortal elves and mortals and by both adults and children. Thus, the *Lost Tales* not only provided personal mythology and fairy stories through which Tolkien recovered from the war but also represent the effective rhetorical and imaginative power of fantasy while mimicking countertraumatic narrative therapy for everyone involved, both storytellers and appreciative listeners.

Setting aside further ventures into its sometimes bewildering details, I claim that Tolkien's original mythology has many of the earmarks of post-traumatic narratives, including fragmentation, reversal of chronology, repetition, and lack of closure. For example, the first element written—the poem about the voyage of Éarendel—would have been the final narrative, but not even its outline was written until the "Sketch of the Mythology" for *The Silmarillion* sometime after 1926. The unfinished state of the *Lost Tales* and their successors, the endless rewriting of the original stories for the rest of Tolkien's life, and his failure to ever find a *readership* for them in his lifetime, exemplifies the difficulty for traumatized writers of meeting the rhetorical conditions outlined by Tal. It is important to emphasize that *The Silmarillion,* the "final" version of the mythology, not only was never published by Tolkien but also was never even *completed* by him for publication despite his wish in 1937 that Allen and Unwin handle it before the later *Lord of the Rings,* on the basis of an uncompleted manuscript (Carpenter 1987, 187–89). And despite Allen and Unwin's eagerness to follow up the success of *The Lord of the Rings* in the 1950s with a completed book (Carpenter 1987, 239), Tolkien was unable to oblige with a completed text after his retirement from Oxford in 1959. Although Christopher Tolkien finally published a coherent edition of the last version of the mythology in 1977, four years after Tolkien's death, it somewhat misrepresents what was "in truth a continuing and evolving creation extending over more than half a century" (Tolkien 1999, viii) that was continuously rewritten by Tolkien but never given closure.

Despite the fragmentary, elliptical, and ever-changing details of the mythology as it developed between 1917 and the 1970s, the proto-*Silmarillion* marked an important new stage in Tolkien's development as a writer, as it took the form of narrative rather than poetry. There are no poems at all within the *Lost Tales,* although some were later to be rewritten in verse, and the posthumous *Silmarillion* authorized by Tolkien has only two (1999, 201–2, 210), both related to the Beren-Luthien story. The experience of war may have helped determine this new phase of Tolkien's imaginative writing, because constructing a coherent narrative of events is essential to post-traumatic recovery, and the war itself provided a terrible but ultimately positive completed narrative that Tolkien's own life narrative may reflect. "The Fall of Gondolin," the first tale written, refigured Tolkien's experience of trench warfare, but both the story and the experience needed to be assimilated to a fuller narrative for which the eventual "Tale of Éarendel" provided closure: the defeat and banishment of the satanic Melko after nearly continuous warfare against his attempts to conquer the Great Lands of men and elves. That ending, published only after Tolkien's death in 1973, records a victory, like the armistice of 1918, that was undercut or at least darkened by the catastrophic violence that had preceded it but that was also justifiable and necessary.

Having moved into narrative during the war years, Tolkien began to practice it at home with perhaps his most important intimate audience, his children, who were eight-, five-, and one-year-old when Tolkien began to teach at Oxford in 1925. Annual Father Christmas letters and stories about a dog named Rover, Tom Bombadil, and Mr. Bliss would eventually be published after Tolkien had become a world-famous author, but began as children's tales composed and read within the household. So did *The Hobbit,* which was accepted for publication on the basis of a reading by Rayner Unwin, the ten-year-old son of the publisher. Tolkien's reading of the story to his three boys may have provided fuller personal and discursive recovery from the Great War than did the still uncompleted *Silmarillion,* which Tolkien appears to have abandoned for a time after 1930, even as he found elements of and references to the mythology entering the children's story as he composed it (1994a, xiii).

Tolkien's great triumph in *The Hobbit* derives from an imaginative recovery of childhood that realized the "Cottage of Lost Play" within the Tolkien household as he shared the story with John (now thirteen), Michael (ten), and Christopher (six) while equally enchanting C. S. Lewis, another Great War veteran, who was given the manuscript.[2] Lewis wrote to his friend Arthur Greeves that "reading [Tolkien's] fairy tale has been uncanny—it is so exactly what we would both have longed to write (or read) in 1916: so that one feels he is not making it up but merely describing the same world into which all three of us have the entry" (White 2001, 148). In the destruction of the dragon Smaug, Tolkien reprised and rewrote his first story as a child and the earliest source of his passion for fantasy, Sigurd's slaying of Fafnir. The numerous lyric poems scattered throughout *The Hobbit* represent a return to and recovery of his own first literary work as well, the genre that had been encouraged by and written for the TCBS, here happily integrated with a coherent and complete narrative, although he later regretted the way in which the narrative voice is almost overly familiar and intimate.[3]

Before publication, however, Tolkien extended and finalized the conclusion that he had first sketched, in a way that seems to recall and reflect personal closure of the First World War. Initially, *The Hobbit* would have ended with Bilbo's killing the dragon with his knife; in the end, the archer Bard kills Smaug as he flies to destroy Lake Town. But then Tolkien supplemented the dragon fantasy with the Battle of Five Armies, "a terrible battle. The most dreadful of all Bilbo's experiences, and the one which at the time he hated most—which is to say it was the one he was most proud of, and most fond of recalling long afterward, although he was quite unimportant in it." Instead of killing the dragon, Tolkien's hobbit hero becomes a quasi-pacifist bystander who attempts to prevent a battle between dwarves, elves, and men but is knocked unconscious when the three groups unite to face an army of savage goblins and wolves. Waking up after the terrible battle is over and finding that Thorin Oakenshield, the dwarf leader, is dying, the wounded Bilbo notes that "all was deadly still. There was no call and no echo of a song. Sorrow seemed to be in the air. 'Victory after all, I suppose!' he said, feeling his aching head. 'Well, it seems a very gloomy business'" (1997, 257). And once the casualty of war has returned to the Shire, "He took to writing poetry and visiting the elves; and though many shook their heads and touched their foreheads and said 'Poor old Baggins!' and though few believed any of his tales, he remained very happy to the end of his days, and those were extraordinarily long" (271). Tolkien was later to write "I am in fact a hobbit, . . . in all but size" (Carpenter 1987, 179), a claim that seems nearly literally true in this characterization of Bilbo as the survivor of the Battle of Five Armies and a fantasy writer. Adding this passage to *The Hobbit* more than twenty years after his participation in the Great War, Tolkien likely still hated it more than anything in his life but could also feel some pride in what he and his comrades had accomplished, small as his own role had been, and as a writer at least he had never been more happy or appreciated.

Besides other kudos, *The Hobbit* won the 1937 New York *Herald Tribune* prize for juvenile literature, and what eventually became *The Lord of the Rings* was initially anticipated by Tolkien's publisher and himself as a continuation of or a supplement to its unexpected success. As Shippey (2000, 52–54) and Carpenter (1987, 189–91) have noted, Tolkien didn't know where he was going with the story when he began it over Christmas in 1937, but even as Europe lurched toward a second world war the story began to draw in elements of the earlier dark mythology, and Tolkien found himself extending but also rewriting the earlier mythology, with Sauron replacing Melko/Morgoth and a fellowship of four hobbits heroically reconstituting the TCBS in his great fantasy. His turning from an extension of *The Hobbit*'s fantasy adventure to the darker great war of *The Lord of the Rings* is reflected in two readings by Rayner Unwin, who was asked again to judge a Tolkien manuscript. At the age of twelve he enjoyed the initial three chapters of Tolkien's first version of the work, but complained that there was "too much Hobbit talk" (Carpenter 1987, 190). Ten years later, in 1947, now an undergraduate at Oxford and a war veteran himself, he was entrusted once more with Tolkien's nearly completed manuscript and declared it a "weird" but "brilliant and gripping story" that ought to be published, but he was unsure about its readership, as children might be confused but adults might hesitate to read a one-thousand-page heroic fantasy. In the event, as with *The Hobbit,* Tolkien's work has captivated millions of readers at least as young as twelve and as old as the fifty-six-year-old C. S. Lewis, the first reviewer of the completed Ring trilogy in 1954. In "On Fairy-Stories," his 1939 Andrew Lang Lecture delivered just after *The Hobbit* had been published and just after beginning work on *The Lord of the Rings,* Tolkien had criticized writing childish stories for children and vindicated the value of fairy stories for adults, as if he were defending his own mastery of fantasy.

Tolkien was to claim that he finally had resolved his plot when Bilbo's ring of mere invisibility became Frodo's ring of power and its origin and significance were explained by Gandalf in chapter 2 of *The Fellowship of the Ring*. He added that "little or nothing in it was modified by the war that began in 1939 or its sequels" (1994a, xiv). But according to Christopher Tolkien's study of the composition of the first part of the trilogy, the writing and placement of that chapter underwent great modification as Tolkien finally arrived at his scheme for what he was to finally call "a history of the Great War of the Ring." The eventual title for that chapter, "The Shadow of the Past," resonantly links not only the past and coming war against Sauron but also the war that had summoned Tolkien and the war that was taking place as he wrote *The Lord of the Rings*. Several of the unmistakable World War II references in it are discussed by Janet Croft, including Frodo's echo of Neville Chamberlain's "peace in our time" speech (1994a, 50) and an analogue of the futile Maginot Line outside Minas Tirith (61), but perhaps even more important as an influence upon Tolkien's work was his personal interest in the outcome of the war and his own involvement with it as he wrote his masterpiece. Tolkien himself volunteered for work as a cryptographer in January 1939 and later served as an air raid warden (Croft 2004, 155–56). His oldest son, John (who had been born when his father was recuperating from trench fever in 1917), was studying for the priesthood in Rome when he and his fellow students were evacuated to Lancashire;

Michael withdrew from Trinity College, Oxford, in 1940 to became an antiaircraft gunner, was injured in a military accident, and later underwent cadet training; and his youngest son, Christopher, was sent to South Africa in 1945 to train as a fighter pilot for the Royal Air Force. In addition, future officers were processed through Oxford during the 1940s in short courses that allowed them to receive higher education certificates, and Tolkien devised a syllabus for naval cadets. Not only do Frodo, Sam, Merry, and Pippin more happily reprise the experiences of the TCBS in the first war, but also the fate of his own sons and the young Oxford graduates sent east to fight and die would have been on Tolkien's mind as he composed the work between 1937 and 1945. His correspondence with Christopher in South Africa included copies of *The Lord of the Rings* manuscript and mixes comments on the book with comments on the progress of the war.

A more detailed consideration of *The Lord of the Rings* as a post-traumatic narrative haunted by the Great War, imaginatively influenced by the second, and drawing upon the earlier mythology cannot be accommodated by this chapter. It is revealing that Tolkien's initial titles for *The Fellowship of the Ring* and *The Two Towers* were *The Return of the Shadow* and *The Shadow Lengthens,* however. Whether as public history or personal memory, psychic trauma, moral evil, or simply the endless cycle of war since 1914, Tolkien's works are haunted by such shadows, which he rewrote, revised, supplemented, and extended throughout his career as an imaginative writer. Whatever the darkness that lies behind it, however, the phenomenal success of *The Lord of Rings,* which continues to enthrall new generations of readers (and filmgoers), vindicates and validates Tolkien's choice of fantasy as a means of successfully assimilating and converting his own trauma into a "shadow of war" that is at least imaginatively redemptive.

Notes

1. Tolkien's creation of these languages derives from his interest in words for their own sake. Judging from their dates of origin, however, they may also be connected with the trauma of World War I. Christopher Tolkien believes that his father began the first "Qenya Lexicon" in 1915, the year before his service in France; the Goldogrin dictionary was compiled in 1917, during Tolkien's convalescence from trench fever. See Tolkien (1983, 280–81).
2. Tolkien seems to have begun reciting the tale about 1930 from a written text. The original typescript appears to have been completed before 1933, when C. S. Lewis read it. See Carpenter (1987, 181) and Bramlett (2003, 27).
3. For example, in a draft of a letter to Walter Allen of the *New Statesman* requesting a written contribution to a 1959 symposium on children's books, Tolkien claimed that *The Hobbit* was flawed by being self-consciously addressed to children, that it began in a whimsical register that became "more serious or significant, and more consistent and historical" and concluded with the comment: "But I regret much of it all the same" (Carpenter 1981, 298).

Figure 3.1. *The Young Soldier*. London? ca. 1815.
Reproduced by permission of the Cotsen Children's Library, Princeton University Library.

Figure 3.3. Frontispiece for William Francis Sullivan, *Pleasant Stories, or, The History of Ben the Sailor and Ned the Soldier.* London: Dean & Munday, 1818. Reproduced by permission of the Morgan Library & Museum.

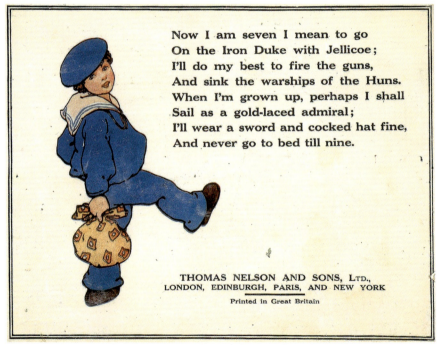

Figure 4.1. Rear wrapper of *The Royal Navy: An ABC for Little Britons.* London: Thomas Nelson and Sons, ca. 1915. Reproduced by permission of the Cotsen Children's Library, Princeton University Library.

INFANTRY WITH GARAND RIFLE, TOMMY GUN, AUTOMATIC RIFLE, MACHINE GUN AND CARBINE

INFANTRY Called "The Queen of Battles," Infantry makes up the bulk of our Army. It is used to attack the enemy and defeat him, or to defend the ground the enemy is trying to capture. Infantry fights by combining fire power, movement and shock attack. This means the Infantry first disrupts the enemy by rifle and machine gun fire. It then moves up to make its fire more effective, and last of all it attacks at close quarters and overwhelms the foe in hand-to-hand fighting.

Modern Infantry is distinguished from Infantry in the past by its armament and equipment. Besides the basic 30-caliber Garand rifles, the Infantry uses semi-automatic rifles, pistols, machine guns and sub-machine guns, trench mortars and anti-tank guns, 77mm and 105mm tank destroyer guns. It has motor trucks of every description from the Jeep to the 6-ton prime-mover. Infantry may use any means of transportation from skis to airplanes.

The Triangular Infantry division is the basic combat organization of the Army. The division is normally composed of Division Headquarters, Headquarters Military Police company, Division Signal company, three regiments of Infantry, Reconnaissance Troop, Engineer Battalion, Division Artillery, Quartermaster Battalion, Medical Battalion, Division Surgeon's Officer, attached medical personnel and Chaplain.

[32]

Figure 4.2. Edward Shenton, *An Alphabet of the Army.* Philadelphia: Macrae-Smith Company, 1943. Reproduced by permission of the Cotsen Children's Library, Princeton University Library.

Figure 4.3. Raul Verdini, illus. *Il caposquadra Balilla*. Rome: L'Opera Balilla, Anno XI [i.e., 1933]. Reproduced by permission of the Cotsen Children's Library, Princeton University Library.

Figure 4.4. *Sillabario e piccole letture*. Rome: La Libreria dello Stato, Anno XI [i.e., 1933]. Reproduced by permission of the Cotsen Children's Library, Princeton University Library.

Figure 4.5. *Sillabario e piccole letture.* Rome: La Libreria dello Stato, Anno XI [i.e., 1933]. Reproduced by permission of the Cotsen Children's Library, Princeton University Library.

Figure 4.6. *Cartilla escolar antifascista.* Valencia: Ministerio de Instrucción Pública y Bellas Artes, 1937. Reproduced by permission of the Cotsen Children's Library, Princeton University Library.

Figure 4.7. *Gloria, Viktoria: Ein Weltkriegs-Bilderbuch.* [Germany? 1915?] Reproduced by permission of the Cotsen Children's Library, Princeton University Library.

Figure 4.8. Hansi, *L'Alsace heureuse.* Paris: H. Floury, 1919. Reproduced by permission of the Cotsen Children's Library, Princeton University Library.

Figure 4.9. Elvira Bauer, *Ein Bilderbuch für Gross und Klein.* Nuremberg: Stürmer-Verlag, c. 1936. Reproduced by permission of the Cotsen Children's Library, Princeton University Library.

Figure 4.10. Wennerwald, illus. Hans Christian Andersen, *Den onde Fyrste.* Copenhagen: Alex. Vincents Kunst-Verlag, 1945. Reproduced by permission of the Cotsen Children's Library, Princeton University Library.

Figure 4.11. L'Oncle Sébastien. *Oui, monsieur le Maréchal.* Grenoble: B. Arthaud, ca. 1942. Reproduced by permission of the Cotsen Children's Library, Princeton University Library.

Figure 4.12. L'Oncle Sébastien. *Oui, monsieur le Maréchal.* Grenoble: B. Arthaud, ca. 1942. Reproduced by permission of the Cotsen Children's Library, Princeton University Library.

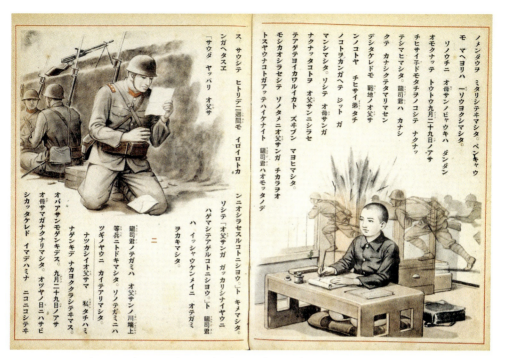

Figure 4.13. Yoshitara Takagi, ed. *Shina Jihen taishō kinengō*. Tokyo: Dai Nihon Yūbenkai Kōdansha, 1938. Reproduced by permission of the Cotsen Children's Library, Princeton University Library.

Figure 4.14. Yoshitara Takagi, ed. *Shina Jihen taishō kinengō*. Tokyo: Dai Nihon Yūbenkai Kōdansha, 1938. Reproduced by permission of the Cotsen Children's Library, Princeton University Library.

Figure 8.1. Raynolt, illus. "Injured soldiers." from Marcel Mültzer, *Avec les poilus: Maman, la soupe et son chat Ratu.* Paris: Roger and Chernovitz, 1916.

Figure 8.2. "Réfugiés couchés sur de la paille dans une classe. Exposition de may 1917." By permission of the Archives de Nantes.

Figure 8.3. "Execution of mother and son." Drawing by Choffget, 11 1/2 years old. (1915–16). By permission of the Archives de Nantes.

Figure 8.5. "Battle of three planes: Boche–Belgian–French, August 1914. Seen by a Belgian girl from Staden Dixmude." Drawing by Célina Terrÿn. By permission of the Archives de Nantes.

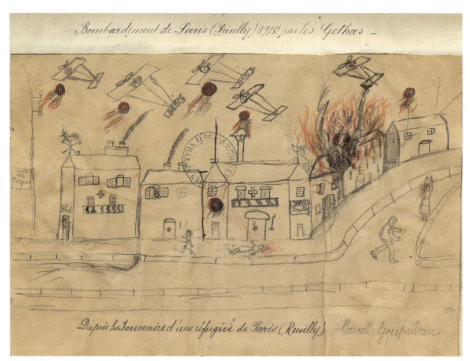

Figure 8.6. "Bombardment of Paris (Reuilly) 1918 by Gotha planes, drawn from memory by a refugee from Paris" (Reuilly). Drawing by Marcelle Goupilleau. By permission of the Archives de Nantes.

Figure 8.7. Charlotte Schaller-Mouillot. "Liège." *En guerre!* Paris: Berger-Levrault, ca. 1915.

Figure 8.8. Henriette Damart, illus. "When the Germans came people left." Lucie Paul-Margueritte *Toinette et la guerre.* Paris/Nancy: Berger-Levrault, 1917. Reproduced by permission of the Cotsen Children's Library, Princeton University Library.

Figure 8.9. Henriette Damart, illus. "A strange night (Une drôle de nuit)." Lucie Paul-Margueritte, *Toinette et la guerre.* Paris/Nancy: Berger-Levrault, 1917. Reproduced by permission of the Cotsen Children's Library, Princeton University Library.

remuait pas. Jean n'osait pas l'appeler. Une fusée monta. Jean ouvrit les yeux tant qu'il put. L'homme avait les lèvres qui grimaçaient, un petit trou noir au milieu du front et une grande figure toute verte.

— 39 —

Figure 8.10. Picart le Doux, illus. "The man had grimacing lips, a little black hole in the middle of his forehead, and a great face turned all green." Paul Vaillant-Couturier, *Jean sans pain*. Paris: Clarté, 1921. Reproduced by permission of the Cotsen Children's Library, Princeton University Library.

III

THE HOLOCAUST IN HINDSIGHT

10

A is for Auschwitz

Psychoanalysis, Trauma Theory, and the "Children's Literature of Atrocity"

Kenneth Kidd

Since the early 1990s, children's books about trauma, and especially the trauma(s) of the Holocaust, have proliferated, as well as scholarly treatments of those books. Despite the difficulties of representing the Holocaust, or perhaps because of them, there seems to be consensus now that children's literature is the *most* rather than the *least* appropriate literary forum for trauma work. Subjects previously thought too upsetting for children are now deemed appropriate and even necessary. Thus in "A New Algorithm of Evil: Children's Literature in a Post-Holocaust World," Elizabeth R. Baer emphasizes the urgency of "a children's literature of atrocity," recommending what she calls "confrontational" texts and proposing "a set of [four] criteria by which to measure the usefulness and effectiveness of children's texts in confronting the Holocaust sufficiently" (2000, 384).[1] *A* is now for Auschwitz, and *H* for Holocaust (and sometimes for Hiroshima). And *B* is still for book, though no longer necessarily the Bible.[2] Baer sees as exemplary texts such as Roberto Innocenti's picture book *Rose Blanche* (1985), Seymour Rossel's nonfiction history *The Holocaust* (1992), and Jane Yolen's novel *The Devil's Arithmetic* (1988). Such books emphasize their protagonists' direct experiences of the Holocaust, experiences that extend to and presumably interpellate the child reader outside the story.

How does one explain this shift away from the idea that young readers should be protected from evil and toward the conviction that they should be exposed to it, perhaps even endangered by it? It's almost as if we now expect reading about trauma to be traumatic itself—as if we think children can't otherwise comprehend atrocity. Just how new is this faith in exposure, experience, and confrontation, and what is the best way to assess its significance with respect to contemporary children's literature and trauma studies?

Many people believe that the Holocaust fundamentally changed the way we think about memory and narrative as well as human nature. Presumably the exposure model became necessary because we no longer have the luxury of denying evil or postponing the child's confrontation with such. Certainly the Holocaust helped make the often entangled projects of literature, and psychoanalysis especially, ever more anxious and serious. Adorno's infamous declaration that "[to] write poetry after Auschwitz is barbaric" was received more as a call to narrative arms than a moratorium; Holocaust scholars have long insisted that Adorno was speaking *poetically* and not literally, saying we *must* write poetry after Auschwitz, just as we must put psychoanalysis to good use.[3] Even so, the Holocaust has only recently become a coherent narrative project in literary, psychological, and theoretical discourse. Lawrence L. Langer's foundational study *The Holocaust and the Literary Imagination* was published in 1975 and is one of the earliest long critical treatments of the "literature of atrocity." If Western culture has only lately come to terms with the Holocaust, those terms are largely literary and psychological, beginning with Holocaust memoirs and diaries, then historical analyses, and finally fictionalized treatments alongside academic trauma theory.

Only now can Baer insist that there's such a thing as "sufficient" confrontation with the Holocaust. Not everyone would agree; one of the countertropes of Holocaust narrative is that confrontation is impossible or always insufficient, that such faith in literature is foolish, even unethical. In any case, the Holocaust has arrived as a legitimate subject and has ushered in the wider sense that trauma writing can be children's literature. It's not surprising that the Holocaust has functioned as a sort of primal scene of children's trauma literature, through which a children's literature of atrocity has been authorized within the last decade, asserted around both the power and limitations of narrative.

The psychoanalytic conceit is not accidental. The recent surge of Holocaust and trauma writing has many causes and vectors, among them the success of the progressive social movements of the 1960s and 1970s, and the residual faith in literature as a form of identity, empathy, and community in a pluralist society. Holocaust writing would be unthinkable without the therapeutic ethos that at once nurtured this progressive culture and formed its popular and institutional corrective (in the form of Cold War psychology, for instance). As social historians have shown, the helping professions have engendered a belief in the complexity of psychic life and interpersonal relations, a belief with both progressive and reactionary tendencies. Psychoanalysis has long been wildly popular in the United States and now has a diffuse cultural life. Thanks in part to the dissemination of psychoanalysis and the professionalization of mental health work, trauma is a key concept in our life and literature. Not surprisingly, recent academic theory privileges literature and psychoanalysis as interrelated forms of trauma "testimony."

For better and for worse, the Holocaust has become nearly coterminous with the idea of the unconscious. Like the unconscious as theorized by Freud, the Holocaust is at once history and the never-ending story, the primal scene forever relived and reconstructed. It is something that must be spoken about but that remains inaccessible. The Holocaust is simultaneously an event that we've moved beyond and one that we cannot and must not forget: this is the necessary paradox of Holocaust writing, akin to the idea of the unconscious, the central and necessary conceit of psychoanalysis. Baer points to the promotional buttons for the United States Holocaust Memorial Museum, which read "REMEMBER" and "NEVER AGAIN"; the museum is a walking and talking cure, one that asserts the preventative as well as recuperative power of memory.[4]

This chapter, however, does not argue for the supremacy of psychoanalysis as a tool for representing and understanding trauma in and around Holocaust literature. Instead, I show how, for better and for worse, psychoanalysis and children's literature have been mutually enabling, alongside and through academic trauma theory, which rewrites the "crisis" of representation in signal ways. Children's literature, of course, has been very usefully understood as therapeutic and testimonial. Certain genres seem to function much like the dreamwork as Freud described it, acknowledging but at the same time distorting or screening trauma. Drawing upon Freud, Bruno Bettelheim famously suggested that fairy tales help children work through both painful experiences and everyday psychic trouble. And fairy-tale motifs surface in other kinds of texts about war and especially the Holocaust. Thus Donald Haase, among others, examines "the fairy tale's potential as an emotional survival strategy" (2000, 361) in and around Holocaust narrative.[5]

But because psychoanalysis and literature are so enmeshed, this kind of treatment begs the analytical question in a sense, using one discourse to discover in the other analogous procedures and truths. To take the case of the fairy tale, we might also examine how fairy tales have helped articulate psychoanalytic discourse. And in the case of trauma writing more broadly, we might ask—as have Holocaust scholars Adrienne Kertzer and Hamida Bosmajian in recent studies—how our understanding of trauma is discursive as well as lived, shaped by cultural pressures alongside personal experiences. What if psychoanalysis *isn't*, in fact, the best treatment for trauma, but rather is one of its privileged modes of presentation? Do we usually now expect children's literature to testify to trauma in psychoanalytic fashion? Why not turn instead to alternative discourses of trauma work, among them "narrative medicine" and "narrative therapy"?[6] Or why not abandon psychological approaches altogether in favor of sociohistorical analysis? In *An Archive of Feelings: Trauma, Sexuality, and Lesbian Public Cultures,* Ann Cvetkovich advocates what she calls "critical American Studies," which would provide "a fuller examination of racialized histories of genocide, colonization, slavery, and migration that are part of the violences of modernity, and whose multigenerational legacies require new vocabularies of trauma" (2003, 37).[7] Is it time to leave psychoanalysis behind?

Cvetkovich's work demonstrates the value of an integrative approach to trauma, one in which psychoanalysis doesn't dominate the interpretive scene and is understood as one heuristic among many. As I've argued elsewhere, psychoanalysis and children's literature share many of the same central themes, conceits, and institutional practices, which means we can't treat one discourse as method and the other as material. Psychoanalysis is not just a method of interpretation but a foundational set of texts, ideas, rules, and habits; psychoanalysis is at once subject, method, and field. We can't either simply apply or renounce it; it's part of our heritage. We can, however, examine the interdependence of psychoanalysis and children's forms. And we can question their testimonial equivalence as asserted by contemporary trauma theory, as trauma theory has its own investments and adapts from literature and psychoanalysis certain conventions and tropes.[8]

While it looks as if we've fashioned a more serious and sophisticated children's literature, what we're seeing is not only a breakthrough in the field but also a particular moment in the ongoing collaborative project of psychoanalysis and literature—both of which take the Holocaust as, in the words of Shoshana Felman and Dori Laub in their book *Testimony* (1992), "the watershed of our times . . . whose traumatic consequences are still actively *evolving*" (xiv; italics in original). That project is articulated in theoretical texts such as *Testimony*, which, despite its sophistication, seems to celebrate testimony as a kind of antidote to the otherwise troubling uncertainties of memory, history, and representation, attributing to testimony the very agency at issue in psychoanalysis and much trauma literature. Such upbeat, personifying theory perhaps parallels the "Americanization" of Holocaust narrative.

Although children's books differ from psychoanalysis and trauma theory, all three projects now make trauma more personal than political. After examining at length trauma theory's complicity with an Americanized, fairy-tale inflected psychoanalysis, I consider first recent young adult novels about genocidal trauma and then picture books about September 11, 2001. Whereas trauma theory is unconsciously sentimental, the young adult novels and especially the September 11 books are openly so, appropriating the vulnerable/dead child as the representative American—as, in Lauren Berlant's formulation, "the infantile citizen." I conclude the chapter by turning to a trauma text that urges communal rather than infantile citizenship, Lois Lowry's *The Giver* (1993). Lowry affirms our faith in testimony but protests the privatization and infantilization of the public sphere.

Trauma/Testimony/Theory

A key lesson of recent trauma theory is that psychoanalysis offers the best clinical and theoretical treatment of trauma. In *Testimony*, Shoshana Felman and Dori Laub propose that psychoanalysis is a form of testimony to the unspeakable, one that recognizes the unconscious witnessing of the subject. In their view, psychoanalysis acknowledged "for the first time in the history of culture, that one does not have to *possess* or *own* the truth, in order to effectively *bear witness* to it; that speech as such is unwittingly testimonial; and that the speaking subject constantly bears witness to a truth that nonetheless continues to escape him, a truth that is, essentially, *not available* to its own speaker" (1992, 15; italics in original). Put another way, the speaker does not possess the truth; the truth possesses the speaker. The traumatized speak in spite of themselves, and psychoanalysis is there to witness that event. *Traum* (the base word for *trauma*) is German for *dream,* and dreams and nightmares help make possible psychoanalysis and much trauma theory after it. Felman and Laub also describe literature as testimony, remarking that "psychoanalysis and literature have both come to contaminate and to enrich each other"; both function "as a mode of *truth's realization* beyond what is available as statement, beyond what is available, that is, as a truth transparent to itself and entirely known" (15–16).

Felman and Laub are right to see psychoanalysis and literature as entangled forms of trauma testimony. High tragedy and other literary genres have long functioned as such, sometimes self-reflexively and sometimes not, and that's largely why Freud repeatedly drew from folklore and literature to dramatize his theories. But Freud's very invocation of folklore as evidence points to the limits of a standard psychoanalytic reading. Furthermore, even if psychoanalysis and literature testify to trauma, are we really reliable witnesses? And how much can we ever know about ourselves or about others?

Consider against Felman and Laub's optimism these characteristically apt words of Janet Malcolm in *Psychoanalysis: The Impossible Profession.* Her subject is transference, but her comment applies to psychoanalysis more broadly:

> The idea of infant sexuality and of the Oedipus complex can be accepted with a good deal more equanimity than the idea that the most precious and inviolate of entities—personal relations—is actually a messy jangle of misapprehensions, at best an uneasy truce between solitary fantasy systems. Even (or especially) romantic love is fundamentally solitary, and has its core a profound impersonality. The concept of transference at once destroys faith in personal relations and explains why they are tragic: we cannot know each other. We must grope around for each other through a dense thicket of absent others. We cannot see each other plain. A horrible kind of predestination hovers over each new attachment we form. "Only connect," E. M. Forster proposed. "Only we can't," the psychoanalyst knows. (1982, 6)

Malcolm takes her book title from Freud's description of psychoanalysis as one of three "impossible professions," after education and government (Freud 2002, 203). Drawing from Freud's work and other materials, she authenticates what many Americans would see as the pessimism of classical psychoanalysis, pointing to the consistency of Freud's sense of the psychotherapeutic project as announced in the early work *Studies on Hysteria* (1899), cowritten with Josef Breuer: "transforming your hysterical misery into common unhappiness" (Breuer and Freud n.d., 305). With the exception of Jacques Lacan and a few others, most post-Freudian psychoanalytic thinkers have embraced a more hopeful psychoanalysis. This is particularly true of Americans, who tend to confuse psychoanalysis with self-help. Most historians of psychoanalysis underscore the positive (perhaps wishful) thinking that marks American variants. At the least, then, the tribute of Felman and Laub needs to be tempered, as does much poststructuralist theory about trauma and disaster, which seems strangely detached from the gravity of its subject.

A return to the pessimistic Freud is not, however, a solution to the problem of voluntarist or utopian trauma theory. It might even be a distraction, as critical theory more broadly, not just trauma theory, is indebted to psychoanalytic and psychological narrative. Critical theory, of course, is a rich amalgam of philosophical and disciplinary projects, but chief among them is psychoanalysis, especially the work of Freud and Lacan, whose writings on subjectivity, desire, and language have been enormously generative. The influence of psychoanalysis on critical theory is both direct and indirect, acknowledged and unremarked.

For example, as Jane F. Thrailkill has very persuasively shown, a particular psychoanalytic trope runs from Freud to Lacan to the work of contemporary trauma theorists: the figure of the dead/wounded child. Long a literary staple—think Stowe's little Eva, for instance, or any of Dickens's angelic and doomed children—the trope of the dead/wounded child entered the psychoanalytic domain in Freud's dream of the burning child in *The Interpretation of Dreams* (1900). As Freud reports, a sleeping father is mourning his dead child, whose body lies in state in the next room. The father wakes up when he dreams this anguished plea: "Father, can't you see I'm burning?" But he cannot save his son, who is already dead, or even his corpse, now being accidentally burned by sacramental candles. "What is [the child] burning with," writes Lacan after Freud, "if not that which we see emerging at other points designated by the Freudian topology, namely, the weight of the sins of the father, borne by the ghost in the myth of Hamlet, which Freud couples with the myth of Oedipus?" (Lacan 1998, 34). For Lacan, the dream illustrates the ethical nature of the unconscious and the existential state of humanity. In her influential study *Unclaimed Experience* (1996), trauma theorist Cathy Caruth in turn interprets and appropriates the dream, remarking, "If Freud asks, *What does it mean to sleep?* Lacan discovers at the heart of this question another one, perhaps even more urgent: *What does it mean to awaken?*" (99; italics in original).

They mean about the same thing for Caruth, who adopts the wounded child as a metaphor for the impossibility of trauma's conscious and localized apperception.[9] Rather than coming to terms with trauma, she says, we pass trauma along to the next person (here, the next theorist), keeping trauma unconscious and always moving. Caruth sees such transmission as an enabling sort of anxiety of influence (and in fact she thanks Harold Bloom in her book's acknowledgments). Such transmission is not just productive but also ethical, in her view. "In thus relating trauma to the very identity of the self and to one's relation to another," she writes, "Lacan's reading shows us, I will suggest, that the shock of traumatic sight reveals at the heart of human subjectivity not so much an epistemological, but rather what can be defined as an *ethical* relation to the real" (1996, 92; italics in original). For

Caruth, the impossibility of sufficient response to and representation of trauma is itself traumatic and inaugurates an ethics of collective memory and cultural work. In her analysis of what we might call the sentimental unconscious of trauma theory, Thrailkill shows how Caruth's reading privileges psychoanalysis:

> Caruth suggests that contemporary theory-reading "trauma experts" have the following role: to take the traumatic death of the child and see that it is "transformed into the imperative of a speaking that awakens others" (1996, 108). This speaking is, as Caruth explains, "the passing on of psychoanalytic writing," which is intriguingly cast as something more akin to inspiration than interpretation. . . . Theory in this account becomes a means of transcendence, and would appear to fulfill a psychoanalytic critic's dream: direct correspondence with Freud. . . . Writers of trauma theory, and by extension, their audience of committed readers, are clearly designated as the keepers of the flame, the memorializers of not just this particular dead child, but of what that figure embodies and indeed etches on the body of the receptive reader. (Thrailkill 2003, 138–39)

Whereas for Malcolm transference is the ultimate downer, for Caruth it is what makes intellectual life worthwhile. We might add that Lacan's discussion of the ethical nature of the unconscious is much more detached than Caruth implies; Lacan even suggests that to understand that ethical dimension, we must break with the understanding of Freud as intrepid explorer. "When I say that Freud's approach here is ethical," writes Lacan, "I am not thinking of the legendary courage of the scientist who recoils before nothing" (1998, 34).

The sentimental invocation of the dead/wounded child is characteristic not just of trauma theory, as Thrailkill shows, but of a certain strain of poststructuralist critical theory. Consider, for instance, Maurice Blanchot's *The Writing of the Disaster* (1980), a poststructuralist theoretical meditation in the form of fragments. Blanchot's mode of critical theory likewise depends on psychoanalysis, and particularly on the writing of Serge Leclaire and D. W. Winnicott. About midway through his text, Blanchot takes up the subject of "impossible necessary death" and turns to Serge Leclair for wisdom: "According to him, one lives and speaks only by killing the *infans* in oneself (in others also): but what is the infans? Obviously," Blanchot continues, "that in us which has not yet begun to speak and never will speak; but, more importantly, the marvelous (terrifying) child which we have been in the dreams and desires of those who were present at our birth (parents, society in general)" (1995, 67). The child as theorized by Blanchot is linked with "primary narcissistic representation" but is neither a child nor a childlike state; rather, it is a metaphor for "impossible necessary death," one with "the status of an ever-unconscious, and consequently, forever indelible, representation" (67)—and one presumably transmitted through experimental forms of theory writing, despite Blanchot's declared resistance to "therapeutic" appropriation.[10] Blanchot even furnishes his own recollection of childhood, introduced parenthetically as "A primal scene?" (see 72).

Lacan and Blanchot costar in Christopher Fynsk's *Infant Figures* (2000), a fascinating if also exasperating exploration of language and its discontents. Pairing up Blanchot's primal scene and the dream of the wounded child as reclaimed by Lacan, Fynsk claims that "all human speech and psychic life are haunted by the death of a child, a being whose passing is the condition of speech, and who is therefore, of necessity, without speech: *infans*" (2000, 3; italics in original). Fynsk extrapolates this idea from Lacan and Blanchot, as well as from literary and artistic treatments of dead children. He insists upon its universal truth against a more historicized analysis of the trope's intellectual and imaginative career. "A theoretical presentation that would attempt to read Blanchot from Lacan or Lacan from Blanchot," he writes, "would lose precisely what is at stake, whatever it is that lies in the resonance of those two phrases ('a child is being killed,' and 'Father, don't you see I'm burning?') as they are brought to sound in the respective texts" (91). Fynsk holds that the death of the *infans* haunts psychoanalysis precisely to the degree that psychoanalysis is concerned with language as the marker of the human.

His formulations are quite engaging, perhaps when most diffuse ("whatever it is"), but like Caruth before him, Fynsk appropriates the trope of the wounded/dead child as a sentimental figure, as a pure or transcendent site of narrative engagement. "No one can say fully, intelligibly, what the death of a child is, for all saying proceeds from such a death. But all saying is haunted by it" (2000, 50). While he acknowledges that Freud's burning child might be voicing abandonment ("Father, don't you see I'm burning?"), Fynsk holds that there "is also a kind of 'pure desire'" for death voiced in the dream (118). What Thrailkill says apropos of Caruth applies here: trauma promises a "point of contact or 'transmission' between the dead and the living; the theorist of trauma, then, might be said to act as Virgilian guide to his realm" (2003, 134–35).[11] *Infant Figures,* in fact, is dedicated to the memory of Fynsk's friend Jean-François Lyotard. "The words in this volume that were written for him are now left like orphans," writes Fynsk. "But I take solace in the thought that some of those who knew him (and perhaps even some who know only his writings) will recognize a trace of his gift in the many pages he rendered possible here, and I will listen for the sound of his humor in their reactions."

The trope of the wounded/dead child is but one index of the mutuality of psychoanalysis and critical theory. As Peter Ramandanovic underscores in his introduction to a special issue of *Postmodern Culture,* the term *trauma* first became an important keyword of critical theory with Shoshana Felman's essay "Education and Crisis, or the Vicissitudes of Teaching," first published in 1991, just as the new "children's literature of atrocity" was appearing on the scene. Felman's essay, which presented psychoanalysis as a form of unconscious testimony, was reprinted in *Testimony,* cowritten by Felman and clinician Dori Laub. In the essay, Felman returns to Mallarmé's lecture "La Musique et les lettres" and a later text, both of which had already loomed large in Paul de Man's essay "The Crisis of Contemporary Criticism" (1967). In his many writings, de Man insisted that the role of theory and criticism is to "trouble and reinvent writing" (Ramadanovic 2001, 2), and Felman, in turn, troubles and reinvents "crisis," turning it into trauma/theory.

"If de Man establishes criticism as the 'rhetoric of crisis,'" writes Ramadanovic, "Felman proceeds to relate the crisis—that is, theory—to education, and, more importantly, she takes the term crisis in a new direction as she focuses on the presence of history in writing" (3). Crisis thus yields to trauma. If we believe Felman, theory more broadly is trauma theory, at least to some degree. Theory is also framed as traumatic: it ostensibly traumatizes literature and those who love it (do we not all know academics who lament the profession's tragic fall into theory?).

Like de Man, notes Ramadanovic, Felman turns theory back upon itself, raising necessary questions about the limits as well as the possibilities of analysis.[12] Ramadanovic seems optimistic about the prospects of trauma theory that foregrounds its own "constitutive limitations" (2001, 9). That optimism, and that formulation of theory's "self-consciousness," ratify intellectual work as a form of academic testimony, even for those outside the clinical fold. Critical theory demands transference and ensures its own transmission, especially when concerned with trauma or psychoanalysis. It is simultaneously a form of cultural capital and a mode of transmission/acculturation.[13] Trauma theory appropriates the ethical discourse of testimony that is largely the legacy of the Holocaust and an international commitment to human rights. If *A is for Auschwitz*, *T* stands not only for trauma, testimony, and theory but also for transference and transmission.

The Uses (and Abuses) of Enchantment

The sentimentality of the wounded child trope, the ease with which some theory sees the dead child as necessary to language, the rewriting of crisis as trauma, and the incestuous kinship of psychoanalysis and theory all helped inspire as much as they explain the contemporary "children's literature of atrocity." To give a proper account of that literature's emergence, of course, we'd also need a thorough psychosocial history of childhood in the United States, dating at least from the end of the nineteenth century. Thrailkill gestures toward such a history, locating her critique of recent trauma theory in the larger context of American literary sentimentalism, showing how the realist tradition that Mark Twain introduced against the excesses of "feminine" sentimentality has nonetheless made way for the reincarnation of the wounded/dead child in that most unlikely of places, critical theory. As Thrailkill has it, the suffering literary child made thinkable the wounded child of social reform around the turn of the century and now survives as the traumatized child of theory. Writing about the sudden popularity in the 1990s of adult trauma stories in which childhood looms large, Patricia Pace similarly points to the historical transformation of the American child from "economically useful" to "emotionally priceless" (1998, 238), drawing from Viviana Zelizer's work on the subject. Clearly, the emergence of a trauma literature for children is part of this complex history of childhood's revaluation, of its merger with the idea of interiority. As Thrailkill, Pace, and other scholars working in the 1990s point out from various angles, childhood is now imagined as a psychic-developmental space at once sacrosanct and violated.

If that larger sociohistorical picture is beyond the scope of this essay, I can at least outline some of the more recent factors in the rise of a children's literature of atrocity. As I've shown, trauma has been authorized by psychoanalysis and as critical theory, as well as by adult literature. Published one year after Langer's *The Holocaust and the Literary Imagination* was Bruno Bettelheim's even more influential study *The Uses of Enchantment* (1976), which codified but also revised the trope of the wounded child. *The Uses of Enchantment* was published to wide acclaim and has had significant influence on how fairy tales signify. Even if Bettelheim knew nothing about children's literature—and in fact posed fairy tales against it—*The Uses of Enchantment* attests to the growing force of that expectation in the 1970s and continues to shore it up.

Bettelheim had no interest in fairy tales originally, but he had long been preoccupied with what I've elsewhere called the "feral tale." Bettelheim was fascinated by accounts of wolf children and argued as early as 1959 that such accounts were really stories of autistic children. He was also preoccupied with the experiences of Holocaust survivors and the ways in which their behavior resembled that of emotionally disturbed children. The feral tale provides a useful bridge from his studies of particular experiences of trauma, especially in concentration camps, to his more professional focus on everyday trauma and how to manage it. A particular "wolf girl" case, about a girl who lived in a bunker in Poland during the war, allowed Bettelheim to move from Holocaust trauma to autism to a more generic sense of trauma and dysfunction—at which point developed his interest in the fairy tale. Put another way, the dead/wounded child of Holocaust experience and of residential clinical work merges in *The Uses of Enchantment* with the traumatized but resilient child of psychoanalysis as theorized by Freud. Freud's detractors have long argued that, by emphasizing the power of oedipal fantasy, Freud denied or downplayed child abuse. Rather than take up that issue, Bettelheim blurs the distinction between fantasy and reality, abuse and everyday angst, by turning to the fairy tale.

The Uses of Enchantment thus evades as much as registers the overdetermined, incestuous history of psychoanalysis and children's literature and represents the kind of personalized theorizing that risks trivializing individual as well as social history. *The Uses of Enchantment* gave pop-intellectual affirmation to the now commonplace idea that fairy-tale reading amounts to self-help or bibliotherapy. Recent revelations that Bettelheim plagiarized and was an often nasty character have not tempered the public's enthusiasm for the uses of enchantment; rather, Bettelheim has become the Big Bad Wolf.

This contemporary tradition of child figuration, of course, differs from the trope of the dead child that drives the poststructuralist theoretics of Blanchot and Fynsk. But just as the dead child trope enables a theoretics of academic transmission and transference, so too does the wounded-but-resilient (inner) child of pop psychoanalysis enable a poetics of popular transmission and transference, whose major genre is the fairy tale. Through the fairy tale, people tell stories about challenge and survival, hardship and hope. By the 1990s, the fairy tale was ever more entrenched in U.S. pop-literary culture, in the form of novelizations, films, "politically correct" satires, and so on. Most of these new fairy tale forms claim psychological and historical relevance both, and usually vis-à-vis each other. Thus in her afterword to *Briar Rose* (first published in 1992), Yolen can write, "This is a book of fiction. All the characters are made up. Happy-ever-after is a fairy tale notion, not history. I know of no woman who escaped from Chelmno alive" (2002, 241). Yolen can repudiate the happy-ever-after scenario precisely because we now expect fairy tales to be both *not happy*—that is, therapeutic rather than conventionally satisfying—and *history*. It's as if Yolen is suggesting that while this particular plot element isn't accurate, the novel is still true to history, that is, to deeper psychological truths.

In this novel, ostensibly a variant of "Sleeping Beauty," a young woman does escape from Chelmno alive—an unthinkable and perhaps irresponsible plot, as Adrienne Kertzer argues in *My Mother's Voice: Children, Literature, and the Holocaust*. Kertzer chastises Yolen for pandering to the naïve American desire for a happy ending in Holocaust narrative. And yet Yolen clearly sees her work as legitimately historical as well as imaginative. So does her editor Terri Windling, in her introduction to the 2002 edition of *Briar Rose*. "Way back in the 1980s," writes Windling, "I was a young book editor in New York City, and Jane Yolen was one of my heroes. Not only was she, quite simply, one of the finest writers I'd ever read, but her knowledge of the world's great wealth of fairy tales was second to none. Like Jane, I was crazy about fairy tales, and so I had the notion of publishing a series of novels based on these classic stories. Thus the Fairy Tale series was born" (Yolen 2002, xiii–xiv). Windling furnishes a nutshell history of the fairy tale, pointing to its juvenilization by Disney and hinting that its legitimacy is now being restored through her series. She implies that Yolen's novel will return to the fairy tale its rightful European seriousness, against Americanizations "stripped of moral ambiguities" and narrative complexities" (xiii). There's even an epigraph from Jack Zipes's *Spells of Enchantment*, which suggests how closely our faith in the sociological and historical significance of the fairy tale is entangled with our faith in its psychological import.[14] Whereas Kertzer sees the novel as a typically American exercise in imaginative denial, Yolen and Windling position *Briar Rose* as a higher truth. Kertzer and Bosmajian are right to point out that such texts are problematic, even if our disappointments with, as much as our praise of, children's literature confirm our faith in its testimonial power.

Among the confrontational texts recommended by Baer are a group of time travel and/or "trading places" novels that operate in a magical realist register and emphasize an experiential, healing relation to Holocaust-related trauma. I don't mean the Time Warp trio books of John Sczieska, but rather Yolen's *The Devil's Arithmetic* (1988) and Han Nolan's *If I Should Die before I Wake* (1994). These titles represent not a simple banalization of the personal, as with the September 11 titles I discuss next, but rather the expectation that young readers must find history personally traumatic in order to know it. It's as if Santayana's famous remark has been amended to "Those who *want* to remember the past are condemned to repeat it."[15]

I should first note that, as Kate Capshaw Smith pointed out in response to an earlier version of this chapter, faith in the power of travel/trading narratives stems in part from the success of similar texts about African American historical trauma published decades ago, such as Virginia Hamilton's *House of Dies Drear* (1968) and especially Octavia Butler's *Kindred* (1979), arguably a text cross-written for (or at least cross-read by) adolescents. In the latter, the protagonist Dana is transported to and from 1976 California to 1815 Maryland so that she—and by extension, the reader—can experience firsthand the terrors of slavery. Another example is Hamilton's *Sweet Whispers, Brother Rush* (1982), in which the female protagonist Teresa (Tree) learns through a sort of psychological time travel of her family's traumatic history of porphyria as well as abuse. Even when time travel or place exchange is not a central element, many if not most contemporary children's books about African American life are historical and often traumatic in emphasis, so pervasive is the legacy of slavery, Reconstruction, and the fight for civil rights. Tellingly, these books have yet to be reclaimed by the emergent field of trauma studies, suggesting again the dominance of Holocaust narrative. Though familiar with all three of these novels, I too failed to see them as trauma texts.[16]

The more contemporary protagonists of Yolen and Nolan are subjected through their Holocaust exposure to a splitting, even shattering of their subjectivity, from which they must assemble a more adult self. Here, as in the texts of Hamilton and Butler mentioned earlier, the psychoanalytic-literary collaboration is productive and admirable. In Yolen's novel, a bored Jewish girl named Hannah opens the door for Elijah during her family's Passover seder and finds herself in Nazi-occupied Poland in 1942. With another Polish villager, Hannah—now Chaya—is rounded up and taken to a concentration camp. Eventually, she sacrifices herself to save her friend Rivka. When she walks into the door leading to the gas chambers, she suddenly returns to her real life in the Bronx, with a new appreciation for history and modern rituals. Nolan's novel likewise whisks a contemporary teen girl back to wartime Poland, but this time that girl, named Hilary, belongs to a white supremacist group. She becomes Chana, a young Jewish girl, and learns some valuable lessons about racism and genocide. Unlike Hannah, Hilary trades ethnicity as well as place, in keeping with other trading places texts. I found this aspect of the transformation unbelievable and wonder if ethnicity should be so easily transferable.

These stories are effective precisely to the degree that they capitalize on our conviction that historical trauma should be personal, in ways that are often surprising or unpredictable. Although I don't know enough about the genre, my sense is that historical fiction for children has become more than ever a metadiscourse of personal suffering that in turn demands pain from readers as proof of their engagement. Whether about the impact of slavery, the Holocaust, or other horrific world events (as in the recent spate of Great Depression stories), the genre seems now to thematize the reader's own exchange with the child protagonist. And such personalization, which seems consonant with post-1960s identity politics and the faith in empathy, can sometimes lead to a denial of history's complexities, which aren't always so easily plotted.

Much as I admire the work of Yolen and Nolan, I find the same conceit of split subjectivity disturbing in another young adult text, Marsha Forchuk Skrypuch's *The Hunger* (1999), in which a fifteen-year-old Canadian girl named Paula simultaneously becomes anorexic and learns about the Turkish massacre of Armenians during the years 1915–23. Half realistic, "problem teen" fiction and half historical fiction, the novel opens as the standard story of a perfectionist girl increasingly preoccupied with her body image but soon takes on another dimension. As she gets sicker, Paula learns more about the massacres online. After a dangerous run, Paula has a heart attack, passes out, and travels through a time tunnel. She finds herself face to face with "a mirror image of herself" (98), named Marta. "Paula stepped into the mirror image of herself and felt a loving warmth envelop her," writes Skrypuch. "'Paula' no longer existed. She had just stepped inside of Marta" (99). Paula-Marta then wakes up in a Turkish orphanage in 1915, where her hellish history lesson begins. The brutalities she experiences link her specifically to her grandmother Pauline, who emigrated from Armenia in 1923 with her adoptive parents at the age of seven (meaning that she was born the same or subsequent year in which the novel is set). Paula's grandmother Pauline is the daughter of Mariam, Marta's older biological sister, which makes her grandmother Paula's niece in the temporal logic of the story. (To make matters more complicated, Marta was not merely Pauline's aunt but also her adoptive mother.)

The Hunger is commendable for raising consciousness about the massacres, which have long been a taboo subject, especially in Turkey. Even so, I doubt that "real hunger" can or should serve as a wake-up call for teen girls with eating disorders in contemporary North America. When offered food, Marta seizes it eagerly, thinking, "The Turks may wish us to die . . . but I'm not about to cooperate" (115). Her brutal experiences with the Turks inspire in her a new will to live and therefore to eat. She learns how to keep food down: "This is medicine, medicine, medicine, she chanted" (160–61). Eventually she's returned to the present and to Paula, her struggle not over but her fatal aversion to food overcome. The novel enacts a split subjectivity only to portray eating as a matter of willpower and personal/familial experience of history. Clearly eating disorders are cultural in part, but the will to live and the will to eat are not so transcendent of historical context. Yet Amazon.com reviewers call the book a "skillful blend of the contemporary and the historical" and "an especially suitable gift for a young person struggling to overcome an eating disorder or to deal with personal or family trauma." *Any* personal or family trauma? Skrypuch herself weighs in as a reviewer, describing her research and naturalizing the link between Paula's story and the historical trauma that Paula (re)lives. Asserting that Hitler modeled the Holocaust on the Armenian massacre, Skrypuch claims an even earlier primal scene of genocide, then uses it to authorize an object lesson for contemporary teens. The personal, it seems, is the historical, and both are billed as traumatic.

Why are Yolen and Nolan successful where Skrypuch is less so? Skrypuch isn't as masterful a writer as Yolen, to begin with, and *The Hunger* is her first novel. But it's also possible that Skrypuch can take greater license with her story because the

Turkish massacre of the Armenians is only now being acknowledged publicly. Even now, perspectives are sharply divided along nationalist and political lines.[17] *The Hunger* at least attempts to grapple with the event and its consequences; it is a consciousness-raising book and was surely published to that end. Another, somewhat contradictory explanation is that whereas the Holocaust is entangled with our ideas about memory, repression, and the intransigence of the unconscious, the Armenian tragedy seems more urgent (as un- or undertold) and also more open to invention, less haunted by mass trauma. I'm probably overlooking other possibilities, but in any case, *The Hunger's* ostensible "historicity" feels almost painfully voluntarist and presentist.

And yet *The Hunger* is but one example of the ease with which historical trauma is used to authorize personal loss in contemporary young adult literature. In Edward Bloor's recent novel *Crusader* (1999), to take another, fifteen-year-old Roberta Ritter reconstructs the horrific murder of her mother through the supportive "screening" of Mrs. Weiss, the daughter of Holocaust survivors. Mary Ann Ritter was murdered while working one night in the family arcade, and the case has never been solved. Seven years later, Roberta begins to figure it all out. Just after watching for the first time a news broadcast about her mother's murder (through a video archive), Roberta cries for the first time in those seven years, then stumbles to the home of Mrs. Weiss, who serves as a surrogate mother. Mrs. Weiss just happens to be watching Holocaust footage on television, and a long conversation ensues about human evil and accountability. "I had come here to get away from a horrible video," thinks Roberta, "and I had found another one" (204). The link is awkward, one of many problems with the book. To make matters worse, Uncle Frank, one of two problematic father figures, hosts parties in the new arcade that revolve around racist/genocidal virtual reality "experiences," among them "White Riot," "Lynch Mob," and "Krystallnacht." Roberta prefers unmediated reality, whatever that might be. *Crusader* is a novel of empowerment, and Roberta's growth depends upon her ambivalence about "enchantment" and her repudiation of her biological family, who are linked to history's worst villains—even as Bloor criticizes anti-Arab sentiment.

Picturing September 11

Of all contemporary genres of children's literature, the picture book offers the most dramatic and/or ironic testimony to trauma, precisely because the genre is usually presumed innocent. A picture book about the Holocaust has greater power to shock and presumably to educate. Innocenti's picture book *Rose Blanche,* for instance, tells the story of a young German girl who secretly feeds concentration camp victims and is then mistakenly shot by Americans soldiers who liberate the prisoners. Her death is abrupt and upsetting, and the book seems to affirm the idea that children should be exposed to rather than protected from trauma. Or consider Toshi Maruki's *Hiroshima No Pika* (1980), a devastating account of a seven-year-old Japanese girl's experience of the Hiroshima bombing. Young Mii "saw children with their clothes burned away, lips and eyelids swollen. . . . There were heaps of bodies everywhere." Those heaps evoke the mass graves of the Holocaust, complicating any "adult" argument about the necessity of such drastic retaliation against the Japanese. In more recent picture books about the Holocaust, the photograph has become the preferred visual form, in keeping with a faith in the realism of photography (a realism that Kertzer and others usefully question).

If the Holocaust is now understood as the horrific event with which we have slowly come to terms—as the structuring and residually unconscious trauma of the twentieth century—then the terrorist attacks of September 11, 2001, in our very American society of the spectacle, constitute the ultimate and easily knowable affront to self and nation. Whereas the Holocaust slowly became an acceptable topic for children's literature, no such lag occurred between September 11 and the publication of children's and young adult books about that tragedy and the so-called war on terrorism. More than twenty such books have appeared so far—the majority of them published in 2002—mostly picture books but also diary anthologies, graphic novels, and comic book issues (single and serialized). These titles are largely disappointing as art and as social commentary. Many claim September 11 both as a simple story and as personally traumatic, figuring the nation as a wounded innocent and ignoring our complicity in the exploitation of the world's people and resources.

In *The Queen of America Goes to Washington City,* Lauren Berlant (1997) argues that "infantile citizenship" has displaced any meaningful participation in American public life. With the rise of the Reaganite right, she holds, "a nation made for adult citizens has been replaced by one for fetuses and children. . . . Portraits and stories of citizens-victims . . . now permeate the political public sphere, putting on display a mass experience of economic insecurity, racial discord, class conflict, and sexual unease" (1). In other words, privileged citizens claim, in the name of children born and unborn, to be traumatized—by progressive social politics, for example, such as feminism and affirmative action, and more recently by the events of September 11. "Mass national pain threatens to turn into banality," writes Berlant, "a crumbling archive of dead signs and tired plots" (2).[18] Berlant even holds that the "ur-infantile citizen narrative is actually the presidential autobiography" (37), as if anticipating the election of President Bush.

The title of Rosina Schnurr's contribution to the growing body of September 11 children's books nicely sums up the collective spirit: *Terrorism: The Only Way Is through a Child's Story.* Another title, *911: The Book of Help,* is a collection of essays, poems, short fiction, and drawings created by young adult writers in response to the attacks—sort of a *Chicken Soup for the Traumatized Teen Soul.* Then there's Latania Love Wright's *A Day I'll Never Forget: A Keepsake to Help Children Deal with September 11, 2001 Attack on America.* I couldn't find the book in my library (or bring myself to buy it), but according to the publisher's description, "this is a book intended for every child between the ages of 4 to 10 years old who watched the worst attack on America . . . from their television set. This book is a keepsake in which the child's name, date given, and who the book was given by can be recorded. The fact that it is a coloring book involves the child in the reading and is a very educational resource. . . . It is a resource that allows children to express their own individual feelings about that horrible day. Children of all races and ages are captivated by this book." Not one of these books seems to grapple with the political contexts of the attacks and certainly not with the United States' own bullying practices or support for such. Instead young readers are urged only to express their feelings and to appropriate September 11 as a personal trauma—no matter what their own experiences have been: Choose (and color in) your own September 11 adventure.

One of the better September 11 books is *The Day Our World Changed* (2002), an anthology of children's art that confirms our faith not only in the picture book as testimony but in children as reliable witnesses, if not expert interpreters. The book is a joint project of the NYU Child Study Center and the Museum of the City of New York, which suggests again how psyche and history convene of late. The book features gorgeous artwork by children alongside essays by therapists, journalists, teachers, politicians, and historians (including former mayor Rudy Guliani, novelist Pete Hamill, and Senator Charles Schumer). The book does represent varied perspectives on the attacks and their import, but once again, there's no attention to geopolitical context, and its language is relentlessly pop therapeutic. In his foreword, Harold S. Koplewicz, explains that "In a single day, the illusion of our nation's invincibility was shattered for them. How they handle this new sense of vulnerability and, more importantly, how we as adults help them find their way, will have a tremendous influence on our country's future" (Goodman and Fahnestock 2002, 10).

There are a few signs of intelligent life in this anthology. In "Children as Witnesses to History," Sarah Henry traces the history of our national interest in children's voices; she even mentions the importance of *St. Nicholas,* as well as Freud, Dewey, progressive education, and the infamous 1913 Armory Show. Debbie Almontaser's "Growing Up Arab-American" is a welcome contribution about anti-Arab and anti-Muslim backlash after the attacks, even if Almontaser keeps her piece focused on strategies for preventing such bigotry rather than narrating actual incidents. For most of the adult contributors, however, the title of *The Day Our World Changed* is not ironic but a straightforward description of innocence lost that makes possible innocence regained. Pete Hamill titles his piece "Horror through Innocent Eyes." Rhapsody displaces analysis throughout the book. "So much that informs the great works of art of our time," writes Arthur L. Carter in his piece, "comes from the innocence, humor, primal joy, fear, and innate sense of humanity that children typically have. . . . Many adults have tried to respond to the day, but few have done it as eloquently as our children. What a lesson! Their instincts have an emotional incisiveness that few adults can match" (Goodman and Fahnestock 2002, 107).[19]

In his spirited interpretation of September 11, *Welcome to the Desert of the Real!,* Slavoj Žižek proposes that terror has lately been made into "the hidden universal equivalent of all social evils" (2002, 111), in keeping with what he calls "the subjective economy of the realization of the Self's inner potentials" (77). For Žižek, Lacanian psychoanalysis is the cure for traumatic political realities. He puts his faith in the Lacanian Real against the "hegemonic liberal multiculturalist logic" (64), which, he says, makes more feasible notions of Absolute Evil. Counterintuitively he asks, "Is it not that today, in our resigned postideological era which admits no positive Absolutes, the only legitimate candidate for the Absolute are radically evil acts?" (137). He strenuously objects to the elevation of September 11 to that status, as well as to comparisons of September 11 to the Shoah (the Holocaust). Though he admires some articulations of the Holocaust as the great singularity, he stresses the need to keep historical perspective on this event, against the kind of personal relativizations that make evil too easily Absolute, as in these children's books.

We don't have to share Žižek's faith in the recuperative power of psychoanalysis, but what better evidence is there of that "subjective economy" than these September 11 titles? If the only way to understand terrorism is through a child's story, then we need children's books that actually reckon with the horrific world violence to which our nation handily contributes and that challenge the master plot of childhood innocence that has transformed our very understanding of citizenship. Instead we have books that promote infantile citizenship, that resort to a thematic of absolute evil and absolute innocence. Among them are books about the bravery of firemen and rescue dogs, alongside *Fireboat: The Heroic Adventures of the John J. Harvey*, the vacuous *On That Day* by Andrea Patel, and the twelve-book "War on Terrorism" series published by ABDO and Daughters. The titles in the latter series, perhaps the most reactionary of all the September 11 books so far, include *Ground Zero, Heroes of the Day, Operation Noble Eagle, United We Stand,* and *Weapons of War* (all published in 2002—a book per month for a full year). This series is dumbly patriotic, with its stars-and-stripes covers and its jingoistic support for America's war machine. President Bush comes off as a hero rather than a war zealot or just a politician. These books have wide distribution, as ABDO is a privately held company that publishes children's nonfiction for the school library market. As reported on the ABDO Web site (www.abdopub.com), the "War on Terrorism" series has garnered praise from the American Library Association's *Booklist* magazine.[20]

Instead of nuanced history we get The Big Scary Picture Book of Terrorism.[21] The child inside and outside the text is at once the wounded/dead child of trauma theory and the endangered child of our reactionary national imagination. All this picture book talk of injury and vulnerability is cause for alarm, especially because such talk is supposed to be reassuring. Picture books about September 11 insist upon a traumatized reader, but they also redefine trauma as the stuff of pop psychology, emphasizing—and delimiting—choice, pleasure, and action. We want books to give children hope, to nurture them and aid their development. But a coloring book about September 11? A personal "keepsake"? Complexity and collectivity are refused in the name of the infantile citizen.

Trauma and Memory in *The Giver*

One of the best-known Holocaust titles for children, and so far the only one to be honored with the prestigious Newbery Medal, is Lois Lowry's *Number the Stars* (1989). Set in 1943, *Number the Stars* tells the story of a Danish family and their friends who help smuggle Jewish neighbors out of Nazi-occupied Denmark and into Sweden. Ten-year-old Annemarie Johansen becomes involved with the Resistance when her family hides Annemarie's best friend, Ellen Rosen, from the Nazis. As the novel unfolds, Annemarie comes to terms with the terrors of their situation.

Lowry alternately safeguards her protagonist Annemarie and puts her in harm's way, through changes in place and an emphasis on the defensive power of ignorance rather than innocence. Midway through the book, Annemarie discovers that her Uncle Henrik has been lying to her about their mysterious family business near the sea and confronts him. "How brave you, little Annemarie?" he asks, saying that the larger truth of their situation is too much for anyone, much less a child, to bear. Annemarie accepts this explanation, thinking "they protect[ed] one another by not telling" (1989, 91)—by not knowing or claiming too much individually, they avoid giving others away through German torture. In the book's climactic event, Annemarie is instructed to take a basket of food to her uncle on a docked boat. She knows her task is dangerous, but not why. Hidden in the basket is a handkerchief soaked with a concoction designed to throw off the German dogs brought aboard the boats to sniff out stowaways headed across the sea to Sweden. On her way she encounters German soldiers, who confiscate the lunch but let her take the basket to her uncle. The handkerchief arrives in the nick of time and prevents the dogs from sniffing out the Rosen family members hiding in a secret compartment. While on the path, Annemarie realizes that she must seem as ignorant as possible. She thinks of herself as Little Red Riding Hood, and even tells herself that story as she walks along. Remembering the childishness of her younger sister, Annemarie feigns anger and confusion when the soldiers confiscate the lunch: "'*Don't!*' she said angrily. 'That's Uncle Henrik's lunch!'" (114–15). Innocence, she knows, is a defense. Some critics even hold that *Number the Stars* is not a story of lost innocence at all but a meditation on the uses and abuses of innocence.

Unlike other Holocaust narratives for children, *Number the Stars* is not set in Germany and does not address life in concentration camps. For better or for worse, its indirection or remove helps explain its success. Unlike Baer, who argues for direct confrontation with trauma, Lowry hopes details will suggest the larger picture. In her Newbery acceptance speech for *Number the Stars*, Lowry remarks: "As a writer I find that I can cover only the small and the ordinary—the mittens on a shivering child—and hope that they evoke the larger events. The huge and the terrible are beyond my powers" (1990, 416). Lowry poses the question with which we've been concerned: How, when, and why to speak the unspeakable, especially to and for and in the name of children? In my view, Lowry does more than just "evoke the larger events," and her images of child innocence and vulnerability engender a strong sense of community.

Number the Stars shows how the infantilizing loss of freedom goes hand and hand with pain and hardship. So too does Lowry's second Newbery Medal winning novel, *The Giver,* published four years later. Whereas *Number the Stars* is historical fiction, *The Giver* is a dystopian novel in the tradition of *Brave New World* (1932) and *1984* (1949). Even so, the continuities of theme are strong. In *The Giver,* twelve-year-old Jonas is selected to be the Receiver of Memory for his community, the bearer of his culture's collective consciousness. His culture has gone to Sameness, refusing pain and poverty but also variety and choice. He begins his training with the current Receiver, whom he calls the Giver. Day by day, the Giver, weary from decades of pain and isolation, transfers memories and impressions to Jonas, in a manner reminiscent of the Vulcan mind-meld, Socratic pedagogy/pederasty, and the evangelical laying-on of hands. Everyone else in the community is shielded from pain and trauma, and soon Jonas finds his new burden intolerable. "I think it would be easier if the memories were shared," he tells the Giver. "You and I wouldn't have to bear so much by ourselves, if everybody took a part" (1990, 112). "The worst part of holding the memories is not the pain. It's the loneliness of it. Memories need to be shared" (153). The Giver agrees, and they carry out a plan to restore memories to the community and force people to make their own decisions. The conclusion is ambiguous, suggesting at once the success and failure of their mission, the survival and the death of Jonas and of the baby boy, Gabriel.

Ideologically, *The Giver* is an ambivalent text. On the one hand, it echoes the classic story of the chosen child, nearly always a boy, who becomes a savior figure by sacrificing himself for the greater good. The exceptionality of Jonas and the "newchild" he nurtures is very seductive, such that it's easy to miss the critique of heroic individualism central to the book. That is, *The Giver* is at once the pleasurably familiar story of the special/gifted boy and a critique of said story.[22]

In the context of contemporary trauma literature, however, *The Giver* looks more progressive than not. The sequence of *Number the Stars* and *The Giver* points to their shared project of ratifying the political sphere against privatization and the banalization of trauma. In *The Giver,* the specific lessons of history take backstage to a generic respect for the importance of collective rather than individual memory. The Giver gives memories to Jonas slowly, unwilling to burden the boy with humanity's painful and largely unspecified past. Even so, in this book there are traces of war and even the Holocaust. The most upsetting memory that Jonas receives is of a brutal battle scene evocative of the Civil War. And the devastating secret that Jonas learns in his training is that people in his community are "released" or put to death when they are too old, too immature, or just troublesome. In horror he watches a videotape of his own father killing a baby by lethal injection, and it's hard not to think here of Nazi eugenics and medical experimentation. (This scene, incidentally, is often criticized as too horrific.)

The Giver is a novel of the education of the senses. At first pain is "beyond [Jonas's] comprehension" (Lowry 1993, 70), but through transmitted memories of sunburns and broken arms, Jonas learns physical pain first; in the novel, physical pain provides a baseline for pain more generally. As he becomes more aware of human frailty and suffering, he becomes more impatient with the empty rituals of family life that merely gesture toward emotion. At one point, his little sister claims to be "angry," but Jonas realizes that she feels only irritation. He reacts "with rage that welled up so passionately inside him that the thought of discussing [his sister's experience] calmly at the dinner table was unthinkable" (132). As he shares physical and emotional pain with the Giver, Jonas gains wisdom, specifically the wisdom that pain must be shared if humans are to have authentic selves. The privatization of pain/wisdom does not a legitimate culture make.

Thus Lowry dismantles the very pedagogical scene that is so seductive in the novel. (Even after finishing the book, my students often tell me they'd like to be Givers.) Like so many heroes of fantasy and utopian narrative, Jonas is the chosen one, destined to assume the most urgent role in his community, to his own surprise and growing dismay. With great power, after all, comes great responsibility: we know the cliché. But while Lowry never dislodges Jonas as the redeemer hero of her story, she does interrogate the classic male homosocial fantasy of private instruction and social stratification that ensures a dead public sphere. Against that classic fantasy she urges the redistribution of knowledge and memory, the sharing of pain and/as wisdom, even if her vision for the redemption of culture still depends, curiously, on both man-boy love and a highly sentimentalized portrait of family life—namely, a Christmas story, a memory of family intimacy and warmth that the Giver transmits to Jonas. Against its own custodial investments, we might read *The Giver* as a cautionary tale about contemporary U.S. culture and about the need for a thoughtful literature of atrocity. *The Giver* offers an allegorical, abstract solution to the problem of narrating trauma and, by being less "historical" than other trauma texts, is less easily made into a keepsake.

Lowry concludes her afterword to *Number the Stars* by quoting Kim Malthe-Bruun, a young man killed for his participation in the Resistance. "I want you all to remember," he writes in a letter to his mother, "that you must not dream yourselves back to the times before the war, but the dream for you all, young and old, must be to create an ideal of human decency" (cited in Lowry 1989, 137). Resistance to nostalgia and emphasis on human decency distinguishes Lowry's ethic of transmission from the ethic of transmission that marks trauma theory and the more banal, politically empty rhetoric of sharing and caring typical of the September 11 books. Lowry is not the hero of my story, but her work offers an engaging model of children's literature as trauma testimony—one that is necessarily imperfect but that reckons with the difficulty of memory and narration—against that "subjective economy of the realization of the Self's inner potentials" (Žižek 2002, 77).

My thanks to Katharine Capshaw Smith and Richard Flynn for their feedback and support. I dedicate this chapter to the memory of Patricia Pace and Mitzi Myers.

Notes

1. Baer adapts Lawrence Langer's phrase "the literature of atrocity," as formulated in *The Holocaust and the Literary Imagination* (1975).
2. In the *New England Primer, A* stands for Adam and original sin: "In Adam's fall / We sinned all." Early children's books on both sides of the Atlantic were largely exercises in shame and abjection, written to subdue children and curb their sinful nature. In a sense, children's literature has always been both traumatized and traumatizing, at once an affirmation of evil and its narrative antidote. As Baer likewise notes, contemporary young adult fiction especially seems preoccupied with social ills, at once protecting and exposing teen readers to pain, loss, and alienation. But if original sin still lurks in the collective unconscious of children's literature and popular culture (think of all the "bad seed" movies, from *Rosemary's Baby* to *The Good Son*), the idea of human depravity was given new and distinctive affirmation by Hitler's genocidal program. Rather than argue for the newness of evil or trauma, Baer introduces into her analysis a mathematical conceit; what the twentieth century bears witness to during and after the Holocaust, she holds, is a new "algorithm" of evil, a new configuration or formula.
3. Adorno later revised this formulation, remarking in *Negative Dialectics* that "it may have been wrong to say that after Auschwitz you could no longer write poems. But it is not wrong to raise the less cultural question whether after Auschwitz you can go on living" (1973, 362–63).
4. The Holocaust is also represented as proof of humans' inherently sinful nature, in keeping with a Calvinistic worldview residual in but not identical to psychoanalysis: here the analogy between the Holocaust and psychoanalysis falters somewhat.
5. Haase looks at imaginative literature as well as autobiographies of war survivors; among the texts he treats is the Sendak-illustrated edition of *Dear Mili* by the Brothers Grimm.
6. Although inspired by many disciplines and practices, narrative medicine is largely the brainchild of Dr. Rita Charon, whose narrative medicine program at Columbia University emphasizes the importance of "narrative competence" for physicians in training. After practicing medicine as an internist for a number of years, Dr. Charon took a doctoral degree in English and has since devoted herself to bringing the two disciplines closer together. Students of narrative medicine take clinical cue from literature as well as the stories of their patients, learning how to interpret the languages of the body and the mind. Narrative therapy, by contrast, is more closely affiliated with humanist psychology and with poststructuralist theory; founding figures Michael White and David Epston emphasize the "disciplinary" work of narrative even as they stress the freedom of individuals to create their own meanings and tell multiple stories. Without further study, it's hard to say if either of these movements offers much by way of content or method; most of the descriptions I found seem pretty generic.
7. Cvetkovich points out that most contemporary discussions of trauma in the academy are psychoanalytic rather than sociocultural or political in emphasis. Her own allegiances—feminism, critical race theory, Marxism, and queer theory—help position trauma instead as "a social and cultural discourse that emerges in response to the demands of grappling with the psychic consequences of historical events" (2003, 18). She names as traumatic not only the usual historical suspects but also the everyday events of sexual, racial, class-based, and homophobic violence. These events are often

not perceived as traumatic because they don't always demand dead or even damaged bodies, and/or because those bodies don't add up to "mass" trauma.

8. In an essay on the "storying of war," the late Mitzi Myers notes that war-themed writing for the young "coincides with accelerating late-twentieth century violence and reflects adult preoccupations with human evil: all forms of moral, psychological, and material destruction; past and present genocides, from the Holocaust to more recent 'ethnic cleansings'; the ever-present possibility of nuclear disaster" (2000b, 328). "Adult social history," she continues, "cultural studies, and postmodern/postcolonial literary theory—all much concerned with redefining what counts as 'war' and with exploring how conflicts escalate and how war is represented in history, memory, and words—filter into the expanding and impressive volume of war stories for the young" (328). The storying of war, she suggests, is entangled not just with social history and with literature but also with theory.

9. Caruth's scholarship "has circulated within a milieu that includes work by Geoffrey Hartman, Dominick LaCapra, Shoshana Felman and Dori Laub, Lawrence Langer, and others that is centered on the Holocaust" (Cvetkovich 2003, 27). Among this group LaCapra has been the most critical of the privileging of psychoanalytic method in Holocaust criticism and, as Cvetkovich notes, has also tried to historicize the place of the Holocaust in trauma theory. Even so, LaCapra turns to a psychoanalytic conceit in his analysis, remarking that the Holocaust "stands as the repressed event that guides poststructuralist theory, particularly in its European contexts—a historical locatedness that is especially likely to be lost in the translation to a U.S. context" (LaCapra 2001, 27). Cvetkovich eschews the conceit of the return of the repressed, noting only that the Holocaust "offers validation of theory's applicability to concrete and pressing historical circumstances, and it serves as a compelling example that unrepresentability and aporia can be integral to lived experience rather than the deconstruction of experience" (2003, 27). She gives trauma theory a hopeful countenance while stressing the importance of developing alternative trauma projects such as her own work on trauma and lesbian public cultures.

10. Blanchot takes issue with Winnicott's "impressive" but faulty formulation of childhood as an individual existential experience, calling it "a fictive application designed to individualize that which cannot be individualized or to furnish a representation for the unrepresentable: to allow the belief that one can, with the help of the transference, fix in the present of a memory (that is, in a present experience) the passivity of the immemorial unknown. The introduction of such a detour is perhaps therapeutically useful, to the extent that, through a kind of Platonism, it permits him who lives haunted by the imminent collapse to say: this will not happen, it has already happened; I know, I remember. It allows him to restore, in other words, a knowledge which is a relation to truth, and a common, linear temporality" (Blanchot 1995, 66).

11. Fynsk also justifies his project as the legacy of Hegel as well as Lacan, remarking that "if there is anything legitimate in the link between death and language that Hegel established for us, then I believe we have the grounds to pursue this problematic of the *infans* through the vast literature devoted to the death of children, and that such a reading would be 'responsible' in the deepest senses of the term" (2000, 88).

12. Felman's most recent contribution to trauma theory is *The Juridicial Unconscious*, which examines how twentieth-century law and jurisprudence respond to as well as perpetuate trauma in the public sphere.

13. In *Cultural Capital,* John Guillory argues that theory more broadly is a form of literary language, a kind of intellectual capital. He proposes, vis-à-vis de Man and Lacan, that theory effects a sort of "transference of transference," displacing the student's love for the teacher—the first transference necessary to successful to pedagogy—onto the love of the teacher's discourse, thus dispensing with (denying) the problems of both transference and countertransference. We don't love the teacher or student; rather, we love literature and/or theory (1993, see especially 176–98).
14. The epigraph also suggests that Zipes has displaced Bettelheim as the fairy tale critic of choice in this particular series.
15. Santayana's actual line: "Those who cannot remember the past are condemned to repeat it."
16. "A trauma history of the United States," writes Cvetkovich, "would address the multigenerational legacies of the colonization and genocide of indigenous peoples as well as of the African diaspora and slave trade—a project, it should be noted, that is necessarily transnational in scope" (2003, 119).
17. Another recent and higher profile return to this tragedy is the documentary film *Ararat* (2002), directed by the Armenian-Canadian director Atom Egoyan. In January 2004, Turkish Minister of Culture and Tourism Erkan Mumcu gave official and controversial permission to Turks wanting to see the film, emphasizing that Turkey is now a democracy. By and large, Turks and Armenians have told different stories about the events beginning in 1915; Armenians avow that they were chased out of their ancestral homeland and executed brutally, whereas the official Turkish line is that the Armenians, encouraged by Russia, were rebelling against the Ottoman Empire and were thus suppressed. Egoyan himself likened the film to *Schindler's List,* Steven Spielberg's Holocaust film, adding more fuel to the political fire. Belonging to the more skeptical genre of political documentary, the film raises consciousness not only about this traumatic episode but also about the difficulties of coming to terms with history and/as trauma.
18. In her chapter "America, 'Fat,' the Fetus," Berlant notes that "the pregnant woman becomes the child to the fetus, becoming more minor and less politically represented than the fetus, which is in turn made more *national,* more central to securing the privileges of law, paternity, and other less institutional family strategies of contemporary American culture" (1997, 85; italics in original).
19. Another such collection of children's testimony is *Messages to Ground Zero: Children Respond to September 11, 2001* (2002), featuring writings by children collected by Shelley Harwayne in cooperation with the New York City Board of Education.
20. Here's the magazine's review of *Weapons of War,* as cited on the ABDO Web site: "Clear and well focused, this highly accessible text delivers the basic facts and the advantages of various craft. Excellent color photos show a dozen different planes, as well as five helicopters, and four support planes in flight, and the others [*sic*] major weapons in use" (http://www.abdopub.com/c/@tBd4Eoatol4KA/Pages/pressmay.html).
21. ABDO and Daughters is not the only children's publisher to join the bandwagon; there's also Scholastic, oft championed as socially progressive. In his very engaging paper "Marketing 9/11: Children as Victims, Agents, and Consuming Subjects," Richard Flynn turns his attention to "the good corporate citizen" Scholastic, which "mobilizes" its resources on behalf of the wounded nation and the vulnerable child (Flynn n.d., 2–3). As Flynn points out, Scholastic.com constructs the child as not

only vulnerable but already traumatized and in need of expert help, shopping incentives, and patriotic pedagogy. Speaking more broadly about corporate children's culture, Flynn holds that such materials "reinforce an image of children as infantile, vulnerable, voracious consumers" (10). Flynn presented this paper at the Children's Literature Association Annual Conference in 2002.

22. In a recent Foucauldian reading of the novel, Dan Latham argues that the novel seems both a narrative exercise in discipline and punishment and a refusal of such, and that it "both resists and fulfills the role of the typical adolescent novel . . . namely to integrate adolescents into the power structure of society" (2004, 149).

13. In *Cultural Capital,* John Guillory argues that theory more broadly is a form of literary language, a kind of intellectual capital. He proposes, vis-à-vis de Man and Lacan, that theory effects a sort of "transference of transference," displacing the student's love for the teacher—the first transference necessary to successful to pedagogy—onto the love of the teacher's discourse, thus dispensing with (denying) the problems of both transference and countertransference. We don't love the teacher or student; rather, we love literature and/or theory (1993, see especially 176–98).
14. The epigraph also suggests that Zipes has displaced Bettelheim as the fairy tale critic of choice in this particular series.
15. Santayana's actual line: "Those who cannot remember the past are condemned to repeat it."
16. "A trauma history of the United States," writes Cvetkovich, "would address the multigenerational legacies of the colonization and genocide of indigenous peoples as well as of the African diaspora and slave trade—a project, it should be noted, that is necessarily transnational in scope" (2003, 119).
17. Another recent and higher profile return to this tragedy is the documentary film *Ararat* (2002), directed by the Armenian-Canadian director Atom Egoyan. In January 2004, Turkish Minister of Culture and Tourism Erkan Mumcu gave official and controversial permission to Turks wanting to see the film, emphasizing that Turkey is now a democracy. By and large, Turks and Armenians have told different stories about the events beginning in 1915; Armenians avow that they were chased out of their ancestral homeland and executed brutally, whereas the official Turkish line is that the Armenians, encouraged by Russia, were rebelling against the Ottoman Empire and were thus suppressed. Egoyan himself likened the film to *Schindler's List,* Steven Spielberg's Holocaust film, adding more fuel to the political fire. Belonging to the more skeptical genre of political documentary, the film raises consciousness not only about this traumatic episode but also about the difficulties of coming to terms with history and/as trauma.
18. In her chapter "America, 'Fat,' the Fetus," Berlant notes that "the pregnant woman becomes the child to the fetus, becoming more minor and less politically represented than the fetus, which is in turn made more *national,* more central to securing the privileges of law, paternity, and other less institutional family strategies of contemporary American culture" (1997, 85; italics in original).
19. Another such collection of children's testimony is *Messages to Ground Zero: Children Respond to September 11, 2001* (2002), featuring writings by children collected by Shelley Harwayne in cooperation with the New York City Board of Education.
20. Here's the magazine's review of *Weapons of War,* as cited on the ABDO Web site: "Clear and well focused, this highly accessible text delivers the basic facts and the advantages of various craft. Excellent color photos show a dozen different planes, as well as five helicopters, and four support planes in flight, and the others [*sic*] major weapons in use" (http://www.abdopub.com/c/@tBd4Eoatol4KA/Pages/pressmay.html).
21. ABDO and Daughters is not the only children's publisher to join the bandwagon; there's also Scholastic, oft championed as socially progressive. In his very engaging paper "Marketing 9/11: Children as Victims, Agents, and Consuming Subjects," Richard Flynn turns his attention to "the good corporate citizen" Scholastic, which "mobilizes" its resources on behalf of the wounded nation and the vulnerable child (Flynn n.d., 2–3). As Flynn points out, Scholastic.com constructs the child as not

only vulnerable but already traumatized and in need of expert help, shopping incentives, and patriotic pedagogy. Speaking more broadly about corporate children's culture, Flynn holds that such materials "reinforce an image of children as infantile, vulnerable, voracious consumers" (10). Flynn presented this paper at the Children's Literature Association Annual Conference in 2002.

22. In a recent Foucauldian reading of the novel, Dan Latham argues that the novel seems both a narrative exercise in discipline and punishment and a refusal of such, and that it "both resists and fulfills the role of the typical adolescent novel . . . namely to integrate adolescents into the power structure of society" (2004, 149).

11

The Hansel and Gretel Syndrome

Survivorship Fantasies and Parental Desertion

U. C. Knoepflmacher

"Hansel, we're saved! The old witch is dead," Gretel triumphantly shouts as she opens the door to release her brother. The children promptly plunder the house of the crone Gretel has just killed. The happiness of these little survivors is unbounded. Even Wilhelm Grimm seems to want an editorial share in their expressions of fraternal glee: "How thrilled they were: they hugged and kissed and jumped up and down for joy!" (Tatar 1999, 189).[1]

But one slight obstacle remains. The children still must find their way back to the home of the parents who have twice left them to perish in a dark forest. How can the trauma of such a desertion be resolved? As Maria Tatar has suggested, perhaps more than any other Grimm fairy tale, "Hansel and Gretel" seems to "perpetuate strangely inappropriate notions about what it means to live ever happily after" (1999, 182). The fairy tale's ostensibly happy ending asks us to become as forgetful of the trauma of abandonment as the story's child protagonists. The alacrity they display upon coming home thus seems even more surprising than that of the returning Dorothy, who, after her own witch killings, so eagerly hugs Aunt Em. When all four versions of Grimm's story ask us to believe that Hansel and Gretel joyfully throw their arms around their father, we are invited to repress parental betrayal just as much as the sturdy children who have, against all odds, managed to survive extinction.[2]

Wilhelm Grimm's masculinist narrative conflates the witch with the children's bad mother and exculpates a husband who allows himself to be dominated by his wife: "The man had not had a happy hour since the day he had abandoned the children in the forest. His wife had died. Gretel emptied her apron and the pearls and jewels rolled all over the floor" (Tatar 1999, 189–90). A derelict father is not only showered with diamonds but is also awarded a more pliable replacement for the spouse who had tyrannized him. Not one, but two witches have been expunged from the narrative: the gluttonous child devourer who fattened Hans for eating and the bread-denying child starver whom Grimm had alternately presented as the children's biological mother and as their stepmother. By offering her father a dowry of jewels, Gretel can now become his "little missus," as Captain Crewe, the imprudent diamond-mine investor, used to call the daughter he, just as imprudently, handed over to a witch, in Frances Hodgson Burnett's *A Little Princess*. But Burnett compensates Sara, and not her father, for the traumas he has induced. Indeed, in a poignant reversal of Gretel's act of bribery, Sara enlists another unhappy and weak father figure, her guardian Carrisford, to help her spread her newfound wealth. The new heiress wants to feed masses of "hungry children" on "days" as "dreadful" as those behind her (2002, 185). Sara is as unembittered as little Gretel. But, unlike Gretel, she refuses to forget her protracted servitude as a starving slave laborer. Whereas the ending of Grimm's tale invites us to repress the past, Burnett's narrative keeps alive a child's memory of betrayal, abuse, and deprivation.

In November 2003, when Maurice Sendak appeared with Tony Kushner after a performance of the Theresienstadt child-opera *Brundibar* at New York's 92nd Street "Y," he invoked the story of "Hansel and Gretel" as an analogue for the new picture book he and Kushner were presenting to the public. The links are certainly there. Pepicek and Aninku, the brother-sister pair in *Brundibar,* also must thread back to the cottage of a starving parent. But it is now a needy peasant mother, not a guilt-ridden woodcutter father, who becomes revitalized by returning offspring. And, whereas a witch was required to obtain the nourishment denied to Hansel and Gretel, the children in the Sendak/Kushner book are cast as nourishers from the very start. Nor will this pair be alone, for they eventually count on child allies far more numerous than Sara Crewe's small band of friends. All threats are removed when a flock of blackbirds, depicted earlier as wresting children away from parents, chases away the Hitlerian bully Brundibar. Evil has been purged. There is no need for a little duck such as the one that ferried Hansel and Gretel back to their father. Aninku and Pepicek require no further help to facilitate their own happy return to a parental home. Brother and sister drag a huge canister of milk to their debilitated mother's bedside. She can now follow the milk cure prescribed by a rotund and jolly doctor whose yellow star suggests that he himself is under the threat of death. Shouting a hopeful "Mazel Tov," this Sendakian look-alike dances off but reappears, still gleefully gyrating, in the book's very last panel. Is a scribbled message from *Brundibar,* promising revenge, now meant to arrest the doctor's ebullience? Can we, in other words, trust this opera/picture book's happy ending?

I.

Sendak told his New York audience that he regarded *Brundibar* as a reassuring closure for lifelong cultural and personal traumas inflicted by the Holocaust. The book's wishful happy ending, he hinted, offered him, Kushner, and readers young and old a link to the invincible hopefulness of the opera's Jewish child actors, most of whom perished at Auschwitz.[3] The illustration of the blackbird-transported children and another drawing of a sad-faced Aninku and Pepicek among heaps of empty shoes in a deserted alley, Sendak conceded, might remind an adult reader that these children could never have survived their ordeal: "like Hansel and Gretel," Sendak ruefully claimed, "in my mind, they died." But the fantasy of their triumph over a Hitlerian bully, Sendak insisted, as he warmed up to his 92nd "Y" audience, should nonetheless become as uplifting as "the fantasy of killing the witch—for the witch-mother can't get away with this thing!"

By alluding to a single "witch-mother" in the Grimm text, Sendak displays the Freudian credentials he shares with other revisionist readers of "Hansel and Gretel," notably, Randall Jarrell, Anne Sexton, and Bruno Bettelheim. Like Kushner today, Jarrell was once an esteemed literary partner whose verbal texts Sendak illustrated. Even after the poet's 1965 death, Sendak drew Gretel and the witch for Jarrell's translation of "Hansel and Gretel" in *The Juniper Tree*; he also appropriated the text of *Fly By Night* to license a lavish dramatization of his own ambivalence toward nurturing domineering mother figures. The matriarchal closure of *Brundibar* thus not only replicates a formula Sendak had amply used in his own children's books (by dramatizing Max's return to the "still hot" supper left by his mother, for example, or by uniting Jenny with a Baby turned into a fat Mother Goose that resembles Sarah Sendak) but was also familiar from the endings of the three Jarrell fantasies for children he had illustrated, *The Animal Family, The Bat-Poet,* and *Fly By Night*.

Like the case studies of Anna and Sigmund Freud, "Hansel and Gretel" offered a crucial impetus for Randall Jarrell's creation of a host of adult poems that obsessively revisited his grim recollections of the childhood trauma of his own abandonment and of the wishful escapes that he had vainly concocted. A poem such as the 1955 "A Quilt Pattern" weaves the Grimm fairy tale into the liminal consciousness of a boy whose mother has tried to lull him to sleep, perhaps by telling him this "oldest tale of all" (1970b, line 10). "The blocked-out Tree / Of the boy's Life" is not just depicted on his "tangled quilt" (ll.1–2), but becomes transformed into the unblocked, terrifying dream-forest into which his aroused mind now wanders, a primal wood of witches, cages, and open graves.

The boy who "sucks at the finger" in Jarrell's poem is, like Hansel, asked to hold it out for inspection by a female presence that supervises his growth into manhood (1970b, l.50). Deemed immature, however, he must withdraw this protrusion from the seductively feminine house that has called to him "in its slow singing voice" (l.51). The boy wants to arrest his sexual awakening: the pleasures of a maternal bath quickly turn into his fear that "my mother is basting / Bad me in the bath-tub" (ll.38–39). A world of death has taken over: Hansel's imaginary "white cat" is now eating his equally imaginary "white pigeon," and the boy whose mother calls him "my little mouse" has himself become a small furry thing, like rabbits "That are skinned, but that never die at all" (ll.31, 78, 18). Yet beyond a little boy's terror lies an adult consciousness of the cultural aftermath of this scary tale. The obsession with hair (even the forest's blackberries are "small hairy things") or lost baby teeth thus does not just betoken the onset of puberty in a child beset by Oedipal feelings. The hair, not yet severed from still unskinned creatures who crouch in cages before their slaughter, evokes Holocaust imagery as much as the "thousand stones" resembling "just-brushed, just-lost teeth" (ll.55, 57) that have replaced the white pebbles left behind by Hansel. It is the oven, however, that Jarrell's boy most fears. Read merely from a Freudian perspective, this cavity represents the maternal genitals that the boy's "bad me" covets yet fears. But read from a post-Holocaust perspective, that oven also marks the resting place of those whose hair, teeth, and skins were removed by later killers of witchlike undesirables, of the "bad" Other:

> He has moved. . . .
> He is still now, and holds his breath.
> If something is screaming itself to death
> There in the oven, it is not the mouse
> Nor anything of the mouse's. Bad me, good me
> Stare into each other's eyes, and timidly
> Smile at each other: it was the Other. (ll.71–76)

Anne Sexton's "Hansel and Gretel," the next-to-last poem in the 1971 volume *Transformations,* also opens with a conflation of the witch with a mother whose devouring love for her little boy rapidly moves from cloying excess to vampiric threat. The first lines of the poem seem innocuous enough:

> Little plum,
> said the mother to her son,
> I want to bite,
> I want to chew,
> I will eat you up. (ll.1–5)

Such exaggeration hardly appears to be any more frightening than that of the teeth-grinding Wild Things who implore little Max, "Oh please don't go / we'll eat you up—we love you so!" But a subtle shift occurs when the mother who has just proclaimed her "little nubkin" to be as "sweet as fudge" suddenly calls him "my blitz" rather than her "bliss." The Freudian slip is followed by a more concrete evidence of an aggressive disregard of her child's psychology:

Survivorship Fantasies and Parental Desertion

> I have a pan that will fit you.
> Just pull up your knees like a game hen.
> Let me take your pulse
> and set the oven for 350.
> Come, my pretender, my fritter,
> my bubbler, my chicken biddy! (ll.17–22)

Sexton's satirical preamble, however, is followed by her more sardonic retelling of the Grimm tale. We are made uneasy as we join Hansel in overhearing the parental discussion of how best to dispose of docile undesirables. For Sexton's phrasing forces us to recognize the makings of a Nazi parable:

> The final solution,
> their mother told their father,
> was to lose the children in the forest.

When a Gretel who "bided her time" tricks the witch, however, she proves herself to be her mother's worthy offspring: "Ja, Fräulein, show me how it could be done," the child says cunningly (Sexton 1971, l.101):

> The witch thought this fair
> and climbed in . . .
> Gretel,
> seeing her moment in history,
> shut fast the oven,
> locked fast the door,
> fast as Houdini,
> and turned the oven on to bake. (ll.102–10)

And yet, Sexton wryly suggests, this historical triumph of the will leaves a slightly tarnished aftermath. Back with their no-longer-famished father, the overstuffed children are faintly reminded of the atrocity that has led to their present bliss. Still, unlike Jarrell's disturbed boy, they are not exactly troubled:

> Only at suppertime
> while eating a chicken leg
> did our children remember
> the woe of the oven,
> the smell of the cooking witch,
> a little like mutton,
> to be served only with burgundy
> and fine white linen
> like something religious. (ll.123–30)

The ingestion made possible by their former host seems to ratify their communion with evil.

Whereas post-Freudians such as Sexton and Jarrell are determined to revive the trauma that Wilhelm Grimm would encourage us to forget, Bruno Bettelheim curiously endorses Grimm's patriarchal slant in his reading of "Hansel and Gretel" in his widely circulated *The Uses of Enchantment* (1989). While Sendak, Jarrell, and Sexton suggest that the revivification of a mother, whether threatening or herself threatened, might offer an antidote for childhood wounds, Bettelheim all but sidesteps the major roles played by both Gretel and the dead mother whom the little girl replaces in her father's house. The conversation overheard by Hansel and Gretel is dismissed as a mere fantasy concocted by a small child who, "awakening hungry in the darkness of the night," justifiably "feels threatened by complete rejection and desertion" (160). The Grimm story presumably offers a healthy counterfantasy to direct children away from "oral greediness" and "immature dependence": "A witch as created by the child's anxious fantasies will haunt him; but a witch he can push into her own oven and burn to death is a witch the child can believe himself rid of" (161, 166; italics mine). Bettelheim's odd fusion of Gretel and Hansel into a single "he"-child here is as remarkable as his lack of interest in the mother-witch conflation he simply cites as a foil for Gretel's helpful services to her male "age mate." Since witch slayers strike him as heroic figures, the child-psychologist endorses the utility of a story that, according to him, can contribute to the "emotional well-being" of maturing sons such as Hansel (165)—and presumably of male Holocaust survivors, such as Bettelheim himself.

II.

Let me create a brief interlude to assess some of the implications of the materials I have been rehearsing. If the survivorship of Hansels and Gretels is to be refigured in narratives that promote the transformation of thinking children into thinking adults, such a narrativizing must presumably confront, however indirectly, the childhood trauma induced by parental desertion and the threat of annihilation. I have been suggesting that Wilhelm Grimm elided a residual anguish from the dubiously happy ending that Jarrell and Sexton, but not Bettelheim, tried to interrogate and transform. The difference between Bettelheim and the two poets, however, goes back to a fundamental contradiction already embedded in Freud's own work on trauma, a contradiction that has divided modern trauma theorists into what Ruth Leys labels mimeticist and antimimeticist camps. Put simply, this contradiction pits those who believe that a victim of trauma is capable of reprocessing the original experience of shock against those who, much like Bettelheim, regard all accounts of trauma as fictive deflections from an unsettling past that has become unrepresentable. For, according to Bettelheim, Hansel and Gretel are themselves fantasizers fearful of the painful separation that accompanies all growth: the children merely think that their parents want to starve them.

Survivorship Fantasies and Parental Desertion

Sendak and Kushner's Brundibar picture book, I would argue, steers between these two camps. The authors endorse the fantasies of the opera's original child performers because they hail their defiance of trauma as a wholesome and even heroic action. Yet, with the hindsight of history, they also know, as do their book's adult readers, what many of the Jewish children who were later killed were unable to anticipate: namely, that their fear of death could neither be allayed nor vanquished by a defiant imagination. Compensatory fantasies of rescue and of revenge could hardly overrule the reality of gas chambers and crematoria. Sendak and Kushner must therefore produce what might be called a double text. The disparity between a linear prose narrative set in dark capital letters and the occasional dialogue that is set, comic-book style, in cartoonish drawings that hark back to Sendak's earlier work in the mini-texts of The Nutshell Library creates an almost schizophrenic split between a child's consciousness and that of an adult.

As I have already suggested, even the drawings—the empty shoes left behind in a depopulated alley or those blackbirds that waft child riders above the heads of their wailing mothers—inevitably evoke grim Holocaust icons. Yet the anxieties of a child-parent separation—always a major component of Sendak's work—are also mitigated somewhat by the fact that in *Brundibar,* as in the unabashedly joyous *Where the Wild Things Are* and *In the Night Kitchen,* it is the children, Aninku and Pepicek, rather than a paralyzed or debilitated parental figure, who boldly initiate the journey away from the family home.[4] This sister-brother pair thus is much closer to rebellious escapists such as Max or Mickey or Jenny and to the heroic Ida of *Outside Over There* than to Hansel and Gretel, children deprived of the agency they require in order to survive parental desertion. Despite their appropriation of a maternal role, Aninku and Pepicek do not have to grow up. By finding strength in numbers and forming an alliance with other children, they cease to be the victims of either adult neglect or the abuse of the adolescent Brundibar, the would-be adult whom Sendak planned to endow with the same Hitlerian mustache he had given to the trio of Oliver Hardy bakers who had shoved a defiant and unbattered Mickey-in-Batter into a steaming Mickey-Oven to bake a "delicious Mickey-Cake" in *In the Night Kitchen.*[5]

As Christian Czechs, Pepicek and Aninku can be more plausibly cast as triumphalist leaders of a fantastic child crusade against Brundibar than the original Jewish child performers who found themselves confined behind barbed wire in a Nazi concentration camp. Their real-life anguish had to be avoided in a children's book, for it could be neither graphically reproduced nor transmuted by surrealist art. It is another Christian child in another text by Wilhelm Grimm, therefore, whose story more closely approximates little Gretel's. Pushed into a forest by a young mother who tries to shield her from the conflagration of war, the nameless girl victim in Sendak's 1988 picture book *Dear Mili* dies of starvation, yet lives on in a Judeo-Christian limbo supervised by a nurturing St. Joseph. When she returns to a dying mother who is now depicted, in Sendak's last illustration of the book, as just as old and wrinkled as the witch he drew in *The Juniper Tree,* the little girl has become an angel child. She is as dead as Anne Frank and all the other Holocaust child victims whom Sendak so lovingly planted into the gardenlike forest that the bearded St. Joseph has tended. And yet, like these child martyrs, she is also beatified, made immortal through the conjunction of verbal and visual art. Wilhelm Grimm's text of *Dear Mili* characteristically absolves the mother who has failed to save her child. But Sendak's illustrations for that text actually go far beyond that absolution, as he also wants us to forgive the European motherlands that so recklessly sacrificed both their Jewish and Christian children. By purging anger and sorrow, Sendak's exquisite rendering of this fable of reconciliation tries to come to terms with Germany's legacy of child abandonment.

And yet, when Wilhelm Grimm wrote down this saint's tale for a motherless girl named Mili, he must have realized the story's proximity to his more punitive legend, "Saint Joseph in the Forest." There, a bad mother and her equally wicked oldest daughter are mortally stung by snakes unleashed by the same kindly hermit whom Grimm describes, and Sendak draws, as a protector of neglected and homeless children. Misogyny, racism, and witch hunts that push imaginary child killers into fiery ovens can often come perilously close to narratives that purport to be conciliatory or therapeutic. Bettelheim's confident reading of "Hansel and Gretel" as a text that validates his prescriptions for "emotional well-being" seems subverted, whether intentionally or not, by Sendak's Brundibar representations of the rotund and childlike doctor who happily dances away after Aninku and Pepicek have followed his therapeutic directions. Is this physician naively overconfident about his own chances of becoming a survivor? Is his ludic vitality endorsed or called into question by the book's darker subtext? The Sendak/Kushner text seems to straddle carefully these two alternative possibilities.

III.

What defensive weapons, then, are available to the child who is determined to survive the real or the perceived trauma of abandonment? How can that fearful child acquire a sense of empowerment?[6] Gretel and Hansel bribe their weak father with treasures stolen from the witch they have killed; Sara Crewe redistributes the wealth she has regained in order to erase her memories of a double trauma: the loss of her father and the abuses she suffered at Miss Minchin's. Reparation and forgiveness are dramatized in *Dear Mili* when the nameless waif returns as a ghost child to ease her mourning parent's passage into the same death world into which she was prematurely thrust. The fatherless Aninku and Pepicek also return from an order that is potentially one of deprivation and death. They restore their mother to life by supplying her with the milk they had obtained, as babies, from her depleted breasts. Like Max's defiance of mother and monster or Sara's earlier resistance of Miss Minchin's abuse, these are fantasies of empowerment that those gifted ex-children who turn into adult authors try to share with young and old through their rich narratives and lush illustrations. Wounds, these survivors seem to insist, can be healed by both oblivion and wishfulness.

Survivorship Fantasies and Parental Desertion

There are, however, as I have already suggested by introducing the verses of Jarrell and Sexton, texts that tap what I have called the "Hansel and Gretel Syndrome" in ways that are decidedly nontherapeutic. By suggesting that psychic wounds may be irreparable or only partially capable of healing, an adult poem such as Jarrell's "A Quilt Pattern" contradicts the same writer's efforts to seek out child readers for his fables of restoration, *The Animal Family* and *The Bat-Poet*. In the first of these books, the wounded Hunter, scarred by the absence of dead parents whose desertion he cannot forget, is unable to replace the lost trinity of father, mother, and child until the miraculous appearance of a baby boy whose own lost parents he and the Mermaid can now replace. That couple's earlier two "children," the doglike Bear and the catlike Lynx, could not satisfy a lack produced by their intraspecies sterility, their inability to create a hybrid offspring. Now, however, a growing human boy can straddle—as Aninku and Pepicek did—what is presented as a double reality, his hunter "father's" land and his mermaid "mother's" more dangerous and more turbulent, because far more fantastical, sea world. And the couple's pets, the Bear and the Lynx, can now acquire new responsibilities of their own as the boy's loving guardians by operating as avuncular figures, much as Baloo and Bagheera, the caretakers of Mowgli the wolf boy, had done in *The Jungle Books* that Jarrell knew so well.

Mowgli, the baby abandoned by Indian woodcutters in the Seonee forest, is adopted by an animal family almost as fantastic as that concocted by Randall Jarrell. Rudyard Kipling's fantasies of restitution stemmed, as I have suggested in two earlier discussions of his work in *Children's Literature,* from memories of the physical abuse and emotional deprivation he suffered when his loving Anglo-Indian parents so abruptly left an unsuspecting Ruddy and his little sister Trix at the witch's abode he would later so bitterly call "the House of Desolation." Kipling's first account of that degradation in the 1888 novella *Baa, Baa, Black Sheep* (a fiction apparently stimulated by his reading, earlier that year, of Frances Hodgson's story of an Anglo-Indian child's desertion in her own novella *Sara Crewe,* the ur-text of *A Little Princess*) was separated by a half-century from the second account he reserved for the posthumous publication of his 1937 autobiography *Something of Myself.*

The decision to cast *Baa, Baa, Black Sheep* as a grim anti-Christmas story in which Ruddy became Punch and Trix became little "Ju" (or Judy) was a risky act of exorcism for Kipling. He had never told his parents what had happened after they inexplicably left him at the mercy of the child beater he drew as a witch in the manuscript illustrations reproduced in Thomas Pinney's fine edition of Kipling's autobiographical writings. Yet the story bitterly yokes a boy's rosy memories of a benign father and mother to their parental surrogate, the decidedly unrosy Aunty Rosa, Punch's relentless tormentor. Beaten with a cane and left alone "to weep himself into repentance," the boy makes a connection that proves far more painful than any of the blows he has received: "Aunty Rosa, he argued, had the power to beat him with many stripes. It was unjust and cruel, and Mamma and Papa would never have allowed it. Unless perhaps, as Aunty Rosa seemed to imply, they had sent secret orders. In which case he was abandoned indeed" (Kipling 1991a, 149,

150).

Randall Jarrell's wonderfully perceptive essay "On Preparing to Read Kipling" captures the dilemma of a writer who considered his artistic and gifted parents as his ideal readers. How could Kipling blame these "best of parents" for the severe trauma they had induced? It is exactly this contradiction, Jarrell shrewdly suggests, "that made Kipling what he was: if they had been the worst of parents, even fairly bad parents, even ordinary parents, it would all have made sense, Kipling would have made sense out of it. As it was, his world had been torn in two: for under the part of him that extenuated everything, blamed for nothing, there was certainly a part that extenuated nothing, blamed for everything—a part whose existence he never admitted, more especially not to himself" (Jarrell 1970a, 341).

Jarrell is correct here, yet Kipling did acknowledge that his childhood denigrations by a witchlike tormentor converted him into a successful fiction maker. The "bullying" he tried to offset by fibbing, Kipling claims in his autobiography, "made me give attention to the lies I soon found it necessary to tell: and this, I presume, is the foundation of literary effort" (Kipling 1991b, 6). The 1888 *Baa, Baa, Black Sheep* relies on artful deformations of the narrative that Kipling retold at the end of his life. Whereas the autobiography makes much of the refuge provided every December for five entire years by the boy's loving aunt, Georgina Burne-Jones, the story offers Punch no such shelter from child abuse. And, in a minor, yet telling change, the book that a loving father sends from India to England is none of the texts recalled and assessed in the autobiography. Instead of sending *Robinson Crusoe* or Mrs. Ewing's *From Six to Sixteen,* a work as important to Kipling as to Burnett, the father in *Baa, Baa, Black Sheep* sends his son a collection of Grimm fairy tales. Presumably, the volume contained "Hansel and Gretel," a story Kipling certainly remembered when he decided, a few years later, to cast Mowgli as an abandoned woodcutter's son. The story of a brother and a younger sister who are confused by the abrupt disappearance of their parents was a fictional analog for a real-life event that the young writer clearly could not bring himself to forget.

Kipling found it difficult to write more children's books after the Great War in which Europe betrayed millions of its young. But the carnage that claimed his son was followed by an even more massive betrayal that he, for all his bitter forebodings about German fascism, did not live to see. Hindsight, as Hamida Bosmajian and Adrienne Kertzer have shown in their recent studies of Holocaust representations in children's literature, has helped us reassess yet also disguise and sublimate the past for a generation of new young readers. Given her own adult readership, Louise Murphy's extraordinary novel, *The True Story of Hansel and Gretel,* published the same year as the Sendak/Kushner collaboration, allows her relentlessly to confront the atrocities that *Brundibar* tries to soften.

Amnesia becomes a leitmotif in a novel that boldly reconfigures as Jews the parents and children of Wilhelm Grimm's fairy tale. The mother—a stepmother, once again—who pushes the children into the dark forest hastily renames them and commands them to forget their actual Jewish names. The newly named "Gretel," now the older of the two siblings, blonde and blue-eyed, protects her younger and darker brother "Hansel." But, on being brutally raped in a Polish forest as treacherous as any of the dense woods in German fairy tales, the traumatized girl loses all memory of the past. In a further reversal of Grimm's emphasis, Murphy vindicates not only heroic stepmothers but also so-called witches. The crone who shelters the renamed children nurtures and tutors them and finally dies in their stead; she is a "righteous Gentile" whose act of sacrifice will remain anonymous and unrecorded. After this old gypsy woman, Magda, has been gassed at Auschwitz, an inmate prepares the corpses for cremation. "He tugged at the bodies," writes Murphy. "There weren't many children anymore. Most were dead already, he guessed. He wondered if there were any children left in the world, but he stopped his mind from the thought. Thoughts were luxuries that led to death" (Murphy 2003, 253).

Murphy's powerful revisions of "Hansel and Gretel" suggest that repression may, after all, be trauma's best antidote. Aided by dimmed recollections of his past, the boy called Hansel manages to recognize his surviving father at the end of the novel. But such a "happy" recognition is denied to the girl called Gretel, his older sister. She has no pearls and jewels to offer the weeping father who is reunited with the child he thought to have lost. Her identity has been erased. Her biological mother, her stepmother, and her surrogate mother, Magda, have all been killed. Forced to forget more than her own, long discarded, Jewish name, this young amnesiac is at least spared the horrors of her recent past.

Notes

1. Although Tatar's translation of the story's final 1857 version in *The Classic Fairy Tales* is much closer to the German original, I do like Jack Zipes's freer rendition of Wilhelm's enthusiasm in *The Great Fairy Tale Tradition:* "My, how happy they were!" (2001, 716).
2. Jack Zipes's "The Rationalization of Abandonment and Child Abuse in Fairy Tales" offers an extremely helpful overview of the various versions of Wilhelm Grimm's text, its indebtedness to antecedents in Perrault and Basile, as well as its relation to other nineteenth-century German texts such as August Stauber's 1842 "Das Eierkuchenhäuslein" and Adelheid Wette's libretto for the 1893 Humperdinck opera. Zipes's contention that the narrative was meant to offer "some form of justification, legitimation, and apology in the minds of parents" (1997, 60) for their abusive practices strikes me as plausible, even though my own emphasis and approach are substantially different. As a Jewish boy saved from Nazi extermination by his father and mother, I am understandably less interested in anatomizing parental betrayal than in recovering a child reader's baffled response to wider and scarier forms of adult treachery. A story that encouraged generations of future adults to exult in the incineration and plunder of fellow humans demonized as cannibalistic witches fascinates and repels me for reasons that are obviously as personal and idiosyncratic as those that have prevented me from regarding another German child-text of my boyhood, Heinrich Hoffmann's *Struwwelpeter,* as a production as delightfully grim as any work by Edward Gorey (see Knoepflmacher 2000, 88–92). One's critical shortcomings, however, can often prove to be quite instructive.

3. One of the few child survivors not killed at Auschwitz was in the audience. I asked "Ela" (who had sung the role of the Cat in the concentration camp's production of Brundibar) to sign my copy of the Sendak/Kushner book. I am honored to share her inscription with the readers of Children's Literature: "REMEMBER ME & MY FRIENDS."
4. In *Higglety Pigglety Pop!* Jenny, too, initiates a journey away from the home where she had "everything." But the sprightly dog does not know what her artist "master" knows, namely, that her translation to Castle Yonder has moved her into an everlasting bourne from which no earthly traveler can return.
5. Sendak told his audience at the 92nd Street "Y" that he did not want to be too overt in representing Brundibar as an Adolf Hitler look-alike. The Oliver Hardy baker, however, does make a reappearance in *Brundibar,* where he is shown loaded with a huge tray of pastries and confections that he has elevated above the reach of the hungry children. The visual resemblance between his Hitlerian mustache and Brundibar's fake whiskers is readily established by flipping over the subsequent four pages.
6. Another German text, also illustrated by Sendak, Wilhelm Hauff's *Dwarf Long Nose* (or *Zwerg Nase*), comes to mind. As I have elsewhere explained, this "odyssey of [a] boy who is abducted, deformed, and yet endowed with superior powers by an aged sorceress who stamps him with her own [Semitic] features meant much to me" as a refugee child (Knoepflmacher 2002, 8). It only now occurs to me that this other German storyteller called "Wilhelm" may well have written his *kunstmaerchen* about a boy called "Jacob" as a wry challenge to the 1812 or 1819 versions of "Hansel and Gretel" in order to express his dissatisfaction with the conformist ideology of the brothers Wilhelm and Jacob Grimm. His naming of the metamorphosed boy, however, also carries other connotations. The biblical Jacob underwent a momentous transformation after the flight from his parental home led to his renaming as "Israel," a fact that did not escape me as a child reader traumatized by the sudden disenfranchisement of Vienna's Jews. I desperately clung to fables that would counter the trauma of dispossession and disempowerment.

   Maureen Thum (1997) has valuably connected *Dwarf Long Nose* to other instances of Hauff's persistent fascination with Jewishness. She also notes that in his collection of fairy tales, the story of little Jacob's magical enchantment is followed by a more realistic tale called "Abner, the Jew Who Saw Nothing." That wry attack on blind bureaucrats who abuse a shrewd detective for his superior powers of observation was another, much reread, favorite of mine. I regarded Hauff's fairy tales as a welcome antidote to the anti-Semitic portraits in the otherwise attractive *kunstmaerchen* of Clemens von Brentano.

12

Gila Almagor's *Aviyah*

Remembering the Holocaust in Children's Literature

NAOMI SOKOLOFF

In recent years the field of children's literature has expressed special fascination with cross-writing. This term refers to texts that address a dual audience of children and adults, or ways in which literature travels across age boundaries. Studies in this area focus, for example, on children's books that are designed to appeal to adults, on adult literature that has been appropriated for young audiences, and on authors who have produced various versions of their own work with different readers in mind.[1] Thinking about cross-writing is a useful way to approach Gila Almagor's art as it deals with Holocaust survivors and with the continuing effects of war trauma on children.

Almagor, often called the leading lady of Israeli cinema, is best known as an actress. She is also the author of two bestselling works of fiction, *Hakayits shel Aviyah* (translated from the Hebrew as *The Summer of Aviya*), and *'Ets hadomim tafus* (translated as *Under the Domim Tree*). Both contributed significantly to a transformation in Israeli attitudes that took place in the 1980s and 1990s toward the Holocaust. During those years an intense new attention to the second generation emerged in literature and film, popular song, documentaries, and school curricula. This interest was accompanied by a new empathy for survivors and a new degree of identification with their experiences. *The Summer of Aviya,* telling the story of a little girl whose mother is a survivor, helped pioneer this trend. Gaining prominence in several cultural arenas, it appeared first as a novel for children (1985) and then as a play that was attended by both adults and children. A film version that achieved international fame came out in 1989. Crossing genre boundaries, the "Aviyah" phenomenon reached wide audiences of many ages. *Under the Domim Tree* (from 1992), is geared to young adult readers and further explores the experience of Holocaust survivors in Israel. It focuses on adolescents who are refugees from Hitler's Europe as they build a new life for themselves in a youth village. This novel, too, became a highly successful film, which was released in 1994.[2]

The Summer of Aviya

What is most striking about *The Summer of Aviyah* as a crossover phenomenon is how similar the various versions are to one another. The book, the play, and the film are exceptionally close in content. This can be ascribed partly to the fact that the author also served as screenwriter and producer. Furthermore, Almagor performed in the one-woman play as both mother and daughter, and in the film she stars as the mother. There, in addition, she provides voice-over narration to convey the words of the daughter who, as a grown-up, recounts the story of her childhood. In various capacities, then, and at several levels, Almagor's creative hand was central to this project, and she took relatively few liberties in terms of changing plot elements, characters, scenes, and even dialogue. Still, the different versions target different audiences. The book is clearly marketed as reading for children. The large font, the illustrations, the child protagonist, the chronological plot, the simple vocabulary, the narrative voice that patiently explains events—all are earmarks of children's literature. This text has also become required reading in Israeli schools. In other words, it is children's literature by virtue of the fact that adults believe young people should read it.[3] The film, in contrast, is geared toward grown-ups, both in its intensity and seriousness and in the way it assumes certain historical knowledge on the part of the viewers. The stage production falls in between. It has been performed at children's theaters and also at mainstream theaters.[4]

What, then, do all three "Aviya"'s have in common, what shifts from one version to the next, and how do these issues tie in with the treatment of trauma?

One factor that makes for closeness is that the book addresses very mature issues from the start. The plot in a nutshell is as follows: The year is 1951. Aviya, who is nine going on ten, has been living at an agricultural boarding school. Her mother, Henya, suffers bouts of mental illness. However, when she is well enough to leave the psychiatric hospital she brings Aviya home for a summer. In the following months the little girl oscillates between joy and heartbreak as she tries to forge a relationship with her loving yet emotionally fragile mother. Henya has been traumatized by her experiences during the Holocaust. The information about what she has gone through is sparse, but she bears a tattooed number on her arm, and Aviya's aunt reports that Henya fought bravely with the partisans. What Aviya knows firsthand is that her mother is by turns anxious, overprotective, neglectful, and filled with rage. At the end of the summer the mother's mental health deteriorates, and Aviya returns to the boarding school, her hopes dashed. In addition to offering an unusually unhappy ending for children's literature, this text engages boldly with the family's protracted mourning for Aviya's father, who died before she was born. Much of children's literature, even on the topic of the Holocaust, evades dealing with unrelieved grief. That this is so in the United States is not surprising, as optimism and hopeful endings are powerful dominant conventions in American children's literature and, more broadly, in American interpretations and approaches to the Holocaust.[5] But even in Israel—a more tragic society, where children are exposed early to stories of war and the Holocaust—*The Summer of Aviya* differs significantly from such well-known juvenile fiction as Uri Orlev's *The Island on Bird Street* (1981) or Tamar Bergman's *The Boy from Over There* (1983). Both of those Holocaust stories offer more upbeat accounts of youthful resilience. All told, *The Summer of Aviya* as a juvenile novel deals with sober themes and dramatic events that can readily speak to adults without major modification.

Moreover, the same story is effective for both children and adults, inviting a dual audience response, because informed grown-up readers will see more in the imagery here than young readers do. Take, for example, one of the central incidents of the plot, when the mother fetches Aviya from her school and, to her horror, finds lice in her daughter's hair. Muttering, "What is this, a concentration camp?" she roughly and without warning or explanation shaves Aviya's head. For months afterward this causes the little girl endless shame. Narrating retrospectively, Aviya refers to this time in her life as the "summer of baldness." Children may or may not associate baldness with images of concentration camps, and such associations are not spelled out in the book, but for adults the connection is clear and in the film it is visually inescapable. Furthermore, adults are more likely to know that in the camps lice were linked to disease, especially typhus. Lice therefore could be truly deadly and not just an ordinary nuisance. Mature readers may recall, too, that the shaving of heads was carried out as a deliberate humiliation of prisoners. Dealing as it does with such issues, *The Summer of Aviya* blurs boundaries between what is a child's text and what is an adult's. Again, this quality makes the novel highly adaptable for older audiences.

What, then, shifts from one version to the next? Almagor's shifting roles are key to understanding this issue. First, the mother becomes increasingly more visible. Henya, played by Almagor, comes to life much more in the play than in the book. The text primarily emphasizes the child's experience and features limited descriptive passages (as is typical of much contemporary children's literature).[6] In contrast, nuanced visual dimensions of this character are immediately evident in the theater; viewers can see love, worry, tension, toughness, beauty, craziness, harshness, and sexuality all at once as part of who Henya is. The film then extends focus on the mother through close-ups and camera work that directs our gaze to her. This shift of emphasis to the mother reveals that each new format reworks the mother-daughter relationship, exploring and redefining the boundaries between the two characters.

To see how this works, we should note that in the novel Aviya identifies intensely with her mother, yearns for her, and wants to understand her. These impulses culminate in the telling of the tale itself: the text is constructed as Aviya's memoir. In other words, Aviya as a grown-up continues to be riveted by her mother and attempts to interpret what happened between them. The same could be said of the author, for "The Summer of Aviya" was based on Almagor's own childhood. In the stage production Almagor plays both the mother and the daughter. Accordingly, the performance physically blurs the boundary between the two characters, casting both as aspects of one person (the adult who carries memories of her mother and of herself when she was a child). In the film, Almagor the actress moves even closer to the position of the mother. She is now separating from the child, who is played by someone else. In this way it is as if the film brings about a realization of young Aviya's intent to understand Henya. Internalizing the maternal character more and more, Almagor in effect takes on the mother's identity and becomes her.

This dynamic invites the kind of feminist interpretation that investigates fluid boundaries of mother-daughter relationships. For example, we might explore the work of Chodorow, Cixous, and Irigaray in this regard.[7] Here the phenomenon is especially charged because the daughter's identification with the mother is amplified by her hunger for parental love and role models and because of the emphasis on transmission of trauma. These add special urgency to the questions "How much are the two characters alike?" "How much are they different?" and "Where does one stop and the other begin?" Trauma in the plot blurs boundaries as it leads to a painful inversion of roles. Henya, in her illness, is referred to as a child who needs protection (Almagor 1991, 87). For her part, Aviya sees her mother's suffering and takes on the responsibility of caring for her, as if she were the adult. Further drawing together adult and child realms is the peculiar timelessness of trauma itself. Traumatized people often experience the past as continually recurring in the present. They relive painful events, frequently in the form of intrusive flashbacks and nightmares, or as vivid yet wordless images and sensations (Herman 1992). Certainly Henya, burdened with memories, relives the past as if it were present, and so she egregiously overreacts to the danger of the lice. This episode humiliates Aviya and has far-ranging ramifications. Other children torment and tease her about the baldness. Tensions build. Finally, excluded and scorned, Aviya hurls a rock at them in anger and hits a neighbor in the eye. Henya in turns hits her daughter for "the first time" with a brutality the little girl has never seen before (1985, 48 [original Hebrew version]). The violence the mother suffered during the war thus leads Aviya to uncover a capacity for brutality within both herself and her mother. The ripple effect demonstrates a direct line of transmission from the past to the present, as the child in the second generation shares in the trauma of the first. "The Summer of Aviya" dramatically underscores the ongoing effects and long-term impact of wartime suffering.

One of the ways that the film explores these ongoing effects on the second generation, while shifting the spotlight onto the mother and also separating the two characters, is by adding historical context. In the juvenile novel much is ahistorical. The little girl registers painful encounters from her childhood, but without much interpretation. The film, in contrast, explores more factors in the social environment that shape the lives depicted. This happens as the film tinkers with the plot and particularly as it introduces a subplot about a camp survivor who comes to the town. Henya takes care of this fellow, for he is completely traumatized, incapable of communicating with others. In this task she gets help from another neighbor, a man who shares her past and seems to have met her or heard of her back in Europe. A romantic connection between these two then adds another dimension to the story, further bringing out the common experiences of new immigrants to Israel who endured the Holocaust in Europe. Opposing newcomers with old-timers, these narrative moves help build the viewer's awareness of the historical moment and the social milieu in which the narrative events take place.

The setting for the story is the formative years of the 1940s and 1950s, when Israel was intent on nation building. During this period the young Jewish state set about constructing a new proud, militarily strong society, and Israelis conceived of themselves as a new breed, a kind of person who would be unlike the victimized Jews of the past. The Diaspora Jew, in this worldview, was associated with shameful passivity and weakness. Literature and film of that era often depicted refugees through the lens of such assumptions; new arrivals were viewed as unfortunates in need of rescue, new names, new homes, and new training so that they might become pioneers and soldiers in the Israeli mold. The film *Aviya* brings out these issues more extensively than the book, indicating pointedly that Henya and her two companions are outcasts. The film presents the mother as a once heroic partisan, recognized as such by her fellow refugees, but seen by the townsfolk as a pathetic and contemptible madwoman. The move, then, from book to play to cinema thereby illuminates the pressures on the child from the second generation. It is not just the trauma of the mother's past that shapes Aviya's misery but the response of her own society to Holocaust survivors that prolongs and complicates the trauma. This is the story of a child who has absorbed long-lasting effects of war, has suffered misunderstanding from her compatriots, and has grown up to recount her childhood, at long last expressing those painful, formative experiences and critiquing ways in which that society was unwelcoming of her and her mother.

In the late 1980s such stories show up with increasing frequency in Hebrew fiction, poetry, pop music, and documentary film. As they remembered their childhoods and their parents, second generation writers such as Nava Semel, Yehuda Polliker, and Savyon Liebrecht helped foster a reorientation in Israeli thinking about the Holocaust. They cultivated a new receptivity to the survivors' own stories, which were recognized and validated only belatedly as Israelis came to identify more closely with the Jewish past and with a history of persecution and victimization.[8] Almagor's novel was one of the first to deal with these issues. Consequently, this story, concerned with the transmission of trauma, played an important role in passing on stories of the Holocaust, transmitting them to a new generation, and mediating public understanding of Holocaust traumas and their long-term effects. We should note that, as children's literature, the book by definition engaged directly with the question of what to transmit to the next generation. It forcefully conveyed a message of empathy and compassion both for the mother and for the daughter who lives in the shadow of war, though she has had no direct experience of it herself.

Seeing the children's novel in relation to the play and the film encourages us to appreciate memory as a dynamic process and autobiographical fiction as part of an ongoing engagement with the past. The reworkings follow a therapeutic trajectory as the author gains distance from her childhood and greater understanding. However, the dynamics of cultural transmission are more complicated than my remarks so far have indicated, due to the complex relationship between Almagor's personal experience and her artistic material. *The Summer of Aviya* was promoted as autobiographical fiction, and the public received it as Almagor's own memoir of growing up. According to published accounts, though, Almagor's was not exactly the childhood recounted in the novel. Her family came to British Mandatory Palestine in 1936, and she was born in 1939.[9] This means that her mother could not have been a World War II partisan and also that she had left Europe before implementation of the Final Solution. It is true that Almagor's father died before she was born and that her mother did suffer from mental illness. In addition, Almagor had firsthand experience living in a youth village, an institution about which she has written with warm appreciation (1995, vii–ix). *The Summer of Aviya* thus grafted autobiographical elements onto a more prototypically second generation story. This move provides an interesting measure of changing attitudes in Israel since the period portrayed in the fiction. In the 1950s Aviya finds it shameful and isolating to have a mother who is a camp survivor. Yet, in the 1980s, Almagor makes special effort to reach out and integrate such a character deliberately into her plot, claiming this legacy as her own. As Almagor overlays the collective experience onto personal memories, she creatively mines her own feelings of orphanhood, loss, and exclusion to explore the situation of the second generation with sensitivity and imagination. Ultimately, it turns out, the restless rewritings are a way to come to grips both with her own personal childhood traumas and with collective Jewish traumas. By conflating them, Almagor constructs a story that is cathartic on both accounts.

Under the Domim Tree

The author's second novel presents an artistic reconfiguration of this same material, which extends the sympathetic treatment of survivors. At the same time it offers tribute to the child from a troubled family who, through personal tragedy, also suffers a great sense of displacement and loss. Following the main character into adolescence, *Under the Domim Tree* ostensibly provides a sequel to *The Summer of Aviya*. It, too, is conceived as Aviya's memoirs and explores her troubled relationship with her parents. However, a number of basic narrative elements have changed. The first story takes place in 1951. Now the year is 1953, but Aviya is already in high school and quite a bit older than she was before. Furthermore, her mother is not a Holocaust survivor. The second novel, then, is less a sequel than a reimagining of the Aviya character and her relationships with her family and with refugees. Her classmates, many of whom are Holocaust survivors and orphans, are haunted by their war-torn past and share with Aviya a desperate wish for parental love. Because of her father's death, and because of her mother's psychotic delusions of being a Holocaust survivor, Aviya feels a special affinity with her classmates. She respects their experiences at a time when they are still outsiders in the eyes of most Israelis. Wrestling with their grief and their individual tragedies, the young people quarrel and often feel lost, but ultimately they come together and serve as substitute family for one another. All are welcomed into the group. Even the most scarred among them, who by night endure nightmares and madness, by day adjust to the routines of the youth village and feel accepted into the community.

Under the Domim Tree is a celebration of Youth Aliyah, the Zionist effort to save Jewish children from Hitler and to absorb them into Israeli life. Often such children were placed in agricultural schools or kibbutzim. Earlier Hebrew literature that dealt with this theme emphasized the goal of redeeming youngsters and bringing them from death to rebirth by transforming them into the ideal of the New Israeli Jew, the sabra. Almagor introduces a vital new element to this familiar tale of rescue as she emphasizes the experiences and perceptions of survivors. Unlike the prevalent ideology of the 1950s that urged refugees to forget their former lives, *Under the Domim Tree* respects the integrity of their past and affirms the individuality of these characters. The significance of the title is that the tree on the hill is a place to find solitude within communal life. It is there that the kids go for contemplation, to be alone with private feelings, and to accord their memories a special place of honor.

Almagor thus renews and revises a cherished national self-narrative even as she redefines her own artistic use of autobiographical material. In the process she moves from children's literature to young adult fiction. The book bears a number of distinguishing features of young adult (YA) writing: the text is longer and the font is smaller than in *The Summer of Aviya*. There are no illustrations. The plot revolves around an adolescent protagonist, and it follows a typical YA formula, defined by Perry Nodelman as "a combination of underdog wish-fulfillment fantasy and therapeutic parable, that centers around a protagonist faced with one specific problem and a message of self-understanding [and] self-acceptance" (1992, 41). Almagor, it must be acknowledged, beautifully expands on this formula by juxtaposing four or five such stories. (All of the major characters want to find family. Aviya succeeds by identifying who her father was and where he is buried. The others similarly find out important information about their lost relatives.) By exploring variations on a theme and weaving them together, the author creates a rich narrative suite in which young people reconcile with their pasts and embrace the present. Still, for all its accomplished elegance, the novel remains in the YA category. Even while delving deeply into themes of loss and grief, Almagor produces a hopeful, inspirational message of a sort we might expect authors to direct at adolescents. The film too is YA. The plot remains much as it was, and the music adds a clearly didactic dimension. Together with the slow motion, it tells viewers what to feel, defining moments of angst and emphasizing moments of triumph.[10] In particular, the last scene shows tulips growing in the desert, under the domim tree, symbolizing the young people who have begun to blossom despite the barrenness in their lives.

The age orientation of this material is particularly significant here for, in arriving at young adult fiction, Almagor also arrives at a kind of resolution of earlier conflicts. This is a tale about making peace with trauma. The thematic emphasis is on acceptance of self and others—in particular, Holocaust survivors. In the plot, the native Israeli Aviya is accepting of her classmates. The author herself has also moved toward greater recognition of Holocaust survivors in that she deals with such characters in their own right rather than with the second generation. Furthermore, she proves more accepting of her own biographical background by disengaging from personal claims of being a second generation child herself. Finally, she accepts the national myth of Israel as redemptive haven, integrating that collective ideal with the story of adolescent self-acceptance. And, because both the book and the film are YA, the two versions are consistent with one another and reinforce one another rather than operating at cross-purposes. In contrast, *The Summer of Aviya* is more conflicted. Its three incarnations, at variance with one another, convey a restless, ongoing struggle on the part of the artist to come to terms with a painful past.

Despite all the acclaim Almagor has received, as a writer she has attracted very little serious literary interpretation or criticism.[11] Perhaps this is not surprising, given the generally low status of children's literature within literary studies. It rarely draws much substantive analysis from scholars outside the field of children's literature itself. Yet I would argue that children's literature and cross-writing merit particular attention here. It is specifically the unsettled quality of Almagor's creative process, the very experimenting with different media and audiences, that puts into relief the artist's effort to grapple with trauma. She engages and reengages with childhood memories, turning them this way and that, until she finally achieves a new sense of closure in her storytelling. Almagor is one particular case that richly illustrates why it is important to consider children's literature in relation to other literary and artistic production— so as to both understand the writer's creative process and gauge broad shifts in cultural outlook. *The Summer of Aviya* and *Under the Domim Tree* were stunning successes. Influential, beautifully crafted, humane, and moving, they become only more fascinating when we recognize the ways in which the stories about Aviya evolved, traveling across age boundaries and genres.

Notes

1. See especially Knoepflmacher and Myers (1997) and Beckett (1999).
2. *Under the Domim Tree* won the National Jewish Book Award in the United States after its 1995 publication in English.
3. See Nodelman (1996) and Nikolajeva (2003) on definitions and distinguishing features of children's literature.
4. The play has been performed in English for children's theater and was performed for

general audiences in September 2003 by the Habima Company in New York City.
5. Kertzer (2002) discusses the treatment of grief in children's literature that deals with the Holocaust. She points out how writing for adults and children often differ on this point. Mintz (2001) and Stier (2002) provide very useful overviews and assessments of American perspectives on the Holocaust.
6. Nikolajeva (2003).
7. Halpern (1995) pursues this line of inquiry.
8. For discussions of the second generation in Hebrew literature and changing attitudes toward the Holocaust in Israeli society, see Holzman (1992), Morahg (1997), Sicher (1998), Avisar (1998), Yaoz (1998), and Brenner (2002).
9. For biographical information on the author, I am relying on Avisar (1998), Chalvany (2003), and a personal conversation with Gila Almagor.
10. The film in fact modifies the ending, making this didactic point even more emphatically than the book does. Hunt (1996) considers the development and history of young adult fiction as a distinct genre of writing.
11. When scholars address her work, it is usually in connection with the films, and these are seen as part of a wider panorama of transformed Israeli attitudes toward the Holocaust (for instance, Avisar 1998). Other writers, including David Grossman and Savyon Liebrecht, have gotten significantly more attention. Sokoloff (2002) argues for the inclusion of Almagor in the canon of important Holocaust literature. Sokoloff (2004) presents discussion of narrative voice in *The Summer of Aviya*.

13

The Anxiety of Trauma in Children's War Fiction

Adrienne Kertzer

The Anxiety of Trauma, or Is It History?

Concerned that literary genres striving to make "history personally traumatic" (133) risk ignoring history's complexities, Kenneth Kidd (2005) observes that "historical fiction for children has become more than ever a metadiscourse of personal suffering that in turn demands pain from readers as proof of their engagement" (134). Speculating whether "we now expect reading about trauma to be traumatic itself" (120) and whether an apparent consensus exists "that children's literature is the most rather than the least appropriate literary forum for trauma work" (120), Kidd challenges my understanding of the representation of trauma in children's war fiction. For if his statements are true, then children's war fiction must be the exception to the norm, given how such fiction continues to be dominated by a variety of narrative strategies intended to soften the depiction of trauma and thereby negate the likelihood of secondary traumatization. The protagonist in most children's war fiction is rarely traumatized, and if she is, she very quickly recovers.

Rukhsana Khan's picture book *The Roses in My Carpets* is typical. Beginning with a traumatic, repetitive nightmare of a child fleeing a bomb-pitted landscape, Khan ensures that neither the reader nor the protagonist is left in this terrifying space. Barely able to run because he is dragging his mother and sister, the child protagonist is terrified that the jets overhead will kill him: "just as I'm about to die, or sometimes just after, I awake." Although we learn that the child fled Afghanistan, we never are told the identity of those flying the planes. This refusal to provide the specific historical context—exactly why are these people in a refugee camp?—is as characteristic of children's war books that depict trauma as is the promise that trauma can be overcome. For when the nightmare returns at the end, the child dreams a more hopeful version in which his mother and sister no longer hold him back: "While running, we find a space, the size of a carpet, where the bombs cannot touch us" (n.p.).

The reassuring ending of *The Roses in My Carpets* is consistent with the pedagogical intent of a recent anthology, *Lines in the Sand: New Writing on War and Peace:* "The writers and artists who have contributed to this anthology want you to know. . . . But they don't want to make you despair" (Hoffman and Lassiter 2003, 4). A recent study by Kate Agnew and Geoff Fox of twentieth-century children's books about war barely mentions trauma. The authors conclude that the writers they examine share a belief that "young readers need narratives which explore the nature and experience of war if they are to make sense of the world they have inherited and the future they confront" (Agnew and Fox 2001, 179). Presumably depictions of traumatized experience do not contribute to this need. Observing that there has been a "gradual shift . . . from the cultural certainties of 1914 to the pluralism and ambiguities of 2000" (1), they do not address what place, if any, the representation of trauma has played in this shift.

In children's war fiction, sustained exploration of psychological trauma remains the exception rather than the rule. Situating the limited treatment of trauma within a discourse of explanatory knowledge is also strikingly different from the representations of subjective experience we have come to expect and valorize in adult texts. However, the distinction between trauma as subjective experience and trauma as an event is not simply a generic difference between children's and adult texts; the meaning of trauma continues to be contested, and this ongoing debate has obvious implications for representational practices.[1] Patrick J. Bracken, the author of several works critical of universalizing Western therapeutic models of trauma, ends *Rethinking the Trauma of War* by quoting a Rwandan child's plea "not for therapy, but for justice" (Bracken and Petty 1998, 192). This plea for justice may well be served by the explanatory model that is the norm in children's war fiction.

Ruth Leys, noting the instability of the concept of trauma, challenges "the currently modish idea that the domain of trauma is the unspeakable and unrepresentable" (2000, 304). The notion of the unrepresentable derives from a distinction between traumatic and ordinary memory, one that may seem to privilege adult texts' representations but really makes all narrative representations of trauma—not just children's war fiction—necessarily inadequate. According to this distinction, traumatic memories "may have no verbal (explicit) component whatsoever" (van der Kolk 1996, 287), and trauma is something we experience but cannot narrate in any coherent fashion. The moment that we can narrate it, it becomes something else, a story that we can control. To talk about trauma is always to substitute a narrative for what cannot be narrated.

But if van der Kolk is wrong, then what we find in children's war fiction is troubling not necessarily because of its strategies for representing trauma but because its commitment to depicting trauma apparently exists in an inverse ratio to its willingness to probe the historical details that directly contribute to the trauma.[2] *Lines in the Sand: New Writing on War and Peace* definitely acknowledges that traumatic experience is a part of war; it also subscribes to the belief that "names and dates don't matter" (Hoffman and Lassiter 2003, 35). Traumatic representations become problematic precisely when we shift from what we perceive as individual trauma to cultural, historic, or collective trauma.[3] Many North American children's books successfully explore trauma in relation to family dynamics, for example, the death of a parent (Zibby Oneal's *A Formal Feeling*) or a sibling (Tim Wynne-Jones, *The Maestro*). The same is true of classics of British children's literature—Frances Hodgson Burnett's *The Secret Garden* is one canonical text that depicts traumatized children; J. K. Rowling's Harry Potter books are others.

Anxieties regarding both history and trauma emerge as soon as adult books touching on historical trauma are rewritten for child or young adult readers. For example, when the Canadian Métis author Beatrice Culleton published *In Search of April Raintree,* her treatment of racial and sexual abuse was viewed as too disturbing for many adolescent readers.[4] Culleton agreed to the request of the Manitoba Department of Education to produce a revised text, *April Raintree.* It is likely that the impossibility of separating the trauma of the protagonist's brutal rape from historical trauma (the treatment of Canada's First Nations) helped to make the original text controversial. Culleton's revisions may be comparable to the choices made when other historical trauma narratives are rewritten for young readers.

Joy Kogawa's *Obasan,* an adult novel much praised for its exploration of Japanese-Canadian trauma in World War II, is another text that has been rewritten for children. Kogawa's adaptation for young readers, *Naomi's Road,* confirms that in children's war fiction both the vicious details of historical events and the traumatic responses/perceptions of the witnesses to those details are subdued. In *Naomi's Road,* war is vague, "a terrible terrible thing" (1986, 13). Just as no adult answers the child protagonist's questions about the continuing absence of her mother, the text does not give child readers any answers about what happens to Naomi's mother after the bombing of Nagasaki. *Naomi's Road* ends with the minister's pronouncement, "The world is full of signs. We have to know how to read them" (82), but history in this children's book remains secretive, and it is history itself that is the secret. Like many authors who rewrite their own disturbing historical texts for children, Kogawa is unwilling to disturb her young readers by revealing that Naomi is traumatized or that she ever learns about the horrific death of her mother.

Naomi's Road begins with a letter to child readers reassuring them that "we are all Canadians together," but that long ago, there was a "sad" situation that was "hard to understand" in which Japanese-Canadians were regarded as enemies. The refusal to depict either the trauma or the facts contributing to it produces a narrative traumatized in its very telling but inadequate as historical fiction for that very reason. Just prior to her departure for Japan, Naomi's mother tells her, "A match is safe if you know how to blow it out" (7). After the war, when the mother fails to return, Naomi wonders, "But what if the whole world was on fire? How could you blow that out?" (70). Only readers familiar with the details of the adult text, *Obasan,* would understand this allusion or Naomi's later dream about her mother singing in a burning rose, as references to the bombing of Nagasaki.

Signs of our anxiety regarding children's exposure to trauma appear not only in war fiction. On September 11, 2001, North American children repeatedly watched television footage of the World Trade Center imploding and the consequences of the Pentagon having been attacked. It quickly became evident that adults were both distressed by their own viewing and worried about the psychological impact on children. Newspaper articles the morning after reported how teachers handled students' questions; some quoted psychologists giving advice to parents; columnists who were also parents wrote of their own dilemma in speaking to children about what they had seen. Within days, the inability of the ongoing television coverage to distinguish between adult viewer and child viewer produced further concern about the exposure of children to traumatic viewing. Mr. Rogers was asked his advice on how to calm children's fears. *Sesame Street* introduced episodes to assist children in dealing with post-traumatic anxiety.

Similar adult interventions have continued to appear. In *130 Questions Children Ask about War and Terrorists*—a 2002 adaptation of their 1991 text, *The War Is Over but Children Still Have Questions*—Stephen Arterburn and David Stoop promise to make parents and teachers "instant expert[s] in the areas of war and terrorism" (xvi). Only one of their recommended resources for further information is described as helping children ages six to twelve to deal with trauma, and only two of their questions incorporate traumatic responses: the question "When will my nightmares stop?" (66), and the question "Why am I still mad even though the war is over?" (69). Perhaps the authors' religious faith accounts for their desire to reassure children that God still cares. However, a comparable impulse governs the dominant depiction of trauma in children's war fiction to such a degree that the muted representation of trauma currently functions as a generic characteristic. In contrast to a willingness to set aside other narrative conventions that might distinguish between children's literature and adults' literature, we remain far more reluctant to abandon self-imposed limitations upon depicting trauma.

Trauma and History in *I Am David*

The belief that children's war fiction only needs to communicate generalized truths about war has resulted in fantasy being far more adept at complex representations of trauma. In fantasy, faithfulness to historical details is irrelevant. In contrast, the facts—what happened when—do matter in historical fiction. We might believe that they belong more in history textbooks, but to ignore them completely produces fiction that seems unable to tell children more than universal statements about the horror of war. The anxiety about representing trauma in historical fiction then may point to a deeper uncertainty regarding the nature of historical evidence.

Lydia Kokkola proposes in her work on Holocaust children's literature that the "understanding of history's factuality [is] more relevant than a precise understanding of when the events took place" (2002, 49). It is difficult to comprehend how we can separate the one from the other. How do readers separate their understanding that a novel is based on something that really happened from attentiveness to what really happened? A "precise understanding" does matter, both of history and of trauma as something that occurs within a particular history to particular individuals. Kokkola's perspective is in part a response to Holocaust denial, yet indifference to historical precision in trauma-inflected war fiction can encourage us to give children amazingly confused texts. Furthermore, appreciation of their depiction of trauma can lead readers—because so many tend to be historically ignorant—to mistake the relationship between the texts and historical events.

This misreading is aggravated because many children's war books cannot decide if they are allegorical examinations of the universal horrors of war or realist, factual depictions. The best example of a genre-confused and historically misleading text is Anne Holm's *I Am David*. An award-winning novel first published in Denmark in 1963 as *David* and published in England in 1965, it is sold in the United States under the title *North to Freedom*. Under the latter title, it appears in Edward T. Sullivan's bibliography, *The Holocaust in Literature for Youth*. What is odd about this inclusion is that Sullivan acknowledges that Holm's protagonist, David, escapes from an "eastern European concentration camp" (1999, 54), most likely a Stalinist camp, but Holm's vagueness encourages confusion. All that readers are told is that David is mysteriously allowed to escape the only place he has ever known. He does this by following the instructions of an unnamed guard (a man he hates), who tells him to go south to Salonica, board a ship going to Italy, and then go north to Denmark. Sullivan is not the only one to categorize *I Am David* as Holocaust fiction. Although Lydia Kokkola observes that "it is offensive to describe this book as being 'about the Holocaust'" (2002, 55) and condemns its historical inaccuracies, she accepts that the book was "one of the first attempts to write about the Holocaust for young readers" (57). In contrast, Agnew and Fox identify the setting of *I Am David* as postwar Europe but praise the novel's universal and allegorical aspects.

Confusion about the novel's setting also characterizes the earliest reviews where we find a debate about whether the camp David escapes from was a concentration camp, a deported persons camp, or a camp in an unspecified Iron Curtain country. The central issue discussed is whether children's fiction suffers if the historical location is so indeterminate.[5] Given that *I Am David* has been translated into more than twenty languages and "has sold over one million copies" (Kokkola 2002, 55), the novel clearly appeals to many either in spite, or because, of its factual confusion. Pedagogical articles are still written in which teachers are instructed on how to use this novel in their Holocaust units.[6]

This amazes me. If Holm knows anything about conditions in Nazi concentration camps, she is unwilling or unable to tell child readers what she knows. David's limited memories are totally inappropriate to conditions in Nazi camps.[7] The novel's depiction of trauma is also significantly different from our current understanding of it. Despite the constant reference to David's strangely vacant eyes, his fear of being touched, and his inability to smile, despite the repeated comment, "I don't think you're all there" (1965, 24), Holm presents David's problems with memory as the consequences of choice. While this emphasis on choice may account for the novel's success as a children's book, it also reduces our ability to regard David as traumatized. In most instances, he has either deliberately chosen not to remember or has been protected by not being informed. Choice and human freedom—learning to think for oneself—are the central issues. David knows the name of the guard who releases him; as a matter of principle, he refuses to use the guard's name just as he refuses to name the country that has imprisoned him or identify the language that "*they* spoke" (32). We immediately learn that the unnamed language cannot be German because David is willing to admit that he can speak German. We also learn that he is not Jewish.[8]

As in many children's books, Holm provides numerous clues about the unnamed people who are David's enemy, but readers require prior historical knowledge to recognize the clues. For example, David knows that his enemy hates Americans more than other people. He trusts a priest because "a priest was never one of *them*" (1965, 107). He also believes that only countries that have kings are free and that the only books worth reading were published prior to 1917. When David picks a book, he checks the date of publication "because he wanted to be sure that what was in it was true and not something *they* had made up" (85). After the success of the novel, Holm expressed concern that teachers gave the book to immature nine-year-olds ("Anne Holm" 2002). It is not clear why a mature older child would recognize that David's enemy is the freedom-hating Communist when mature adult readers still refer to her novel as a Holocaust text.

A romantic fairy tale about a child's quest for his mother, *I Am David* represents David's inability to recall the past as a protective strategy. David does not know who he is because he has not been told. In light of Holm's confession regarding her own "miserable childhood" ("Anne Holm" 1989, 123)—"I was never taught to think; I suppose that's why I don't remember much" (125)—David may also not remember because he has been taught not to think. Only one narrative detail supports a traumatic reading; it is the way that David, who was separated from his mother at age one, instinctively pauses when he stumbles upon her photograph eleven years later.

Rather than dismiss this moment as just one more example of Holm's excessive reliance upon coincidences, I prefer to read it autobiographically. In the account of her life that she wrote for Gale, Holm briefly mentions that during World War II, her first husband and baby fled to Sweden. She is very reticent, explaining only that they did it "for safety" and that after the war she divorced this husband and was never able to find out what had happened to her son ("Anne Holm" 1989,

133). The traumatic moment of recognition in *I Am David* may be a response to this experience, the way a child immediately recognizes the image of his mother and then does not stop until he finds her. At the end of this very peculiar novel, a mother who has not seen her son for nearly ten years opens the door and confirms his identity, "My son David" (Holm 1965, 159). No further dialogue ensues to trouble the perfect fantasy reunion and recognition. David does not need to ask questions; the mother does not need to justify her own behavior. In contrast, in her autobiographical account for Gale, Holm mentions that her son contacted her in 1964, one year after the publication of *I Am David* ("Anne Holm" 1989, 135). Whether this was a consequence of her sudden fame is not clear; she does not say what they talked about or what the result of the meeting was.

Once David is told the story behind the photograph, he suddenly and coherently understands that a camp guard, in love with his mother, ensured the murder of his father, the escape of his mother, and his own survival. The adult who tells David this "grown-up story" (Holm 1965, 122) also assures him that "all suffering has an end" (122). This assurance is as characteristic of children's fiction as it is alien to our current focus on the endless repetitions of trauma. Managing to conceal the historical and minimize the traumatic, Holm constructs a plot that hinges on the prison guard's ambivalence. The guard hates David yet feels responsible for him, and both feelings are attributed to the "mother who would have nothing to do with him" (124). Is this not the way a woman who has had nothing to do with her son might construct an ideal narrative that puts her back into the picture? The mother just waits, and one day the son returns.

Angry Protagonists, Traumatized Others, and Lessons about Trauma

In the decades since Holm's novel was published, children's writers have become more willing to represent the specific historical horrors of the past century. The child in the concentration camp no longer resembles Holm's David, who thinks that he is being punished when he is forced to drink his milk and swallow his vitamins. Our conception of trauma as something over which we have no control, however, continues to conflict with our insistence that stories offer child readers narratives of choice. As a result, in recent children's war fiction, trauma remains predominantly the story of the Other, the one who is traumatized and therefore is both unable to narrate her own story and unable to act. In such cases, the protagonist is relatively free of trauma and survives because of that freedom; the traumatized self is another, whom the narrator or protagonist observes and explains to the reader.

Instead of a traumatized child, we find an angry child protagonist (the child narrators of Carol Matas's *Daniel's Story* and Jane Cutler's picture book, *The Cello of Mr. O,* and the child protagonist, Clara, in Kathy Kacer's *Clara's War*). The depiction of modern war that the child reader is offered increasingly acknowledges the legitimacy of anger. But if anger is acceptable, trauma remains dangerous. Inevitably these books offer an unintentional warning about the inverse relationship between trauma and survival. Kacer repeatedly reminds the reader that Clara survives Terezin because of luck; it is hard not to conclude that the bad luck of Clara's friend, Hanna, a child who does not survive, extends to her susceptibility to trauma when she arrives in the camp.

Our reticence regarding trauma also affects our willingness to explore postwar lives. Certainly in the case of North American children's books about the Holocaust, the child survivor's postwar trauma was for many years a story that was rarely told, particularly from the protagonist's perspective.[9] A discourse in which children were meant to learn the "lessons" of the Holocaust did not regard lessons about postwar trauma as a priority. Growing adult interest in the memoirs of child survivors has started to alter this situation. One example is Lillian Boraks-Nemetz's trilogy about Slava Lenski, a child survivor whose traumatic memories continue after she immigrates to Canada. Drawing on her own experience as a child survivor, Boraks-Nemetz insists that "the child survivor never recovers, though he or she may find a way to live that is least painful" (1999, 163). This may explain why the first novel about Slava, *The Old Brown Suitcase: A Teenager's Story of War and Peace* "received twenty-five rejections from Canadian publishers, many saying that the young adult audience wouldn't identify with this type of story or with its victim protagonist" (1999, 163). Boraks-Nemetz uses a retrospective narrative in which traumatic flashbacks of hiding from the Nazis are framed by an ultimately hopeful story of immigration in which the adolescent protagonist learns to adjust to her new Canadian identity. The distance of postwar Canada from the traumatic site clearly enables the novel's relatively safe exploration of trauma. The safety, however, is ambiguous because Slava's traumatic memories are nearly always prompted by the anti-Semitism that she experiences in Canada. What also makes Boraks-Nemetz's depiction unusual is that she insists that Slava will never recover from the loss of her sister. In the third part of the trilogy, *The Lenski File,* Slava is eighteen years old and still searching for her sister.[10] Boraks-Nemetz dedicates this novel to the "memory of my grandmother who saved my life and my sister whom I shall always seek."

Representing Trauma and History in World War I Fiction

Like fiction on the Armenian genocide, children's fiction about the Holocaust may be more reluctant to represent trauma than other children's historical fiction.[11] The paradoxical simultaneity of Holocaust denial and the widespread discourse that refers to the Holocaust as "unbelievable" and "unimaginable" has definitely muted the representation of trauma in these books, but conventions for representing trauma in children's war fiction may be war specific in that we may be more willing to expose readers to the experience of trauma in one war than in another. Yet if we consider the evidence of Canadian children's novels about World War I, we find that they too prefer minimal and factual depictions of trauma. Agnew and Fox observe that children's books about World War I published in the last thirty years are far "less romanticized and more ambivalent" (2001, 14) than those written earlier. Recent fiction's ambivalence toward World War I does not lessen its reticence regarding trauma.

Consider three recent examples published in Canada about boys' participation in World War I. The first, Sharon E. McKay's *Charlie Wilcox,* won the 2001 Geoffrey Bilson Award for Historical Fiction for Young People, stresses the naïveté of the young Newfoundland men who expected war to be their "great adventure" (2000, 129), and provides a lesson about the carnage of war. Told by his father to learn to see, not merely look (93), Charlie Wilcox, the fourteen-year-old protagonist, is a model observer, but he is never a soldier. Thinking that the ship he has boarded will enable him to join the seal hunt, he is surprised to learn that he is accompanying the Newfoundland Regiment to England. Charlie remains a fairly comic protagonist, experiencing the war as a medical assistant only because he is so recklessly determined to go to France that he boards another ship by wearing a stolen Red Cross armband. Despite what he then sees at the Battle of the Somme, he remains reckless and stays at the front only because he foolishly decides that he must not lose the spyglass his father has given him.

McKay conveys little interest in depicting trauma other than giving Charlie a few bad dreams. She also avoids narrating trauma by leaping suddenly from the beginning of the Battle of the Somme, in July 1916, to April 1919. In the conclusion, we learn that Charlie witnesses numerous battles, but how or whether they psychologically affected him we never know. Even at the Battle of the Somme, he serves as an observer, the one who sees others die and attends the wounded, all the time drawing appropriate lessons about the futility of war: "There's got to be another way" (2000, 199). By the time he returns home to Newfoundland, he is wounded and unrecognizable to his mother. Thus despite its critique of war, *Charlie Wilcox* ends both comically and conventionally, both in its avoidance of trauma and its gendered depiction of war. Charlie's mother does not recognize him because he comes home a man. That Charlie in 1916 heroically gives up his return ticket so that a pregnant nurse can go home only reinforces the latter convention.

Iain Lawrence's *Lord of the Nutcracker Men,* through its reliance upon fantasy and the relative safety of its English setting, is more willing to explore war's trauma than many of the novels that take their protagonists to the front. Yet the story of Murdoch, the doubly traumatized soldier who wounds himself in order to escape the battlefield, remains the story of the traumatized other. The account of his suffering and his fugitive return to England where he fears being executed for desertion is framed through the narration of the ten-year-old protagonist, Johnny. Sent to his aunt's house while his mother works in a factory, Johnny entertains himself by playing with the toy soldiers that his father sends him from the front. In an early letter, his father introduces the dilemma about what to tell Johnny about war: "I want so badly to tell you that everything is fine, that I'm having a splendid adventure" (2001, 38). A toy soldier accompanies each of the father's letters. One figure, formed with hands still trembling after a disastrous attack, is so horrifying that Johnny's aunt destroys it: "That's not fit for a boy to play with" (130). In his next letter, Johnny's father apologizes: "It was one thing to set out to tell you the truth about the war; but another thing altogether to weigh you down with all my fears and worries" (138).

Despite the efforts of his aunt and his father, Johnny cannot be protected; Murdoch's voice and body function to contest the truth of the father's letters. The next time that Johnny encounters Murdoch, he sees a double of the twisted toy soldier: "He was the dog-faced soldier my father had made, a weary and horrid thing that groped along, that . . . stopped, and moaned, then started again" (Lawrence 2001, 145). Yet the novel's main interest lies elsewhere. Two questions obsess Johnny and deflect attention from Murdoch. The first is Johnny's growing suspicion about his father's letters; the second is his fear that the games he plays with his toy soldiers have given him an ability to control the events of the war. Taught that Homer in the *Iliad* depicts the gods as playing with people, treating them as "pieces in a great game" (60), he imagines destroying all the German toy soldiers in a single battle. The fantasy reveals his real desire: "My little wooden father would be right at the center; he would kill half of them himself, and my real dad would come home a week later, with medals all over his chest" (152).

As Johnny comes to discredit his father's letters (including the letter that reports the strange but true Christmas day in 1914 when soldiers temporarily stopped fighting in order to exchange "presents and photographs" [Lawrence 2001, 204]) and finds Murdoch's account of the war to be more convincing, he stops playing war games. But when Johnny decides to put away his toy soldiers that same Christmas day, his fantasy regarding his power as the lord of the nutcracker men to affect the outcome of the real battles is left open: "I really didn't want to know" (204). In the final paragraphs of the novel, we learn that after the war, Murdoch writes poetry that makes people cry. One poem is about the resemblance between the toy soldiers and the real soldiers of the war, but it is a poem that we cannot read. Murdoch is the real nutcracker man; to end with his traumatized voice would be to move outside the discourse of children's books. The one time that Johnny observes Murdoch having a flashback, he acknowledges, that "what he was seeing I couldn't even guess" (168).

The third example of World War I fiction, John Wilson's *And in the Morning*, is more willing to disrupt the conventions governing the representation of trauma and the gendered depiction of war. Nevertheless, Wilson relies on a narrative frame to distance the reader: the story of the traumatized protagonist/adolescent soldier, Jim Hay, is presented to the sixteen-year-old narrator as a gift from his long-dead great-grandfather. In a sense, the temporal distance is doubled because the great-grandfather gave the narrator his World War I diary when he was just a baby, but left instructions that he not receive it until he turned sixteen. The diary enables the narrator to learn the secret of his great-grandfather's identity, who is also named Jim. It also allows Wilson to provide a relatively safe and therefore more thorough representation of war trauma than is usually found in such books.

When World War I starts, the fifteen-year-old Jim is delighted. But after his father dies in action, Jim watches hysteria destroy his mother. Although this does

The Anxiety of Trauma in Children's War Fiction

not stop him enlisting, he begins to notice how some faces of wounded soldiers resemble his mother's during her illness. Later forced to watch a soldier shot for deserting, Jim draws on the experience of his mother's illness, to recognize the shell shock that caused the soldier's behavior. Nightmares of a black dog start to torment him, and when he finally faces battle (like Charlie Wilcox, Jim is a participant in the Battle of the Somme), he is traumatized and eventually court-martialed for desertion. Wondering if his madness is inherited, he goes to his death still traumatized. The inability to see that hysteria and shell shock are related disorders is the subject that Wilson explores. The crime his novel condemns is how this failure allowed armies to execute their own men.

Trauma and Maternal Voices

In both *And in the Morning* and *The Lord of the Nutcracker Men,* the depiction of war trauma includes maternal experience. The narrator of *And in the Morning* observes his mother's breakdown upon hearing of her husband's death. In *The Lord of the Nutcracker Men,* Johnny's mother plays a minor role; only in the conclusion do we learn that his father survived the war but his mother did not, having died from the effects of working with chemicals at a shell factory. In comparison, Mirjam Pressler's *Malka* goes much further in its attentiveness to maternal narratives and its willingness to represent trauma as the experience of the protagonist. While it may be too early to tell whether September 11, 2001, and the subsequent "War on Terror" will produce a greater willingness to represent trauma in children's war fiction, I read *Malka* as exemplifying what a less anxious narrative might entail.

Malka bears a Young Picador imprint, but its depiction of trauma is what we are more likely to find in adult literature. Pressler, the editor of Anne Frank, *The Diary of a Young Girl: The Definitive Edition,* has written a novel about a hidden child, Malka Mai, that is simultaneously the story of a mother, Hannah Mai. The mother leaves her child behind during her escape from Poland to Hungary and then desperately tries to find her.[12] Taking place between September 1943 and March 1944, *Malka* is exceptional for giving equal time to the perspectives of the seven-year-old, bewildered Malka and her equally confused mother, Hannah. It is also unusual in its exploration of trauma, both the child's and the mother's, and its refusal to give easy lessons—should Hannah be blamed for abandoning her child when Malka is too ill to journey over the mountains? Should Malka be blamed for rejecting her mother at the end?

In her afterword, Pressler explains the relationship between the novel and the real Malka Mai's story, including the fact that the real Malka Mai was both too young to remember and had "suppressed much of what had happened" (2002, 245). Although she informs us that the real Malka "was brought by her mother from Poland a second time and taken to Hungary" (245) and eventually to Palestine, Pressler does not mention that after March 1944, Hungary became as dangerous for Jews as Poland. Telling us that Malka's real mother did not immigrate to Israel until after 1948 and that, when she did, she did not live with her daughter,

Pressler implies that the real mother and daughter remained alienated. She also never tells the rest of the mother's Holocaust story—was she deported after she arranged for her daughter's escape? Did she spend the rest of the war in hiding? Pressler's narrative omissions reflect the dilemma regarding historical knowledge in children's fiction—how much history do readers need to know in order to understand the fictional characters' story?

Pressler does not address how historical ignorance affects our recognition of the bleakness of the ending. Like Malka's mother, we are sufficiently disturbed by what we do know. Instead, Pressler focuses on the trauma of her central characters. Inspired by the real Malka Mai's disjointed memories, she structures a narrative in which the fictional child's story is presented as a series of fragments. She foregrounds questions of memory even before Malka is abandoned by her mother and left to fend for herself in several ghettos, for Malka's narrative begins with a series of contradictory statements regarding one's ability to control memory. Malka thinks that she will "never forget that day at the beginning of last winter when she had nearly drowned" (Pressler 2002, 2). Going to play that morning, she is told by her mother not to forget that she is expected elsewhere in the afternoon, and she promises "I won't forget" (4). Yet Pressler quickly reveals that Malka cannot remember her father and is soon shocked into suppressing the painful memory of the mother who has left her behind when her feet were so swollen and infected that she could not walk. As far as Malka is concerned, the doctor who made this medical decision is someone other than the woman who was once her mother. The child is never able to understand her mother's behavior, just as she is not able to understand what occurs in the ghettos.

Initially, the angry and confused Malka invents picture games as a strategy for reducing the boredom she feels in the ghetto: "If she saw something she really liked, so much that she never wanted to forget it, she looked at it for a long time" (Pressler 2002, 85). This game accounts for the fragmented images of the traumatized self. When Malka is later imprisoned, she turns to memories of her collection of pictures. But as her experience worsens, she becomes unable to control them; images recur that she does not want to see. Numerous adults state that "nobody notices children" (68), and this both contributes to Malka's trauma and reflects its nature. Looking at herself in a pool of water, she sees fragments and soon not even that. The child who once nearly drowned sees her identity vanish; she becomes invisible. The greater trauma of her wartime experiences triggers her traumatic memory of the suppressed earlier anti-Semitic incidents that provoked her near drowning. Trying to hold the self together, Malka believes that excretion will destroy her, until finally, ill with typhoid, she concludes, "I've crapped myself away" (193). She observes that she is no longer the child she once was: "No longer was she Malka Mai, the daughter of Doctor Hannah Mai; she was some other girl who happened to be called Malka Mai" (204). She is the traumatized child, shocked into dissociation, tormented by nightmares, unable and unwilling to speak.

What permits this unusually detailed exploration of the subjective experience of trauma is the equal attention given to the mother's experience. Through this narrative strategy, Pressler can provide some of the historical information that is often minimized in children's fiction. She does not set up a structure in which the child is traumatized and the mother is not. Instead she deconstructs their difference, depicting Hannah as equally naïve and childlike —both in her prewar confidence that Nazis would never target her and in the parallel between the mother's wartime flight to Hungary and back to Poland and that of her daughter. Hannah and Malka repeatedly mirror each other. Both keep their heads down, berate themselves for their abandonment of others (in Malka's case, the doll Liesel), desperately mistake others for the one they most desire, and are so traumatized that they feel invisible. What differentiates them is the way their trauma reverses their parent-child roles, so that by the time Hannah cries "as a child" (Pressler 2002, 221), Malka has lost the very ability to cry or respond. Toward the end of the novel, Hannah is forced to acknowledge "what she had been suppressing all this time" (233), that even if she can rescue Malka, her daughter will be transformed, forever scarred by what has happened.

The ending of *Malka* disrupts many of the conventions regarding the depiction of trauma and the representation of mothers in children's war fiction. In contrast to the mother at the end of *I Am David*—"the woman whose eyes had seen so much and yet could smile" (Holm 1965, 159)—Hannah in *Malka*, returning to Poland and managing to find her daughter, bursts into tears when Malka refuses to acknowledge her and calls in panic for another female caregiver. In the novel's final sentence, Malka, who has never been able to comprehend her mother's behavior, "look[s] up in bewilderment" (244) at this strange woman crying. Depicting the mother's traumatized quest as well as the daughter's, Pressler rejects the clarity and triumph of Holm's ending to *I Am David* and rethinks the war-related trauma of children's fiction. In so doing, she emphasizes how the traumatic effect of war includes both mother and child and demonstrates how to explore this subject without sacrificing historical precision. The space of trauma opens as Pressler challenges us to think about children's war fiction differently, as a space in which trauma is one of the truths of war, and neither parent nor child is safe.

Notes

1. For a useful overview of current scientific research on trauma, see McNally (2005).
2. I argue that this is also true of Louise Murphy's *The True Story of Hansel and Gretel*, discussed by U. C. Knoepflmacher in this volume.
3. The notion of cultural trauma is also contested. See Kansteiner (2004).
4. The critical edition of *In Search of April Raintree* refers to the author as Beatrice Culleton Mosionier.
5. For some examples of early reviews, see "Anne Holm" (2002).
6. See, for example, Mortimer (2001). Mortimer identifies the setting as taking place during World War II, finds the book relevant to the persecution of Jewish people, and suggests that Anne Frank's *Diary* is a related text that students would find helpful.
7. For example, David recalls that the prisoners refused to talk about food: "When you had nothing but bread and porridge . . . you did not want to talk about the kind of

food you used to have when you were free" (Holm 1965, 31). The evidence of Holocaust memoirs, particularly those by women, challenges this assertion.

8. Supporting evidence that David is not Jewish is stereotypical, for example, reference to the light color of his hair.
9. More examples of texts that examine post-Holocaust trauma are published in Europe, for example, the fiction of Ida Vos. In contrast, we find greater willingness to explore post-traumatic stress disorder in American children's books about Vietnam. This is not just because post-traumatic stress disorder was labeled as a medical disorder after the Vietnam conflict but because, when war-related trauma happens close to home, it is more likely to be acknowledged and examined in that culture's reading for young people.
10. The second novel in the trilogy is *The Sunflower Diary* (Montreal: Roussan, 1999).
11. Children's fiction on the Armenian genocide includes Bagdasarian (2000). Bagdasarian bases the novel on his great-uncle's experience.
12. Pressler is also the author of *Shylock's Daughter,* a novel that revisions *The Merchant of Venice* and focalizes the daughters' perspective, both Jessica, the daughter found in Shakespeare's play, and that of another young woman, whom Pressler imagines as a substitute daughter.

IV
STORYING HOME

14

A Physician's Take on *Ferdinand*

JOHN GALL

I took my pediatric training at the Mayo Clinic, way back in the days when it was called a fellowship, not a residency. I had just completed a brutal internship, and I showed up promptly at 7 AM on the first day wearing a clean, starched white coat. The attending physician stared at my coat, then he did something that shocked me and changed my life and attitude forever. He reached out his hand and shook mine and said, "Dr. Gall, I'm Haddow Keith. Welcome to the Mayo Clinic. We're all licensed physicians here, so you don't need to wear any kind of uniform, just your everyday jacket."

I felt ten feet tall. All of us in the program did too. We were going to be treated like human beings. We strove to be worthy of that status of equality that had been conferred on us. In fact, we strove so hard that in a year or two we began to think we really were the equals of those gods of medicine. Then I encountered something that shook me to the core.

A little eight-year-old boy had been brought into the hospital late the night before with what looked for all the world like epileptic seizures. A look of terror would come over his face, he sat bolt upright in the bed, stiffened, jerked convulsively, then shrank back and tried to bury himself in the pillow. After a few minutes he would recover enough to sit up again.

He had been sent for an emergency brain wave test that showed some type of spikelike abnormalities, but no true epileptic pattern. The neurologist had done an emergency neurological exam and found no abnormality.

The nurse who had been with him all night reported that she had finally been able to make sense of his shrieks. A giant black widow spider, six feet tall, would suddenly appear in the room and lunge at him, trying to bite and kill him.

So what were we seeing? Some bizarre form of epilepsy or some sort of hallucinatory panic reaction or what? How would the physicians at the Mayo Clinic respond to this utterly unclassifiable mystery?

Then the social worker came into the room. (I might comment that this is what made the Mayo Clinic so great. Where else in the world could you get a neurologist, an electroencephalographer, and a social worker to show up at 2 AM and work for six hours straight to solve an emergency problem that no one could understand?) The boy's mother was living alone in an isolated farmhouse. Her husband had deserted her, it was midwinter in Minnesota, and she didn't know how she was going to feed her three children. She began to believe enemies were surrounding her home and flashing lights into her eyes to confuse her. She gathered her three children together and ran with them through the snow to the barn, where she thought she was safe. (This was in the days of the Cold War.) The nearest neighbors saw the commotion and drove over to help her. Their headlights made beams in the icy fog and the mother thought the CIA and the Communists had finally come to kill them all. At least she could protect her children by killing them before they could be captured. She had already killed two of them before the neighbors ran up and stopped her. Our eight-year-old patient was being strangled by his own mother when they rescued him.

And now here he was, being persecuted by fantasies of a giant black widow spider trying to kill him. Fate had forced into his conscious awareness one of those fantasies that for the sake of sanity must remain forever unconscious—the image of the devouring mother.

I must say that the Mayo Clinic responded beautifully to such a challenge back in those primitive days of the 1950s. They didn't medicate the little boy, the didn't treat him as if he had a disease; they provided him with support and security and a chance to tell his story over and over, day after day, until he was able in some way to assimilate what had happened to him.

That was the day on which I learned that I didn't know it all, I didn't know anything, I didn't even know the name of the game I was trying to play, or the rules by which it was played. That little boy haunted me for decades until I finally decided to make the break from academic medicine and go into practice on my own and try to learn how to understand what's really going on in this world.

Some years later I was located in a university town and some of the parents in my practice were adopting children from Vietnam, Korea, even Russia. I remember an infant who had been brought directly from the airplane to my office. At six months of age he was refusing to make eye contact. When someone approached he jerked his head to the left or to the right to avoid eye contact. He was six years old before he would willingly walk into my office, and at sixteen he was haunted by fantasies of suicide even though his new parents were loving, sensitive, and stable.

But I also saw many babies who were not traumatized, who had been gladly brought into this world and had been welcomed and loved for their own sake. What is life like for such a child? What specifically happens when a baby is *not* living in fear, anxiety, and oppression?

Life is so short when you look back on it. Ten years went by before I realized that I wasn't even noticing what was happening as I met with my patients and their parents. I bought a video camera and hung it on rails from the ceiling. That way I could review what had actually happened each day.

It didn't work. There was no time for reviewing videotapes. They began to pile up, but I kept the camera running, and in another fifteen years I was seventy-five years old and ready to retire.

Now I'm retired and have enough videotapes to review to at least age one hundred.

When I finally found the time to begin reviewing the tapes, my very first tape showed me things I never expected to see. For some totally inexplicable reason, when I had first set up my office I had hung musical mobiles above the examining table—you know, the kind where you pull a little chain and the stuffed toy begins to play a tune. Before my very eyes my patients were dancing the dance of life and I was not seeing it. But now I see it, and I can show it to you to prove it really happens.

Now I know what Ferdinand was doing as he smelled the flowers to his heart's content. He was doing what every living creature does that is allowed to live without fear—he was dancing. He was dancing to the music and the rhythm of his own life. Maria Tatar has told us what Nabokov said—that literature was born when the first boy cried, "Wolf!" But before literature there is Dance, and Dance begins when the child is born, or perhaps even earlier. The newborn baby dances, and if his parents know how to dance with him or her, there is the possibility of great joy from the very beginning.

15

Breaking the Cycle

MARK JONATHAN HARRIS

At the age of twelve my grandfather left his widowed mother in Hungary and sailed alone to America. He spoke no English and had only distant relatives in this country. But like many of the 2 million eastern European Jews who immigrated to the United States in the decades after 1880, he established a new life for himself and a new family; eventually he even brought his mother to join him in America.

I was very close to my grandfather as a child. He lived a block away from us and I saw him almost daily. Sadly, he died when I was only six, and most of what I know about his history has come to me secondhand. I never had the opportunity to ask him directly what it was like to arrive at Ellis Island, to work in a cigar factory as a boy, to become a millionaire, and then to lose all his fortune in the Great Depression.

Deborah Oppenheimer's mother also left home as a child and fled to a country whose language she did not speak to live with people she had never met. The circumstances were very different, though. It was 1939 and Deborah's mother lived in Chemnitz, Germany. In a desperate effort to save their eleven-year-old daughter from Hitler's murderous intentions, Deborah's grandparents put her on a train and sent her to England to live with strangers. She arrived as part of a remarkable British rescue mission known as the Kindertransport, which saved ten thousand (mainly Jewish) children from Germany, Austria, and Czechoslovakia in the nine months prior to World War II.

Growing up in Long Island, New York, Deborah and her brother and sister knew fragments of their mother's history, but whenever they questioned her about her childhood or the Kindertransport, she would begin to cry. The children understood that the subject was too painful to discuss and tacitly agreed not to bring it up. Like my grandfather, Deborah's mother died without ever imparting to her the full story of her separation from her parents, whom she never saw again after leaving Germany, and her life as a heartbroken refugee in England.

This gap, this emotional lacuna, in both our family's histories was one of the principal reasons Deborah and I set out to make the documentary film *Into the Arms of Strangers: Stories of the Kindertransport*. We both wanted to know more about the seminal experiences that had shaped our families. I learned a great deal about the immigrant journeys of children in the two years I spent researching and directing the film, yet the discovery that made the most impact on me came after the film was released.

When the documentary screened in the United States and England, the film was a revelation to many children whose parents had escaped to England before the war. Like Deborah's mother, a majority of the Kindertransport survivors we interviewed had not talked extensively to their children about their experiences during the war years. Both parents and children had feared that such a discussion might set off feelings in the other that would be unbearable, so they avoided the subject. For several children, seeing the film was their first time hearing their parents' detailed stories; for others, it was the first time hearing the stories recounted with so much emotion, because even though their parents had told them about the Kindertransport, they had often held back the extent of the loss and loneliness they had suffered.

After the premiere in London, the eldest daughter of one of the Kinder in the film invited my wife and me to tea. We sat in her kitchen on a gray, rainy afternoon while she served us fresh-baked scones. "I want to tell you my perceptions of my mother," she began. Her mother had had a harrowing childhood as one of a very few Jewish children in a small town in northwest Germany. Her early years were marked by isolation and anti-Semitism. On *Kristallnacht,* her father was arrested and murdered. She and her sister were later placed in an orphanage by their mother. Eventually, the two teenage girls were sent to England on the Kindertransport. Their wrenching parting with their mother at the train station was the last time they would ever see her. Yet, in England, for the first time in her life, the woman felt accepted. In the film she says, "Nobody's ever said to me, 'Well, you weren't born in this country.' I was as entirely accepted as everyone else. And I gradually felt that I had somewhere I belonged."

Her daughter had a very different view. "I want you to know my mother was never accepted here in England," she said emphatically. "My parents were always outsiders, foreigners. They always stood out. My mother may have felt that our family was part of the community, but growing up I saw we didn't fit in. I saw how others scorned us." The daughter's experience of growing up in Manchester mirrored her mother's growing up in Germany. Although the discrimination and isolation she experienced were not as intense, she too felt that she didn't belong.

Even more striking was the separation anxiety the woman's daughters experienced. Whenever she left the house for any length of time, one of her two daughters would cry hysterically. Without being aware of it, their mother had communicated to her daughters her own fears about leaving them. Even short separations from her children brought back the trauma of that final goodbye to her mother at the railroad station in Germany. The fact that this anxiety was conveyed nonverbally, and never discussed among mother and children, made it even more powerful.

I was stunned by the daughter's disclosures because I had never questioned her mother's statement of acceptance in England. Now I realized how hard that acceptance had been to gain, how much her refugee's gratitude to England for rescuing her had blinded her to the prejudice she had faced there. Yet despite her efforts to spare her daughters the pain of her own childhood, she had unconsciously perpetuated it.

Returning to our hotel, I remembered a conversation I'd had with my father the year before he died. Knowing that his health was failing, I had brought a tape recorder to collect some family history. Among the questions I asked was how my grandfather had lost his dry goods store during the Depression. My father blamed it on the perfidy of his partner and the incompetence of my grandfather's lawyer. My grandfather was left bankrupt and with a bleeding ulcer. Years later this same lawyer had become a U.S. attorney and brought charges against one of my father's clients. The incompetent lawyer had now become a vindictive prosecutor with a lust for publicity. The long trial was a terrible ordeal for my father. Although his client was eventually acquitted, shortly afterward my father had to be hospitalized for depression.

Arriving in the United States at twelve, my grandfather had learned to survive by staying out of trouble. He had succeeded by accommodation and ingratiation, not confrontation. My father had followed his example. Decent, trusting men, both were vulnerable to being bullied and taken advantage of by other people. Uncomfortable with their anger, they had turned it inward, one developing ulcers, the other depression. I remember thinking to myself: Is this my fate as well?

Maybe my father was thinking along similar lines, for he suddenly stood up and ended our conversation. "But this is all past history," he said irritably. "What's the point of talking about it now?"

The point, I might have said, is to keep your children from suffering the same distress. Or I could have quoted psychologist Bruno Bettleheim: "What cannot be talked about can also not be put to rest. And if it is not, the wounds continue to fester from generation to generation." But I saw that our conversation had upset my father, and I said nothing, withdrawing in much the same way my father and my grandfather had in situations that discomforted them.

In an effort to shield their children from the anguish of their past, many Kindertransport survivors retreated behind a similar "wall of silence." Yet, despite their attempts to protect their families, the Kinder often unwittingly transferred their anxieties and depression to their children. In making *Into the Arms of Strangers,* Deborah discovered that she was not alone among the second generation in carrying her mother's unexpressed grief.

Sixty-five years after the Kindertransport, we know much more than we did then about the long-lasting impact of childhood loss and trauma. By now it is clear how porous the "wall of silence" is, how flimsy a defense against our worst fears and nightmares. Though the physical scars of war may be more visible, the psychic scars can last much longer, passed on from parent to child to grandchild.

The woman from the Kindertransport I described earlier had not talked very much about the traumas of her youth until she was in her seventies. Before her interview for our film, she had recurring nightmares about Hitler's Germany. After the interview, in which she grieved and wept openly about her childhood, she was surprised to find that her nightmares ceased.

Breaking that silence, in itself, will not heal all the festering wounds of the past. Bearing witness will not end war or barbarism or cruelty or the tribal, religious, racial, and ethnic hatreds that divide us. It may not even keep our children from repeating our mistakes or suffering the same losses, but it is a beginning.

The historian Lord Macaulay insists that it takes five generations to destroy the memories of earlier times. That is a long time to maintain a legacy of fear and suffering.

16

Please Don't Touch My Toys

Material Culture and the Academy

Mitzi Myers

For many years I've been researching historical children's literature and culture in one of the world's best libraries for that purpose, the University of California, Los Angeles, CBC—short for Children's Book Collection, a world-class repository of material stuff—games and such as well as books, many of these the only known copies in the world. Laughingly, I would always say to the long-suffering staff who needed the shelf space full of my stuff: Please don't touch my toys—that, is, keep what I called up from storage on hold: I *need* them. Unsurprisingly and symbolically, the CBC is located in the basement of the URL, the University Research Library. There are no windows looking out on campus, and it's possible to be on the faculty for years and to graduate as a student without ever knowing that the library exists, much less visiting and using it. Although I and many others have been working for years to change this isolation and are having some success, the enclosed and unseen cubicle below ground emblematizes the relationship between the beloved books I write about—my toys, my intellectual playthings—and the larger university world.

The library's spatial position always reminds me of Mole's home, hidden and special to those in the know. When Rat gives Mole back his subjectivity, his self-hood, by investing the old home place with value, he performs a huge service for his friend, who had momentarily doubted his roots, now having been introduced to a larger world aboveground, the River world where public life goes on. Rat shows you need both: the hidden roots of childhood and the public world. We partisans here must play Rat and teach the university and the public to value where we begin, with the artifacts of childhood.

Like many others who care about children's literature and culture and who hope to make these topics central to a reimagined cultural studies, I've been romancing children's literature studies as crucial to the curriculum for years. I introduce my students to the material artifacts and urge them to use the books, toys, puzzles, games, and so forth for special projects in the three huge classes I teach: children's literature, young adult literature, and growing up multicultural. My students are easily and readily hooked by books—my own obsession with these material artifacts is evidently catching. And their projects win prizes: their research is original and highly sophisticated. They've won fellowships and grants playing with these toys. Microfilm and digital versions won't do: we need to devote special attention to preserving and collecting the real thing. So many books are full of childish scribbles, inscriptions, math problems solved on blank pages, marks of personality and usage. Real children read these books, used them, were shaped by them. A lot can be learned about past cultures by careful examination of material objects. For example, what pages are quite clean and what sections are dirty from childish use, who gave what to whom, what was the history and circulation, and so on. This is a material culture marked by wear and tear: rips, dirt, spills, uncensored comments, drawings and scribbles, rude jokes, and missing pages. In these "defacements" we discover the hidden history of childhood. These aren't cute toys; they're real and really valuable research objects.

Upstairs, in the main library, which doesn't define children's culture as a major acquisition area, the toys on the shelves are fewer, though choice. Because of my badgering, the generous humanities bibliographers are beginning to make it possible to do real research by providing the books, journals, and so on that students need for projects. After many years I got sick of lugging my own copies of journals and books to school to photocopy for students because the library system didn't subscribe. I won't be doing that anymore, for now this paper takes a very different turn from that initially planned.

However, I hope what we can learn from one scholar's lifelong obsession with physical books, objects owned and cherished as far back as memory goes, can speak to those of us concerned with children's studies in a culture that's increasingly online and net bound, little concerned with real books or imaginative reading, troublingly materialist and conformist. I remember feeling murderous when my *Bambi* was defaced by my little sister, who wrote her name inside in crayon. My mother reminded me that I was bigger and therefore should forgive, but to deface a loved toy seemed wicked to me then and still does. I don't think that passion for reading and for owning books is as common today; I feel passionately that we must cherish it if we are to survive as a healthy culture. I hope I will survive to see that culture; I hope I will be able to continue to contribute to humanizing the university and the world through tirelessly emphasizing the foundational importance of children's literature and related disciplines.

Once upon a time, I had a house with toys in every room, yes, including both bathrooms. Once upon a time, I had something like thirty-five thousand volumes, including my dead husband's library, the acquisitions of my own from childhood days on, complete runs of every major and minor journal or newsletter concerned with children's literature and culture, all the major reference volumes, and a fair number of historical volumes painstakingly found at prices I could afford. Needless to say, I was beloved by every bookstore and publisher in the world. I had paperbacks by the yard of every important book that anyone could name; I bought books for youth by the pound. I could reach out my hand and find whatever I needed. My toys were my life (and took almost all of my salary). Now there's nothing at my old address but a concrete slab, and I'm struggling very hard to recover from the physical and mental trauma that resulted when a fire caused by a gas leak consumed everything I had. The fireman thought I might be mad when I kept going back in, hair aflame, and had to be physically restrained. They kept asking "Are there pets?" and I kept screaming, "No, no my books are my life: *Do something*!" When nothing was saved, I wanted to die. You can see from the pictures that my whole life is ashes.

When you lose the material books and work that define who you are, you lose your identity. The Stones sang (they and my music collection burned too), "Lose your dreams, lose your mind." And my "nineteenth nervous breakdown," to steal another Stones' title, except this time it's for real, shows, I believe, that what we read determines who we are. I don't exist right now without those material objects. I can't be the grand old queen of footnotes today because I don't have anything to footnote (the audience is probably grateful). I know all the criticism about the cultural construction of subjectivity; I know all the postmodern stuff about consumer culture and the sameness of everyone as products thereof. I know too about the critics who argue that consumers are not passive responders but take and use in their own ways. I can't cite anyone, as they're all toast too.

But I can use the homely image that I use with students about reading and stuff we acquire and the postmodern self. I do this when we are reading about Mole's home and how it defines him and how he is given back his selfhood by his friend. I point out that dorm rooms and apartments (and houses that your insurance company finds for you as shelter) are neutral spaces, devoid of your personality. But no sooner does anyone move in than subjectivity, a collage of objects taken from a seemingly homogenizing culture, begins to emerge. Each dorm room is a little bit different, each apartment acquires a flavor. My naked space now has a few volumes, thanks to the kindness of friends. And I'm shamelessly asking for every journal, every book. I ruined my health trying to save the books I love so well and have tried so hard to serve. Weirdly, that *Bambi* was one of a handful that survived unscathed. (It was in a closet in a plastic container in the least gutted room.)

I made a vow that I wouldn't kill myself till I tried to get back who I was by getting ahold of books. I shall never be able to replace them all, and other things may now kill me, ironically, when I so much want to live. I want to get still more personal while I simultaneously argue for the importance of books in the formation of selfhood, the furnishing of those dorm rooms with bits and pieces of who I am kidnapped from a conformist culture. I want to use Harry Potter to do so. I also criticize myself while I tweak my friend Jack Zipes, whose fine chapter in *Sticks and Stones* I just read. Like most of you, I am disgusted and completely put off by the hype of Harrymania. But mine is not to reason why about the media and their weird ways and banal stupidities. I owned all of Harry Potter before the fire. Bought them because they were important—was too damn put off by all the hoopla to read them. After the fire, when I was taken in by friends who thoughtfully hid all the sharp knives and made me promise to at least give life a try, my room had no books. What can I read, said I—try this, said they (the parents of two boys) handing me a volume. And so the day I was released from the regional burn center, I began reading someone else's Harry Potter. And I'm sorry, folks, but I was hooked. I bought the whole thing again. Harry saved my life, as much by his kinship with the moral tales and historical didactic literature I love so well as by anything. When Harry is the good Boy Scout for right against mounting evils, I felt, OK, I'll try to hang in there. (Like most women, I'm a very agile reader; I have no problems identifying with the hero, though my critical self knows very well that's sexist. However, if Harry is the Christian Knight—there was also a Britomart.) I won't give up, I thought, even though the odds are against me. Before the fire, I would have agreed wholeheartedly with Jack's chapter, because we are all snobs, and God knows, I've been the worst. But in my misery of loss, I became a child and read like a child. And yep, I do think it was good for me. Nor do I buy the argument that adults buy books and kids don't read them. I bought once and have rebought a book about Harry by kids. There are still readers out there hooked on the experience of reading. I guess in losing everything, I regained my innocence. I cry now, like a child; I'm scared a lot, like a child; I'm lonely and need reassurance a lot, like a child. These were not things characteristic. My reversion scares me; I can't read much criticism now. I can read stories. I think my experience says something about the primal experience of storying in forming selfhood, maintaining sanity, undergirding civilization itself. I have reached out my hand at almost every line I've written—the first time I've tried to write, as I've been too ill—for a good quote—and it's not there. I want to check such and such, but I don't have it anymore. And I felt naked, bereft, selfless, and terrified. I don't think the feeling of security kids (and I) gain after reading Harry's repetitive success is a bad thing. Kids now and always have read selectively for what they need. Often, the textual marks in the material object literally inscribe a selfhood. The new copies of the books I've bought or been sent scare me. They aren't "mine" yet; I haven't written my self on them. No marks and scribbles in the margins; no pages festooned with every color of self-adhesive note.

My life experience with material books, historical research, and the cultural narrative of childhood reverses the conventional structure of the fairy tale. It is a tale of riches to rags. Cinderella doesn't get the handsome prince (actually she did briefly, though he died tragically young of cancer, but that's another tale). Cinderella in this 2000 version is very literally and permanently reduced to the Ashbottom—that's her name in some versions. A few years back, I used the term *cross-writing*, and Uli Knoepflmacher may remember this differently, but I think I made that term up, and then we did the volume together that I still think was among Yale's best. But I don't have it, so I can't check. I've become myself a cross-writer and cross-reader, for now I've read and written as both a child and an adult; I have been personal on this panel and I've also given some raw ethnographic field data for you to chew over. I look forward to hearing what you think can be learned from this sad case; I'm struggling to find something positive. I know I can't go home again (that novel burned too), but I hope I can make a new home in the world. May you, good fairy godmothers and godfathers among the audience, wave your wands (phallic symbol or no) and waft good thoughts my way. Keep up your good work; I will be with you in spirit, though the body is too sick and skeletal to travel. I think I know now why so many kids' books have orphans as the central figure, with the plot featuring the orphan's triumph. I think one of the areas I shall concentrate on is the experience of being homeless, a war victim, a refugee, a displaced person. I understand these kinds of storying as I never did before. I understand too what I thought I knew and didn't. Books matter; storying makes the world. When a child or a list person creates selfhood, the process comes about through narrative. Lose your stories, lose your mind—or never grow a mind. What will the new century bring to children's studies? Let my experience demonstrate the primal importance of the book and the tale.

17

"Appointed Journeys"

Growing Up with War Stories

Maria Tatar

In a wartime meditation on fairy tales and fantasy, J. R. R. Tolkien worried about what we should read to children in times of crisis. He lamented that the older stories had been "mollified" and "bowdlerized" in order to court the favor of grown-ups. Concerned that authors were patronizing their readers instead of challenging them, he sounded the alarm about "a dreadful undergrowth of stories" that had been written to conform to adult beliefs about what children want to read. Tolkien never identified the older stories or the "dreadful undergrowth," but he made it clear that efforts to purge tales of cruelty inevitably leads to a "falsification of values." Children are not meant to become Peter Pans, he insisted: "Their books like their clothes should allow for growth, and their books at any rate should encourage it." Stories allow children to embark on "the appointed journey"—voyages of discovery that secure wisdom for them through encounters with "peril, sorrow, and the shadow of death" (Tolkien 1966, 42–44).

The shadow of death has always posed a challenge for writers of children's literature. It may be true that many children's books engage with anxieties about violence and death in profound ways that sometimes escape the notice of adults. Even Margaret Wise Brown's *Goodnight Moon,* for example, with its concluding image of a dim, silent room, has the capacity to arouse fears about whether light and sound will ever return. And yet we tend to align children's literature with fantasy, magic, enchantment, and imagination, with stories designed to arouse wonder and hope—the promise of "the fresh morning, and the light that returns with day" at the end of White's *Trumpet of the Swan* (White 1970, 210). Henry Wadsworth Longfellow captured in his poem "Morituri Salutamus" the notion of literature as a safe haven when he wrote of "the love of learning, the sequestered nooks, / And all the sweet serenity of books" (Longfellow 1914, 313).

Tolkien himself identified four important ingredients—each made more authoritative through the use of uppercase—in fairy tales and literature for children: Fantasy, Recovery, Escape, and Consolation. He did not include in this classic formulation "peril, sorrow, and the shadow of death," nor did he seek to explore the value of struggle, trauma, and violence in stories for children. Instead he emphasized the primacy of Fantasy, suggesting that children's literature may engage real-life fears and passions, but never in a way that impinges on reality. It is the duty of authors of children's books to *avoid* reality and historical referentiality and instead to produce plots that symbolically enact what is bewildering and even terrifying for the child. As importantly, children's stories need to end by producing the "catch of the breath, a beat and lifting of the heart" that comes with the joy of a happy ending (Tolkien 1984b, 69).

Vladimir Nabokov tells us that literature was born on the day "when a boy came crying wolf, wolf and there was no wolf behind him" (1980, 5). Nabokov was, to be sure, thinking about how literature creates artificial worlds through strategies of deceit and misrepresentation, but he must also have understood, at a very deep level, that storytellers get the attention of their audiences by invoking primal fears. One could assert that children's literature was born on the day that a child came running home crying wolf, wolf—and that the wolf haunting the child's imagination, far more than any real wolves, is what inspires stories for children. It is no accident that "Little Red Riding Hood"—in all its cultural variation—has become the most widely disseminated of all fairy tales, for children's literature so often draws on encounters with monsters that no one ever encounters in reality (wolves that talk) to show how real fears can be banished or tamed. Many writers have seen it as their mission to produce stories that help manage the monsters that beleaguer every child's mind—the lions, tigers, and bears, oh my! that come to life when everything is, as in Roald Dahl's *BFG*, "deathly still." Whether those fiends go by the name of Lord Voldemort, the Wicked Witch of the West, or Captain Hook, they are the embodiments of the many wolves that haunt the child's imagination.

But what about real wolves? What about the child caught in a story that does not take place in Neverland, Oz, or Hogwarts but on the home front, at a time and place that has real historical referentiality? How does the representation of real-world trauma and conflict affect the child reading that story? And what about the child who is not caught in a story but trapped in the real-life menace of war? What is the function of storytelling for that child? Can it serve as an antidote to the feelings of defenselessness that are magnified—indeed doubled—in times of war? War is, after all, precisely the situation in which even adults lose a sense of agency, becoming as vulnerable and powerless as children.

In the last century, it was relatively easy for those living in the United States to draw a distinction between children who are on the home front—safe, sheltered, protected, even if frightened and confused by the words they read and the images they see in the media—and children who are, as we know all too well from looking at those images in the media, caught in combat zones, some of them at home. Now that the notion of a contained war has vanished and terrorist threats have turned every home front into a potential battle zone, we face hard choices about what to read children. Should we retreat into the untroubled pleasures of *Curious George* or *The Cat in the Hat*? Is it more appropriate to worry about moral guidance and turn to what William Bennett offers up in his *Children's Book of Hearth and Home*? Should we revive *Hansel and Gretel* as a tale that endows children with the power to escape monsters? Or should we pay attention to the gritty realism of *Shattered: Stories of Children and Wars,* which gives us testimony from children who have been in the line of fire as well as on the sidelines of war? It is not at all clear whether we relieve anxieties by offering children the pleasures of winning real-life battles by proxy in Neverland or Narnia or whether we intensify them by going down the path of escapist fantasy and choosing stories determined to avoid what is in the headlines. Nor is it self-evident that we fuel or ease children's fears with stories that aim to instruct them about the realities of war.

In a bold account that documents the shift from fantasy to "problem novels" in children's literature, Barbara Feinberg quotes from a reference book that commends the realistic turn taken by children's books in the 1960s: "Realistic fiction helps children enlarge their frames of reference while seeing the world from another perspective. Stories . . . help young people develop compassion for an understanding of human actions. . . . For many years, death was a taboo subject in children's literature. Yet, as children face the honest realities of life in books, they are developing a kind of courage for facing problems in their own lives" (Huck et al. 1997, 455). Books addressing death will, we are told, inspire compassion, which will in turn produce courage. There is no consideration at all of the possibility that the representation of death and dying in children's books might give rise to dread, alarm, or anxiety—or to fears about dying before awakening.

Feinberg was inspired to write *Welcome to Lizard Motel* because, as a parent, she observed firsthand the toxic effect of problem novels on children. The ethos of many of these books, she reports, "seems not to be 'Love Makes the World Go Round,' or 'Only Connect,' or 'There's No Place Like Home,' or even primarily 'Be Brave.' Instead, 'Only Survive' or 'At Least You Have Yourself (since you can't rely on anyone else)'" (Feinberg 2004, 41). Most of these books focus on a rite of passage, showing how death, loss, and trauma test a child's ability to cope. The protagonist generally inhabits a world of pathologies and is defined by what Sheila Egoff describes as the "terminology of pain" (1981, 14). And the goal is to help child readers develop compassion, which has become the cardinal virtue of our culture.

This new literary culture resists the protective stance toward real-life violence once taken in books for children. Instead it endorses the view that children can cope better with pain if they encounter trauma and tragedy rooted in the here and now rather than in "once upon a time." Or as Anne Macleod has put it: "By the middle of the 1960s, political and social changes leaned hard on the crystal cage that had surrounded children's literature for decades. It cracked and the world flowed in" (1994, 59). These books, among them Paula Fox's *Monkey Island,* Sharon Creech's *Walk Two Moons,* Paul Zindel's *The Pigman,* and Katherine Paterson's *Bridge to Terabithia,* may engage the perils and shadows that Tolkien declared to be necessary for children's stories, but they do so without recourse to the fantasy that he also declared to be an indispensable ingredient. Lacking a "happily ever after," they can be, as one child declared to Barbara Feinberg, "weird" and "depressing." (2004, 59)

Children seem to throw their votes consistently at books that combine the drama of high peril with the vibrant allure of fantasy. They cast their lot with stories that address lurking fears but also avoid unmediated engagement with them. We err when we give them too strong a dose of reality, but we also make a mistake when we pretend that nothing is or ever will be out of order in the world. A scene of reading from a film that won the Oscar for best motion picture of 1942 captures earlier views on what to read to children in times of crisis and war and reveals the powerful appeal of retreating into sheltered innocence. Greer Garson, who plays the indomitable Mrs. Miniver in the film of that title, takes refuge underground with her husband and children during the aerial bombardment of England. Providing shelter—both physical and emotional—is presented as the first response to children under fire. In inimitable British fashion, Mrs. Miniver and her husband sip tea while bombs blast their home and its surroundings. As the children sleep, Mr. Miniver opens the volume by his side, and the camera pans to the title page of *Alice in Wonderland.* Mr. Miniver reads from the book's last page, and, when he pauses, Mrs. Miniver recites the final words about how Alice would keep "through all her riper years, the simple and loving heart of a child; and how she would gather about her other little children, and make their eyes bright and eager with many a strange tale, perhaps even with the dream of Wonderland of long ago."

What becomes clear in this scene of reading is that stories can serve as a protective layer, building intimacy and warmth. The bomb shelter may be the first line of physical defense, but reading provides an emotional sanctuary, one that strengthens the adults (as much, if not more, than the children) as they steel themselves for the air raid. *Alice in Wonderland* may divert the children from wartime anxieties and provide the soothing comforts of a story read by their mother, but, for the parents, the words on the page evoke the utopian wonders of childhood, creating a powerful sense of nostalgia for the "long ago" dream of peacetime. Lewis Carroll's book is mobilized to ease anxieties and provide comfort, and the book itself, like the classics of children's literature, becomes a trope for the pleasures of an untroubled era, of an idealized world that is described in the words that open the film: "This story of an average English middle-class family begins with the summer of 1939; when the sun shone down on a happy, careless people, who worked and played, reared their children and tended their gardens in that happy, easy-going England that was so soon to be fighting desperately for her way of life and for life itself."

Alice in Wonderland, as many will recall from their own childhood reading of the book, is in fact no paradise of utopian delights. Alice's world has been correctly described as violent, anarchic, nonsensical, and frightening, and her travels through Wonderland leave her feeling by turns mystified and mortified. But in the cinematic world of *Mrs. Miniver,* the book becomes a fetishized prop invested with the power to conjure a mythical past linked to childhood purity and Edenic innocence—not unlike the "happy, easy-going England" of the opening title. Like the blankets enfolding the children in their beds, it covers up and shields the children from reality—appropriately so in times of aerial bombardment but less so when children are navigating the ordeals of everyday life.

If we move to another scene of reading, one taken from *The Children's Book of Heroes,* edited by William J. Bennett, we discover that the sheltering impulse operates far more powerfully in wartime than in times of peace. Bennett's volume, which ends with an image of mother and son reading together, includes the boy's gloss on the experience:

> When Mother reads aloud, the past
> Seems real as every day;
> I hear the tramp of armies vast,
> I see the spears and lances cast,
> I join the thrilling fray. (Bennett 1997, 110)

For this parent, stories also look backward—not to a mythic past but to a very real history of military engagement and conflict. In the one instance, a family is in the midst of war, with the story used as a means of providing hope for the future, a hope that is embodied in the utopian dream of Wonderland. In the other, mother and child are in the safe haven of home, with the child expressing a sense of longing to enter a battle in which spears and lances are cast but which is nonetheless a "thrilling fray." In the film, nostalgia for peace in wartime; in the poem, excitement about war in times of peace.

These two scenes of reading should not delude us into thinking that the plots of diversions and entertainments for children are driven solely by the desire for peace and stability ("the simple and loving heart of a child") or by the desire for adventure and conflict (the "thrilling fray"). The two dominant genres of children's literature—fairy tales and fantasy—have always relied on blending utopian aspirations with discord and strife. Fairy tales, as Donald Haase has argued, serve as appealing structures for war narratives precisely because they map a symbolic geography that captures the competing energies of wartime experience: "Children who have been *displaced* by violence may perceive an affinity between their traumatic experience and utopian projections, on the one hand, and the landscape of the fairy tale, on the other" (Haase 2000, 362). Beginning at home, a site of danger, distress, and trauma, the fairy tale takes advantage of the "liberating potential of the fantastic" to produce a second home, one that functions as a place of permanent safety and security (Zipes 1983, 170–92). Danger, distress, and trauma are located, not in the here and now but in "once upon a time," at a vast remove from reality.

"Once upon a time," "At a time when wishes still came true," "Deep in the forest," "When animals still talked to each other"—the reassuring certainty of a "happily ever after" is embedded in these formulaic beginnings. The vague, generic quality at the start of every fairy tale makes it clear to the child that the story is *not* grounded in reality. As Bruno Bettelheim explains in *The Uses of Enchantment* (1976): "The old castles, dark caves, locked rooms one is forbidden to enter, impenetrable woods all suggest that something normally hidden will be revealed, while the 'long ago' implies that we are going to learn about the most archaic events" (1989, 62). More importantly, Bettelheim argues that fairy tales function like dreams, helping children to work out by proxy the problems with which they struggle: "Maybe someday we will be able to demonstrate . . . that children are much worse off when deprived of what these stories can offer, because the stories help the child work through unconscious pressures in fantasy" (63).

It may be true that fairy tales and fantasy offer attractive structures for helping children manage anxieties both conscious and unconscious, but they function just as importantly as "stories to think with, stories that do not necessarily determine lives but can give children (and adults) a way to read and understand them" (Harries 2000, 124). There is, as Bettelheim himself concedes, little clinical evidence available to instruct us on exactly how children process fairy tales or how they can function as what Carolyn Kay Steedman calls an "interpretive device" (1997, 142–43). What we do know is that fantasy allows children to enter other worlds, where they encounter desires and fears—for which they may not yet have names—in the embodied forms of ogres, grinches, wizards, and dragons, as well as of helpful foxes, munificent trees, and charming princes. As they navigate a world of mystery and magic, they explore an alternate reality that creates a certain friction with real life but also models what could be.

Ernst Bloch found the utopian fantasies of fairy tales symptomatic of a revolutionary urge to create a new social order. "Wishful thinking," Bloch asserted, "is capable of revolutionary awareness, and can enter the chariot of history without necessarily abandoning in the process the content of dreams." In other words, fairy-tale fantasies can engage with gritty historical realities and point the way to "a remote realm that appears to be better." There may be suffering in fairy tales, but "it never returns." And finally: "Fairy tales always end in gold. There is enough happiness there" (Bloch 1988, 168). Childhood stories traffic in fantasies and dreams, projecting into the future a world without the suffering, violence, and conflict that fired its plot.

Bloch relies on fairy tales from the Brothers Grimm to demonstrate his thesis, but he might have found gratifying evidence for his views about the utopian function of children's literature—of fantasy as well as fairy tales—in C. S. Lewis's *Chronicles of Narnia,* published from 1950 to 1956. Lewis's *The Lion, the Witch and the Wardrobe* gives us an antidote to what we saw in the scene from *Mrs. Miniver,* using children's literature at dusk (Bloch's magical time for telling stories) not to put children to sleep but to awaken them with a call to action. The narrative begins in "the heart of the country," where Peter, Susan, Edmund, and Lucy have been sent to escape air raids in wartime London. There the four children resist the serenity of the British countryside and end up fighting the world war by proxy against the armies of the White Witch. And, even if they do not always feel brave or clever, they triumph: "In the end all that foul brood was stamped out" (Lewis 1950, 200). Reigning supreme as kings and queens of Narnia, they govern Narnia well, and "long and happy was their reign." Establishing a model United Nations, they make good laws, keep the peace, drive back giants, and enter into "friendship and alliance with countries beyond the sea and paid them visits of state and received visits of state from them" (201). Unlike the happily ever after of fairy tales, the utopia established in Narnia receives real elaboration. If it is fantasy, and if the children must eventually return to reality, they have still managed to develop a plot that does not simply look back with longing to a simpler, happier time, but rather looks ahead and builds a constructive fantasy that allows for the triumph of hope.

I turn now from the notion of literature as escape (*Mrs. Miniver*) and literature as enabling fantasy (*The Lion, the Witch and the Wardrobe*) to some texts that engage in a very different way with how children cope when living in times of war or in war zones. The children in these stories are not physically or emotionally sheltered—instead they face real dangers as they make their way, in fairy-tale fashion, through woods and encounter the enemy. But theirs is no fairy-tale world. Instead of entering a magical, imaginative counterworld in which the child is never really alone and always has recourse to a providential nature, the protagonists in these stories inhabit a realistic world, one that, in all three cases, engages with the experience of World War II and of the Holocaust. We are in a world where there is neither an imaginative "once upon a time" nor the certainty of "happily ever after." How have authors risen to the challenge of representing the realities of the Holocaust, and have any managed to escape the charge of being "weird" and "depressing"?

Lois Lowry's *Number the Stars* (1989) takes place in Denmark in 1943, during the German occupation. This is a narrative that captures the realities of what it was like for a child to live in Copenhagen during a time of "relocations," food shortages, and Nazi soldiers posted on street corners. For ten-year-old Annemarie Johannsen, the return home from school can be fraught with dread: "Annemarie looked up, panting, just as she reached the corner. Her laughter stopped. Her heart seemed to skip a beat" (2). The occupation has had a transformative effect on her life: "The whole world had changed" (17). The only constant for her are the stories she tells her younger sister Kirsti: "The fairy tales remained the same" (17).

Fairy tales are a source of stability for the Johannsen girls, and Annemarie is an experienced raconteur who recites stories on a nightly basis for Kirsti, always ending her stories with "and they lived happily ever after." Andersen's "Little Mermaid" is a favorite with her sister, but the "Little Red Riding Hood" of the Brothers Grimm turns out to be the story that inspires and guides Annemarie's real-life rescue effort. Annemarie Johannsen is given agency, not in a fantasy world but in the very real world of wartime Denmark, where she must intercede as messenger in order to save Jewish refugees trying to reach safety in Sweden. "I can run like the wind" (Lowry 1989, 104): these are the words Annemarie uses to reassure her mother that she will get a vital packet to the refugees. Annemarie's ability to run means the difference between life and death.

Number the Stars is one of a small number of books that shows how children can make a difference, that the courage and cunning endorsed by Ernst Bloch and his contemporary Walter Benjamin as the captivating traits of fairy-tale heroes can be mustered in real-life situations. In Lowry's novel, as in some of the other works, it is a fairy-tale heroine who is invoked as a model of courageous action and shrewd behavior. "'Once upon a time there was a little girl,'" Annemarie recites to herself as she enters the woods, carrying the straw basket containing the drug that will be used to deaden the scent of the guard dogs used to search boats crossing from Denmark into Sweden. Annemarie must get the basket to her uncle in order to secure the safe passage of refugees, and she uses the fairy tale not just because she identifies with the girl in its title but because the story ends with rescue, liberation, and "happily ever after." Annemarie understands that the forest through which she is traveling is not at all "like the woods in the story," and yet the story fortifies her and prepares her for encounters with wolves. And, indeed, while she is running through the woods with her basket, she meets the wolf in the form of Nazi soldiers and their dogs.

Annemarie draws on the strategy of many a fairy-tale hero in the Grimms' collection of tales: she plays dumb. Think of the youngest of three sons—invariably called Dummy—and how he outwits everyone around, including his two older and wiser brothers. When confronted with the soldiers and their dogs, Annemarie finds her mind racing: "She remembered what her mother had said. 'If anyone stops you, you must pretend to be nothing more than a silly little girl.'" Using her wits to outsmart the grown-ups, she acts like a silly little girl in order to allay suspicion and to try the patience of the soldiers. If Annemarie's story deviates from that of Little Red Riding Hood by showing a child who obeys mother's orders and who does not need a hunter to rescue her and others, it nonetheless shows how children can draw on the wisdom of fairy tales to inspire confidence and lay claim to real agency in a situation that leaves even adults powerless.

In the afterword to *Number the Stars,* Lowry wrote about a young man named Kim Malthe-Bruun, a youthful leader of the Danish Resistance who observed, on the night before he was put to death: "And I want you all to remember—that you must not dream yourselves back to the times before the war, but the dream for you all, young and old, must be to create an ideal of human decency, and not a narrow-minded and prejudiced one" (1989, 137). For the child reading the book, this is a powerful call to avoid the dream of Wonderland and instead to look ahead to utopian ideals, not as fantastic as the ones worked out in Narnia, but utopian nonetheless.

Growing Up with War Stories

In Peter Rushforth's novel *Kindergarten* (1979), the boy Corrie, whose grandmother is a Holocaust survivor and whose mother is the victim of terrorists, contrasts stories that end with the triumph of good over evil with those in which the innocent perish: "In fairy-tales collected by the Brothers Grimm, the innocent and the pure in heart always seemed to triumph, even after much fear and suffering: Hansel and Gretel outwitted the witch and escaped; the seven little kids and their mother destroyed the wolf; the three sisters in 'Fitcher's Bird' overpowered even death to defeat the murdering magician." Corrie contrasts the Grimms' tales with Hans Christian Andersen's fairy tales, which he read again and again, hoping that the ending would change.

> But the endings never changed: the little match-girl died entirely alone, frozen on New Year's Eve, surrounded by burned-out matches; the little mermaid melted into foam after bearing her suffering bravely; and the steadfast tin soldier and the ballerina perished in the flames of the stove, leaving only a little tin heart and a metal sequin behind. He had been unable to put them away and forget about them. He had been drawn, compulsively, to read them with engrossed attention, and had wept as he found himself realizing what the inevitable and unchanged end of the story would be. (112)

Rushforth's description of the boy's response to the Grimms' tales and to Andersen's stories deeply complicates what makes for appropriate reading matter for children. Corrie finds that "Hansel and Gretel," which depicts how a witch is shoved into an oven, is reassuring, while Andersen's "Little Match Girl," with its frozen corpse of a child, creates a sense of "mounting desolation." The child claims to feel better off with the Grimms than with Andersen. Yet some would argue that the boy's compulsion to read Andersen is part of a need to work through a mortality crisis, to master the anxieties raised by what is not only the "inevitable and unchanged end" of Andersen's stories, but of all of our lives. Reading the Grimms would, in this view, promote sadistic fantasies, while reading Andersen would constitute a form of empowering bibliotherapy.

Corrie's distinction is nonetheless telling. Many would argue that there is only one real requirement when it comes to children's books, and that is that the child protagonists survive the horrors threatening to overwhelm them. In an earlier era, children's books almost always ended in the cemetery. Beginning with James Janeway's *A Token for Children: Being an Exact Account of the Conversion, Holy and Exemplary Lives, and Joyful Deaths, of Several Young Children* (1642), literature for children was intent on converting carefree infidels into pious Christians. "They are not too little to die," Janeway gleefully warned. "They are not too little to go to Hell" (1825, 3–4). The boys and girls in *A Token for Children* spend their last days and hours reading scripture and exhorting others to follow their good example. The Puritans were not unique in their focus on dying children. Nineteenth-century children's literature is littered with corpses: think of Little Eva, Little Nell, the Little Mermaid, the Little Match Girl, one of the Little Women, and all those other diminutive nineteenth-century heroines for whom the term *little* functions as a death sentence. Today, we seem be reviving stories that break one of the most powerful taboos in cultural production—the representation of the death of a child. Until the 1960s, as noted, it was unusual to find children's books with deathbed scenes. Still, there are powerful exceptions to the rule, and many of those exceptions come in the form of books engaged with the historical realities of the Holocaust.

Naomi Sokoloff tells us that "there is an undeniable possibility of doing genuine damage to children by shocking them and exposing them to unbearable details at too young an age" (1994, 267). Even if some children benefit from books that engage issues of persecution, suffering, and death, it seems unlikely that children in the age range of four to seven have much to gain from learning about the unspeakable events of the Holocaust. And so it is something of a shocker to come across *Rose Blanche,* published in 1985, which gives us a picture book about the Holocaust, with a text by Christophe Gallaz and illustrations by Roberto Innocenti. With its large format, copious illustrations, and sparse text, the book is clearly intended for an audience of children—its U.S. publisher is Creative Education.

The dust jacket to *Rose Blanche* gives an account of Innocenti's own wartime experiences as child witness to the horrors of Nazism:

> I was a little child when the war passed in front of my door. One day, two very young German soldiers, wearing gray uniforms, came to our house and begged us to hide them. They probably weren't even 18 years old. They wanted to surrender to the English troops. And they kept repeating: "Stop the war." We were hiding them in the basement when we saw a German truck passing by, taking away a family. The mother was holding a tiny baby wrapped in a pink blanket.
>
> My father did not want to answer my questions, but I knew then that something terrible was happening.

Innocenti, born in 1940, must have been less than five years old as he watched the truck pass by, yet he instantly comprehended that "something terrible was happening"—that "tiny baby wrapped in a pink blanket" was a clear signal that something was awry.

Innocenti further comments on the genesis of the book—on what moved him to produce *Rose Blanche:* "In this book I wanted to illustrate how a child experiences war without really understanding it. After drawing the first page I chose Rose Blanche as its title, because of the significance of the name. 'Rose Blanche' was a group of young German citizens protesting the war."

Innocenti portrays a heroine who is both bewildered by the transformations taking place in her home town and wise beyond her years in the compassion and courage she mobilizes in response to the sight of human suffering. The doubled narrative voice (the text switches from a first-person narrative to a third-person narrative) is matched by a dualistic view of the child as mystified observer (experiencing the war "without really understanding it") and as prescient agent (knowing the "real face" of war). *Rose Blanche,* in sum, explores the emotions of a child in real historical circumstances—a child frightened and made anxious by the war experience. But it also narrates the actions of an idealized child, boldly resourceful in taking the lead where adults have failed.

Innocenti's picture book takes us to a small town in Nazi Germany. There the heroine named in the title witnesses the arrest of a boy by a Nazi soldier pointing a gun at him (a reprise of the famous photograph worth a thousand words in its arousal of existential shock and moral outrage), follows the tracks of the truck transporting him to a concentration camp, brings food to starving children at the camp, and perishes while searching for camp survivors after the Russian invasion. The pronounced historical referentiality of this text (townspeople display swastika armbands, Nazi propaganda banners are everywhere in sight, concentration camp inmates wear striped uniforms with yellow stars) makes it obvious that we are in the Third Reich. Yet Innocenti—in a move that suggests an investment in preserving the naïve point of view of a child—never once uses the terms *Nazis* and *Jews.* That Rose Blanche perishes becomes clear from the shot that rings out in the final pages, the report that "Rose Blanche's mother waited a long time for her little girl," the bright red poppy that blooms precisely where she once stood, and the final illustration showing the signature blue flower carried by the heroine drooped over a barbed wire fence.

The book's final illustration, which shows beads of water resembling tears dripping from the barbed wire on which Rose Blanche's flower has been caught, clearly alludes to Christ's martyrdom. The heroine is positioned as a savior figure, one whose death transforms the unrelieved brown drabness of the earlier illustrations (we are, after all, in a world created by "brown shirts") to a soothing green, dotted with red, white, and blue. Like Dickens's Little Nell and Stowe's Little Eva before her, Rose Blanche becomes a savior figure who redeems the adult sinners of her social world. That a message about salvation in a book about the Holocaust should be funded by allusions to Christ's sufferings is more than odd, though some Holocaust reminiscences are surprisingly rich in references to Christ's martyrdom. Rose Blanche, who distributes bread to the concentration camp inmates and who dies at a site covered with angled wooded crosses, becomes identified with the (com)passion and suffering of Christ.

The title vignette for the story alerts us to the presence of another, very different cultural story used by Innocenti to construct the figure of Rose Blanche. Beneath the title the reader sees the picture of a long, muddy road, at the end of which appears Rose Blanche, running into the woods with a bag of provisions and a red ribbon adorning her head. The allusion to Little Red Riding Hood, on the road with her basket of bread and wine and her red adornment, is unmistakable. The folkloric code running through the narrative becomes complicated by the visual link between Rose Blanche's ribbon and the red armbands worn by soldiers, along with the red flag Rose Blanche waves on the first page of her story, before she witnesses the arrest of the Jewish boy. Red literally becomes the badge of the rescuers as well as the persecutors—the Russian soldiers (both invaders and saviors) wear red stars on their hats. Finally, red is also the color of the poppy that signals salvation and hope at the site of Rose Blanche's death.

That Innocenti must have been aware of the two competing discourses in the text—the one folkoric, the other theological—becomes evident from the pairing of the opening vignette, with its clear citation of the story of Little Red Riding Hood, and the closing vignette, with its unambiguous evocation of the crown of thorns. The heroine of his narrative begins as a girl trickster (a courageous young girl who defies both parental and civil authority) but ends as a martyr (falling prey to a voracious military power). She is the savior and also the character with whom children reading the story will most readily identify. That *Rose Blanche* quickly went of print and now cannot be found in most public libraries suggests that few adults were willing to test a child's tolerance for learning about the Holocaust through this particular book, in which both the Jewish children and the heroic child who tries to sustain them through the winter all presumably die. That their deaths are only implied makes the book all the more unsettling. Rose Blanche's death is never clearly spelled out, and we never know for certain that she has perished. That uncertainty (as adult readers polled testify) produces an effect even more disturbing than a clear resolution of the events.

Maurice Sendak's *Dear Mili*, like Innocenti's *Rose Blanche,* is another children's book that invokes the Holocaust, but in ways so subtle that few are aware of the work's historical referentiality. *Dear Mili* represents an effort to work through personal distress about a historical event. In Sendak's case, it was not until his bar mitzvah in 1941 that he became aware of the Holocaust and of the relatives in Europe whose lives it had claimed. *Dear Mili,* with its numerous embedded pictorial allusions to victims of the Holocaust, addresses an event that had a considerable impact on Sendak as boy.

It is noteworthy that both Innocenti and Sendak write Holocaust books featuring little *girls* who become victims of war and that they—perhaps not coincidentally—depict redemption in seasonal terms through the rebirth of nature. Both Rose Blanche and Mili also operate as martyred savior figures in narratives embellished with allusions to Christianity. Sendak himself did not produce the text of *Dear Mili,* but instead undertook the project of illustrating a story written in the early part of the nineteenth century by Wilhelm Grimm. Although reportedly disturbed by the "Christian themes" in the Grimms' tale, Sendak's discovery that St. Joseph (the principal male character in the story) was Jewish seemed to lift his illustrator's block about this text and to authorize the use of a nineteenth-century tale about Christian salvation to come to terms with the Holocaust.

The pictorial energy of Sendak's *Dear Mili* is focused on the last days of Mili's apprenticeship in the woods. Mili, who has been sent by her mother into the woods to escape marauding soldiers, spends her days in the cottage of St. Joseph. Before coming upon this cottage, Mili is shown resting in the woods, contemplating a desolate landscape in which the roots and branches of trees resemble skeletal remains. What Mili does not perceive and what will escape most children looking at the double-page textless illustration is the allusion to the tower of Auschwitz-Birkenau in the background. This turns the bedraggled group of wanderers crossing the footbridge into camp inmates who wearily contemplate the dreary landscape. That site of colorless desolation will undergo a transformation while Mili is in the woods working her way toward salvation. As Mili and her guardian angel contemplate sylvan wonders near a Jewish cemetery several pages later, they are unaware of a lush flowering lily behind them, beyond which a choir of children sings under the direction of a pig-tailed choirmaster—perhaps Mozart?

The choir of children in Sendak's *Dear Mili* has been identified as standing in for the forty-four children of Izieu who perished in a concentration camp after Klaus Barbie ordered their transport. Two of the girls in that choir bear a distinct resemblance to two different, well-known photographs of Anne Frank. In St. Joseph's wooded preserve, the dwelling that housed the children of Izieu remains intact, and they, like Mili, have found safety at last. The woods, once the locus of ghoulishly threatening presences and affiliated with such sites as Birkenau and Buchenwald, have been turned into a divine sanctuary, one overseen by St. Joseph and an eighteenth-century choirmaster. This solemn yet playful promise of salvation (St. Joseph) and transcendence (Mozart) seems designed to neutralize the bleak realities of both the Holocaust and of Mili's life. Mili's return home to her mother, her discovery that she has been gone three decades rather than three days, along with the death of mother and child that evening, reveal that the sojourn in the woods has been little more than a cover for Mili's death.

Sendak's text, read without knowledge of its source, would seem to be a throwback to earlier consolatory stories written for children living in an age with a mortality rate far higher than our own and with a more steadfast faith in the afterlife. It thus comes as no surprise to learn that the text itself was written in 1816 and that it comes from the pen of Wilhelm Grimm. What Sendak does is to preserve the words of that text, which is anchored in a specific time and place, and to illustrate them in such a way as to transfer the original pious sentiments about eternal life to the context of another historical event, the murder of the children of Izieu. What Innocenti starkly reveals, Sendak effaces. *Dear Mili* has no barbed wire, no children in prisoners' uniforms, no emaciated forms and faces. Instead we have a smiling chorus, cheerfully following the instructions of a choirmaster who is lounging about in an enchanted woodland setting that is meant to represent the transcendent beauty of life after death.

Innocenti's grim realism stands in sharp contrast to Sendak's stylized romanticism, although both illustrators reach for redemption in the face of horror. If *Rose Blanche* gives us an unvarnished version of the fate of Jewish children in the Holocaust, *Dear Mili* tries to find beauty and transcendent meaning in those deaths. Rose Blanche dies in her rescue efforts, though her spirit presumably remains alive in the blue flower caught in the barbed wire and in the regeneration of nature; the child in *Dear Mili* perishes in the woods but finds eternal life in the woodland splendors of St. Joseph's abode. Innocenti's text refuses to soften our collective cultural memory of the Holocaust, exposing us to its most brutal reality: the murder of children. Sendak, by contrast, seeks to find a redemptive moment, aestheticizing our cultural memory of the Holocaust with consolatory images of the children of Izieu singing in a chorus. Both authors—in their efforts to confront and represent what François Mauriac called "absolute evil" (1960, vii–viii) and what the narrator of William Styron's *Sophie's Choice* described as the "unpardonable sin"—work through their own childhood anxieties. But both books, in representing children who, despite their courage, do not survive and become martyrs, are problematic as children's books. Lacking the utopian impulse of *The Lion, the Witch, and the Wardrobe,* the healing force of fairy tales, and the empowering energy of *Number the Stars,* they seem to function as picture books designed as therapeutic exercises largely for the adults who wrote them and for adult readers.

Fantasy, Recovery, Escape, Consolation: Tolkien, as noted, identified these four elements as key ingredients in children's stories. He reminded us that the "joy of the happy ending" is something that fairy tales produce "supremely well." Neither escapist nor falsely consolatory, that happy ending gives us "a catch of the breath, a beat and lifting of the heart," reminding us that, where there is suffering and loss, there is also courage and hope, even deliverance and restitution.

Longfellow's "sweet serenity of books" refers us to those happy endings, to the consolation that comes, not in the form of treacly sentimentalism or stern political correctness but in inspired adventures that tug and pull at children, drawing them into a safety zone where the conflicts they encounter in real life are enacted on a larger, more expansive stage. Those symbolic battles may be very different from the real ones at home or in the headlines, but they create a space for identifying and managing fears, for engaging in dialogue about what matters to us, and for imagining the utopian possibilities we abandoned on the way to becoming adults.

Afterword

Pamela Reynolds

Our understandings of the past inform our literature, which in turn influences our interpretations of the past. In this cyclical process, the question of narrative and history is vital, especially the manner in which truth, explanation, and rhetoric (in the sense of storytelling) is handled. A major question in relation to the concerns of this volume is whose truth is recorded and how faithfully changes in attitudes toward war are reflected in the present writing of history. Until recently, histories dealing with war seldom touched on its effects on children. The chapters in this volume attest to the fact that authors are beginning to pay specific attention to it. As changes in attitudes toward topics such as a warrior's honor, loyalty to the sovereign, nationalism, and early entry into military training schools are incorporated into accounts of the recent past, so there will be reverberations in narratives written for children that reflect on these issues. We might profitably ask how the history of war, including children's roles in it, is written? How is war documented in the archive? How are its effects on the young measured and weighed? Without some understandings of these matters, we may suppose, it will be unlikely that the authors of children's books will represent the changes in the ways in which we conceive of the reality of war.

Afterword

Concerning truth and the writing of history, Bernard Williams asserts that

> the truths in any history are at the very least a selection, and indeed that is an understatement, since they are not simply waiting to be selected. In any text, there is a question of what is left out, above all what is left out and can be claimed to be relevant. There is also a question of what is added, what is inferred to fill the gaps. Over all that, there is the question of what story is being told. It is not a matter of leaving truths or reality or past happenings out of it, of generating a *detached* fiction. As Clemenceau famously said at Versailles to a German who wondered what future historians would say about all this, "They won't say that Belgium invaded Germany." (2002, 243)

I wish to emphasize that the narratives of the experiences of women and children in war have barely entered the archive. They have been left out for a range of reasons, one of which is that they are difficult to document given the parts they have played in wars until recently (see Ross 2003). Traditional definitions of war no longer apply to many current conflicts, and it is difficult to apply international rules of conduct to them. Skepticism has grown as to the efficacy of the laws of war (*jus in bello*) or the reliability of the honor of warriors in protecting children in the past and the present. The "law of the innocents" seems to have been most honored in the breach unless applied only to formal battles of specific kinds in particular eras and, even then, the destruction of children's lives and the harm they suffered as armies moved to the battlefield (one army almost always invading another country's territory and therefore passing less than lightly through their homes, fields, and businesses). As Paul Celan said, "The spectre of war goes through the land" (1999, 9). Children are always in the paths of armies, and some are engaged on their peripheries. In the different kinds of wars we see in modern times, children die in great numbers and few commanders of national armies or of warring groups are held accountable, once conflict has ceased, for the harm done to children. While significant progress has been made in promulgating international measures to protect children, it is salutary to observe the struggle that has been waged over raising the age, as laid down in the United Nations' Convention on the Rights of the Child, when the young can participate in formal armies from fifteen years to seventeen years. The main protagonists of the optional protocol to the Convention on the Rights of the Child on the involvement of children in armed conflict wanted to achieve the prohibition of recruitment of children into the armed forces and a prohibition of their participation in hostilities, but they failed. Armies do not record the effects of armed conflict on children, claiming, under the guise of euphemisms, that all wars produce "collateral damage" despite attempts to avoid harming civilians.

There is a conundrum that puzzles many writers on the predicament of children in armed conflict. On the one hand, there is a desire to assert children's innocence and call for their protection; on the other hand, is the need to acknowledge that a young person under eighteen years of age can become engaged for a variety of reasons that cannot be disregarded. Coercion is, of course, a major reason, but other reasons can include the child's perceived need to protect the family and a way of life from predators or oppressors, the necessity to protect self, the desire to secure political liberation, or to revolt against domination. It is a moot point as to what choice means within the context of disorder and destruction, but the implication for the treatment of the child seen as a participant in conflict differs according to whether he or she is described as having been an involuntary conscript or a warrior (for a discussion of responsibility and choice, see Scanlon 1998, 256–67). Some of the children who have been involved in Africa's armed clashes and who have then responded to demobilization campaigns have subsequently been excluded from benefits or opportunities offered to older recruits and have not received the acknowledgment they felt was their due in having fought for a worthy cause.

It is difficult to document children's experiences in, and the effects on them of, war. Most accounts necessarily rely on recall after the cessation of fighting. Even attempts to count how many children were involved in a conflict are fraught with problems: it is, for example, difficult to identify the age of many children, and conflicts often last for years and someone may have begun to participate while a child but may no longer be a child at the time the conflict ends. Besides, the remembrance of harsh experiences often requires time in a supportive context for it to be shaped into a narrative that can be shared. As a consequence, little is known about the actual nature of the effects of and responses to violence, or the forms of recovery from trauma, or the extent to which sound ethical sets of behavior can be acquired despite engagement in dreadful events. We require more careful documentation that includes children's accounts of their experiences throughout the period of conflict (and not just of particular incidents of trauma), that tracks sets of relationships that may have held them through conflict or afterward, that maps their movements and contacts, that chronicles their actions and the context in which they occurred, and that outlines their emotional and ethical responses. The record should place these small histories within the context of local histories of the recent past.

Given the paucity of our knowledge, it is likely that children's literature will be constrained in its ability to reflect on the issue; not that there is a direct connection but that, with a more widespread understanding of the situation of children, the literature may touch on a greater variety of perspectives of war than it might otherwise and, in turn, influence attitudes to war, although it is not possible to predict in which direction.

"Things by Their Right Names"

John Aikin and Anna Letitia Barbauld

Charles.
Papa, you grow very lazy. Last winter you used to tell us stories, and now you never tell us any; and we are all got round the fire quite ready to hear you. Pray, dear papa, let us have a very pretty one.

Father.
With all my heart—What shall it be?

Charles.
A bloody murder, papa!

Father.
A bloody murder! Well then—once upon a time, some men dressed all alike . . .

Charles.
With black crapes over their faces?

Father.
No; they had steel caps on:—having crossed a dark heath, wound cautiously along the skirts of a deep forest . . .

CHARLES.
They were ill-looking fellows, I dare say?

FATHER.
I cannot say so; on the contrary, they were as tall, personable men as most one shall see:—leaving on their right hand an old ruined tower on the hill . . .

CHARLES.
At midnight, just as the clock struck twelve: was it not, papa?

FATHER.
No, really; it was on a fine balmy summer's morning;—they moved forwards, one behind another . . .

CHARLES.
As still as death, creeping along under the hedges?

FATHER.
On the contrary—they walked remarkably upright; and so far from endeavouring to be hushed and still, they made a loud noise as they came along, with several sorts of instruments.

CHARLES.
But papa, they would be found out immediately.

FATHER.
They did not seem to wish to conceal themselves; on the contrary, they gloried in what they were about. They moved forwards, I say, to a large plain, where stood a neat pretty village which they set on fire.

CHARLES.
Set a village on fire, wicked wretches!

FATHER.
And while it was burning they murdered—twenty thousand men.

CHARLES.
O fie! Papa! You don't intend I should believe this; I thought all along you were making up a tale, as you often do; but you shall not catch me this time. What! They lay still, I suppose, and let these fellows cut their throats?

FATHER.
No, truly, they resisted as long as they could.

CHARLES.
How should these men kill twenty thousand people, pray?

"Things by Their Right Names"

Figure 19.1. Detail from a writing sheet *The Blessings of Peace and the Calamities of War.* London: J. Hawkins, 1762. Reproduced by permission of the Cotsen Children's Library, Princeton University Library.

FATHER.
Why not? the *murderers* were thirty thousand.

CHARLES.
O, now I have found you out! You mean a battle.

FATHER.
Indeed I do. I do not know any *murder*s half so bloody.

From *Evenings at Home; or The Juvenile Budget Opened,* 1807.

Works Cited

Adorno, Theodor W. 1973. *Negative Dialectics.* New York: Continuum.
Aelred de Rievaulx. 1958. *Quand Jésus eut douze ans.* Ed. and trans. Anselme Hoste and Joseph Dubois. *Sources Chrétiennes,* 60. Paris: Éditions du Cerf.
Agnew, Kate, and Geoff Fox. 2001. *Children at War: From the First World War to the Gulf.* London: Continuum.
Aikin, John. 1792–96. "The Price of a Victory." Vol. 4, 51–61. In John Aikin and Anna Laetitia Barbauld, *Evenings at Home; or, The Juvenile Budget Opened. Consisting of a Variety of Miscellaneous Pieces, for the Instruction and Amusement of Young Persons.* London: J. Johnson.
Aikin, John, and Anna Laetitia Barbauld. 1792–96. *Evenings at Home; or, The Juvenile Budget Opened. Consisting of a Variety of Miscellaneous Pieces, for the Instruction and Amusement of Young Persons.* 6 vols. London: J. Johnson.
Alington, Gabriel. 1977. *Willow's Luck.* London: Heinemann.
Allan, Mable Esther. 1976. *Sara Goes to Germany.* London: White Lion.
Almagor, Gila. 1991. *Hakayits shel Aviyah.* Tel Aviv: Am Oved. Trans. Hillel Halkin as *The Summer of Aviya.* London: Collins. (Orig. pub. 1985).
———. 1995. *'Ets hadomim tafus.* Tel Aviv: Am Oved. Trans. Hillel Schenker as *Under the Domim Tree.* New York: Simon and Schuster. (Orig. pub. 1992).
Alphandéry, Paul, and Alphonse Dupront. 1995. *La chrétienté et l'idée de croisade.* Paris: Albin Michel.
Andersen, H. C. ca. 1945. *Den onde Fyrste: Eventyr for Børn og Voksne.* With a foreword and moral by A. Hermann. Illustrated by Palle Wennerwald. Copenhagen: Alex. Vincents Kunstforlag.
"Anne Holm." 1989. *Something about the Author Autobiography Series.* Ed. Joyce Nakamura, 123–37. Detroit: Gale.
"Anne Holm." 2002. *Children's Literature Review.* Ed. Rebecca J. Blanchard, 123–41. Detroit: Gale.
Anonymous. 1801. *Juvenile Stories and Dialogues, composed chiefly in Words of Two Syllables, for the Use of Schools, and Young Readers.* London: Vernor and Hood and E. Newbery.
———. ca. 1803. "The Minor's Soliloquy." Bound in the British Library's collection of "Broadside ballads, etc., in response to the projected invasion of Britain in 1803."

BL 1851.c.3, f.3.

———. 1808. *The Pictures in the Hermitage; or, the History of George Meadows*. London: J. Harris.

———. 1812. *My real friend; or, incidents in life, founded on truth, for the amusement of children*. 2nd ed. London: Darton.

———. 1816. *The Funny Old Man Who Had Apples to Sell*. London: Wallis and Son.

———. ca. 1819. *The Little Deserter; or, Holiday Sports: Dedicated to all good boys*. Edinburgh: Oliver and Boyd.

———. ca. 1822. *The Good Child's Delight; or, Joy to the Eye and Delight to the Mind: A Collection of Curious Engravings, and Amusing Original Stories*. London: Hodgson.

Armitage, Doris Mary. 1939. *The Taylors of Ongar: Portrait of an English Family of the Eighteenth and Nineteenth Centuries. Drawn from Family Records by the Great-great Niece of Ann and Jane Taylor*. Cambridge: W. Heffer and Sons.

Arterburn, Stephen, and David Stoop. 2002. *130 Questions Children Ask about War and Terrorists*. Rev. ed. London: Tyndale House.

Auden, W. H. 1945. *The Collected Poems of W. H. Auden*. New York: Random House.

Audoin-Rouzeau, Stéphane. 1993. *La guerre des enfants 1914–1918*. Paris: Armand Colin.

———. 1996. "French Children as Target for Propaganda." In *Facing Armageddon: The First World War Experienced*, 767–79. London: Cooper.

Avisar, Ilan. 1998. "Personal Fears and National Nightmares: The Holocaust Complex in Israeli Cinema." In *Breaking Crystal: Writing and Memory after Auschwitz,* ed. Ephraim Sicher, 137–59. Urbana: University of Illinois Press.

Bagdasarian, Adam. 2000. *Forgotten Fire*. New York: Dorling Kindersley.

Barbauld, Anna Letitia. 1792–96. "Things by Their Right Names." In John Aikin and Anna Letitia Barbauld, *Evenings at Home; or, The Juvenile Budget Opened. Consisting of a Variety of Miscellaneous Pieces, for the Instruction and Amusement of Young Persons*. Vol. 4, 51–61. London: J. Johnson.

Barchilon, Jacques. 1993. "Children and War in the Fairy Tale." *Merveilles et contes* 7:17–39.

Barney, John. 2000. *The Defence of Norfolk, 1793–1815*. Norfolk: Mintaka Books.

Bauer, Elizabeth R. 2000, September. "A New Algorithm in Evil: Children's Literature in a Post-Holocaustal World." *The Lion and the Unicorn* 24, no. 3:378–401.

Bauer, Elvira. 1936. *Trau keinem Fuchs auf grüner Heid und keinem Jud bei seinem Eid! Ein Bilderbuch für Gross und Klein*. Nuremberg: Stürmer-Verlag.

BBC Radio 4 programme. Interview with the archbishop of Canterbury on September 4, 2004.

Becker, Annette. 2000. "The Avant-garde, Madness and the Great War." *Journal of Contemporary History* 35, no. 1:71–84.

Beckett, Sandra, ed. 1999. *Transcending Boundaries: Writing for a Dual Audience of Children and Adults*. New York: Garland.

Belardinelli, Dina Buciarelli. 1931. *Sillabario e piccole letture*. Rome: La Libreria dello Stato.

Bellamy, Carol. 2001. *The State of the World's Children, 2001*. New York: UNICEF.

Bennett, William J. 1997. *The Children's Book of Heroes*. New York: Simon and Schuster.

Bériou, Nicole. 1998. *L'avènement des maîres de la Parole: La prédication à Paris aux XIIIe siècle*. Collection des Études Augustiniennes, Série Moyen Âge et Temps Modernes 31, vol. 1. Paris: Brepols.

Works Cited

Berlant, Lauren. 1997. *The Queen of America Goes to Washington City: Essays on Sex and Citizenship.* Durham, NC: Duke University Press.

Berquin, Arnaud. 1788. *Ami des enfans.* In *The Children's Friend. Translated from the French of M. Berquin,* vol. 3, 64–73. London: J. Stockdale.

Bettelheim, Bruno. 1989. *The Uses of Enchantment: The Meaning and Importance of Fairy Tales.* New York: Random House, Vintage Books. (Orig. pub. 1976).

Blanchot, Maurice. 1995. *The Writing of the Disaster.* Trans. Ann Smock. Lincoln: University of Nebraska Press.

Bloch, Ernst. 1988. *The Utopian Function of Art and Literature: Selected Essays.* Trans. Jack Zipes and Frank Mecklenburg. Cambridge, MA: MIT Press.

Bloor, Edward. 1999. *Crusader.* New York: Scholastic.

Boraks-Nemetz, Lillian. 1994. *The Old Brown Suitcase: A Teenager's Story of War and Peace.* Brentwood Bay, BC: Ben-Simon.

———. 1999. "The Child as the Hero/Victim of the Dark Planet—the Holocaust." *Canadian Children's Literature* 25, no. 3:161–64.

———. 2000. *The Lenski File.* Montreal: Roussan.

Bosmajian, Hamida. 2002. *Sparing the Child: Grief and the Unspeakable in Youth Literature about Nazism and the Holocaust.* New York: Routledge.

Bracken, Patrick J., and Celia Petty, eds. 1998. *Rethinking the Trauma of War.* London: Free Association.

Bramlett, Perry C. 2003. *I Am in Fact a Hobbit: An Introduction to the Life and Work of J. R. R. Tolkien.* Macon, GA: Mercer University Press.

Brauner, Alfred, and Françoise Brauner. 1991. *J'ai dessiné la guerre: Le dessin de l'enfant dans la guerre.* Paris: Expansion Scientifique.

Brenner, Rachel. 2002. "The Holocaust and Its 50 Year Commemoration." In *Traditions and Transitions in Israel Studies: Books on Israel VI,* ed. Laurie Z. Eisenberg, Neil Caplan, Naomi Sokoloff, and Mohammed Abu-Nimr, 43–66. Albany: SUNY Press.

Breuer, Josef, and Sigmund Freud. n.d. *Studies on Hysteria.* Trans. James Strachey. New York: Basic.

Brogan, Hugh. 1989. "Tolkien's Great War." In *Children and Their Books: A Celebration of the Work of Iona and Peter Opie,* ed. Gillian Avery and Julia Briggs. Oxford: Clarendon.

Brontë, Charlotte. 1996. *Jane Eyre.* Ed. Michael Mason. New York: Penguin Classics Edition.

Bruce, Dorita Fairlie. 1942. *Toby at Tibbs Cross.* London: Humphrey Milford/Oxford University Press.

Bunting, Eve. 1995. *Spying on Miss Müller.* New York: Clarion.

Burnett, Frances Hodgson. 2002. *A Little Princess.* Ed. U. C. Knoepflmacher. New York: Penguin.

Burney, William. 1806. *The Naval Heroes of Great Britain; or, Accounts of the Lives and Actions of the Distinguished Admirals and Commanders who have Contributed to Confer on Great-Britain the Empire of the Ocean.* London: Richard Phillips.

———. 1807. *The British Neptune; or, A History of the Achievements of the Royal Navy, for the Earliest Periods to the Present Time.* London: Richard Phillips.

Cadogan, Mary, and Patricia Craig. 1978. *Women and Children First: The Fiction of Two World Wars.* London: Gollancz.

Carpenter, Humphrey. 1987. *J. R. R. Tolkien: A Biography.* Boston: Houghton Mifflin.

———, ed. 1981. *The Letters of J. R. R. Tolkien.* Assisted by Christopher Tolkien. Boston:

Houghton Mifflin.

[Carter, T.] 1845. *Memoirs of a Working Man.* Ed. Charles Knight. London: Charles Knight.

Cartilla escolar antifascista. 1937. Illustrated by Mauricio Amster. Valencia: Ministerio de Instruccion Publica y Bellas Artes.

Caruth, Cathy. 1996. *Unclaimed Experience: Trauma, Narrative, and History.* Baltimore: Johns Hopkins University Press.

Celan, Paul. 1999. *Collected Prose.* Trans. Rosmarie Waldrop. Manchester: Carcanet.

Chalvany, Shoshana. 2003. "'Hakayits shel Aviya' me'et Gila Almagor–hasefer vehaseret." In *Merging Voices: Voices from the Ashes,* ed. Yaakova Sacerdoti, 66–74. Cranston, RI: Writers Collective.

"Charlotte Elizabeth." 1841. *Personal Recollections.* London: R. B. Seeley and W. Burnside.

Chronicon rhythmicum Austriacum (to 1267). 1880. Ed. W. Wattenbach. *Monumenta Germaniae historica, Scriptores.* Vol. 25.

Cole, Tim. 1999. *Selling the Holocaust from Auschwitz to Schindler: How History Is Bought, Packaged, and Sold.* New York: Routledge.

Coleridge, Samuel Taylor. 1988. "Fears in Solitude." In *Poetical Works,* ed. Ernest Hartley Coleridge, 259–60. Oxford: Oxford University Press.

Congar, Yves. 1997. *Journal de la Guerre, 1914–1918.* Ed. Stéphane Audoin-Rouzeau and Dominique Congar. Paris: Cerf.

Cookson, J. E. 1982. *The Friends of Peace: Anti-war Liberalism in England, 1793–1815.* Cambridge: Cambridge University Press.

Cooper, Thomas. 1971. *The Life of Thomas Cooper: Written by Himself.* Reprinted in facsimile with an introduction by John Saville. Leicester: Leicester University Press. (Orig. pub. 1872).

Corelli, Marc. 1917. *Mémoires du Général Joffre en Plomb.* Illustrated by H. Gray. Paris: Ramel.

Cormier, Robert. 1979. *After the First Death.* New York: Pantheon.

———. 1991. *I Have Words to Spend: Reflections of a Small-Town Editor.* Ed. B. Constance Senay Cormier. New York: Delacorte.

———. 1992. "A Book Is Not a House: The Human Side of Censorship." In *Author's Insights: Turning Teenagers into Readers and Writers,* ed. Donald Gallo, 64–74. Portsmouth, NH: Heinemann, Boynton/Cook.

———. 1999a. *Frenchtown Summer.* New York: Delacorte.

———. 1999b. *Probing the Dark Cellars of a Young Writer's Heart: Frances Clarke Sayers Lecture 1998.* Los Angeles: UCLA Department of Library and Information Science.

Croft, Janet Brennan. 2004. *War and the Works of J. R. R. Tolkien: Contributions to the Study of Science Fiction and Fantasy,* Number 106. Westport, CT: Praeger.

Cronin, Michael. 1998. *Against the Day.* Oxford: Oxford University Press.

Culleton, Beatrice. 1992a. *April Raintree.* Winnipeg: Peguis. (Orig. pub. 1984).

———. 1992b. *In Search of April Raintree.* Winnipeg: Pemmican, Winnipeg: Peguis. (Orig. pub. 1983).

Cutler, Jane. 1999. *The Cello of Mr. O.* Illustrated by Greg Couch. New York: Dutton.

Cvetkovich, Ann. 2003. *An Archive of Feelings: Trauma, Sexuality, and Lesbian Public Cultures.* Durham, NC: Duke University Press.

Dancel, Brigitte. 2003. "L'enfant, l'ecole et la grande Guerre." In *Les enfants dans la Grande*

Guerre: exposition du 20 jun au 26 octobre 2003, 71–81. Peronne: Historial de la grande guerre.

Danks, Carol, and Leatrice B. Rabinsky, eds. 1999. *Teaching for a Tolerant World, Grades 9–12: Essays and Resources.* Urbana, IL: National Council of Teachers of English.

Day, Thomas. 1867. *The History of Sandford and Merton.* Edinburgh: Gall and Inglis. (Orig. pub. 1783–89).

Des écoliers dans la Grande Guerre: enfance et adolescence à Sainte-Croix-du-Verdon. 1997. Mane: Alpes de Lumière.

Dickson, Gary. 1992. "Stephen of Cloyes, Philip Augustus, and the Children's Crusade of 1212." In *Journeys toward God: Pilgrimage and Crusade,* ed. B. N. Sargent-Baur, 83–105. Kalamazoo, MI: Medieval Institute Publications, Western Michigan University.

———. 1995. "La genèse de la croisade des enfants (1212)." *Bibliothèque de l'École des chartes* 153:53–102.

———. 1997. "Shrines and Revivals." In *Atlas of Medieval Europe,* ed. Angus MacKay and David Ditchburn. London: Routledge.

———. 1999–2000. "Prophecy and Revivalism: Joachim of Fiore, Jewish Messianism and the Children's Crusade of 1212." *Florensia* 13/14:97–104.

———. 2000a. *Religious Enthusiasm in the Medieval West: Revivals, Crusades, Saints.* Abingdon: Ashgate.

———. 2000b. "Revivalism as a Medieval Religious Genre." *Journal of Ecclesiastical History* 51:473–96.

———. 2002. "Innocent III and the Children's Crusade." In *Innocenzo III: Urbs et orbis, Atti del congresso internazionale, Rome, 9–15 Sept., 1998,* ed. Andrea Sommerlechner, 586–97. Rome: Instituto storico italiano par il Medio Evo e Societa romana di storia patria.

———. Forthcoming. *The Children's Crusade: Medieval History, Modern Mythistory.* Basingstoke: Palgrave-MacMillan.

Dudley, Martin R. 1994. "*Natalis Innocentum:* The Holy Innocents in Liturgy and Drama." In *The Church and Childhood, Studies in Church History* 31, ed. Diana Wood, 233–42. Oxford: Blackwell.

Dumesnil, René, and Thomas Simon. 1918. "La guerre vue par les écoliers." *Mercure de France* 1.

Dupont, Roy. n.d. *Bombs on Berchtesgaden.* London: W. Barton.

Edgeworth, Richard Lovell, and Maria Edgeworth. 1798. *Practical Education.* 2 vols. in 1. London: J. Johnson.

Egoff, Sheila. 1981. *Thursday's Child: Trends and Patterns in Contemporary Children's Literature.* Chicago: American Library Association.

Eiss, H. 1989. *Literature for Young People on War and Peace: An Annotated Bibliography.* New York: Greenwood.

Elliott, Mary Belson. ca. 1823. *Plain things for little folks; seasoned with instruction, both for the mind and the eye.* London: William Darton.

Evans, Reverend John. 1811. *The New Geographical Grammar; or, Companion and Guide Through the various Parts of the Known World.* London: Albion.

Ewing, Juliana Horatia. 1912. "Friedrich's Ballad: A Tale of the Feast of St. Nicholas." In *Melchior's Dream and Other Tales,* by Juliana Horatia Ewing, 47–83. London: Bell.

(Orig. pub. 1862).
Faron, Olivier. 2001. *Les enfants du deuil: Orphelins et pupilles de la nation de la première guerre mondiale (1914–1941)*. Paris: La Découverte/Syros.
Feinberg, Barbara. 2004. *Welcome to Lizard Motel: Children, Stories, and the Mystery of Making Things Up*. Boston: Beacon.
Felman, Shoshana, and Dori Laub. 1992. *Testimony: Crises of Witnessing in Literature, Psychoanalysis, and History*. New York: Routledge.
Firchow, Peter Edgerly. 1986. *The Death of the German Cousin: Variations on a Literary Stereotype, 1890–1920*. Lewisburg: Associated University Presses.
Flynn, Richard. n.d. "Marketing 9/11: Children as Victims, Agents, and Consuming Subjects." Unpublished essay. Cited with permission.
Foreman, Michael. 1989. *War Boy*. London: Pavilion.
Foss, Clive. 1997. "Teaching Fascism: Schoolbooks of Mussolini's Italy." *Harvard Library Bulletin* 8, no. 1:5–30.
Fox, Carol, Annemie Leysen, and Irene Koenders, eds. 2000. *An Anthology of War and Peace in Children's Literature*. London: Pavilion.
Fox, Geoff. 2001. "From the Great War to the Gulf, 1914–2000." In *Children at War: From the First World War to the Gulf*, ed. Kate Agnew and Geoff Fox, 3–54. London: Continuum.
Freud, Sigmund. 2002. "Analysis Terminable and Interminable." In *Wild Analysis*, trans. Alan Bance, 171–208. New York: Penguin.
Froelich, Jules. 1913. *Le Pangermaniste en Alsace*. Paris: Berger-Levrault Éditeurs.
Fynsk, Christopher. 2000. *Infant Figures*. Stanford, CA: Stanford University Press.
Gallo, Donald R., ed. 1992. *Author's Insights: Turning Teenagers into Readers and Writers*. Portsmouth, NH: Heinemann, Boynton/Cook.
Garth, John. 2003. *Tolkien and the Great War: The Threshold of Middle-Earth*. Boston: Houghton Mifflin.
———. 2006. Review of *War and the Works of J. R. R. Tolkien* by Janet Brennan Croft. *Tolkien Studies* 3:234–38.
Gilson, Capt. Charles. 1915. *A Motor-Scout in Flanders: or, Held by the Enemy etc*. London: Blackie.
———. 1941. *Through the German Hordes*. London: Blackie.
Gloria, Viktoria: Ein Weltkriegs-Bilderbuch. ca. 1915. N.p.
Goddard, Julia. 1863. "Peter's Story: The Poor Musician." In *More Stories*, 57–77. London: Hall, Smart, and Allan.
Goffman, Erving. 1961. *Asylums: Essays on the Social Situation of Mental Patients and Other Inmates*. New York: Doubleday/Anchor.
Goodenough, Elizabeth, ed. 2003. *Secret Spaces of Childhood*. Ann Arbor: University of Michigan Press.
Goodenough, Elizabeth, Mark Heberle, and Naomi Sokoloff, eds. 1994. *Infant Tongues: The Voice of the Child in Literature*. Detroit: Wayne State University Press.
Goodenough, Elizabeth, and Mitzi Myers, eds. 2000. *Violence and Children's Literature: The Lion and the Unicorn* 24, no. 3:v–ix, 327–464.
Goodman, Robin F., and Andrea Henderson Fahnestock, eds. 2002. *The Day Our World Changed: Children's Art of 9/11*. New York: Harry N. Abrams.
Gordon, Mary. 2005. "Appetite for the Absolute." In *The Best American Spiritual Writing*

2005, ed. Philip Zaleski, 89–97. Boston: Houghton Mifflin.

Greene, Bette. 1973. *The Summer of My German Soldier.* New York: Dial.

Greene, Graham. 1951. *The Lost Childhood and Other Essays.* London: Eyre and Spottiswoode.

Grimm, Wilhelm. 1986. "Hänsel und Gretel." In *Kinder-und Hausmärchen.* Vol. 1. Zurich: Manesse.

———. 1986. "Der heilige Joseph im Walde." In *Kinder-und Hausmärchen.* Vol. 2. Zurich: Manesse.

———. 1995. *Dear Mili: An Old Tale.* Trans. Ralph Manheim. Illus. Maurice Sendak. New York: HarperCollins.

Guillory, John. 1993. *Cultural Capital: The Problem of Literary Canon Formation.* Chicago: University of Chicago Press.

Guthrie, William. 1806. *A Geographical, Historical and Commercial Grammar; and Present State of the Several Kingdoms of the World.* 20th ed. London: J. Walker.

———. 1819. *A Geographical, Historical and Commercial Grammar; Exhibiting the Present State of the World.* 23rd ed. London: F. C. and J. Rivington.

Guyvarc'h, Didier. 1993. *Moi, Marie Rocher, écolière en guerre, dessins d'enfants 1914/1919.* Rennes: Apogée.

Haase, Donald. 1998. "Overcoming the Present: Children and Fairy Tales in Exile, War, and the Holocaust." In *Mit den Augen eines Kindes: Children in the Holocaust, Children in Exile, Children under Fascism,* ed. Viktoria Herling, 86–99. Amsterdam: Rodopi.

———. 2000. "Children, War, and the Imaginative Space of Fairy Tales." *The Lion and the Unicorn* 24:360–77.

Hadley, Frédérick. 2003. "Dessiner pendant la guerre: L'encadrement des enfants." In *Les enfants dans la Grande Guerre: exposition du 20 jun au 26 octobre 2003,* 47–68. Peronne: Historial de la grande guerre.

Halpern, Roni. 1995, December. "The Summer of Aviya: Writing the Storms." Paper presented at the Association for Jewish Studies Annual Meeting.

Harries, Elizabeth W. 2000. "The Mirror Broken: Women's Autobiography and Fairy Tales." *Marvels & Tales* 14:122–35.

Harvey, A. D. 1981. *English Literature and the Great War with France: An Anthology and Commentary.* London: Nold Jonson.

———. 1998. *A Muse of Fire: Literature, Art and War.* London: Hambledon.

Harwayne, Shelley, and the New York City Board of Education, eds. 2002. *Messages to Ground Zero: Children Respond to September 11, 2001.* Portsmouth, NH: Heineman.

Hauff, Wilhelm. 1930. "Der Zwerg Nase." In *Werke.* Vol. 1. Berlin, Leipzig: Bong and Co.

———. 1960. *Dwarf Long Nose.* Trans. Doris Orgel. Illus. Maurice Sendak. New York: Random House.

Heberle, Mark. 2001. *A Trauma Artist: Tim O'Brien and the Fiction of Vietnam.* Iowa City: Iowa University Press.

Hérault, Pierre. ca. 1940. *La Vie d'honneur du Maréchal Pétain racontée et illustrée pour les jeunes français.* Cholet: Farré and Freulon.

Herf, Jeffrey. 2006. *The Jewish Enemy: Nazi Propaganda during World War II and the Holocaust.* Cambridge, MA: Harvard University Press.

Herman, Judith Lewis. 1992. *Trauma and Recovery.* New York: Basic.

Higonnet, Margaret. 1987. "Narrative Fractures and Fragments." *Children's Literature*

15:37–54.

———. 1998. "War Games." *The Lion and the Unicorn* 22:1–17.

———. 2005. "Time Out: Trauma and Play in *Johnny Tremaine* and *Alan and Naomi*." *Children's Literature* 33:151–71.

———. 2006, October. "Child Witnesses: The Cases of World War I and Darfur." *PMLA*: 1565–76.

Hill, J. R., ed. 1995. *Oxford History of the Royal Navy.* Oxford: Oxford University Press.

Historial de la grande guerre. 2003. *Les enfants dans la Grande Guerre: exposition du 20 jun au 26 octobre 2003.* Peronne: Historial de la grande guerre.

The History and Adventures of Little Henry, Exemplified in A Series of Figures. 1810. 2nd ed. London: S. and J. Fuller.

Hoffman, Mary, and Rhiannon Lassiter, eds. 2003. *Lines in the Sand: New Writing on War and Peace.* New York: Disinformation.

Hollebecque, Marie Lahy. 1916. *La jeunesse scolaire de France et la guerre.* Paris: Didier.

Holm, Anne. 1965. *I Am David.* Trans. L. W. Kingsland. London: Methuen.

Holsinger, M. Paul. 1995. *The Ways of War: The Era of World War II in Children's and Young Adult Fiction.* Lanham, MD: Scarecrow.

Holzman, Avner. 1992. "Nosei hasho'ah basiporet hayisra'elit." *Dapim lemehkar besifrut* 10:131–58.

Huck, C., S. Hepler, J. Hickman, and B. Ziefer, eds. 1997. *Children's Literature in the Elementary School.* Madison, WI: Brown and Benchmark.

Hunt, Caroline. 1996. "Young Adult Literature Evades the Theorists." *Children's Literature Association Quarterly* 21, no. 1:4–11.

Husemann, Harald. 1986. "When William Came; If Adolf Had Come: English Speculative Novels on the German Conquest of Britain." *Anglistik & Englischunterricht* 29/30:57–83.

———. 1995. "The Colditz Industry." In *Anglo-German Attitudes,* ed. Cedric Cullingford and Harald Husemann, 141–63. Aldershot: Avebury.

I Dream of Peace: Images of War by Children of Former Yugoslavia. 1994. Preface by Maurice Sendak, Introduction by James O. Grant. New York: UNICEF/HarperCollins.

Ienaga, Saburo. 1978. *The Pacific War, 1931–1945: A Critical Perspective on Japan's Role in World War II.* New York: Pantheon.

Il capo-squadra Balilla. 1932. Illus. Raul Verdini. Rome: L'Opera Balilla.

Innocenti, Roberto, illus., and Christophe Gallaz. 1985. *Rose Blanche.* Mankato: Creative Education.

Iritani, Toshio. 1991. *Group Psychology of the Japanese in Wartime.* London: Kegan Paul International.

Isnenghi, Mario. 1977. *Giornali di trincea (1915–1918).* Torino: Einaudi.

Janeway, James. 1825. *A Token for Children: Being an Exact Account of the Conversion, Holy and Exemplary Lives, and Joyful Deaths, of Several Young Children.* London: Francis Westley.

Jarrell, Randall. 1965. *The Animal Family.* New York: Alfred A. Knopf.

———. 1970a. "On Preparing to Read Kipling." In *Kipling, Auden & Co.: Essays and Reviews, 1935–1964,* 332–45. New York: Farrar, Straus and Giroux.

———. 1970b. "A Quilt Pattern." In *The Complete Poems,* 57–59. New York: Farrar, Straus and Giroux. (Orig. pub. 1955).

Johannessen, Larry R. 1992. *Illumination Rounds: Teaching the Literature of the Vietnam*

War. Urbana, IL: National Council of Teachers of English.

Johns, Capt. W. E. 1941. *Biggles Defies the Swastika.* London: Oxford University Press.

Kacer, Kathy. 2001. *Clara's War.* Holocaust Remembrance Book for Young Readers. Toronto: Second Story.

Kamenetsky, Christa. 1984. *Children's Literature in Hitler's Germany: The Cultural Policy of National Socialism.* Athens: Ohio University Press.

Kansteiner, Wulf. 2004, June. "Genealogy of a Category Mistake: A Critical Intellectual History of the Cultural Trauma Metaphor." *Rethinking History* 8, no. 2:193–221.

Kennedy, Grace. 1824. *Anna Ross; a Story for Children.* Edinburgh: William Oliphant.

Kennemer, Phyllis K. 1993. *Using Literature to Teach Middle Grades about War.* Phoenix: ORYX Press.

Kertzer, Adrienne. 1999. "'Do You Know What "Auschwitz" Means?' Children's Literature and the Holocaust." *The Lion and the Unicorn* 23, no. 2:238–56.

———. 2002. *My Mother's Voice: Children, Literature, and the Holocaust.* Peterborough, ON: Broadview.

———. 2004. "The Problem of Childhood, Children's Literature, and Holocaust Representation." In *Teaching the Representation of the Holocaust,* ed. Marianne Hirsch and Irene Kacandes, 250–61. New York: Modern Language Association.

Khan, Rukhsana. 1998. *The Roses in My Carpets.* Illustrated by Ronald Himler. Toronto: Stoddart.

Kidd, Kenneth. 2005. "'A' is for Auschwitz: Psychoanalysis, Trauma Theory, and the 'Children's Literature of Atrocity.'" *Children's Literature* 33:120–49.

Kilner, Elizabeth. 1808. *A Visit to London, containing a Description of the Principal Curiosities in the British Metropolis. By S. W.* London: Tabart and Co. (Orig. pub. 1805).

Kipling, Rudyard. 1892. *Barrack-Room Ballads.* London: Methuen.

———. 1987. *The Jungle Books.* Ed. Daniel A. Karlin. London: Penguin.

———. 1991a. "Baa, Baa, Black Sheep." In *Something of Myself and Other Autobiographical Writings,* ed. Thomas Pinney, 135–70. Cambridge: Cambridge University Press.

———. 1991b. *Something of Myself and Other Autobiographical Writings.* Ed. Thomas Pinney. Cambridge: Cambridge University Press. (Orig. pub. 1937*).*

Klein, Holger. 1984. "Britain." In *The Second World War in Fiction,* ed. Holger Klein, John Flower, and Eric Homberger, 1–46. London, Basingstoke.

Knoepflmacher, U. C. 2000. "Validating Defiance: From Heinrich Hoffmann to Mark Twain, Rudyard Kipling, and Maurice Sendak." *Princeton University Library Chronicle* 62:83–107.

———. 2002. "The Critic as Former Child: A Personal Narrative." *Papers: Explorations into Children's Literature* 12:5–9.

Knoepflmacher, U. C., and Mitzi Myers. 1997. "From the Editors: 'Cross-Writing' and the Reconceptualizing of Children's Literary Studies." *Children's Literature* 25:vii–xvii.

Kogawa, Joy. 1981. *Obasan.* Toronto: Lester and Orpen Dennys.

———. 1986. *Naomi's Road.* Illustrated by Matt Gould. Oxford: Oxford University Press.

Kokkola, Lydia. 2002. *Representing the Holocaust in Youth Literature.* London: Routledge.

Koon, Tracy H. 1985. *Believe, Obey, Fight: Political Socialization of Youth in Fascist Italy, 1922–1943.* Chapel Hill: University of North Carolina Press.

Kushner, Barak. 2006. *The Thought War: Japanese Imperial Propaganda.* Honolulu: University of Hawaii Press.

Lacan, Jacques. 1998. *The Four Fundamental Concepts of Psychoanalysis: The Seminar of Jacques Lacan, Book XI.* Ed. Jacques-Alain Miller. Trans. Alan Sheridan. New York: Norton.

LaCapra, Dominick. 2001. *Writing History, Writing Trauma.* Baltimore, MD: Johns Hopkins University Press.

Langer, Lawrence L. 1975. *The Holocaust and the Literary Imagination.* New Haven, CT: Yale University Press.

Latham, Don. 2004. "Discipline and Its Discontents: A Foucauldian Reading of *The Giver.*" *Children's Literature* 32:134–51.

Lathey, Gillian. 1999. *The Impossible Legacy: Identity and Purpose in Autobiographical Children's Literature Set in the Third Reich and the Second World War.* Bern: Peter Lang.

Lavery, Brian, ed. 1998. *Shipboard Life and Organisation, 1731–1815:* Publications of the Navy Records Society. Vol. 138. Aldershot: Ashgate.

"La vie à Montmartre pendant la guerre racontée par les écoliers montmartrois de la rue Sainte-Isaure." 1915. *Bulletin de guerre du Vieux Montmartre,* no. 18. Fascicule spécial 1914–1915.

Lawrence, Iain. 2001. *Lord of the Nutcracker Men.* New York: Delacorte.

Leaf, Munro. 1936. *The Story of Ferdinand.* New York: Viking.

Leak, Andrew, and George Paizis, eds. 2000. *The Holocaust and the Text: Speaking the Unspeakable.* New York: St. Martin's.

Leaning, Jennifer. 2003, November. "Radcliffe Examines Role of Gender in the 'War Zone.'" *Harvard Gazette,* 13.

Le Cordier, G. 1918. *La classe 1925.* Illustrated by J. Fontanez. Paris: Delagrave.

Leersen, Joep. 1994. "'As others see, amongst others, us': The Anglo-German Relationship in Context." In *As Others See Us: Anglo-German Perceptions,* ed. Harald Husemann, 69–79. Frankfurt: Peter Lang.

———. 2000. "The Rhetoric of National Character. A Programmatic Survey." *Poetics Today* 21:267–92.

Lenz, Millicent. 1990. *Nuclear Age Literature for Youth: The Quest for a Life-Affirming Ethic.* Chicago: American Library Association.

Levi, Primo. 1989. *The Drowned and the Saved.* Trans. Raymond Rosenthal. New York: Random House/Vintage.

Lewis. C. S. 1950. *The Lion, the Witch and the Wardrobe.* New York: Harper Trophy.

Leys, Ruth. 2000. *Trauma: A Genealogy.* Chicago: University of Chicago Press.

Lindsay, W. M., ed. 1911. *Isidori Hispalensis espiscopi, Etymologiarum sive Originum* (Books xi–xx). Oxford: Clarendon.

Lingard, Joan. 1993. *The File on Fraulein Berg.* Harmondsworth: Puffin. (Orig. pub. 1980.)

Loftus, Charles. 1998. *My Youth by Sea and Land* (1876). Quoted in A. D. Harvey, *A Muse of Fire: Literature, Art and War.* London: Hambledon.

L'Oncle Sébastien. ca. 1942. *Oui, monsieur le Maréchal.* Grenoble: B. Arthaud.

Longfellow, Henry Wadsworth. 1914. *The Complete Poetical Works of Henry Wadsworth Longfellow.* Boston: Houghton Mifflin.

Lowry, Lois. 1993. *The Giver.* New York: Dell.

———. 1989. *Number the Stars.* New York: Bantam Doubleday Dell.

———. 1990, July/August. "Newbery Medal Acceptance." Published speech. *The Horn Book Magazine,* 412–21.

Works Cited

Lucas, Annie. 1902. *Leonie: A Tale of the Franco-German War.* London: Nelson and Son.

Lutzeier, Elizabeth. 1984. *No Shelter.* London: Blackie.

MacKay, Angus, and David Ditchburn, eds. 1997. *Atlas of Medieval Europe.* London: Routledge.

Macleod, Anne Scott. 1994. *American Childhood: Essays on Children's Literature of the Nineteenth and Twentieth Centuries.* Athens: University of Georgia Press.

Macleod, Emma Vincent. 1998. *A War of Ideas: British Attitudes to the Wars against Revolutionary France, 1792–1802.* Aldershot: Ashgate.

Mahon, Penny. 2000a. "In Sermon and Story: Contrasting Anti-war Rhetoric in the Work of Anna Barbauld and Amelia Opie." *Women's Writing: The Elizabethan to Victorian Period* 7, no. 1:23–38.

———. 2000b. "'Things by their right name': Peace Education in *Evenings at Home.*" *Children's Literature* 28:164–74.

Maier, Christoph T. 1999. "Mass, Eucharist and the Cross: Innocent III and the Relocation of the Crusade." In *Pope Innocent III and his World,* ed. John C. Moore. Aldershot: Ashgate.

Malcolm, Janet. 1982. *Psychoanalysis: The Impossible Profession.* New York: Vintage.

Malvano, Laura. 1997. "The Myth of Youth in Images: Italian Fascism." In *A History of Young People: Stormy Evolution to Modern Times,* vol. 2 of *A History of Young People in the West,* ed. Giovanni Levi and Jean-Claude Schmitt, trans. Carol Volk, 232–56. Cambridge, MA: Belknap Press of Harvard University Press.

Mante, Thomas. ca. 1803. *The Naval and Military History of the Wars of England; including The Wars of Scotland and Ireland.* 6 vols. London: Champante and Whitrow.

Marryat, Captain. 1829. *The Naval Officer, or Scenes and Adventures in the Life of Frank Mildmay.* London: Henry Coburn.

Marten, James, ed. 1998. *Lessons of War: The Civil War in Children's Magazines.* Wilmington, DE: Scholarly Resources.

Martineau, Harriet. 2000. *Autobiography.* Reprinted in *Records of Girlhood: An Anthology of Nineteenth-Century Women's Childhoods,* ed. Valerie Saunders. Aldershot: Ashgate.

Matas, Carol. 1993. *Daniel's Story.* New York: Scholastic.

Mauriac, François. 1960. Foreword to *Night,* by Elie Wiesel. Trans. Stella Rodway. New York: Bantam.

———. 1969. *Nobel Lectures, Literature, 1901–1967.* Ed. Horst Frenz. Amsterdam: Elzevier.

Mayer, Hans E. 1988. *The Crusades.* 2nd ed. Oxford: Oxford University Press.

McCutcheon, Elsie. 1983. *Summer of the Zeppelin.* London: Dent.

McKay, Sharon E. 2000. *Charlie Wilcox.* Toronto: Stoddart Kids.

McNally, Richard J. 2005. *Remembering Trauma.* Cambridge, MA: Harvard University Press.

Michaud, Eric. 1997. "Soldiers of an Idea: Young People under the Third Reich." In *A History of Young People: Stormy Evolution to Modern Times,* vol. 2 of *A History of Young People in the West,* ed. Giovanni Levi and Jean-Claude Schmitt, trans. Carol Volk, 257–80. Cambridge, MA: Belknap Press of Harvard University Press.

Milosz, Czeslaw. 1983. *The Poetry of Witness.* Cambridge, MA: Harvard University Press.

———. 1991. "A Poet between East and West." In *Seasonal Performances: A Michigan Quarterly Review Reader,* ed. Laurence Goldstein. Ann Arbor: University of Michigan Press.

Mintz, Alan. 2001. *Popular Culture and the Shaping of Holocaust Memory in America.* Seattle: University of Washington Press.

Moeller, Susan D. 1999. *Compassion Fatigue: How the Media Sell Disease, Famine, War, and Death.* New York: Routledge.

Moon, Marjorie. 1987. *The Children's Books of Mary (Belson) Elliott.* Winchester, Hants.: St. Paul's Bibliographies.

———. 1990. *Benjamin Tabart's Juvenile Library.* Winchester, Hants.: St. Paul's Biographies.

Morahg, Gilead. 1997. "Breaking Silence: Israel's Fantastic Fiction of the Holocaust." In *The Boom in Contemporary Israeli Fiction,* ed. Alan Mintz, 143–83. Hanover: Brandeis University Press.

Morpurgo, Michael. 1977. *Friend or Foe.* London: Macmillan Education.

Mortimer, Amy. 2001. "Anne Holm's *I Am David*," *Primary Educator* 7, no. 2:10–17.

Mosionier, Beatrice Culleton. 1999. *In Search of April Raintree.* Critical ed. Ed. Cheryl Suzack. Winnipeg: Portage and Main.

Mosse, George. 2000. "Shell-shock as a Social Disease." *Journal of Contemporary History* 35, no. 1:101–8.

Mültzer, Marcel. 1916. *Avec les poilus. Maman, la soupe et son chat Ratu.* Illus. Raynolt. Paris: Roger et Chernovitz.

Murphy, Louise. 2003. *The True Story of Hansel and Gretel: A Novel of War and Survival.* New York: Penguin.

Myers, Mitzi. 1996. "'Like the Pictures in a Magic Lantern': Gender, History and Edgeworth's Rebellion Narratives." *Nineteenth-Century Contexts* 19, no. 4:373–412.

———. 2000a. "Little Girls and Boys Lost? Growing Up in Cyberspace." *Michigan Quarterly Review* 39, no. 2:422–33.

———. 2000b. "Storying War: A Capsule Overview." *The Lion and the Unicorn* 24, no. 3:327–36.

Nabokov, Vladimir. 1980. *Lectures on Literature.* Ed. Fredson Bowers. New York: Harcourt Brace Jovanovich.

Nikolajeva, Maria. 2003. "Beyond the Grammar of Story, or How Can Children's Literature Criticism Benefit from Narrative Theory?" *Children's Literature Association Quarterly* 28, no. 1:5–16.

Nodelman, Perry. 1992. "Never Going to be Persuaded: A Response to 'Never Going Home.'" *Children's Literature Association Quarterly* 17, no. 1:40–44.

———. 1996. *Pleasures of Children's Literature.* 2nd ed. White Plains: Longman.

Novick, Peter. 1999. *The Holocaust in American Life.* Boston: Houghton Mifflin.

O'Malley, Andrew. 2003. *The Making of the Modern Child: Children's Literature and Childhood in the Late Eighteenth Century.* New York: Routledge.

O'Sullivan, Emer. 1990. *Friend and Foe: The Image of Germany and the Germans in British Children's Fiction from 1870 to the Present.* Tübingen: Narr.

———. 2002. "Comparing Children's Literature." *German as a Foreign Language* 2:33–56.

———. 2005. *Comparative Children's Literature.* London: Routledge.

Overstreet, Deborah Wilson. 1998. *Unencumbered by History: The Vietnam Experience in Young Adult Fiction.* Lanham, MD: Scarecrow.

Owen, Wilfred. 1994. *The Works of Wilfred Owen.* Ware: Wordsworth.

Pace, Patricia. 1998. "All Our Lost Children: Trauma and Testimony in the Performance of

Childhood." *Text and Performance Quarterly* 18:233–47.
Paluel-Marmont, A. ca. 1942. *Il était une fois un Maréchal de France.* Paris: Les Éditions et Publications Françaises.
———. 1942. *Pétain.* Paris: Librairie des Champs-Élysées.
Paul-Margueritte, Lucie. 1917. *Toinette et la guerre.* Illustrated by Henriette Damart. Paris: Berger-Levrault.
Perreau, Robert. 1962. *Hansi; ou L'Alsace révelée.* Meaux.
———. 1994. *Avec Hansi à travers l'Alsace.* Colmar: Editions Alsatia.
Perrot, Victor. 1915. "Introduction." In *La Vie à Montmartre pendant la guerre racontée et dessinée par les ecoliers montmartrois de l'Ecole de la rue Sainte Isaure no 18.* Fascicule spéciale 1914–15. *Bulletin de Guerre du Vieux Montmartre* 88. Paris.
Pétain. 1942. Paris: Librairie des Champs-Élysées.
Pignot, Manon. 2004. *La Guerre des crayons: Quand les petits Parisiens dessinaient la Grande Guerre.* Paris: Parigramme.
Pilkington, Mary. 1799. "The Little Negro Boy; or, Cruelty to Dependents." In *Tales of the Cottage; or Stories Moral and Amusing, for Young Persons. Written on the Plan of that Celebrated Work Les Veillees du Chateau, by Madam Genlis,* 83–103. London: Vernor and Hood.
Powell, James M. 1986. *Anatomy of a Crusade, 1213–21.* Philadelphia: University of Pennsylvania Press.
Présentez armes! Les voyages du Maréchal. ca. 1942. Marseilles: n.p.
Pressler, Mirjam. 2002. *Malka.* Trans. Brian Murdoch. London: Young Picador-Pan MacMillan.
Quayle, Eric. 1973. *The Collector's Book of Boys' Stories.* London: Studio Vista.
Raedts, Peter. 1977. "The Children's Crusade of 1212." *Journal of Medieval History* 3:279–323.
Ramadanovic, Petar. 2001, January. "From Haunting to Trauma: Nietzsche's Active Forgetting and Blanchot's Writing of the Disaster." *Postmodern Culture: An Electronic Journal of Interdisciplinary Criticism.* "Trauma: Essays on the Limit of Knowledge and Experience: A Special Issue." Ed. Petar Ramadanovic. Vol. 11, no. 2:1–19. Available from http://www.iath.virginia.edu/pmc/text-only/issue.101/11.2ramadanovic.txt.
Rees, David. 1976. *The Missing German.* London: Dobson.
Reynolds, Pamela. 2002. "Where Wings Take Dream: On Children in the Work of War and the War of Work." *Journal of the International Institute* 9, no. 2:2–3.
Richeri Gesta Senoniensis Ecclesiae (to 1264). 1880. Ed. G. Waitz. In G. H. Pertz, *Monumentum Germaniae Historica* 25:301.
Riley-Smith, Jonathan. 1987. *The Crusades: A Short History.* New Haven, CT: Yale University Press.
Riordan, James. 1999. *The Prisoner.* Oxford: Oxford University Press.
Roberts, Margaret. [1877.] *Fair Else, Duke Ulrich, and Other Tales.* London: Frederick Warne.
Robertson, Judith P., ed. 1999. *Teaching for a Tolerant World, Grade K–6: Essays and Resources.* Urbana, IL: National Council of Teachers of English.
Roche, Aude. ca. 1942. *Maréchal nous voila!!!* Grenoble: B. Arthaud.
Rodger, N. A. M. 1986. *The Wooden World: An Anatomy of the Georgian Navy.* London: Collins.
Rogers, Deborah Webster, and Ivor A. Rogers. 1980. *J. R. R. Tolkien.* Boston: G. K. Hall/

Twayne.

Rose, Jacqueline. 1984. *The Case of Peter Pan: or, The Impossibility of Children's Fiction*. London: Macmillan.

Rosen, Barbara. 1987. "The Wandering Life of Sanmao." *Children's Literature* 15:120–38.

Rosenfield, Alvin H., ed. 1999. *Thinking about the Holocaust after Half a Century*. Bloomington: Indiana University Press.

Ross, Fiona. 2003. *Bearing Witness: Women and the Truth and Reconciliation Commission in South Africa*. London: Pluto Press.

Rossignol, Dominique. 1991. *Histoire de la propagande en France de 1940 à 1944: L'utopie Pétain*. Paris: Presses Universitaires de France.

The Royal Navy: An ABC for Little Britons. ca. 1915. London: Thomas Nelson and Sons.

Rushforth, Peter. 1979. *Kindergarten*. New York: Avon Books.

Salimbene de Adam. 1966. *Cronica*. Vol. 1. Ed. Giuseppe Scalia. Bari: G. Laterza.

Scanlon, T. M. 1998. *What We Owe Each Other*. Cambridge, MA: Harvard University Press.

Schaller-Mouillot, Charlotte. ca. 1915. *En guerre!* Paris: Berger-Levrault.

Schmidhammer, Arpad. ca. 1914. *Lieb Vaterland magst ruhig sein! Ein Kriegsbilderbuch mit Knüttelversen*. Mainz: Jos. Scholz.

Sendak, Maurice. 1970. *In the Night Kitchen*. New York: Harper and Row.

———. 1985. *Where the Wild Things Are*. New York: Harper and Row.

———. 1994. Preface to *I Dream of Peace: Images of War by Children of Former Yugoslavia*. Introduction by James P. Grant. New York: HarperCollins.

Sendak, Maurice, and Tony Kushner. 2003. *Brundibar: After the Opera by Hans Krása and Adolf Hoffmeister*. New York: Michael di Capua/Hyperion.

Sexton, Anne. 1971. "Hansel and Gretel." In *Transformations*. Boston: Houghton Mifflin.

Shenton, Edward. 1943. *An Alphabet of the Army*. Philadelphia: Macrae-Smith.

Shinners, John, ed. and trans. 1997. *Medieval Popular Religion, 1000–1500: A Reader*. Peterborough, ON: Broadview Press.

Shippey, T. A. 2000. *J. R. R. Tolkien: Author of the Century*. Boston: Houghton Mifflin.

Sicardi Episcopi Cremonensis Cronica (to 1212). 1903. Ed. O. Holder-Egger. In G. H. Pertz, *Monumentum Germaniae Historica* 31:180–81.

Sicher, Efraim, ed. 1998. *Breaking Crystal: Writing and Memory after Auschwitz*. Urbana: University of Illinois Press.

Sinanoglou, L. 1973. "The Christ Child as Sacrifice: A Medieval Tradition and the Corpus Christi Plays." *Speculum* 48, no. 3:491–509.

Singer, P. W. 2005. *Children at War*. New York: Pantheon.

Skrypuch, Marsha Forchuk. 1999. *The Hunger*. Toronto, ON: Boardwalk.

Smith, Charlotte. 1794. *The Wanderings of Warwick*. London: J. Bell.

———. 1795. *Rural Walks: In Dialogues. For the Use of Young Persons*. 2 vols. London: Cadell and Davis.

Société libre pour l'étude psychologique de l'enfant. 1917. *Nos enfants et la guerre*. Paris: Alcan.

Sokoloff, Naomi. 1994. "Childhood Lost: Children's Voices in Holocaust Literature." In *Infant Tongues: The Voice of the Child in Literature,* ed. Elizabeth Goodenough, Mark A. Heberle, and Naomi Sokoloff, 259–74. Detroit: Wayne State University Press.

———. 2002. "Gila Almagor." In *Holocaust Literature: An Encyclopedia of Writers and their Work,* 2 vols., ed. S. Lillian Kremer, 1:14–16. New York: Routledge.

———. 2004. "Voices of Children in Literature: Fiction by David Grossman and Gila Almagor." In *Multiple Lenses, Multiple Images: Perspectives on the Child Across Time, Space and Disciplines,* ed. Hillel Goelman, Sheila Marshall, and Sally Ross, 73–90. Toronto: University of Toronto Press.

South, John Flint. 1884. *Memorials of John Flint South . . . Collected by the Rev. Charles Lett Feltoe.* London: John Murray.

Steedman, Carolyn Kay. 1997. *Landscape for a Good Woman: A Story of Two Lives.* New Brunswick: Rutgers University Press.

Stephens, Elaine C., and Jean E. Brown. 1998. *Learning about the Civil War: Literature and Other Resources for Young People.* North Haven, CT: Shoestring Press.

Stephens, Elaine C., Jean E. Brown, and Janet E. Rubin. 1995. *Learning about the Holocaust: Literature and Other Resources for Young People.* North Haven, CT: Shoestring Press.

Stier, Oren. 2002. "Holocaust, American Style." *Prooftexts* 22, no. 3:354–91.

Styron, William. 1979. *Sophie's Choice.* New York: Random House.

Sullivan, Edward T. 1999. *The Holocaust in Literature for Youth: A Guide and Resource Book.* Lanham, MD: Scarecrow.

Sullivan, William Francis. 1803. *Test of Union and Loyalty, on the Long-Threatened French Invasion.* 4th ed. London: J. Hatchard.

———. 1805. *The Thespian Dictionary: or, Dramatic Biography of the Present Age.* 2nd ed. London: Albion Press.

———. ca. 1818. *Pleasant Stories; or, The Histories of Ben, the Sailor, and Ned, the Soldier. Containing Entertaining and Authentic Anecdotes and Adventures of Real Life.* London: Dean and Munday.

Summerfield, Geoffrey. 1984. *Fantasy and Reason: Children's Literature in the Eighteenth Century.* London: Methuen and Co.

Takagi, Yoshitaka, ed. 1938. *Shina Jihen taisho kinengō.* Tokyo: Dai Nihon Yūbenkai Kōdansha.

Tal, Kalí. 1994. "Speaking the Language of Pain: Vietnam War Literature in the Context of a Literature of Trauma." In *Fourteen Landing Zones,* ed. Philip K. Jason, 217–50. Iowa City: Iowa University Press.

———. 1996. *Worlds of Hurt: Reading the Literatures of Trauma.* Cambridge: Cambridge University Press.

Talbot, Margaret. 2005. "The Candy Man: Why Children Love Roald Dahl's Stories—and Why Many Adults Don't," *The New Yorker* 81, no. 2:92–98.

Tatar, Maria, ed. 1999. *The Classic Fairy Tales.* New York: Norton.

Taylor, Desmond. 1994. *The Juvenile Novels of World War II.* Westport, CT: Greenwood Press.

Taylor, Isaac. 1841. *Memoirs, Correspondence, and Poetical Remains, of Jane Taylor.* 4th ed. London: Jackson and Walford.

Thrailkill, Jane F. 2003. "Traumatic Realism and the Wounded Child." In *The American Child: A Cultural Studies Reader,* ed. Caroline F. Levander and Carol J. Singley, 128–48. New Brunswick: Rutgers University Press.

Thum, Maureen. 1997. "Misreading the Cross-Writer: The Case of Wilhelm Hauff's 'Dwarf Long Nose.'" *Children's Literature* 25:1–23.

Tolkien, J. R. R. 1966. "On Fairy Stories." In *The Tolkien Reader,* 42–45. New York: Ballantine.

———. 1983. *The Book of Lost Tales: Part I.* Ed. Christopher Tolkien. New York:

Ballantine.

———. 1984a. *The Book of Lost Tales: Part II.* Ed. Christopher Tolkien. New York: Ballantine.

———. 1984b. "On Fairy-Stories." In *"The Monsters and the Critics" and Other Essays.* Ed. Christopher Tolkien, 109–61. Boston: Houghton Mifflin.

———. 1994a. *The Fellowship of the Ring: Being the First Part of "The Lord of the Rings."* Boston: Houghton Mifflin.

———. 1994b. *The Return of the King: Being the Third Part of "The Lord of the Rings."* Boston: Houghton Mifflin.

———. 1994c. *The Two Towers: Being the Second Part of "The Lord of the Rings."* Boston: Houghton Mifflin.

———. 1997. *The Hobbit: Or There and Back Again.* Boston: Houghton Mifflin.

———. 1999. *The Silmarillion.* Ed. Christopher Tolkien. 2nd ed. New York: Ballantine.

Tonnelat, E., and J. J. Waltz. 1922. *A travers les lignes ennemies: Trois années d'offensive contre le moral Allemand.* Paris: Payot and Cie.

Trimmer, Sarah. ca. 1800. *Series of Prints of English History, Designed as Ornaments for those Apartments in which Children receive the first Rudiments of their Education.* London: John Marshall.

———. 1803. *The Guardian of Education* 2:343–52.

U.S. Holocaust Memorial Museum. 1995. *Teaching about the Holocaust: A Resource Book for Educators.* Washington, DC: Resource Center for Educators, U.S. Holocaust Memorial Museum.

Vaillant-Couturier, Paul. 1921. *Jean sans pain.* Illustrated by Picart le Doux. Paris: Clarté.

van der Kolk, Bessel A. 1988. "The Trauma Spectrum: The Interaction of Biological and Social Events in the Genesis of the Trauma Response." *Journal of Traumatic Stress* 1:273–90.

———. 1996. "Trauma and Memory." In *Traumatic Stress: The Effects of Overwhelming Experience on Mind, Body, and Society,* ed. Bessel A. van der Kolk, Alexander C. McFarlane, and Lars Weisaeth, 279–302. New York: Guilford.

Ventum, Harriet. 1806. *Tales for Domestic Instruction.* London: J. Harris.

———. 1810. *Charles Leeson: or, The Soldier.* London: J. Harris.

Wall, Barbara. 1991. *The Narrator's Voice: The Dilemma of Children's Fiction.* New York: St. Martin's Press.

Walter, Virginia A. 1993. *War and Peace Literature for Young Adults: A Resource Guide to Significant Issues.* Phoenix: ORYX.

Walteri de Coventria Memoriale. 1873. Ed. W. Stubbs. *Rolls Series,* vol. 2. London: n.p.

Waltz, Jean-Jacques [a.k.a. Hansi]. 1912. *Professor Knatschké: Oeuvres choisies du grand savant allemand et de sa fille Elsa.* Paris: H. Floury.

———. 1913. *Mon village, ceux qui n'oublient pas.* Paris: H. Floury.

———. 1915. *L'histoire d'Alsace: Racontée aux petits enfants d'Alsace et de France.* Paris: H. Floury.

———. 1918. *Le paradis tricolore: Petits villes et villages de l'Alsace déjà délivrée. Un peu de texte et beaucoup d'images pour les petits enfants allis.* Paris: H. Floury.

———. 1919. *L'Alsace heureuse: La grande pitié du pays d'Alsace et son grand bonheur racontés aux petits enfants.* Paris: H. Floury.

———. 1925. *La merveilleuse histoire du bon S. Florentin d'Alsace.* Paris: H. Floury.

Welch, Ronald [i.e., Ronald Oliver Felton]. 1972. *Tank Commander.* London: Oxford

University Press.
Werner, Emmy E. 1998. *Reluctant Witnesses: Children's Voices from the Civil War.* Boulder, CO: Westview.
———. 2000. *Through the Eyes of Innocents: Children Witness World War II.* Boulder, CO: Westview.
Westall, Robert. 1977. *The Machine-Gunners.* Harmondsworth: Puffin. (Orig. pub. 1975).
———. 1982. *Fathom Five.* Rev. ed. Harmondsworth: Puffin. (Orig. pub. 1979).
Westerman, Percy F. 1918. "The Perforated Helmet: An Exciting Story of the War." In *The Secret Channel and Other Stories of the Great War,* 65–82. London: Blackie.
White, Daniel E. 1999. "The *Joineriana:* Anna Barbauld, the Aikin Family Circle, and the Dissenting Public Sphere." *Eighteenth-Century Studies* 32, no. 4:511–33.
White, E. B. 1970. *The Trumpet of the Swan.* New York: Scholastic.
White, Michael. 2001. *Tolkien: A Biography.* London: Abacus/Little, Brown.
Whitehead, Winifred. 1991. *Old Lies Revisited: Young Readers and the Literature of War and Violence.* London: Pluto.
Williams, Bernard. 2002. *Truth and Truthfulness: An Essay in Genealogy.* Princeton, NJ: Princeton University Press.
Wilson, John. 2003. *And in the Morning.* Toronto: Kids Can Press.
Winter, Jay. 2000. "Shell-Shock and the Cultural History of the Great War." *Journal of Contemporary History* 35, no. 1:7–11.
Wyler, William, dir. 1942. *Mrs. Miniver,* MGM.
Wynne-Jones, Tim. 1995. *The Maestro.* Vancouver: Douglas and McIntyre.
Yaoz, Hanna. 1998. "Inherited Fear: Second Generation Poets and Novelists in Israel." In *Breaking Crystal: Writing and Memory after Auschwitz,* ed. Efraim Sicher, 160–69. Urbana: University of Illinois Press.
Yolen, Jane. 2002. *Briar Rose.* New York: Tor.
Zacour, Norman P. 1962. "The Children's Crusade." In *A History of the Crusades,* vol. 2, ed. Kenneth M. Setton, 325–42. Madison: University of Wisconsin Press.
Zipes, Jack. 1983. *Fairy Tales and the Art of Subversion: The Classical Genre for Children and the Process of Civilization.* New York: Wildman.
———. 1997. "The Rationalization of Abandonment and Child Abuse in Fairy Tales." In *Happily Ever After: Fairy Tales, Children, and the Culture Industry,* 39–60. New York: Routledge.
———, ed. 2001. *The Great Fairy Tale Tradition from Straparola and Basile to the Brothers Grimm.* New York: Norton.
Žižek, Slavoj. 2002. *Welcome to the Desert of the Real!* London: Verso.

Contributors

Gary Dickson, F.R.H.S., is currently Honorary Fellow in the School of History and Classics, University of Edinburgh, where he was Reader in History for many years. He delivered *The Wilde Lectures in Natural and Comparative Religion* at the University of Oxford, 1996–97, on "Medieval Pentecostalism." His publications include *Religious Enthusiasm in the Medieval West* (Variorum Collected Studies Series; Abingdon, 2000) and the forthcoming *The Children's Crusade: Medieval History; Modern Mythistory* (Palgrave-MacMillan).

John Gall, M.D., FAAP, retired in 2001 after more than forty years of experience in behavioral and developmental problems of children. His publications include *The Systems Bible (How Systems Work and Especially How They Fail); Elegant Parenting: Strategies for the Twenty-First Century; Dancing with Elves: Parenting as a Performing Art;* and *First Queen: A Historical Novel on the Life of Hatshepsut, Queen of Egypt.* He maintains an online teaching program in parenting at www.higherlevelparenting.com.

Elizabeth Goodenough has taught English and American literature since 1976 at Harvard University, Claremont McKenna College, and the University of Michigan Residential College. A scholar and activist in the emerging field of children's studies, she is the editor of *Secret Spaces of Childhood* (University of Michigan press, 2003) and the forthcoming *Where Do the Children Play?* (Wayne State University Press). She also coedited *Infant Tongues: The Voice of the Child in Literature* (Wayne State University Press, 1994) and a special issue of *The Lion & the Unicorn,* "Children and Violence" (2000). She has developed a film documentary on play for public television, which broadcast in 2007.

M. O. Grenby is a Reader in Children's Literature in the School of English at Newcastle University, United Kingdom. His work focuses on children's culture in the eighteenth century and on Romantic-era novels. He has written and edited articles, collections of essays, and books on these subjects, including *The Anti-Jacobin Novel,* a study of propaganda fiction in the 1790s (Cambridge University Press, 2001). He is currently working on a history of eighteenth-century childhood reading practices.

Contributors

Mark Jonathan Harris is a multiple Academy-Award-winning documentary filmmaker, children's novelist, and distinguished professor in the School of Cinematic Arts at the University of Southern California. He earned his most recent Oscar for writing and directing *Into the Arms of Strangers: Stories of the Kindertransport* (2000). He is currently producing a feature-length documentary on the genocide in Darfur.

Mark A. Heberle is professor of English at the University of Hawai'i at Mānoa, where he teaches courses in literature of the Renaissance and war literature. He is the author of *A Trauma Artist: Tim O'Brien and the Fiction of Vietnam* (University of Iowa Press, 2001) and coeditor of *Infant Tongues: The Voice of the Child in Literature* (Wayne State University Press, 1994) and has published articles on Spenser, Shakespeare, literary biography, and the Vietnam War.

Margaret R. Higonnet, professor of English at the University of Connecticut, and Affiliate at Harvard University's Center for European Studies, has published extensively on children's literature. She coedited *Children's Literature* from 1985 to 1990; *Girls, Boys, Books, Toys* (Johns Hopkins University Press, 1999); and a special *MELUS* issue on the topic of children's literature. Her essays, two of which have won prizes from the Children's Literature Association, span courtesy books, Jules Verne, music albums, history books, and experimental form from Comenius to popups.

Andrea Immel is curator of the Cotsen Children's Library at Princeton University. Her research has focused on the history of children's book publishing, especially the intersections between print, visual, and material cultures. Her publications include *Childhood and Children's Books in Early Modern Europe 1550–1800*, coedited with Michael Witmore (Routledge, 2006), *A Catalogue of the Cotsen Children's Library: The Twentieth Century* (Princeton University Library, 2000), and the chapter on children's books in the *Cambridge History of the Book in Britain V* (forthcoming).

Eric J. Johnson holds a Ph.D. from the University of York (U.K.) and an M.L.I.S. from Rutgers University. He has a long-standing interest in literature about war, including soldiers' memoirs, narratives of survival, and wartime propaganda targeting children. He has written articles for the *Oxford Encyclopedia of Children's Literature*, as well as a piece on Oncle Hansi, a French-Alsatian children's book author and World War I propagandist. Until recently, he worked at Princeton University's Cotsen Children's Library where he cocurated the 2003 exhibition *Brave New World*, including its extensive section on children and warfare.

Adrienne Kertzer is a professor of English and associate dean, Faculty of Graduate Studies, at the University of Calgary. Recipient of the 2003 Canadian Jewish Book Award for Scholarship and the 2004 Children's Literature Association Honor Book Award for *My Mother's Voice: Children, Literature, and the Holocaust* (Broadview, 2002), she teaches courses on the representations of trauma, children's literature, Holocaust literature, and women's writing.

Contributors

Kenneth Kidd is associate professor of English at the University Florida, where he also serves as associate director for the Center of Children's Literature and Culture. He is the author of *Making American Boys: Boyology and the Feral Tale* (University of Minnesota Press, 2004) and coeditor (with Sidney I. Dobrin) of *Wild Things: Children's Culture and Ecocriticism* (Wayne State University Press, 2004). His essay in this volume is part of a book in progress tentatively titled *Freud in Oz: Children's Literature, Psychoanalysis, Queer Theory*.

U. C. Knoepflmacher is Paton Foundation Professor of Ancient and Modern Literature emeritus at Princeton University and the author or editor of ten books and more than one hundred articles on nineteenth-century literature and children's literature. He has recently completed a memoir called *Oruro: Growing Up Jewish in the Andes* (forthcoming) and is currently editing a special issue for the journal *SEL: Studies in English Literature* on the subject of Victorian "hybrids."

Mitzi Myers was lecturer in the writing programs at the University of California, Los Angeles, at the time of her death in 2003.

Emer O'Sullivan is professor of English literature at Lüenenberg University. She has published widely in both German and English on comparative literature, image studies, children's literature, and translation. She lectured at the Institut für Jugendbuchforschung (Institute for Children's Literature Research) at Frankfurt University from 1990 to 2004 and was vice president of the International Research Society for Children's Literature (IRSCL) from 2003 to 2005. Her *Kinderliterarische Komparatistik* (C. Winter, 2000) was awarded the biennial IRSCL Award for outstanding research; an English language version, *Comparative Children's Literature,* was published by Routledge in 2005. The English-language translation won the Children's Literature Association's 2005 book award. She is currently working on a historical dictionary of children's literature for Scarecrow Press.

Pamela Reynolds is professor of anthropology at Johns Hopkins University. Her research interests focus on the ethnography of children and youth in Southern Africa. She is writing a book, *An Ethnographic Study of Truth and Reconciliation Commission in South Africa and the Role of Youth.* She has been involved in the Social Science Research Council (SSRC) and UNO Research Project on Children in Armed Conflict and is working with adolescent girls who have HIV in a four-city project in the United States. Her four books on children in Southern Africa have helped to shape the subdiscipline of the ethnography of childhood.

Lore Segal was born in Vienna, Austria. In 1938, at the age of ten, she was brought to England on a transport of Jewish children. She came to the United States in 1951. A novelist, translator, essayist, writer of children's books, and teacher of creative writing, her books include *Other People's Houses* (Harcourt, 1964) and *Her First American* (Knopf, 1985). Portions of both were serialized in the *New Yorker.* Mrs. Segal is a member of the Academy of Arts and Sciences. Her new book of stories, *Shakespeare's Kitchen,* was published by the New Press in July 2007.

Contributors

Naomi Sokoloff professor of Hebrew and modern Jewish literature at the University of Washington (Seattle). She is the author of *Imagining the Child in Modern Jewish Fiction* (Johns Hopkins University Press, 1992), and she is coeditor of *Infant Tongues: the Voice of the Child in Literature* (Wayne State University Press, 1994) and of "The Jewish Presence," a special issue of the *Lion & the Unicorn* (2003).

Maria Tatar is dean for the humanities and the John L. Loeb Professor of Germanic Languages and Literatures at Harvard University. She is the author of many books on folklore and children's literature, among them *The Annotated Brothers Grimm* (Norton, 2004), *Classic Fairy Tales* (Norton, 1998), *The Annotated Hans Christian Andersen* (Norton, 2007), and *Secrets beyond the Door: Bluebeard and His Seven Wives* (Norton, 2002).

Index

Note: Page numbers in bold refer to figures.

Adorno, Theodor, 162, 181n3
After the First Death (Cormier), 104
Agnew, Kate, 208, 211, 214
Aikin, John, 5, 19, 43, 46, 47, 49–50. *See also* "Things by Their Right Names" (Aikin and Barbauld)
Alice in Wonderland (Carroll), 240, 241
Almagor, Gila, 11, 12–13, 197–204
Alphabet of the Army, An (Shenton), 62, 65, **145**
alphabet books, 60–62, **144–45**
Andersen, Hans Christian, **150**, 245
And in the Morning (Wilson), 216–17
Animal Family, The (Jarrell), 193
Anna Ross (Kennedy), 39, 43
anti-German propaganda, 66–67, **149**
anti-Semitic propaganda, 5, 68–69, 71–72, **150**
April Raintree (Culleton), 209
Archive of Feelings, An (Cvetkovich), 163, 181n7
Armenian genocide, 173–74, 183n17, 220n11
Arterburn, Stephen, 210
Audoin-Rouzeau, Stéphane, 115, 120, 121
Austrian Rhymed Chronicle, 33, 35–36
Avec les poilus (Mültzer), **154**

Baa, Baa, Black Sheep (Kipling), 193, 194
Baer, Elizabeth R., 10, 161, 163, 171
Barbauld, Anna Letitia, 5, 19, 43, 46, 47, 49–50. *See also* "Things by Their Right Names" (Aikin and Barbauld)
Barrack-room Ballads (Kipling), 2–3
Barrault, Jean-Louis, 119

Bauer, Elvira, 68–69, **150**
"Behind Closed Eyes," 2
Behind the Secret Window (Toll), 24
Bennett, William J., 241
Berlant, Laurel, 11, 164, 175, 183n18
Berquin, Arnaud, 49
Bettelheim, Bruno: on fairy tales as helpful in recovery from trauma, 12, 163, 242; on importance of discussing the past, 229; *The Uses of Enchantment*, 170, 190, 192, 242
Beyond the Chocolate War (Cormier), 8, 105
Blanchot, Maurice, 167, 182n10
Blessings of Peace and the Calamities of War, The, **257**
Bloch, Ernst, 242–43, 244
Bloor, Edward, 174
Book of Lost Tales, The (Tolkien), 131, 134, 135, 136–38
Boraks-Nemetz, Lillian, 214
Briar Rose (Yolen), 171, 172
Briggs, Raymond, 25
British children's fiction, portrayal of Germans in, 77–88
British Neptune, The (Burney), 45
Brogan, Hugh, 130
Brown, Margaret Wise, 237
Brundibar (Sendak and Kushner), 12, 186–87, 191, 192, 196n5
Bunting, Eve, 6, 87
Burnett, Frances Hodgson, 186, 209
Burney, William, 45
Butler, Octavia, 172
Butter Battle Book, The (Seuss), 25

Index

capo-squadra Balilla, Il, 63, 64, 65, 75n3, **146**
Carroll, Lewis, 240, 241
Cartilla escolar antifascista, 64–65, 75n4, **148**
Caruth, Cathy, 166–67, 182n9
Case of Peter Pan, The (Rose), 117–18
censorship, 99–101, 119
Charles Lesson (Ventum), 53–55
Charlie Wilcox (McKay), 215
"Charlotte Elizabeth," 41–42
Charon, Rita, 181n6
child crusaders (of 1212), 4, 5, 30, 34–35
Children's Book of Heroes, The (Bennett), 241
Children's Crusade, 29–37
children's drawings: about September 11 attacks, 176; about World War I, 115–16, 119, 120–24, 126–27, **154–56**
children's literature: as a means of escape from trauma, 240–41; as the most appropriate forum for trauma work, 161–62, 181n2, 207; preservation of original copies of, 232; and psychoanalysis as mutually enabling, 162–65; representation of trauma in, 7–13, 207–14; shadow of death in, 237–40; translation of big themes into human terms, 101–2; as a vehicle for propaganda, 59–60, 70–75, **151–53**; wounded child trope in, 169–74, 245–46, 247–48
child soldiers, 1, 4, 5, 253
Chocolate War, The (Cormier), 8, 100, 104, 106
Choffget, **155**
Clara's War (Kacer), 213–14
Coleridge, Samuel Taylor, 42–43
Congar, Yves, 9, 121–24, 126
Cooper, Thomas, 41, 42
Corelli, Marc, 116
Cormier, Robert: *Beyond the Chocolate War,* 8, 105; censorship of works by, 99–101; *The Chocolate War,* 8, 100, 104, 106; didacticism of works by, 111–12; intertextuality of works by, 102–3, 110–11; morality in the books of, 104–7; themes in works by, 97–99; *Tunes for Bears to Dance To,* 22, 105, 107–9
critical theory, psychoanalysis and, 166–69
Croft, Janet, 130, 141
cross-writing for dual audience works, 12–13, 102–3, 110–11, 197–202, 204
Crusader (Bloor), 174
Culleton, Beatrice, 209
Cultural Capital (Guillory), 183n13

Cvetkovich, Ann, 163, 181n7

Damart, Henriette, 125, **157**
Day I'll Never Forget, A (Wright), 175–76
Day Our World Changed, The, 176
dead child trope. *See* wounded child trope
Dear Mili (Sendak), 15, 191–92, 248–50
de Man, Paul, 168–69
Den onde Fyrste (Hermann), 69–70, **150**
Després, Émile, 128n9
Devil's Arithmetic, The (Yolen), 8, 21, 161, 171
Diary of a Young Girl, The (Frank), 23–24
Dickson, Gary, 4
drawings. *See* children's drawings
Dumesnil, René, 117, 118, 127
Dwarf Long Nose (Hauff), 196n6

Edgeworth, Maria, 48, 51, 111
Edgeworth, Richard Lovell, 48, 51
Eight Plus One (Cormier), 102, 103
Ein Bilderbuch für Gross und Klein (Bauer), **150**
elementary primers, propaganda in, 62–65, 68–69, **146–48**
Elliott, Mary, 46
En guerre! (Schaller-Mouillot), 124–25, **156**
Evans, John, 44
Evenings at Home (Barbauld and Aiken), 19, 43, 46, 47, 49–50
Ewing, Juliana Horatia, 84–85

Fade (Cormier), 98, 110
fairy tales, 163, 170–71, 238, 241–44
fascist propaganda, 63–64, 75n3, **146–47**
Fathom Five (Westall), 22, 78
"Fears in Solitude" (Coleridge), 42–43
Feinberg, Barbara, 239
Felman, Shoshana, 164–65, 168–69
File on Fraulein Berg, The (Lingard), 87, 88
Final Journey, The (Pausewang), 23
Fox, Geoff, 208, 211, 214
France: children's drawings depicting World War I experiences in, 115–16, 119, 120–24, 126–27, **154–56**; juxtaposition of trauma experienced by children and soldiers in, 117–19, **154**
Frank, Anne, 23–24
French Revolutionary Wars, 39–40, 55–56
Freud, Sigmund, 163, 165, 166, 170
Fuller, S. and J., 45, 47
Fynsk, Christopher, 168, 182n11

Gall, John, 14, 223–25
Gallaz, Christopher, 25, 246
Garth, John, 130, 132, 133–34, 137
Geographical, Historical, and Commercial Grammar (Guthrie), 44–45
Germans: in British children's fiction, 77–88; in *Den onde Fyrste*, 69, **150**
Gilson, Charles, 77–78, 83, 85
Gilson, Rob, 132–33
Giver, The (Lowry), 11, 164, 179–80, 183n22
Gloria, Viktoria, 65–66, 75n5, **148**
Goffman, Erving, 109
Goodnight Moon (Brown), 237
Goupilleau, Marcelle, 124, 127, **156**
Greene, Bette, 22
Grenby, Matthew, 5
Grimm, Wilhelm, 11, 12, 185–86, 190, 195n2, 248
Guillory, John, 183n13
Guthrie, William, 44–45

Haase, Donald, 163, 241
"Hansel and Gretel" (Grimm), 11, 12, 185–86, 190, 195n2
"Hansel and Gretel" (Sexton), 188–90
Hansi, Oncle, 59, 66–67, 75n1, **149**
Harris, Mark, 14
Hauff, Wilhelm, 196n6
Heberle, Mark, 5, 9
Herman, Judith, 118, 135
Hermann, Aage, 69–70, **150**
Higonnet, Margaret, 5, 8–9, 10
Hiroshima No Pika (Maruki), 25, 174–75
History and Adventures of Little Henry, The (Fuller), 45, 47
Hobbit, The (Tolkien), 130, 132, 139, 140
Hoffman, Mary, 208, 209
Holiday Sports, 42, **43**
Hollebecque, Marie, 119, 120
Holm, Anne, 13, 23, 211–13, 219–20nn7–8
Holocaust: in *Brundibar*, 12, 186–87, 191, 196n5; cross-writing for dual audiences about the, 12–13, 197–202, 204; in *Dear Mili*, 15, 191–92, 248–50; impact of trauma on survivors of the, 96, 197–204, 214, 228–30; literature and psychoanalytic method in studies of the, 162–63, 182n9; number of deaths in the, 26; in *Number the Stars*, 11, 15, 178–79, 180, 243–44; in *Rose Blanche*, 15, 25, 161, 174, 246–48; in time travel novels, 171, 172; truth telling vs. reassurance about the, 10–13, 199, 205n5
Holocaust and the Literary Imagination, The (Langer), 162
Hunger, The (Skrypuch), 173–74

I Am David (Holm), 13, 23, 211–13, 219n7
If I Should Die before I Wake (Nolan), 21, 171, 172
Infant Figures (Fynsk), 168, 182n11
Innocenti, Roberto, 15, 25, 161, 174, 246–48
Innocent III, 31, 36–37
In Search of April Raintree (Culleton), 209
intertextuality, 12–13, 20, 102–3, 110–11, 197–202
In the Night Kitchen (Sendak), 191
Into the Arms of Strangers, 228, 230
Island on Bird Street, The (Orlev), 19, 199
Israel, 197–98, 201–2

Jagout, Théophile, 121
Janeway, James, 245
Jarrell, Randall, 187–88, 190, 193–94
Jean sans pain (Vaillant-Couturier), 125–26, 127, **158**
Johns, W. E., 20, 81, 83
Johnson, Eric, 5
Juvenile Stories and Dialogues, 55
juvenile war stories: depictions of trauma during World War I, 116–19, 124–26, **154, 156–58,** 214–17; during the Napoleonic Wars, 45–46, 55–56; fairy tales as structures for, 241–42; juxtaposition of the child and the soldier in, 117–18; narrative strategies to soften the depiction of trauma in, 207–14, 216–17; overview of themes in, 19–26; truthful vs. reassuring depictions of war in, 7–13

Kacer, Kathy, 213–14
Kennedy, Grace, 39, 43
Kertzer, Adrienne, 10, 13, 163, 171
Khan, Rukhsana, 13, 207–8
Kidd, Kenneth, 11, 207
Kilner, Elizabeth, 45
Kindergarten (Rushforth), 245
Kindertransport, 14, 96, 227–30
Kindred (Butler), 172
Kipling, Rudyard, 2–3, 193–94
Knoepflmacher, U. C., 12
Kogawa, Joy, 209–10

Kokkola, Lydia, 211
Kushner, Tony, 12, 186–87, 191, 192, 196n5

Lacan, Jacques, 166, 167
L'Alsace heureuse (Waltz), 66–67, **149**
Langer, Lawrence L., 162
Lassiter, Rhiannon, 208, 209
Laub, Dori, 164–65, 168–69
Lawrence, Iain, 215–16, 217
Leaf, Munro, 13–14
Leaning, Jennifer, 1
Leclair, Serge, 167
Lenski File, The (Boraks-Nemetz), 214
Levi, Primo, 23, 106
Lewis, C. S., 140, 242–43
Leys, Ruth, 208
Lines in the Sand (Hoffman and Lassiter), 208, 209
Lingard, Joan, 6, 21, 87
Lion, the Witch and the Wardrobe, The (Lewis), 242–43
Little Deserter, The, 42, **43**
"Little Match Girl" (Andersen), 245
Little Princess, A (Burnett), 186
"Little Red Riding Hood," 238
Longfellow, Henry Wadsworth, 238, 250
Lord of the Nutcracker Men (Lawrence), 215–16, 217
Lord of the Rings, The (Tolkien), 129, 130, 131, 132, 136, 140–42
Lowry, Lois: *The Giver,* 11, 164, 179–80, 183n22; *Number the Stars,* 11, 15, 21, 178–79, 180, 243–44

Machine-Gunners, The (Westall), 22, 83, 85, 86
Mai, Malka, 217–20
Malcolm, Janet, 165
Malka (Pressler), 11, 13, 217–19
Malthe-Bruun, Kim, 244
Mante, Thomas, 44
Martineau, Harriet, 40, 46–47
Maruki, Toshi, 25, 174–75
Maus (Spiegelman), 25
McCutcheon, Elsie, 85
McKay, Sharon E., 215
Mémoires du Général Joffre en Plomb (Corelli), 116
Milgram, Stanley, 106
military propaganda, 62–65, 75, 75nn3–4, **146–48**. *See also* war propaganda
"Minor's Soliloquy, The," 40–41

Morning Is a Long Time Coming (Greene), 22
Morpurgo, Michael, 83, 86
Motor-Scout in Flanders, A (Gilson), 85
Mrs. Miniver, 240–41
Mültzer, Marcel, **154**
Murphy, Louise, 194–95
Mussolini, Benito, 63–64, 75n3, **146–47**
Myers, Mitzi, 3, 8, 15, 182n8, 231–35
My Mother's Voice (Kertzer), 171
My Real Friend, 50

Nabokov, Vladimir, 238
Naomi's Road (Kogawa), 209–10
Napoleonic Wars, 39–46, 49–56
narrative medicine/therapy, 163, 181n6
national characters, construction of, 84–85
Naval and Military History of the Wars of England (Mante), 44
Naval Heroes of Great Britain, The (Burney), 45
Nazi propaganda, 68–69, **150**
New Geographical Grammar (Evans), 44
Nicholas of Cologne, 30, 32
Nolan, Han, 21, 171, 172
Number the Stars (Lowry), 11, 15, 21, 178–79, 180, 243–44

Obasan (Kogawa), 209
Old Brown Suitcase, The (Boraks-Nemetz), 214
130 Questions Children Ask about War and Terrorists (Arterburn and Stoop), 210
"On Preparing to Read Kipling" (Jarrell), 194
Oppenheimer, Deborah, 227–28, 230
Orlev, Uri, 19, 199
O'Sullivan, Emer, 5–6
Other Peoples Houses (Segal), 94–96
Oui, monsieur le Maréchal! (Sébastien), 71–72, **151–52**

Pace, Patricia, 169
Paul-Margueritte, Lucie, 125, 127, **157**
Pausewang, Gudrun, 22, 23
"Perforated Helmet, The" (Westerman), 80
Perrot, Victor, 117, 126
Pétain, Henri-Philippe, 70, 71–72, 74, **151**
Picart le Doux, 126, **158**
picture books: about September 11 attacks, 175–77; depiction of trauma from World War I, 124–26, **156–58**; on the Holocaust, 174, 175, 191–92, 246–50; war propaganda in, 5, 65–70, 75, 75n5, **146–50**

Index

Plain Things for Little Folk (Elliott), 46
Pleasant Stories (Sullivan), 50–51, **144**
Practical Education (Edgeworth and Edgeworth), 48
Pressler, Mirjam, 11, 12, 13, 217–19, 220n12
"Price of a Victory, The" (Aikin), 46, 49–50
propaganda: children's literature as a vehicle for, 59–60, 70–75, **151–53**; in *The File on Fraulein Berg,* 88. *See also* war propaganda
psychoanalysis, 162–70, 182n9
Psychoanalysis (Malcolm), 165

Queen of America Goes to Washington City, The (Berlant), 175
"Quilt Pattern, A" (Jarrell), 187–88, 190, 193

Ramandanovic, Peter, 168–69
Reynolds, Pamela, 2, 15–16
Richter, Hans Peter, 23
Rose, Jacqueline, 117–18
Rose Blanche (Innocenti and Gallaz), 15, 25, 161, 174, 246–48
Roses in My Carpets, The (Khan), 13, 207–8
Royal Navy, The, 61–62, 65, **144**
Rural Walks (Smith), 47, 48–49
Rushforth, Peter, 245

Schaller-Mouillot, Charlotte, 124–25, **156**
Sébastien, L'Oncle, 71–72, **151–53**
Segal, Lore, 7–8, 11, 94–96
Sendak, Maurice: *Brundibar,* 12, 186–87, 191, 192, 196n5; *Dear Mili,* 15, 191–92, 248–50; *In the Night Kitchen,* 191
September 11 attacks (2001), 96, 175–77, 210
Serrailler, Ian, 3–4, 21
Seuss, Dr., 25
Sexton, Anne, 188–90
Shenton, Edward, 62, 65, **145**
Shina Jihen taishō kinengō (Takagi), 72–74, **153**
Shippey, Tom, 130
Shoah. *See* Holocaust
Shylock's Daughter (Pressler), 220n12
Sicard, 35
Sillabario e piccole letture, 63–64, 65, **146, 147**
Silmarillion, The (Tolkien), 130, 131, 134, 135–36, 138–39
Silver Sword, The (Serrailler), 3–4, 21
Simon, Thomas, 117, 118, 127

Skrypuch, Marsha Forchuk, 173–74
slavery, 172
Smith, Charlotte, 5, 47, 48–49, 56n2
Smith, Geoffrey Bache, 132, 133
socialist propaganda, 64–65, **148**
Sokoloff, Naomi, 246
South, John Flint, 41, 42
Spiegelman, Art, 25
Spying on Miss Müller (Bunting), 87
Stephen of Cloyes, 30, 31–32, 36
Stoop, David, 210
Story of Ferdinand, The (Leaf), 13–14, 225
Sullivan, W. F., 50–51, **144**
Summer of Aviya, The (Almagor), 11, 12–13, 197–202, 204
Summer of My German Soldier, The (Greene), 22
Summer of the Zeppelin (McCutcheon), 85

Takagi, Yoshitara, 72–74, **153**
Tal, Kalí, 135
Tank Commander (Welch), 80
Tatar, Maria, 15, 79, 185
Taylor, Isaac, 40
Tea Club and Barrovian Society, 132, 133
Tellegen, Duco, 2
Tenderness (Cormier), 101, 106
Terrÿn, Célina, 124, 127, **155**
Testimony (Felman and Laub), 164–65, 168–69
textbooks: military propaganda in, 62–65, **146–48**; portrayal of the Napoleonic Wars, 44–45
"Things by Their Right Names" (Aikin and Barbauld), 16, 19, 49, 255–57
Thrailkill, Jane F., 166, 167, 169
Through the German Hordes (Gilson), 77–78, 83
time travel novels, 21, 171–73
Toinette et la guerre (Paul-Margueritte), 125, 127, **157**
Token for Children, A (Janeway), 245
Tolkien, Christopher, 133, 134, 137, 139, 141, 142
Tolkien, Edith, 132, 134, 137
Tolkien, J. R. R.: *The Book of Lost Tales,* 131, 134, 135, 136–38; childhood of, 131; creation of languages, 132, 133–34, 142n1; *The Hobbit,* 130, 132, 139, 140; influence of trauma on the career of, 9, 129–31, 132–39, 140–42; *The Lord of the Rings,* 129, 130, 131, 132, 136,

Tolkien, J. R. R. (*continued*) 140–42; *The Silmarillion,* 130, 131, 134, 135–36, 138–39; on stories for children, 237, 238, 250; "The Voyage of Éarendel the Evening Star," 133–34
Tolkien, John, 141–42
Tolkien, Mabel, 131, 132
Tolkien and the Great War (Garth), 132
Toll, Nelly S., 24
Tonna, Mrs., 41–42
Tonnelat, E., 59, 75n1
Transformations (Sexton), 188–90
Trau keinem Fuchs auf grüner Heid und keinem Jud bei seinem Eid! (Bauer), 68–69
trauma: anxiety regarding children's exposure to, 7–13, 207–14; from child-parent separation, 190–95; children's literature as a means of escape from, 240–41; children's literature as the most appropriate forum on, 161–62, 181n2, 207; fairy tales as structures for managing, 241–42; historical fiction's personalization of, 169–75, 177–80, 207; influence on Tolkien's career, 9, 129–31, 132–39, 140–42; instability of the concept of, 208–9; integrative approach to, 163–64, 181n7; juxtaposition of children and soldier's wartime experiences of, 117–19, 125, 127, **154**; long-term impact on Holocaust survivors, 96, 197–204, 214, 228–30; narrative strategies to soften the depiction of, 207–14, 216–17; physical effects on children, 223–25; as represented in children's drawings, 119, 120–24, 126–27, **154–56**
Trauma and Recovery (Herman), 118
trauma theory, 10–13, 164–69, 182n9, 190
Trimmer, Sarah, 47–48
True Story of Hansel and Gretel, The (Murphy), 194–95
Tunes for Bears to Dance To (Cormier), 22, 105, 107–9
Turkey, 173–74, 183n17

Unclaimed Experience (Caruth), 166–67, 182n9
Under the Domim Tree (Almagor), 197, 198, 202–4
Unwin, Rayner, 141
Uses of Enchantment, The (Bettelheim), 170, 190, 192, 242

Vaillant-Couturier, Paul, 125–26, 127, **158**
Ventum, Harriet, 53–55
Visit to London, A (Kilner), 45
"Voyage of Éarendel the Evening Star, The" (Tolkien), 133–34

Waltz, Jean-Jacques, 59, 66–67, 75n1, **149**
Wanderings of Warwick, The (Smith), 56n2
"War and Peace" (Berquin), 49
war propaganda: in alphabet books and elementary primers, 60–65, 75, 75nn3–4, **144–46**; in children's literature about exemplary war figures, 70–74, **151–53**; juxtaposition of the child and the soldier in, 117–18, **154**; in picture books, 5, 65–70, 75, 75n5, **146–50**; variety as a condition of success for, 59–60, 75n1
war stories for children. *See* juvenile war stories
Welch, Ronald, 80
Welcome to the Desert of the Real! (Žižek), 176–77
Welcome to Lizard Motel (Feinberg), 239
Westall, Robert, 6, 22, 78, 83, 85, 86
Westerman, Percy F., 80
When the Wind Blows (Briggs), 25
Williams, Bernard, 252
Wilson, John, 216–17
Windling, Terri, 171
Wiseman, Christopher, 130, 132
Worlds of Hurt (Tal), 135
World War I: British children's fiction published during, 78–79, 81; children's drawings about, 115–16, 119, 120–24, 126–27, **154–56**; depictions in children's books of trauma during, 116–19, 124–26, **154, 156–58,** 214–17; propaganda in children's books during, 61–62, 65–67, 71–72, 75n5, **146–49**
World War II: evacuated-British-child genre, 21–22; Japanese-Canadian trauma in, 209–10; number of casualties in, 26; propaganda for children during, 62, 69–70, **144–48, 150.** *See also* Holocaust
wounded child trope: in children's literature, 169–74, 245–46, 247–48; in psychoanalysis and critical theory, 166–68, 182n9
Wright, Latania Love, 175–76
Writing of the Disaster, The (Blanchot), 167, 182n10

Index

Yolen, Jane, 8, 21, 161, 171, 172
Young Soldier, The, **143**

Zipes, Jack, 195n2
Žižek, Slavoj, 176–77

Permissions Acknowledgments

"*A* is for Auschwitz: Psychoanalysis, Trauma Theory, and the 'Children's Literature of Atrocity'" by Kenneth Kidd reprinted with permission from *Children's Literature* 33 (2005): 120–49. © Hollins University Corporation.

"Building the Barricade" by Anna Swirszczynska reprinted with permission. Translation © 1979 by Magnus Jan Krynski and Robert A. Maguire.

"The Hansel and Gretel Syndrome: Survivorship Fantasies and Parental Desertion" by U. C. Knoepflmacher reprinted with permission from *Children's Literature* 33 (2005): 171–84. © Hollins University Corporation.

"'No safe place to run to': An Interview with Robert Cormier" by Mitzi Myers reprinted with permission from *The Lion and the Unicorn* 24, no. 3 (2000): 445–64. © Johns Hopkins University Press.

"Storying War" by Mitzi Myers reprinted with permission from *The Lion and the Unicorn* 24, no. 3 (2000): 445–64. © Johns Hopkins University Press.